*Volume III*

# ACCOUNTANT'S ENCYCLOPEDIA

Prepared by

**THE EDITORIAL BOARD OF
PRENTICE-HALL PROFESSIONAL
ACCOUNTING PUBLICATIONS**

*and*

**A BOARD OF 45 CONTRIBUTORS**
*Consisting of Accounting Practitioners, Educators,
and Advisors to the Accounting Profession*

PRENTICE-HALL, INC., Englewood Cliffs, N. J.

VOLUME III

# Contents

# 26

# Practical Audit Working Papers

**SIDNEY W. PELOUBET**

*Certified Public Accountant; Retired Partner, Pogson, Peloubet & Co., New York; Lecturer in Accounting, Pace College; Co-Author, "Integrated Auditing"*

**HERBERT HEATON**

*Certified Public Accountant; Partner, Pogson, Peloubet & Co., New York; Co-Author, "Integrated Auditing"*

CHAPTER TWENTY-SIX

# Practical Audit
# Working Papers

The purpose of auditing is to arrive at informed opinions about the subject of the audit, whether it be the certification of a balance sheet and income statement, or the investigation of inadequate records and recommendations for the improvement of these records. This is accomplished by the process of selecting, examining, and organizing evidence to the extent necessary to draw inferences and to verify these inferences. Working papers are necessary to describe the process of selecting and examining evidence, to help organize this evidence, to record the inferences drawn, and to verify these inferences.

In other words, proper working papers record the running story of an audit. They aid in the hour-by-hour conduct and organization of the audit as it is performed, and become the organized compilation of support and explanation of the completed audit.

This chapter provides the auditor with the necessary understanding of working paper techniques to enable him to make the best use of working papers as a tool to support his opinion, both from an evidential and working viewpoint. Additionally, the chapter contains a concrete approach to the problem of applying working paper techniques to practical auditing situations.

## WHAT WORKING PAPERS ARE AND WHAT THEY DO

In addition to providing a running story of the audit, as just described, working papers help in:

1. Linking the original transactions to the final reports.
2. Supporting the accountant's opinion.
3. Organizing data.
4. Completing and correcting company records.

▶ NOTE: The legal functions of working papers are covered in Chapter 29.

**Linking the original transaction to the final reports.** Working papers are records. Every record of a business organization, beyond the original entry, can be considered to be a working paper that links the original transactions to the tax returns, SEC filings, stockholders' reports and other final financial reports. In this sense, the function of working papers is to provide the most direct linkage between the transactions as recorded and the financial statements or reports.

Under the linkage concept, the audit as reflected in the working papers consists of two separate functions: *first,* retracing the trail by which an item turned up in the final statements; *second,* after retracing to the record frontier (original cash book or journal entry), using an audit technique to verify the transactions making up the statements.

What then is to be audited? Certainly not the records alone! The actual transactions are audited. This is done by reviewing the records, of course, but the entire endeavor is to go beyond and behind the record to reach concrete evidence of purchase or sale, acquisition and possession. The function of working papers is to provide the most direct linkage between the transactions as recorded and the statements.

*Significance of initial recording of transaction.* The emphasis on tracing statement amounts to original entries of transactions is based on the peculiar significance of the initial recording of a transaction. The description, classification or identification in this initial recording will determine the item's ultimate appearance in the several financial summaries and reports. An error in initial recording will, particularly with the use of machine bookkeeping, almost certainly carry through the entire sorting process and be reflected in the final report or statement.

*Company-produced linkage.* In a well organized company, all working papers (ledgers, cost accounts, work sheets, analytical schedules, distributions) necessary to completely link the original entries in journals to the several financial summaries are prepared currently. In this way, the working papers prepared by such a company are basically the same as those prepared by an auditor, except that an auditor's working papers include comments on the auditing procedures used, the results obtained, and appropriate corrections and suggestions. When a company prepares complete working papers to produce this linkage, this process automatically becomes a form of self-audit, which helps to reduce errors and encourage consistency.

▶ TIME SAVER: The auditor can acquire useful information by obtaining copies of the company's working papers and including them as part of his work papers. He then can write his auditing procedures and comments directly on the copy furnished by the company. The auditor should, however, differentiate between company-furnished working papers and those he prepared by marking the former "Copy Furnished by Client." Both the auditor and the client can benefit from the time saved by using this method.

▶ WARNING: Don't succumb to the tendency to collect copies of company schedules merely for the sake of increasing or "padding" working papers. Only working papers offering concise, pertinent linkage of the underlying entries should be selected.

Many responsible companies also prepare what is termed the "company bible." This is the equivalent of the public accountant's long-form report in which every caption is supported by significant detail and explanation. The formal records are designed to currently furnish all the necessary detail to produce this bible.

When the company does not prepare all the necessary working papers, the auditor, of course, must do so. However, he should point out the safeguards of having complete linkage and support within the company. If not in the first year, certainly later, the auditor should convince the client of the usefulness of company prepared analyses, reconciliations, and other schedules, such as insurance, securities, and plant and depreciation. These statements are particularly valuable if promptly supplied to the party responsible for the function.

**Supporting the accountant's opinion.** In all auditing and accounting, the desired result is the controlling factor. The desired result in a certification of stockholders' report is the conviction that it is safe to sign the opinion (certificate). To arrive at this result, the auditor must be well informed and feel comfortable that:

1. Material amounts have been reasonably stated.
2. Accounting concepts have been reasonably applied, not only currently but also in relation to long-run policy.
3. Disclosure has been made as to certain accounting conventions.
4. The statements are not misleading.

There is but one way to sign an opinion with conviction, and that is to be well informed. There is but one way to be well informed, and that is to learn enough detail to make the whole picture an intelligent, integrated, consistent whole. There is but one way to have sufficient detail, and that is to record it and have it available in the working papers.

The detail in question must be clearly stated, tested, and interrelated to properly support, by schedule, every significant item on the balance sheet and income statement. An auditor should be properly satisfied only when he has gathered enough meaningful detail to enable him, whether necessary or not, to prepare a long-form report without further reference to the client's records.

Moreover, it is not enough to possess merely the detail necessary to understand and explain the whole audit picture. The auditor must reach through and beyond the records to sufficient factual evidence to make him sure of the reality of the multitudinous transactions that took place in the period under audit. Every audit working paper should not only show the significant detail behind an item, but should also tell of the procedures used to test the soundness and validity of the evidence examined by the auditor.

In other words, the greatest purpose of the working papers is to reflect the way the auditor gains conviction and to leave a record of how, why, and when this was gained. An auditor thus prepares working papers to facilitate the gathering of information and to retain the proof of his search of company records and other evidence. From this he gains an informed opinion of the nature and dependability of the company's financial statements.

**Organizing data.** It is not enough to gather great quantities of data. The information must be organized in a manner to facilitate the conduct of the audit, to support the finished audit, and to provide meaningful data for the next auditor, replacement auditors, or other interested parties.

This practical need for organizing and referencing work papers and supporting schedules has resulted in the convention of arranging the working papers in balance sheet and income statement order and assigning a letter of the alphabet to each statement item—say, *A* for cash, *B* for accounts receivable trade, *C* for reserve for receivables, and so on. Double letters are often assigned to income statement items—*AA* for sales, *BB* for cost of sales, and so on. In this way, utilizing planned pigeon holes (schedule letters and numbers) in which to put each completed, or in process, schedule, the invaluable procedures of interrelation, cross indexing, and referencing may be currently carried out. Then, too, the processes of recording audit procedures and writing up schedules are performed in accordance with preplanned symbols, forms, notations, and conventions. (These techniques will be further described in later sections of the chapter.)

All of this is in keeping with the controlling concept of good auditing, which is *careful, meticulous planning*. To thus lay out the pattern and organization of the support for the finished audit, minimizes "backing and filling" on the job, allows the auditor to apply himself to the various auditing functions as the records are completed or are made available to him, and yet allows him to fit any of his work into a prearranged pattern and form. Although audit programs and planning are discussed in Chapter 24, it can be readily seen that the use of audit programs and working paper techniques forms a sound basis from which the auditor can meet the unexpected situations that invariably arise.

*The audit diary.* One of the disadvantages of the use of symbols and other shorthand techniques is that they produce a rather formal, uninteresting format. To counteract this and to aid a replacement auditor, either in the following year or—due to illness or the pressure of work—during the current conduct of the audit, it has been found invaluable to keep a running narrative, in condensed form, of the progress of the engagement. This is practically a diary, giving details on transportation to the engagement, comments on accomodations when out of town, facilities available for washing up, lunch, etc.: the working space, circumstances and impressions upon meeting personnel, availability of records, cooperation of those in custody of records; arrangements for inventory taking as to time, transportation, general methods, cooperative personnel; the assignment of various parts of the audit program; the time of request for information, schedules, copies of statements, when they were promised and when received; comments on personnel, company procedures and doubtful audit procedures; and many other intuitive thoughts that in the pressure and volume of audit work may never recur or may recur too late for proper consideration. When work is done on the road, this diary may be mailed to the supervisor to keep him posted. A promising junior often benefits from reviewing his own work for the purpose of describing it in the diary.

**Completing and correcting company records.** Because many company records are incomplete, lack final adjustments, and may be incorrect due to errors in mechanics, classifications, and accounting concepts, an auditor completes and corrects the records as part of his engagement.

It has been the custom to crystallize the status of records as of the start of an audit by taking a trial balance so that later entries, made either by the company or by the auditor, may be clearly shown, explained, and applied. This custom places emphasis on the auditor's responsibility to justify his acts.

This attitude of segregated responsibility and action is being replaced by a more cooperative concept of the auditing function. The newer concept assumes that, while the company must take full responsibility for its financial statements, it is the auditor's duty to use the perspective of review to bring clarity and consistency of policy to the accounting reports. While it is the sole responsibility of the company to furnish sound, dependable statements, it is the mutual endeavor of both company and auditor to seek the best expression of the true situation.

A number of companies or departments of a large national or international corporation are sometimes combined to give a simple looking set of stockholders' statements. In order to consolidate all the assets, liabilities, income, and expenses of the many parts of the organization, a mass of information must be condensed. By rights, the accountant's working papers necessary to piece and sort out the various trial balances and put them together, perhaps fifty or more in some cases, should be made part of the formal, permanent company records. These working papers support the integrity of the company when it presents financial statements to stockholders, employees, or the public.

## INTEGRATED DATA PROCESSING AND WORKING PAPERS

The phrase "integrated data processing" means simply that one writing serves, by means of carbon copies or other duplicating devices, a sequence of uses. One set of punched cards can serve all the record keeping and reporting functions. (Integrated data processing is covered in Chapter 22, electronic data processing in Chapter 23.)

Practically the same work papers are needed whether records are prepared by machines or by hand. With the speed and adaptability that machines offer, working papers may well be prepared on a current basis. If not prepared routinely, certainly they can be prepared on request. This discussion of integrated data processing and working papers will cover:

1. Double entry theory and working papers.
2. Electronic records and working papers.

**Double entry theory and working papers.** The advent of integrated data processing has not changed the fact that double entry bookkeeping is still the backbone of all accounting and its recording. The purpose of double entry bookkeeping is to record all financial transactions, of whatever nature, and to give consideration to the causes and the effects of these financial acts. This purpose is carried out in terms of the fundamental equation: *Assets = Liabilities + Capital.*

This doctrine of equilibrium, this harmonious balance, establishes what may be called a closed system. After being originally introduced into this system, values may be transferred or combined, but the original amount must remain constant and identified. Any item withdrawn from this closed system must be withdrawn at the original entering value. The remaining items must at all times be identifiable with specific entering items, in much the same manner as a perpetual inventory on the physical identity basis is recorded and accounted for.

This concept of double entry is one of the strongest safeguards enforcing accountability. Under all machine accounting methods, the auditor must be vigilant in observing this enforcement. This is particularly true under the new methods and procedures of electronic data processing where the machine operations so overshadow the double entry concept as to subordinate its constant consideration.

**Electronic records and working papers.** It is difficult to visualize applying conventional patterns of audit procedure and working papers to electronic records. It may be helpful to remember that work papers are records reflecting the two auditing functions. Electronically speaking, these two functions (tracing back to the original entry and verifying the transactions recorded) are practically divorced from each other, since the machine performs all the mechanics within itself from integrated data (punched cards, magnetic or perforated tape, or a memory drum). Even in electronics, the greatest importance is still attached to the evidence contained in the original entries. The recording or punching of this original information calls for accuracy, knowledge of the transaction, and understanding of the accounting and business patterns of the company. This first tabulation must be checked painstakingly by the company at the time the record is made. This is also the most important area for the auditor to challenge.

All recording and processing beyond the preparation and checking of this original tabulation are mechanics, a way of directing items to their right pigeon holes for statements and reports. The mechanics of sorting, matching, classification, costing, and selecting, is done by the machine without leaving a dependable trail, intermediate totals, or a record of the calculations and pricing. There is little or nothing that can be checked at a later time. With conventional written records, these mechanics can be reviewed or tested after the close of the period. In electronic data processing, the machine performs these functions from the punched card deck, or magnetic or perforated tape. Even though a print-out is made, there is but one dependable method of checking the mechanics, a duplicate run. This is wasteful and unsatisfactory and the auditor should have some better assurance of the soundness and dependability of the records.

The greater part of the machine record keeping must be challenged, evaluated, and proved by the company—step by step as the record is being built up. It is necessary for the company to set up total controls, hash totals, and other running proofs to check the accuracy and dependability of machines, and this should be done currently—hour by hour. This is a new adaptation, an extension of internal control and internal auditing—the current control and audit of the mechanical functions. Similarly, the auditor must check these procedures at various times throughout the year, in much the same manner as inventory checking and procedures enforced on a continuing basis. Except for this basic shift in the responsibility for mechanical accuracy, the concepts of auditing and work papers are unchanged.

Basically, auditing and control have to do with the evidence supporting the original entries. The auditor must work with this evidence. The value of working papers and other records depends upon the use and reference to this evidence in analyses, reconciliations, verifications, and calculations.

▶ NOTE: Chapter 28, *Auditing Electronically Processed Data,* contains a full delineation of the techniques involved in this type of audit.

### WORKING PAPERS AND MANAGEMENT SERVICES

The question is often asked today, are auditors competent to render management services? Certainly some are. This competence is demonstrated by the soundness of their working papers and other background material used to support their comments and recommendations. The working papers that have been discussed so far are those prepared or used in examinations certifying the financial statements. During such an examination both the auditor and management often recognize the need for system surveys, including the review of inventory records and cost systems and the improvement of recording routines by the introduction of business machines or other means.

This type of management services work can be accomplished with professional responsibility and skill only when proper working papers are prepared in the same general manner as has already been discussed. These working papers should include a record of the auditor's discussions and conferences, organization charts, instruction manuals, job duties and evaluations, office and plant layouts, and suggestions for new and revised forms.

There is no requirement or skill applicable to certification audits that is not equally applicable to management services work. Even the working papers are similar, with the exception of the emphasis and focus on financial statements in the certification audit.

### PREPARING PRACTICAL AUDIT WORKING PAPERS

Company officials are responsible for reporting to stockholders, for the filing of tax returns, and for reporting to creditors, banks, and government agencies. In discharging this responsibility, the complete support for all such statements should be on file and readily available. The linking and supporting statements, which the auditor prepares because the company does not, should also be in the company files. Better yet, copies of such statements should be put in the files; the originals being retained by the auditor.

There are times when an auditor does routine accounting work, similar to that which might be performed by an employee of the company. In such a situation, the company rarely has an official who is charged with the safekeeping of records. When this occurs it is particularly wise for the auditor to retain his working papers, for he may be called upon to discuss them with taxing authorities, banks, or other interested parties. He should try, however, to establish a company file for their copies of these records and to promote protection and respect for them.

This section will deal with actual techniques of preparing practical working papers, in the following order:

1. General comments on format.
2. Notations.
3. Analysis.
4. Synthesis.
5. Reconciliation.
6. Lists of accounts or items.
7. Flow.
8. Combination schedules.
9. Working trial balances.
10. Accounting policy and control.
11. Permanent file.
12. Indexing.
13. Filing papers at completion.

**General comments on format.** Each working paper should have a uniform heading in the top right hand corner as follows:

Company name.
Description of working paper.
Period under audit, or cut-off date.

Each working paper should have a uniform explanation in the lower left hand corner as follows:

Source (record from which information is drawn).
Who furnished the information.
The verification procedure used.
Legend of auditor's check marks (unless uniform code is used).
Evidence examined.
Initials of auditor preparing work paper.
Date prepared.
Initials of supervisors checking work paper.

*Classification.* The primary mechanical method used in record keeping is classification. This method is based on two assumptions: (1) that there is a preconceived pattern reflecting the ideas and plans of management that may be expressed by sorting out and arranging like transactions, and (2) that there are several levels or degrees of classification depending on the various purposes and reports prepared from the records. The posting of repetitive transactions to the same classification is the most suitable form in which the information may be grasped. This form is much more workable then either totals of cash received or spent, or long chronological lists of expenditures or revenues. It is fundamental that the finest, most detailed classification that is desired must be indicated on the original entry of a transaction. The original entry must also serve for any broader classifications that the entry might be placed under later for the several purposes of reporting.

In a good system of records, this classification of several degrees is carried out, and schedules giving supporting details of accounts are prepared, in the regular course of record keeping. The following is an example of the diversity and detail involved.

▶ EXAMPLE: A simple balance sheet may have some twenty classifications that represent the normal condensed captions. In turn, each of these may have from five to twenty-five sub-classifications to give significant details of the condensed captions. These sub-classifications may easily total more than three hundred for the balance sheet alone. The income account may well have almost as many again. This significant detail is the basis on which the auditor must satisfy his need to be well informed.

There is a deceiving simplicty in the final appearance of completed working papers. With skill and experience an auditor almost instinctively knows what classification or summary of information will give a significant explanation of an account. The process of arriving at this pattern for a working paper is a question of development that approaches a trial and error technique. It is, of course, bound up with the ease or possibility of obtaining adequate proof and evidence of the validity of the information given in the working paper.

In an inferior set of records, where little or no secondary detail or classification is indicated, the auditor must in some way satisfy himself as to the nature and accuracy of the broad classification. He can do this in one of two ways:

1. By carrying out a sub-classification himself on columnar paper, as in Figure 1, Analysis—Office Expense.

2. By one of the other methods of preparing working papers that will be explained in this section—synthesis, reconciliation, lists of sub-accounts, flow, etc.

**Notations.** *Tick marks.* There are two things to consider in establishing a discipline for the use of tick marks. First, use marks that are easy to make and that are easy to distinguish. Second, insofar as possible, use the same tick for the same purpose so as to simplify interpretation by both the auditor who prepares the working paper and his supervisor.

It is wise to use letters to tick off auditing procedures performed; for example, use C for confirming, use V for vouching.

The common check mark ($\checkmark$) can be used for checking off items by comparison with another list or source. If it is necessary to recheck or check with a third source, the tail of the tick may be crossed ($\not\checkmark$). Should it be required to check with still another source or recheck again, a dot may be placed behind the tick($\not\checkmark$.).

Footing checks may be indicated by an arrowhead, made to point in the direction footed. If a column is footed down, the arrowhead should appear below the total $\left(\dfrac{7,684.27}{\vee}\right)$. If a line of figures is crossfooted to a total at the left, the arrowhead should appear pointing into the total ($942.67<$). If a line of figures is crossfooted to a total at the right, the arrowhead should appear pointing into the total from the left ($>6,780.22$). If a line of figures balances out to zero, the arrowhead should point into the column where the total would have appeared, had there been one, left (———.——<), or right (>———.——).

Indicated calculations that have been checked by independent calculation should have a calculation tick ($\wedge$) placed at the right ($31 \times 17 = 527\wedge$).

Should a tick be needed for checking off postings, a left-hand tick (L) may be used. As an alternate, the calculation tick may be made left-handed ($\wedge$).

Even though ticks are used consistently for one purpose, it is best to always include a legend in the lower left corner of any schedule where ticks are used.

*Referencing figures.* In referencing figures back and forth on the same page, both figures should bear an unused letter of the alphabet with a circle ( (A) , (A) ) or if from page to page ( (p6A) (p14A) ). Other signs to indicate reference to a footnote or comment may be used (*, $\phi$ or #), all of which are usually available on typewriters.

**Analysis.** A ledger account usually covers a fairly broad classification. The account usually does not contain sufficient detail for its nature to be easily understood or for efficient auditing. The analysis of such an account is accomplished by the techniques of classification and posting, the same techniques as were used to create the original account. Analysis and classification, in fact, are merely different viewpoints of the same process. Ledgers are used to gather like items from the running chronological record —cash books or other journals. When more than one classification of the same ledger account is needed, as in payroll, for example, first the payroll is spread to processes or jobs, and second to the several payroll classifications required for the payroll tax returns. The working papers must clearly show these two analyses: the second being analyzed and reassembled on a separate schedule.

▶ TIME SAVER: Analytical ledgers are often used to accomplish the classification of items in the initial posting. These have a number of columns to the right of the total or posting column that are used for further detailed classifications of the items posted. This type of ledger provides a running analysis of accounts such as office expense, administrative or selling expense, and plant by location or type of equipment.

The reclassification shown in Figure 1, Analysis—Office Expense, is accomplished by dividing the monthly balances of the account into ten further classifications. The items under the classification *Miscellaneous* comprise four additional classifications. After sorting the individual trans-actions recorded in the account into the ten columns, it is obvious that the items in four of the columns were placed in this account in error. Classifications in other accounts exist for *Taxes, Insurance, Dues and Sub-scriptions* and *Advertising*. The items labeled *Furniture and Fixtures* under the *Miscellaneous* account are also in error. In this manner, analysis indi-cates what belongs in the account, and at least as important, what does not belong in the account. Those items posted in error are transferred by journal entry to the proper account classification, as indicated in Figure 1.

Thus splitting up the account aids in auditing by enabling a pattern of repetition to be observed. In other words, the auditor now has units of classification that can be challenged, checked, or reconstructed; units that, in short, can be audited efficiently. *Cleaning* now appears to be a weekly service with 4 or 5 payments a month being made for a yearly total of 52 weeks @ $12, or $624.

The totals for the prior year's classifications are useful for comparison and should be placed under the totals for the current year. Apparently, *Cleaning* in the prior year did not follow exactly the same pattern as in the current year. The irregularity of one week not paid and $4 paid out of pattern might be caused by changing help and being without cleaning service for several days, matters that could be verified by referring to last year's papers or by inquiry.

This comparison of last year's totals with those of this year seems reasonable as an element of overall proof. The pattern of *Postage* and *Bottled water* makes sense. Examining an early and a late voucher for items in any of the first three columns can help to convince the auditor that the pattern and the total are reasonable. The total for supplies and expenses does not vary much from last year. By checking several vouchers and making inquiries as to authority for ordering, and provisions for receiving, stocking, and issuing, the auditor may feel sufficiently informed about this modest amount.

The full details of *Contributions* are given, of course, as this information is required for tax purposes.

*Supper money* may be checked by comparing the dates for which it was paid with the overtime requirements for staff work. Only one entry occurs for *Salesmen's expenses*. This item should be investigated as to the pattern of procedure. The authorizations for the last two expenses mentioned, as well as *Christmas gratuities,* comes from petty cash. Both their pattern and authority would be brought out in auditing petty cash.

**Synthesis.** Although the term, *synthesis,* may seem unfamiliar in relation to working papers, it is good auditing practice to reconstruct an account or total independent of the mechanical bookkeeping which formed it. While in some cases an account may be reconstructed to the last penny, it is also a very useful method when only 80 or 90% of the total is so validated.

The method of synthesis sometimes involves an element of duplication of the mechanical bookkeeping. But in an audit where the entire field of detail is available, in contrast with the day by day classification and posting that originally formed the account, short cuts are almost always possible.

Figure 2, Examination of Vouchers, illustrates the use of information derived from an interim audit, an examination of 8 months' vouchers. In this company, the vouchers were filed alphabetically rather than in the sequence of their entry in the records.

▶ SUGGESTION: Since many companies file vouchers alphabetically, time can be saved and an invaluable picture of the business pattern obtained if all the bills of one supplier and the corresponding vouchers are taken from the files at one time. This procedure is in place of sorting several months' vouchers by the month drawn. By examining several vouchers of one supplier, the rest of the supplier's bills are quickly analyzed. They may be tested by using the quantity purchased and the average price or some

| | | Total | Cleaning | Postage | Bottled Water | Supplies and Expense | Contributions | |
|---|---|---|---|---|---|---|---|---|
| | | | | | | | Amount | Description |
| | January | 146 00 | 60 00 | 60 00 | 6 00 | 12 00 | | |
| | February | 252 00 | 48 00 | 60 00 | 6 00 | 38 00 | 100 00 | Y. M. C. A. |
| | March | 332 00 | 48 00 | 76 00 | 6 00 | 20 00 | | |
| | April | 200 00 | 48 00 | 90 00 | 6 00 | 14 00 | | |
| | May | 366 00 | 60 00 | 100 00 | 6 00 | 138 00 | | |
| | June | 252 00 | 48 00 | 100 00 | 8 00 | 78 00 | | |
| | July | 290 00 | 60 00 | 60 00 | 10 00 | 50 00 | 40 00 | Boy Scouts |
| | August | 206 00 | 48 00 | 60 00 | 10 00 | 28 00 | | |
| | September | 236 00 | 48 00 | 80 00 | 8 00 | 52 00 | | |
| | October | 398 00 | 60 00 | 100 00 | 6 00 | 10 00 | 150 00 | Red Cross |
| | November | 264 00 | 48 00 | 60 00 | 6 00 | 64 00 | | |
| | December | 428 00 | 48 00 | 110 00 | 6 00 | 24 00 | | |
| | April | -10 00 | | | | | | |
| | | 3360 00 | 624 00 | 956 00 | 84 00 | 528 00 | 290 00 | |
| | Journal entry | -716 00 | | | | | | |
| | | 2644 00 | 624 00 | 956 00 | 84 00 | 528 00 | 290 00 | |
| | Prior year | 2538 00 | 616 00 | 902 00 | 72 00 | 618 00 | 240 00 | |

X See Petty Cash analysis A7 for authority and nature of these items.
Vouchers seen for all entries.
Journal entry corrects wrong distribution to this account.
Furniture and fixtures amounts redistributed to asset account represents
typewriter, table and chair.

Source and Evidence - ledger, vouchers and bills.
Furnished by - J. Brown, Asst. Bookkeeper
Procedure - vouching
Legend - none
Auditor - L. A. P.
Supervisor - M. E. P.
Prepared - 1/6/66

Fig. 1. Analysis

| Taxes | Insurance | Dues and Subscriptions | Advertising | Miscellaneous | |
|---|---|---|---|---|---|
| | | | | Amount | Description |
| | | 8|00 | | | |
| | 170|00 | | 12|00 | | |
| | | | 24|00 | 18|00 | Ⓡ Supper money |
| | | 38|00 | | 24|00 | Supper money |
| | | | | 18|00 | Supper money |
| 70|00 | | | | | |
| | | | 50|00 | 10|00 | Ⓡ Salesmen's expenses |
| | | 30|00 | | 18|00 | Supper money |
| | | | | 24|00 | Supper money |
| | | | | 48|00 | Furniture and fixtures |
| | | | | 86|00 | Furniture and fixtures |
| | | | | 60|00 | Ⓡ Christmas gratuities |
| | | | 60|00 | 120|00 | Furniture and fixtures |
| | -10|00 | | | | |
| 70|00 | 160|00 | 76|00 | 146|00 | 426|00 | |
| -70|00 | -160|00 | -76|00 | -146|00 | -264|00 | Furniture & fixtures, salesmen's expenses |
| – | – | – | – | 162|00 | |
| | | | | 90|00 | |

—Office Expense.

| | Vendor | Description | Total | Raw Material X | |
|---|---|---|---|---|---|
| | | | | Gallons | Dollars |
| | Aaron Assurance Co. | Group life + casualty | 9690 00 | | |
| | Aetna Tool Co. | Small tools | 820 00 | | |
| | Boston Foundry | Castings | 260 00 | | |
| | Broadway Supply Co. | Cleaner, gloves, towels, etc | 1800 00 | | |
| | Continental Glass Co. | Shipping jars | 5986 00 | | |
| | Corn Chemical Co. | | 4716 00 | 9200 | 4716 00 |
| | Craft Stationery Co | Forms, ink, etc | 610 00 | | |
| | Cusard Machine Shop | | 506 00 | | |
| | Catter Distillery | Emergency supply - local | 1790 00 | 3000 | 1790 00 |
| | Dorr Chemical | | 14400 00 | | |
| | Duckee Refining | | 14400 00 | | |
| | Drichen Corporation | | 9420 00 | 18400 | 9420 00 |

| | Vendor | Description | Total | Raw Material X | |
|---|---|---|---|---|---|
| | Strood Electric Co. | | 1704 00 | | |
| | | Total quantities | | 30600 | |
| | | Total amounts | 221513 00 | | 159260 0 |
| | | Per General Ledger | | | 165260 0 |
| | | Per Voucher Register | 223108 00 | | |

* Difference between voucher and general ledger account in Raw Materials X is freight bill. Bills for freight checked but not shown on this schedule.

Source and Evidence - alphabetical file of vouchers
Furnished by - assistant bookkeeper
Procedures - examined eight months vouchers. If vendor's bills for the eight months aggregated $500 or more the vendor was included above. If vendor's eight months bills were under $50 they were omitted.
Legend - none used
Auditor - L. M. G.
Supervisor - S. M. P.
Prepared - 1/29/66

**Fig. 2. Examination**

Manufacturer's Company
Examination of Vouchers
Eight Months to August 31, 1965

| Raw Materials Pounds | Dollars | Factory Supplies and Services | Repairs | Shipping Jars | Office Supplies and Services | Miscellaneous Account Dollars | Number & Name | |
|---|---|---|---|---|---|---|---|---|
| | | | | | | 9690 00 | 861 Group Insurance | |
| | | 820 00 | 260 00 | | | | | |
| | | 1800 00 | | | | | | |
| | | 300 00 | | 5686 00 | | | | |
| | | | | | 610 00 | | | |
| | | | 566 00 | | | | | |
| 16000 | 14400 00 | | | | | | | |
| 16000 | 14400 00 | | | | | | | |
| | | | 1704 00 | | | | | |
| 170000 | | | | | | | | |
| | 15300000 | 5720 00 | 2806 00 | 8300 00 | 1950 00 | 33610 00 | | |
| | 15300000 | 6214 00 | 2890 00 | 8346 00 | 2210 00 | | | |

f Vouchers.

other reasonable evidence. The use of this procedure makes unnecessary the proving of register footings and ledger postings. The nature of any unsupported portion of the total may be determined by scanning some additional vouchers. Since the mechanics of bookkeeping are not repeated in this procedure, the possibility of repeating a bookkeeping error is improbable.

In the working paper shown in Figure 3, Marketable Securities, the method of synthesis is used to determine the profit or loss on the sale of securities. The interest and dividends are determined by an independent calculation of accruals and earnings. The preparation of this working paper also makes use of a combination of analysis, independent calculation, and comparison. In other words, if the dates of purchases and sales of securities are known, calculations may be made to determine the earnings from these securities. The indicated earnings may be proved, in total at least, to the related profit and loss account. This interrelation of pertinent information— the interaction of assets and liabilities upon income and expenses—ties in and proves the soundness of the whole picture.

The working paper shown in Figure 4, Prepaid Insurance, is another example of accounts created without tracing the bookkeeping mechanics. The allocation of insurance premiums paid between expense and unexpired, and the flow of unexpired at the beginning into expense or still unexpired at the end of the year, are the result of independent calculation used synthetically.

**Reconciliation.** Reconciling schedules are generally prepared for cash, confirmations of receivables and inventories, and other items. Their chief use is in situations where information can be drawn from different sources to verify the items under audit. The technique of reconciliation is made use of in the following cases:

1. The audit of cash. The cash accounts are supported by the cash book and also by the bank statements. As these two sources are usually not in agreement, they must be reconciled with each other.

2. When trade accounts receivable are confirmed by correspondence, the customer's figure is frequently in disagreement with the book figures. These must be reconciled.

3. When perpetual inventories are checked by counting specific items, the count and bin card must be reconciled with the balance in the sub-ledger.

The reason for many differences is that parts of the record are kept in two places by different individuals and, consequently, there is a lag in the recording of transactions or the making of adjustments. To reconcile balances from different sources, an analysis is made of each balance. This discloses which items are common to both sources and which items are dissimilar. These differing items are used to reconcile the balances.

Finding the unlike items is but the beginning of auditing. More important, and one of the means of uncovering fraud, are proving the reality of the transactions, and finding the reasons for the delayed recording. Reconciling schedules should show that open items have been followed through, and have been given careful consideration and support.

**Lists of accounts or items.** It is a great convenience to reduce the number of ledger accounts by using a general ledger control account to represent hundreds, perhaps thousands, of individual accounts. This principle may even be used to allow a single general ledger cash account to represent five or ten bank accounts. More frequently, however, a single control account will represent several divisions (alphabetical sections) of customers' trade receivables (accounts or notes), with each division containing hundreds of individual accounts. The same pattern would apply to either accounts or notes payable in a control account for trade payables. It is not always necessary for the working papers to contain complete support of these controls in the form of a listing of individual sub-accounts. But it must be remembered that an auditor is seeking concrete evidence, based upon individual transactions or accounts, to establish a bridge or link between the transaction and a ledger account.

If an auditor is reconciling cash, he must deal with separate bank accounts as well as with the explanation of individual differences. If trade receivables are aged, this test is applied to individual customers' accounts that are still open. In these circumstances, where the company has lists of open accounts to support their controls, it is wise to obtain copies of these lists for inclusion in the working papers. All confirmation work should be related to lists that prove to the ledger balances under audit.

Inventory records are another type of list. Just as cash, receivables, and payables are continuing accounts that deal with the complete flow of transactions, so are perpetual inventory accounts, in a sense. However, because the inventory material accounted for is constantly moving and is recorded piecemeal, the probability of error in record keeping is great and some adjustments are to be expected. Any inventory, therefore, that is tested by count or by confirmation must be considered item by item. The lists that are used to verify items by examination must at least be complete as to control units. In this way the individual item is linked with a sub-control that may be checked as part of the total control, and, thus, identified with the balance on the particular day of the examination.

Ledgers should show the cost of construction and the purchase or

| Description of Security | | December 31, 1964 | | Bought or - Sold | | |
|---|---|---|---|---|---|---|
| | | Face value or number of shares | Book Value | Date | Face value or number of shares | Cost |
| Bonds | Democracy Steel Co 4% Maturity 1984 interest dates Feb. 1 and Aug. 1 Cert. No. 0963 1st Mtg | 18000 | 1755000 | | | |
| | Utility Power Light Co 1st Mtg 6% Maturity 1979 interest dates Apr. 1 and Oct. 1 Cert. N. AC 6421 | 36000 | 3660000 | 3/1/65 ✓ | -36000 00 | -36600 |
| | Nut & Bolt Co ✓ debentures ✓ 5% ✓ Maturity 1974 ✓ interest dates May 15 and Nov 15 ✓ Cert. No. M84335 | | | 12/15/65 ✓ | 3000000 ✓ | 29700 |
| | | 5400000 | 5415000 | | -600000 | -69000 |
| Stock | Columbia Auto Co preferred ✓ 6% Cert. No. P 70062 ✓ | | | 11/1/65 | 600 sh. | 153000 |
| | Totals | | | | | 84600 |
| | Balances per general ledger | | | | | |
| | Journal entries | | | | | |

Source and Evidence - vouchers, brokers' statements, Wall Street Banner of Jan. 3, 1966.
Furnished by - cashier for vouchers, Secretary for brokers' statements
Procedures and Legend -
 Ø checked when securities were counted with Vice-President and Secretary at City Bank, January 7, 1966, 10:00 A.M. Bank card for safe deposit box #334 showed last opened December 20, 1965
 C Confirmed by correspondence with Snake, Shark & Co.
 V Verified by examining invoices and statements

Market values verified in Wall Street Banner, January 3, 1966.
Auditor - E. C. H.
Supervisor - H. M. J.
Prepared - 1/26/66

**Fig. 3. Marketa**

Manufacturer's Company
Marketable Securities
Year 1965

| Profit & Loss on Sale | Face value or number of shares | December 31, 1965 | | Market Price per share or per bond | Value Amount | Interest and Dividends | | | | |
|---|---|---|---|---|---|---|---|---|---|---|
| | | Cost | | | | Accrued 12/31/64 | Purchased | Earned | Received | Accrued 12/31/65 |
| | 18000 00 | 17550 00 | | 1000 00 | 18000 00 | 300 00 | | 720 00 | 720 00 | 300 00 |
| 165 00 | | | | | | 540 00 | | 360 00 | 900 00 | – – |
| | 30000 00 | 29700 00 | | 990 00 | 29700 00 | | 125 00 | 62 50 | | 187 50 |
| 165 00 | 48000 00 | 47250 00 | | | 47700 00 | 840 00 | 125 00 | 1142 50 | 1620 00 | 487 50 |
| | 600 00 | 15300 00 | | 250 00 | 15000 00 | | | 900 00 | 900 00 | |
| 165 00 | | 62550 00 | | | 62700 00 | 840 00 | 125 00 | 2042 50 | 2520 00 | 487 50 |
| 0 | | 62385 00 | | | | | | 1565 00 | | 0 |
| Cr 165 00 | | 12/31 Dr 165 00 | | | | | JE 2 Cr 487 50 | | | 12 Dr 487 50 |

| | | Policy Number | Company |
|---|---|---|---|
| Standard fire coverage | Machinery & fixtures | 611135 | Rutgers Insurance Co. |
| | | 625135 | Rutgers Insurance Co. |
| Standard fire coverage | Merchandise | 772643 | Madison Insurance Co. |
| | | 851283 | Madison Insurance Co. |
| | | 342251 | Greenwich Insurance Co. |
| Use and occupancy | | 425135 | Montrose Insurance Co. |
| | | 916145 | Montrose Insurance Co. |
| Comprehensive | General liability | H 90855 | Hinter Insurance Co. |
| Workmen's compensation | | X 53799 | Hinter Insurance Co. |
| | | X 54797 | Hinter Insurance Co. |
| Total | | | |

\* Workmen's compensation insurance calculated at policy rates on payroll classifications.

Source and Evidence - ledger accounts, vouchers, policies
Furnished by - assistant bookkeeper, policies by Treasurer
Procedures - ledger account analyzed and vouchers checked.
   -unexpired end balances calculated
   -policies examined and numbers, coverage, dates etc. checked.
   -confirmed coverage, premiums and that policies were in force with agency - Falls, Summer & Co.
   -checked coverage as reasonable with related assets etc.
   -discussed insurance requirements and company policy with Treasurer
Legend - not used
Auditor - E.C.M.
Supervisor - J.H.L.
Prepared - 1/22/66

Fig. 4. Prepaid

Ring Register Company
Prepaid Insurance
December 31, 1965

| Insurance | Coverage | Policy Dates From | Policy Dates To | Premiums on dividend — Current year | Unexpired Dec 31 1964 | 1965 | Expense 1965 | | |
|---|---|---|---|---|---|---|---|---|---|
| 90% | 20000000 | 3/27/62 | 3/27/65 | -7980 | 12000 | | 4020 | | |
| 90% | 20000000 | 3/27/65 | 3/27/68 | 141370 | | 106002 | 35368 | | |
| | | | | | | 106002 | 39388 | | |
| 80% | 10000000 | 9/29/64 | 9/29/65 | | 17136 | | 17136 | | |
| 80% | 10000000 | 9/29/65 | 9/29/66 | 21648 | | 16236 | 5412 | | |
| 80% | 22100000 | 6/21/63 | 6/21/66 | | 65500 | 21840 | 43680 | | |
| | | | | | | 39076 | 66228 | | |
| 80% | 20000000 | 3/22/63 | 3/22/66 | | 39000 | 7800 | 31200 | | |
| 80% | 10000000 | 3/22/64 | 3/22/66 | | 21000 | 4200 | 16800 | | |
| | | | | | | 12000 | 48000 | | |
| Bodily injury 50,000/100,000 | | 5/1/64 | 5/1/67 | | 67200 | 38400 | 28800 | | |
| Statutory | | 5/1/64 | 4/30/65 | -8638 | 31370 | | 22732 | | |
| Statutory | | 5/1/65 | 4/30/66 | 94040 | | 23040 | 71000 | * | |
| | | | | | | 23040 | 93732 | | |
| | | | | 240440 | 253226 | 175518 | 276148 | | |

Insurance.

| | Dec. 31, 1964 | Deposits | Disbursements | Dec. 31, 1965 |
|---|---|---|---|---|
| Per bank | 4385 54 | 177113 34 | 177786 36 | 3712 52 |
| Outstanding checks | | | | |
| December 31, 1964 | -2385 54 | | -2385 54 | |
| December 31, 1965 (per list) | | | 1712 52 | -1712 52 |
| Per books | 2000 00 | 177113 34 | 177113 34 | 2000 00 |
| Reconciliation with payroll ledger expense account: | | | | |
| Salaries - sales | 1057 14 | | | |
| production | 2484 07 | | | |
| office | 2979 23 | | | |
| Labor - comparing | 9202 38 | | | |
| machine shop | 1525 92 | | | |
| indirect | 24169 11 | | | |
| direct | 85325 95 | | | |
| shipping and receiving | 8137 08 | | | |
| Commissions - salesmen's | 21576 33 | 22388 461 | | |
| Deduct: | | | | |
| Federal income tax withholding | 33125 04 | | | |
| State withholding tax | 5527 51 | | | |
| Federal Insurance Contribution Act | 6249 34 | | | |
| Employees' loans liquidated from wages | 3928 23 | | | |
| Miscellaneous deductions | 2541 15 | 51771 27 | | |
| Net payroll, as above | | 177113 34 | | |

59 employees are paid weekly by check, some 250 to 300 checks per
month. Check for weekly payroll total is drawn on regular bank
account for deposit in payroll account.

Source and Evidence - bank statements, cash book, general ledger.

Furnished by - cashier and assistant bookkeeper.

Procedure - Deposits to payroll account, four or five monthly, were footed for
twelve months from cash book, reconciled to obtain total of deposits of
$177,113.34. Total disbursements were obtained by adding bank balance,
December 31, 1964 to these deposits and deducting the bank balance, December 31, 1965.

Deposits and disbursements per books were obtained by adding up
twelve monthly totals in check journals. Federal income taxes withheld
were obtained by totaling the twelve credits to the ledger accounts.

Outstanding checks, December 31, 1964 were examined when returned
by the bank in February, 1965 and found in order. Those outstanding
December 31, 1965 were examined in February when January bank statement
was received.

Legal - none

Auditor - R.O.G.

Supervisor - M.A.

Prepared - 1/22/66

Fig. 5. Bank Reconciliation—Payroll Account.

contract price for the various units in the plant account. Good record systems provide controls by building, by type of machinery and equipment, and often by location where there are branch factories. This breakdown into small units gives significance to the movement of values. It is one way of having intelligible working papers to support the informed auditor's opinion, after he has audited some units to familiarize himself with the system routines and the validity of transactions.

**Flow.** In auditing there are two distinct approaches to verification. The first is *balance,* the end result of an accounting period reflected by the net amount left in an account. The second is *flow,* the entire movement in an account during the period under audit. Auditing that uses the balance approach to verify balance sheet items, and the flow approach to verify income statement items is possible, but not entirely workable.

The contradictory element that disrupts this dual pattern is that many items of income and expense move through asset and liability accounts as, for example, prepaid insurance and marketable securities. The working papers illustrating these two accounts on pages 892 to 895 (Figures 3 and 4) are examples of complete flow auditing. Actually there are few asset and liability accounts that would not be better supported in working papers by including some concept and test of flow in auditing them.

In an account like "receivables," flow would be shown by sales (a summary total) increasing the balance and cash collections (another summary total) reducing the balance. Of course, other elements must be included to complete the picture, such as sales adjustments, allowances, discounts, and uncollectible adjustments. The auditor should know the volume, nature, and source of these elements. This gives him a direct approach to internal control of authorization and the other procedures that govern these important and vulnerable activities, and a means of discovering fraud, carelessness, and error.

The flow concept is, of course, essential in auditing property and equipment accounts. The authorization and proper reporting to management of the additions and deductions in these accounts are of great importance. Also, many examples are found in this area of the inconsistent application of company policy regarding the classification of items as additions or expenses.

**Combination schedules.** Figure 6 illustrates the combination of the asset and depreciation reserve with the depreciation charge year by year. By graphically showing the spread of depreciation over the years in which it is to be taken as an expense to wipe out the asset value, a clear pattern is always available to demonstrate accounting policy. Against this pattern, retirements and fully depreciated items may be applied in a simple logical way.

| Year | | | Asset | Reserve | 1964 | 1965 | 1966 |
|---|---|---|---|---|---|---|---|
| | | Brought forward | 1770000 | 997000 | 274000 | 214000 | 154000 |
| 1964 | | Acquisitions | 30000 | | | 30000 | 6000 | 6000 |
| | | Depreciation | | 304000 | -304000 | | |
| | | Balance, Dec. 31 | 2070000 | 1301000 | | 274000 | 214000 |
| 1965 | | Acquisitions | 190000 | | | | 190000 | 38000 |
| | | Depreciation | | 293000 | | -293000 | |
| | | Balance, Dec. 31 | 2260000 | 1594000 | | | 252000 |
| 1966 | | Acquisitions | 400000 | | | | 400000 |
| | | Depreciation | | 292000 | | | -292000 |
| | | Balance, Dec. 31 | 2660000 | 1886000 | | | |
| 1967 | | Acquisitions | 200000 | | | | |
| | | Write off fully depreciated assets | -120000 | -120000 | | | |
| | | Retirement of 1965 addition | -20000 | -8000 | | | |
| | | Depreciation | | 290000 | | | |
| | | Balance, Dec. 31 | 1640000 | 968000 | | | |

Sources of Evidence - ledger accounts & vouchers, related accounts).
Furnished by- assistant bookkeeper
Procedure - summarize ① gross additions, ② retirements ③ fully depreciated assets
- amortize additions over 6 years - #1-6 @ 10%, #6-5 @ 20%
- retirements - reverse depreciation already taken in Reserve column
  - reverse depreciation originally spread over remaining open years of amortization.
- reverse both asset and reserve for fully depreciated assets
- figure depreciation for current year by balancing out current year depreciation column with a negative figure which is this entered in the Reserve column
- rule off single line under current year items and bring down all totals
Legend - none used

| | | | | | | | |
|---|---|---|---|---|---|---|---|
| Auditor | | | | | L.L.H. | M.E.M. | a.n.a. |
| Supervision | | | | | S.H.P. | S.P.P. | N.H. |
| Prepared | | | | | 2/1/65 | 2/3/66 | 2/1/67 |

Fig. 6. Composite Depreciation—

| 1967[2] | 1968 | 1969 | 1970 | 1971 | 1972 | | |
|---|---|---|---|---|---|---|---|
| 94000 | 37000 | | | | | | |
| 60000 | 60000 | 30000 | | | | | |
| | | | | | | | |
| 154000 | 97000 | 30000 | | | | | |
| 38000 | 38000 | 38000 | 19000 | | | | |
| | | | | | | | |
| 192000 | 135000 | 68000 | 19000 | | | | |
| 80000 | 80000 | 80000 | 80000 | 40000 | | | |
| | | | | | | | |
| 272000 | 215000 | 148000 | 99000 | 40000 | | | |
| 20000 | 40000 | 40000 | 40000 | 40000 | 20000 | | |
| -2000 | -4000 | -4000 | -2000 | | | | |
| -290000 | | | | | | | |
| | 251000 | 184000 | 137000 | 80000 | 20000 | | |

a.n.a.
N.H.
2/7/68

**Test Equipment—5 Year Life.**

As this schedule presents the background and the continuing history of an accounting element, it is placed in the permanent file. Consistency in accounting treatment from year to year is obvious. The interrelation of depreciation charges and the growth of the reserve is easily seen.

The remaining net asset balance, asset less reserve, is shown spread over the future years in which it will be charged off as expense. Independent calculation, graphic arrangement and accumulated footings verify the accuracy and reasonableness of the several accounts.

Both Marketable Securities (Figure 3) and Prepaid Insurance (Figure 4) are examples of this concept of combining assets and the related income or expense on the same working paper.

**Working trial balances.** By setting up the accounts in the ledger in statement order, the accounts will, of course, appear in the trial balance in balance sheet and income statement order. By using the familiar device of a horizontal, classifying working-trial-balance, the statements are obtained. The adjustment columns on the usual horizontal working trial balance are merely a way of applying entries and corrections. From this point of view, the ledger has been used as a sorting box to arrive at the right order for the balance sheet and income statement. Various account balances may be bracketed to combine them for one statement caption.

This more familiar horizontal form is used in most schools and textbooks. In this form, the trial balance is adjusted or corrected by entering figures directly to the right of the trial balance columns. The adjusted figures are then carried into the third set of columns for the income statement items and into the fourth set of columns for the balance sheet items. The working trial balance can be reduced in size if instead of having separate columns for debits and credits, the auditor uses black and red ink in a single column.

There are a number of disadvantages to this pattern. If the accounts are not in balance sheet and income statement order a clumsy arrangement may result. If there are a great number of adjustments and corrections, either the working trial balance becomes untidy or separate sheets must be used to accumulate adjustments for those accounts that require considerable attention. If a number of companies or branches are consolidated, the difficulty of entering adjustments for individual companies and on the summary of all companies often results in confusion and failure to keep the statement clean and up to the minute.

A second or vertical form provides columns for the trial balances of both the beginning and end of the period under audit. Debits and credits are indicated by black and red entries. A column between the account titles and last year's trial balance is provided for the notation of working paper index numbers. The columns to the right of this year's trial balance are used to distribute the accounts to the balance sheet captions, a column being assigned each caption in the same order that it would appear on the statement. One account may be distributed under several captions, in which case it would be entered on the same horizontal line under each caption. Adjustments are journalized below the last trial balance account, a full line being used for each entry. This provides a means of making correcting or adjusting entries as they are disclosed by analysis or the examination of other accounts as the audit progresses. The index column is used to index the journal entries to the working papers explaining them. By footing the vertical columns, the totals of the statement captions are obtained. (See Chapter 3 for illustration of the use of vertical working papers in making up consolidated financial statements.)

Figures 7 and 8 illustrate the vertical working trial balance. They show the treatment of the balance sheet page and the income statement page, and demonstrate how the interlocking balance ties the statements together.

Items should be ticked off after figures in the Per Books Current Year column as they are distributed. This permits completing the audit of an item out of turn and shows open items.

Balances given index numbers that include letter *P* indicate they will be found in the permanent file.

In actual practice, credit items are entered and distributed in red ink. For printing convenience, these credits are indicated by a dash preceding them.

In a small company of this type, there are usually more corrections by journal entry, several accounts need to be split by distribution and the accounts are not apt to be in balance sheet classification order. Were these usual confusions illustrated, it is felt the schedule might be more difficult to follow.

**Accounting policy and control.** Brief comments about policy should be made in many of the working papers, as indicated in Figure 10. A discussion with management about their accounting policies is, of course, a necessary part of an audit. The results of this discussion are often put into a separate schedule in the working papers, particularly where these policy matters concern some of the explanatory notes that will be part of the financial statements. The same is true of controls that require tightening or altering, which the auditor brings to the attention of management.

**Permanent file.** The permanent file is a set of working papers in continuing historical form that is used to augment the current working papers.

**Fig. 7. Working Trial**

| | Index | Per Books Dec. 31, 1964 | Per Books Dec. 31, 1965 | A Cash | B Accounts Receivable | C Inventory | D Prepaid Expenses |
|---|---|---|---|---|---|---|---|
| Guaranty National Bank | | | | | | | |
|   Regular account | A 2 | 2655209 | 3018319 | 3018319 | | | |
|   Payroll account | A 3 | 200000 | 200000 | 200000 | | | |
| National State Bank | A 5 | 215845 | 165723 | 165723 | | | |
| Petty cash | A 6 | 5000 | 5000 | 5000 | | | |
| Trade accounts receivable | B 1 | 5145488 | 5574906 | | 5574906 | | |
| Trade bad debt reserve | B 4 | -100000 | -100000 | | -100000 | | |
| Commission advances | B 2 | 134388 | 256447 | | 256447 | | |
| Receivable from employees | B 3 | 7220 | 6130 | | 6130 | | |
| Inventory - raw materials | C 2 | 3035344 | 1555086 | | | 1555086 | |
|   - work in process | C 4 | 949356 | 992592 | | | 992592 | |
|   - finished - orders | C 5 | 2017065 | 1913425 | | | 1913425 | |
|   - finished - stock | C 3 | 696379 | 697091 | | | 697091 | |
|   - packing supplies | C 1 | 584889 | 296367 | | | 296367 | |
| Prepaid insurance | D 1 | 298729 | 203650 | | | | 203650 |
| Travel advance | D 2 | 70905 | 67400 | | | | 67400 |
| Machinery and fixtures | E 1 | 13390590 | 13547549 | | | | |
| Depreciation to date | F 1 | -5649007 | -6421517 | | | | |
| Leasehold improvements | G | 324380 | 365453 | | | | |
| Deposit - gas company | H | 2000 | 2000 | | | | |
| Trade accounts payable | H 2 | -1357014 | -2336128 | | | | |
| Payable on extended terms | H 4 | -3789605 | -897346 | | | | |
| Payroll accrued | H 5 | -178137 | -286054 | | | | |
| Commissions payable | H 6 | -260412 | -95634 | | | | |
| Fed. inc. tax withheld - employees | H 7 | -158134 | -176800 | | | | |
| F.O.A.B. tax withheld - employees | H 8 | -16601 | -17255 | | | | |
| Taxes - Federal income | J 3 | -638730 | -720530 | | | | |
|   Federal unemployment | J 4 | -49067 | -41849 | | | | |
|   Old age benefits | J 5 | -16812 | -16909 | | | | |
|   State income tax | J 6 | -148758 | -127272 | | | | |
|   State unemployment | J 8 | -75170 | -56457 | | | | |
|   City + county property | J 9 | -266840 | -305113 | | | | |
| Note payable - bank | K 1 | -300000 | - | | | | |
| Capital stock | L 2 | -11858613 | -11858613 | | | | |
| Retained earnings | M 3 | -4869892 | -4769892 | | | | |
| Bal. from income worksheet | | | -639769 | | | | |
| | | | | 3389042 | 5737483 | 5454561 | 271050 |
| | | | | | | | |
| Journal entries: | | | | | | | |
| 1. Adjust depreciation | | | | | | | |
| 2. Adjust for physical inventory of raw materials | | | | | | 1261129 | |
| 3. Accrue state franchise tax | | | | | | | |
| 4. Adjust income tax accrual | | | | | | | |
| | | | | 3389042 | 5737483 | 6715690 | 271050 |

**Pacific Printing Company**
**Balance Sheet Working Trial Balance**
**December 31, 1965**

| E | J | G | H | J | K | L | Changes in Retained Earnings in 1965 | | M |
|---|---|---|---|---|---|---|---|---|---|
| Machinery and Fixtures | Depreciation | Other Assets | Accounts and Taxes Payable | Taxes Accrued | Notes Payable | Capital Stock | Balance Dec 31 1964 | Income 1965 | Dividends Paid |
| | | | | | | | | | |
| 13547549 | -6421517 | 365453 2000 | | | | | | | |
| | | | -2336128 -897346 -286054 -95684 -176800 -172500 | | | | | | |
| | | | | -720530 -41849 -16909 -127222 -56457 -305113 | | | | | |
| | | | | | -11858613 | | -4869892 | -639769 | 100000 |
| 13547549 | -6421517 | 367453 | -3809267 | -1268080 | | -11858613 | -4869892 | -639769 | 100000 |
| | -17314 | | | -60988 -140000 | | | | 17314 -126112 7 60988 140000 | |
| 13547549 | -6438831 | 367453 | -3809267 | -1469068 | | -11858613 | -4869892 | -1682596 | 100000 |

Balance—Balance Sheet.

| | | Indexed | Per Books 1964 | 1965 | Net Sales | Cost of Depreciation |
|---|---|---|---|---|---|---|
| Sales | | AA 1 | -5519650 | -6116330 | -6116330 | |
| Sales discount | | AA 1 | 46521 | 63106 | | 63106 |
| Salaries | | BB 1 | 5447827 | 5845752 | | |
| Salesmen's commissions | | CC 3 | 4972926 | 5280609 | | |
| Direct labor | | BB 2 | 7456267 | 7146338 | | |
| Indirect labor | | BB 2 | 6834939 | 4689894 | | |
| Purchases — stock | | BB 3 | 15572081 | 18659497 | | |
| wire | | BB 4 | 1241857 | 1368621 | | |
| other material | | BB 5 | 1236301 | 1472433 | | |
| discount | | BB 7 | -105774 | -192427 | | |
| Factory expenses | | BB 6 | 9638908 | 10156561 | | 791510 |
| Selling expenses | | CC 1 | 919397 | 803064 | | |
| Office expenses | | DD 2 | 1445256 | 1728662 | | |
| Other income and expense | | EE 1 | 189992 | -55359 | | |
| (and other than Fed. inc. tax) | | J 9 | 1162255 | 1143948 | | |
| Change in process & finished goods | | C 4 | -2959457 | 1695976 | | |
| Federal taxes on income | | J 3 | 630000 | 720000 | | |
| Balance | | | 1469561 | 639769 | | |
| | | | | | -6110322 | 791510 |
| Journal entries: | | | | | | |
| 1. adjust depreciation | | | | | | 17314 |
| 2. adjust for physical inventories of raw materials | | | | | | |
| 3. accrue state franchise tax | | | | | | |
| 4. adjust income tax accrual | | | | | | |
| | | | | | -6110322 | 808824 |

Fig. 8. Working Trial Balance

Keeping such papers in a separate file avoids having to repeat the same information year after year in the current papers. Typical contents of the permanent file include the history of and changes in such accounts as:

Land.
Long-term liabilities.
Long-term investments.

Capital stock.
Earned surplus.
Paid-in surplus.

Pacific Printing Company
Income Account Working Trial Balance
Year Ended December 31, 1965

| BB | CC | DD | | EE | | |
|---|---|---|---|---|---|---|
| Sales Other | Selling Expense | Office and Management Expense | Taxes other than Federal Income tax | Interest Expense | Federal Taxes on Income | Net Income |
| | | | | | | |
| 1793757 | 1185776 | 2866219 | | | | |
| 7146238 | 5286602 | | | | | |
| 4689892 | | | | | | |
| 18659492 | | | | | | |
| 1368621 | | | | | | |
| 1472933 | | | | | | |
| -192427 | | | | | | |
| 9365051 | | | | | | |
| | 803064 | 1728662 | | | | |
| | -301850 | | 1143948 | 246491 | | |
| 1695976 | | | | | | |
| | | | | | 720000 | |
| | | | | | | 639769 |
| 45999033 | 6967592 | 4594881 | 1143948 | 246491 | 720000 | 639769 |
| | | | | | | -17314 |
| -126129 | | | | | | 126129 |
| | | | 60988 | | | -60988 |
| | | | | | 140000 | -140000 |
| 44737904 | 6967592 | 4594881 | 1204936 | 246491 | 860000 | 1682594 |
| | | | | | | |

**—Income Account.**

Long-term deferred charges, such as expenses connected with long-term liabilities.

Intangibles.

Sales by product, comparative by years.

Cost of sales by product, comparative by years.

Dividends declared records.

The permanent file is also the proper place to file contracts and agreements such as the following:

| | |
|---|---|
| Corporate history. | Plant and office lay-out charts. |
| Charter and bylaws. | Bonus, profit sharing, and pension |
| Partnership agreements. | plans. |
| Corporate minutes—copies | Labor agreements. |
| or extracts. | Leases. |
| Capital stock records. | Litigation details. |
| Manual of accounts. | Guarantee agreements. |

Lists of books and records identified by name and number, their interrelation, and who keeps or is in charge of them, may be included.

Chart of accounts.
Organization chart.
Survey of accounting system.

Also included in the permanent file, are notes on: accounting policy and methods (inventory, depreciation, and sales bases, etc.); signature or initials of those preparing and responsible for vouchers, checks, notes payable, check signatures, stock and bond authentication, etc.; and in certain cases, maps, depletion schedules, salary schedules, layouts and diagrams, and classified summaries by years of dates and locations selected for surprise testing or interim detail checking.

Figure 9 is an example of a Permanent File Working Paper. This schedule would be set up and started in the initial audit of 1963. Each year figures are added and checked out with sources for proof of validity. Keeping this running information allows the auditor at a glance to see the complete historical background of the account and not only know what *is* included in the account but just as important what *is not* included. The composition of the account by totaled elements is particularly valuable in the case of surplus accounts.

**Indexing.** Preassigning a letter to each caption on the balance sheet and double letters to each caption on the income statement enables the auditor to index a working paper as soon as it is started. By keeping the working papers filed in proper order when not working on them, they remain well organized and can be readily referred to at any time.

Indexing is not a minor matter. It is very valuable in carrying out the following basic functions of working papers:

1. It keeps the work in progress constantly available by filing it in an orderly way.

Manufacturer's Company
Retained Earnings
Permanent Working Papers
Years 1963 to 19...

| Year | Net Income | Dividends | Adjustments | Balance Dec. 31 |
|---|---|---|---|---|
| 1957* | 7720.20 | | | |
| 1958 | 25830.17 | -2710.00 | | |
| 1959 | 30116.90 | -2710.00 | | |
| 1960 | 44311.18 | -5503.00 | | |
| 1961 | 60784.37 | -5830.00 | | |
| 1962 | 58416.13 | -7520.00 | | |
| 1963 | 227380.95 | -24279.00 | | 203,107.95 Ø |
| | 77390.34 | -13610.00 | -63771.80 | |
| 1964 | 305271.29 | -37883.00 | -63771.80 | 203616.49 |
| | 84668.39 | -1796.00 | | |
| 1965 | 389939.68 | -55843.00 | -63771.80 | 270324.88 |
| | 108733.22 | -26310.00 | | |
| | 498672.90 | -82165.00 | -63771.80 | 352746.10 |

* Company incorporated January 17, 1957, income from that date.
Ø Intangible assets written off.
Old ledgers filed in vault in care of controller.

Source and Evidence - ledger accounts, director meetings, annual reports
Furnished by - head bookkeeper and secretary
Procedures -

| | | 1963 | 1964 | 1965 | 1966 | 1967 | 1968 |
|---|---|---|---|---|---|---|---|
| Enter ledger movements gross income, dividends, adjustments etc. | | REC | REC | R.R.B. | | | |
| Check dividends with directors meetings | | REC | REC | R.R.B. | | | |
| Check all account items with stockholders reports as available | | REC | REC | R.R.B. | | | |
| Supervised | | H.P. | M.P. | HH | | | |
| Prepared | | 2/14/64 | 2/5/65 | 2/9/66 | | | |

**Fig. 9. Retained Earnings—Permanent Working Papers.**

2. It makes it easy to find information in the finished working papers, either directly after the audit or at some later date.

The working trial balance is generally used as an index of the various supporting schedules and statements in the working papers. A column is usually provided for this purpose just after that provided for the account titles, as shown in Figures 7 and 8. Sometimes a number of schedules are prepared to support a balance sheet caption for which one letter has been assigned. This is handled by assigning a number to each schedule in addition to the letter. In the case of cash, for example, the summary of cash receipts might be *A1,* the disbursements *A2,* the bank reconciliation *A3,* the list of checks outstanding *A4,* and the petty cash count *A5.* Whatever indexing scheme is used, any person not familiar with the working papers should be able to find any desired information. Cross indexing must be carried out currently in order to serve as a proof of the work and to integrate the various sources of evidence and information.

Some accounting firms use a standard list of letters preassigned to all possible balance sheet and income account titles. This has its advantages in auditing larger companies, particularly when there are multiple operations and several companies are consolidated. In a small job, however, the many alphabetical holes left in the working papers may be confusing.

**Filing papers at completion.** Working papers should be kept in index order during the progress of an audit unless they are being worked on. File folders are sometimes prepared for each item of the statements or for each balance sheet section when there are a great many papers. This is helpful when several auditors are working together and there is a great deal of detail to be dealt with on, say, securities, inventories, or confirmations of receivables.

At the completion of the audit it should be a routine practice to check the working papers for such things as arithmetical accuracy, indexing, cross indexing, program work completion, and the cleaning up of inquiries or open points that have been noted on any of the papers. The bound file of papers should be a neat, orderly set of supporting evidence. It should show clearly the interrelation of all work done, its necessity and result, by whom accomplished, and the source of the information.

The poor appearance and incompleteness of working papers often lead to a misjudgment of the auditor. Frequently, he has used proper auditing procedures and has gathered substantiating evidence. The lack may be due merely to the auditor's failure to promptly and carefully record consecutive, concise support.

### SUMMARY AND CONCLUSIONS

Figure 10, Examples of Accounts, Applicable Audit Procedures, and Types of Working Papers, is a summary of the procedures and types of working papers that are applicable to the auditing of all real and nominal accounts. In a sense, this figure summarizes a great deal of the information contained in this chapter. (See pages 910 and 911.)

*Because audit working papers are records:*

Ideally, a company should prepare, protect, and file all necessary working papers.

Working papers link and explain the original cash and other journal entries with the reports furnished to operating supervisors, company officials, creditors, government, tax and financial agencies, and stockholders.

*The auditor should:*

Encourage the company to take responsibility for complete records and linkage. Use company statements and forms where available. Get the company to adopt statements and forms that are better links and offer more concise, informative explanations.

Encourage the company to improve internal control, current records, and reports that reflect controls. Everyone exercising control should be encouraged to keep a record of how and when this work is done.

Prepare working papers so that they are in good form for adoption by the company. Provide the company with copies of working papers that you wish them to prepare.

*And remember to:*

Make sure he knows what audit procedure is being used and spell out the use in the legend. Challenge the procedures of the present audit. See if time and effort can be saved on the next audit by eliminating procedures or substituting other procedures, samples, analyses, reconciliations, and independent calculations.

EXAMPLE OF ACCOUNTS, APPLICABLE AUDIT

| | Observe or Count | Confirm | Calculate Independently | Verify | Inquire |
|---|---|---|---|---|---|
| **ASSETS:** | | | | | |
| Cash—Bank | | X | | | |
| —Petty | X | | | | |
| Receivables—Trade | | X | | | X |
| —Affiliates | | X | | | X |
| —Employees | | X | | | X |
| Uncollectible—Reserve | | | X | | X |
| Notes | X | X | | | |
| Discounted | | X | | | X |
| Inventories—Raw | X | | | | |
| —In process | X | (2) | X } prices | | |
| —Finished | X | (2) |   and | | |
| —Supplies | X | (2) | extensions | | |
| Securities—Marketable | X | Held by others | X | | |
| —Long-term | X | Held by others | X | | |
| Interest receivable | | | X | | X |
| Land | | | | Changes | |
| Buildings | (1) | | | Changes | |
| Depreciation reserve | | | X | | |
| Machinery, equipment, etc. | (1) | | | Changes | |
| Depreciation reserve | | | X | | |
| Furniture | (1) | | | Changes | |
| Depreciation reserve | | | X | | |
| Prepaid—Insurance | Policies | As needed | X | | |
| —Interest | | | X | | |
| Unamortized bond discount | | | X | | |
| Good Will | | | | | |
| Patents less amortization | | | X | | |
| **LIABILITIES:** | | | | | |
| Payables—Trade | | As needed | | | |
| —Affiliates | | X | | | |
| —Notes trade | | As needed | | | |
| —Notes bank | | X | | | |
| Accrued—Taxes | | | X | | |
| —Wages | | | X | | |
| —Interest | | | X | | |
| Bonds payable | | X | | | |
| **CAPITAL STOCK** | | X | | By minutes | |
| **SURPLUS**—Capital | | | | By minutes | |
| —Earned | | | | By minutes | |
| **INCOME ACCOUNT:** | | | | | |
| Sales | | | | | |
| Cost of sales | | | | | |
| Selling expense | | | | | |
| Administrative expense | | | | | |
| Interest & dividends received | | | | | |
| Other income & expense | | | | | |
| Interest paid | | | | | |

(1) Additions and retirement.
(2) Inventories held by or for others.
(3) Interest and dividends, purchase and sale, profit and loss.

**Fig. 10. Example of Accounts, Applicable**

PROCEDURES AND TYPES OF WORKING PAPERS

| | | | Working Papers | | | | |
|---|---|---|---|---|---|---|---|
| Analysis | Synthesis | Recon-ciliation | Lists of Accounts or Items | Flow | Combination With | Accounting Policy and Control | Permanent File |
| | X | X | | | | | |
| X | | | | X | | X | |
| Aging | | X | X | X | | | |
| | | | X | | | | |
| | | | X | | | | |
| | | | | | | X | X |
| | | | X | | Interest | | |
| | | | X | | | X | |
| | | X | X | | | X | |
| | | | | | | X | |
| | | X | X | | | X | |
| | | X | X | | | X | |
| | | | | X ⎫ | (3) | X | |
| | | | | X ⎬ | | X | |
| | X | | X | | Securities & Notes | | |
| X | | | | | | | X |
| X | | | | X ⎫ | | | X |
| | | | | ⎬ | Interrelate | X | X |
| X | | | | X ⎫ | Interrelate | X | |
| | X | | | ⎬ | | | |
| X | | | | X ⎭ | | | |
| | X | | | ⎫ | Interrelate | X | |
| | X | | X | X | Ins. expense | | |
| | X | | X | | | | |
| | X | | | | | X | X |
| X | | | | | | X | X |
| X | X | | X | | | X | X |
| | | | X | X | | | |
| | | | X | | | | |
| | | | X | | Interest paid | | |
| | | | | | Interest paid | | |
| | X | | | | | | |
| | X | | | | | | |
| | X | | | | Notes | | |
| | | | X | | | | X |
| X | | | X | | | | X |
| X | | | | | | | X |
| X | | | | | | | X |
| X | | | | X | | X | |
| X | | | | X | | | |
| X | | | | X | | | |
| X | | | | X | | | |
| | | | | X | Securities | | |
| X | | | | X | | X | |
| | | | | X | Bonds, Notes, Bank | | |

Audit Procedures and Types of Working Papers.

# 27

# Statistical Sampling Techniques

### HOWARD F. STETTLER

*Certified Public Accountant; Professor of Business Adminis-*
*tration, The University of Kansas; Author, "Auditing Principles"*

CHAPTER TWENTY-SEVEN

# Statistical Sampling Techniques

Although the use of *sampling* or *test-checking* is now within the concept of generally accepted auditing standards, the use of statistical techniques in audit tests did not receive extensive consideration until about 1950. In fact, the Committee on Statistical Sampling of the American Institute of Certified Public Accountants was not appointed until late in 1956. Since 1950, research and experimentation have demonstrated the applicability of statistics to audit sampling and limited applications have been regularly made. It has, therefore, now become necessary for the public accountant to learn these techniques and to consider using them in his practice.

The proper application of statistical techniques can assist the auditor in determining sample size (often pointing the way to savings through justifiable reductions in sample size), and in arriving at more reliable interpretations of sampling results. Similarly, knowledge of the techniques may prove helpful in recommending applications to clients within their accounting or other operations.

This chapter will explain the basic concepts of statistical sampling, describe the various sampling and sample evaluation techniques, and show the accountant how to apply these techniques in his auditing practice.

## HISTORICAL DEVELOPMENTS

To clearly establish the relationship of statistical techniques to present day auditing practice, a brief account of historical developments is first presented.

**Examinations to detect fraud and errors for business owners.** The ownership of private property and the advantages of specialization of labor led to the development of individually owned and operated businesses. As these enterprises prospered and expanded, the owners frequently found it desirable to delegate money handling and record keeping to employees who were skilled in such matters. Then, to gain assurance that the records were

**913**

properly kept and all monies fully accounted for, the owners turned to auditors who reviewed the accuracy of the bookkeeping and ascertained that no funds had been misappropriated. These early audits involved the *detailed examination of all transactions* that had occurred.

**The impact of the industrial revolution.** The industrial revolution had an important bearing on auditing practice. The extensive use of machinery resulted in larger businesses and increased output, with an attendant increase in the number of business transactions. This increase in accounting activity permitted some division of labor within the office, and opened the way to the introduction of internal control in the handling of money and in the accounting records. Capital requirements increased beyond the personal means of the individual entrepreneur, leading to the formation of partnerships and joint stock companies, as well as to reliance upon borrowed funds.

The effect of these changes on the practice of auditing was threefold:

1. The complete verification of all transactions became increasingly costly.

2. The introduction of various internal checks to assure that records were accurate and that all funds were properly accounted for, alleviated the need for the detailed audit of all transactions.

3. Newly emergent partners, stockholders, and creditors became interested in the credibility of financial statements in view of the importance of such statements to their investment decisions. Consequently, the formulation of independent opinions on financial statements became the prime concern of public accountants. The attendant audits were less concerned with defalcations and accounting accuracy than in the past, because financial statements could be corroborated by *tests* of supporting data coupled with reliance on the system of internal control.

**The introduction of statistical concepts and techniques.** Although testing, or sampling, has long been accepted as an appropriate auditing technique, the selection of items to be tested has almost invariably been made on a judgmental or haphazard basis, and the results of such tests have been evaluated judgmentally.

The shift to more scientific audit sampling had its origin in events associated with World War II. Statistical quality control, which had been introduced prior to the war, received considerable research and further development during the war from governments faced with the task of inspecting the vast outpouring of war material. Manufacturers became increasingly interested in statistical quality control as a device to control production and to anticipate the sampling by government inspectors.

The end of the war offered individuals an opportunity to examine these new sampling techniques from the standpoint of other fields in which testing was carried on, including accounting and auditing. In 1950, L. L. Vance prepared the first major publication dealing with statistical sampling in accounting and auditing. This volume was followed by two more significant and extensive works in 1956 and 1957:

Robert M. Trueblood and Richard M. Cyert, *Sampling Techniques in Accounting.* Prentice-Hall, Inc., 1957.

Lawrence L. Vance and John Neter, *Statistical Sampling for Auditors and Accountants.* John Wiley & Sons, Inc., 1956.

Throughout this period, numerous articles appeared in accounting and statistical periodicals. A bibliography of such material is available from the American Institute of Certified Public Accountants.

**Statistical techniques in relation to generally accepted auditing standards.** The future use of statistical sampling techniques in both auditing and accounting seems quite promising. Although there is no official position on the place and usefulness of statistics in auditing, the consensus of those in the forefront of this development may be summarized as follows:

1. There should be no conflict with generally accepted auditing standards in the use of statistical techniques, particularly since such standards recognize the propriety of the basic concept of sampling.

2. In any given audit situation, the use of statistical techniques in one area carries no obligation to use the techniques in other areas where they are inappropriate.

3. Even though the present use of statistical concepts in auditing is essentially on a voluntary and experimental basis, their use in any one area of an audit may make it necessary for the auditor to be prepared to defend his decision not to use these techniques in other audit areas involving the use of sampling.

4. Any single statistical technique (e.g., random selection of a sample) may be used without necessitating the use of other statistical techniques, such as statistical determination of the size of the samples or statistical evaluation of the results of the sample.

5. Statistical techniques are most readily applied when voluminous data are involved and the tests bear only on a single aspect of the audit. Present knowledge is insufficient to establish a quantitative relationship between the results of one audit test and the results of other closely related tests. For example, it isn't possible to statistically correlate the results of the confirmation of receivables with the results of tests of postings to the accounts receivable records.

6. Although it appears desirable that auditors have sufficient knowledge of statistical techniques to use them in appropriate circumstances, an auditor can effectively use statistical techniques without being a trained statistician.

7. When an auditor has only a general understanding of statistics, a trained statistician should be consulted in resolving difficult or unusual applications of statistical techniques.

**Use of statistics by clients and in management services.** The main concern of this chapter is with the use of statistical sampling in auditing. However, it should be recognized that there are other possibilities for the use of statistical techniques. A very common application is in quality control over repetitive clerical operations such as billing, or transcribing data onto punched cards. Other applications include the development of cost data, aging accounts receivable, auditing accounts payable invoices, and developing physical inventory balances.

The existence of such applications prompts the auditor to be prepared to recommend statistical techniques if they would be beneficial to clients. Such recommendations might arise during an audit engagement or as part of a specific management services assignment.

## BASIC STATISTICAL CONCEPTS

Sampling may be conducted scientifically through the use of statistical methods or informally on a judgmental basis. In either case, it ordinarily involves working with a group of items, customarily referred to as the *population*. Sampling attempts to arrive at an *inference* about the make-up of the population by examining items selected from the population, the selected items being known as the *sample*. The inference about the population derived from the sample may pertain to (1) the number of items present in the population, (2) the total amount or value of the population, or (3) the rate of occurrence or non-occurrence of some characteristic of the items making up the population.

**Theory of probability.** Probability statistics reflect essentially common sense notions about the occurrence of some specified characteristic within a population. The advantage of interpreting common sense in statistical terms is that the mathematical processes make it possible to express conclusions in a meaningful and concrete form.

The two following examples will illustrate the simple logical principles underlying statistical sampling:

▶ EXAMPLE 1: The probabilities are 1 in 52 of predicting which card will be drawn out of a well-mixed deck of playing cards. The odds in attempting to predict two consecutively drawn cards are determined by multiplying the probabilities of drawing the first by those of the second. Since there are 1 out of 52 chances of predicting the first card, and 1 out of 51 chances of picking the second, the probabilities of drawing them consecutively are 1 in 2,652 [$\frac{1}{52} \times \frac{1}{51}$].

▶ EXAMPLE 2: Both the color and the quantity of a number of balls in a bowl are unknown. By dipping into this bowl (the population) for a handful of balls and examining this sample, one may form the following conclusions (inferences) about the balls in the bowl:

1. Assuming that both black and white balls are present in the sample, the inference is that the population consists of black and white balls.
2. If the balls in the sample are about evenly divided between black and white, there is an inference that the balls in the bowl are also divided somewhat equally.
3. If there are more white balls than black in the sample, one would undoubtedly infer that a similar condition probably exists in the entire bowl.

If the theories of probabilities illustrated above are applied on a statistical rather than on the judgmental basis that was used here, inferences about populations can be expressed quantitatively, thus making them more useful.

**Measures of statistical inference.** Clearly, statistical inference is capable of producing a more precise indication of the characteristics of a population than intuition or judgment. Yet it must be realized that sampling can never produce an estimate that is absolutely correct. Only 100% inspection of a population will insure completely accurate results. The advantage of statistical inference is that measures can be calculated showing the maximum difference that is likely to exist between the sample estimate and the true characteristics of the population. Two measures are involved. They are usually referred to as *precision* and *reliability*.

*Precision.* The precision of an estimate represents the maximum difference that is likely to exist between the results determined from a sample and the true condition of the population.

▶ EXAMPLE: An auditor wishes to arrive at an estimate of the total dollar amount of a group of accounts receivable ledger cards. Since the *exact* amount of receivables cannot be determined from his sample, he must be content with an approximation. His calculation shows that the estimate of the total receivables, based on his samples, is within plus or minus $x$ dollars of the true receivables figure. This range of possible values represents the precision of his estimate.

Precision is also a factor when the estimate to be made involves some characteristic of the population; for instance, errors occurring in the extension inventory quantities and prices. If the sample contains $x$ percent errors, the precision of this estimate is the range within which the actual rate of error in the population is likely to fall.

▶ EXAMPLE: If a sample reveals a 2% error rate, the auditor's concern usually would be about the maximum rate of error that exists in the population as a whole. Therefore, if the population error were estimated to be a maximum of 5%, the precision of the estimate would be plus 3% (5% — 2%). The error rate might also be less than 2% shown by the sample, and the minimum rate of error in the population could also be determined to complete the precision limits, but an auditor would seldom be interested in this opposite limit.

*Reliability.* Sampling always involves uncertainty, and the measurement of this uncertainty represents the second measure involved in sampling. Thus, statistical inference must deal with both the precision of the estimate arrived at, as well as the possibility that the actual make-up of the population may lie outside the limits stated in the measure of precision. Again, absolute certainty about the population is attainable only by 100% inspection of the items in the population.

The reliability of an estimate may be expressed in terms of *confidence* that the population actually is within the limits of precision related to the sample. Thus, 90% confidence that the true value of a population lies within plus or minus $5,000 of a figure implies that there are 90 chances in 100 that the actual value of the population lies within the specified precision limits. Conversely, there are 10 chances in 100 that the true value lies outside the precision limits, or in statistical terms, there is a 10% risk that the conclusion reached from the sample may be wrong.

**Interrelationship of precision, reliability, and sample size.** Precision and reliability are interdependent in that for a given sample the precision of the estimate may be increased (the range between the limits made smaller) only at the expense of a reduction in confidence that the population actually is within the limits specified. By the same token, if greater confidence is desired, the precision of the estimate is reduced accordingly (the range between the limits made larger).

Precision and reliability are in turn influenced by a third factor—the size of the sample. As shall be explained in greater detail shortly, the larger the sample, the more meaningful are the sample results. In other words, increased sample size affords either greater precision, greater confidence, or increases in both of these factors, although to a lesser degree than if only one of the factors is adjusted.

**Probable characteristics of many samples drawn from the same population.** Assume that a sample of 100 balls is drawn from a bowl containing 9,000 white balls and 1,000 black balls thoroughly mixed together. The number of black balls in the sample is noted, the balls are returned to the bowl, and the sampling process is repeated until 100 samples have been taken. The probable results of such a process can be approximated mathematically in a number of ways. One such approximation, the *Poisson distribution* (explained on page 928), shows that the results would probably be as shown in Figure 1.

| Number of black balls in sample of 100 | Number of times in 100 samples that stated number of black balls would probably appear | Cumulative number of times that stated number of black balls or fewer would probably appear |
|---|---|---|
| 0 | 0 | 0 |
| 1 | 0 | 0 |
| 2 | 0 | 0 |
| 3 | 1 | 1 |
| 4 | 2 | 3 |
| 5 | 4 | 7 |
| 6 | 6 | 13 |
| 7 | 9 | 22 |
| 8 | 11 | 33 |
| 9 | 12 | 45 |
| 10 | 13 | 58 |
| 11 | 12 | 70 |
| 12 | 10 | 80 |
| 13 | 7 | 87 |
| 14 | 5 | 92 |
| 15 | 3 | 95 |
| 16 | 2 | 97 |
| 17 | 2 | 99 |
| 18 | 1 | 100 |
| 19 | 0 | 100 |

**Fig. 1. Expected Results Based on Poisson Distribution of Drawing 100 Samples of 100 Balls from a Bowl Containing 9,000 White Balls and 1,000 Black Balls.**

Perhaps the first observation that should be made about the probable results, or probabilities, shown in Figure 1 is that although the bowl from which the samples were drawn contained 10% black balls, only 13 of the 100 samples would contain the identical 10% proportion of black balls. Of the remaining samples, 45 would contain less than 10 black balls and 42 would contain more than 10 black balls. Also, only rarely (less than once in 100 samples) would the sample contain as few as 2 black balls or as many as 19 black balls.

With the probabilities available in a series of tables similar to Figure 1, it is possible to illustrate one form of statistical inference. Assume that an auditor is testing the accuracy of a client's physical inventory count to ascertain that not more than 10% of the items counted are in error. If 100 different inventory items are test counted and 5 errors are found, what can reasonably be ascertained about the inventory on the basis of this sample?

The obvious tendency is to conclude that if 5% errors are present in the sample, 5% errors are present in the entire population. Figure 1 suggests, however, that this conclusion is not particularly sound. Figure 1 shows that in taking repeated samples from a population that has 10% defectives (black balls), only 13 in 100 samples would show the same percentage of defectives as exist in the entire population. By the same token, in drawing samples from a population that contains 5 percent defectives, presumably only a small proportion of the samples would contain 5 percent defectives.

It would, of course, be entirely reasonable to conclude that the sample of 100 inventory items *could* have come from a population of 5% defectives. But such a conclusion is not particularly helpful in deciding whether the inventory counting was sufficiently accurate to permit acceptance of the client's figures. Other tables similar to Figure 1 would show that a sample of 100 containing 5 defectives might be drawn from a population containing as few as 2% errors or as much as 14% errors—again not very helpful information.

Recall, however, that certainty is possible only through complete inspection, and that there is always a possibility of reaching an incorrect conclusion in resorting to sampling. The advantage of a statistical approach is that the risk of reaching an incorrect conclusion can be stated quantitatively, permitting a reasoned decision of whether or not to accept the amount of risk involved. Risk is, of course, merely the complement of confidence; the lesser the risk of a wrong decision, the greater the confidence that the decision is correct.

Returning to the sample inspection of the client's inventory count, it can be seen from Figure 1 that if exactly 10% of the inventory items were actually counted incorrectly, a sample of 100 items would show 5 or fewer errors 7 times in 100, or 7% of the times. In other words, it would be relatively rare to draw a sample of 100 with 5 defectives from a population that is 10% defective, and even more rare to draw such a sample from a population that is more than 10% defective. On this basis it is reasonable to conclude, with considerable confidence, that it is not likely that the population contains more than 10% defectives. Quantitatively, the conclusion can be stated to be based on 93% confidence, or conversely, to involve 7% risk.

A statistical inference of the type being discussed does not ordinarily involve the question of precision. Nevertheless, the precision of the inference can be determined. From additional tables similar to Figure 1, it can be determined with 93% confidence that the percentage of defectives in the inventory situation that has been discussed is no greater than 10% (as already mentioned) and no less than 3%. The range of these two figures may be considered the precision of the estimate of the true condition of the inventory, based on the stated sample of 100, and with a confidence (reliability) of 93%.

**Relation of sample size to size of population.** The reader may have wondered why no mention was made of the total number of inventory items in the preceding illustration, and whether meaningful results can actually be obtained without reference to population size. The question is particularly appropriate since audit sample size is commonly specified in audit programs in terms of a percentage of the total population.

This question can best be answered by returning to the example of the bowl containing 9,000 white balls and 1,000 black balls. With slight oversimplification, it can be said that the results obtained in the repeated samples of 100 are dependent upon the proportion of white and black balls in the bowl and not the number. So long as 10% of the balls are black, it makes relatively little difference whether the sample of 100 is drawn from a bowl containing 1,000, 10,000 or 100,000 balls, provided that the balls are thoroughly mixed before the sample is drawn.

The oversimplification in the above analysis becomes apparent, however, in sample sizes that represent a relatively large proportion of the population. This is best demonstrated by the obvious fact that a sample of 100 drawn from a population of 100 has a reliability of 100%, whereas a sample of 100 drawn from a population of 1,000 will have less than 100% reliability in reaching an inference about the make-up of the population as a whole. Reliability decreases as the sample becomes a smaller proportion of the population, decreasing until the population becomes infinite in size. This decrease, however, becomes relatively insignificant in populations of 1,000 or more, and in samples that constitute no more than 10% of the population. The Poisson distribution from which Figure 1 was prepared assumes an infinite population, and as a result, inferences drawn from samples selected from finite populations will have slightly greater reliability than the reliability determined from use of Poisson's figures. Again, however, the difference will not be significant if limits of 1,000 for population size and 10% for the proportion included in the sample are observed.

An important corollary to the above conclusions is that the absolute size of the sample is the principal factor affecting the reliability of an inference. Thus, the larger the sample the greater the reliability of any inference based on the sample. A related aspect is that as additional items are included in a sample, the sample results achieve greater stability. The bowl of balls may again be called upon to illustrate the point. If the sample is drawn one ball at a time, the proportion of black and white balls in the sample can be computed after each ball is drawn. After the first draw, the sample will be either 100% black or 100% white, but as additional balls are drawn, the percentage will tend to move toward the 10% proportion represented in the entire bowl. Also, since the influence of each successive ball on the percentage will be decreased, the changes in the percentage will be less erratic, and if balls continue to be drawn from the bowl, the percentage would become exactly 10 upon drawing the 10,000th ball.

Very obviously, the size of the sample to be drawn is a key factor in any type of sampling, and it is in the area of determining sample size that statistical methods can be of particular help to the auditor. The manner in which sample size can be determined is covered in a subsequent section of this chapter that describes various sampling plans.

**Advantages of using statistical techniques.** The advantages to the auditor of using statistical techniques may be broadly summarized in one word: *control.* The selection of items on an objective basis that can be readily followed by others, permits control over work that has been delegated. Sample size can be effectively controlled so that the sample size dictated by formula or table is neither too large and hence wasteful of audit time, nor too small and hence inadequate for a sound inference about the population.

Although the two considerations just listed may suggest that statistics can displace judgment, statistics do not and can not actually achieve such displacement. Instead, judgment is emphasized, with statistics providing a sounder basis for the exercise of judgment. The use of statistics might be likened to the installation of a speedometer in an automobile. The driver must still exercise judgment as to the speed at which he decides to drive, but his control over the situation is increased because he can determine with the aid of the speedometer precisely the speed at which the automobile is moving.

*The comparable control over sampling is achieved by the specification of reliability and precision in quantitative terms, these factors in turn de-termining sample size.* Conversely, if a sample has been taken, the reliability and precision of the inference drawn from the sample can be expressed quantitatively, thus permitting the auditor to determine on a meaningful basis whether there is adequate justification for accepting and using the inference involved. Again, control over the situation is the advantage gained by translating these factors into quantitative terms.

With this background, we may proceed to the actual mechanics of statistical sampling.

### SELECTING ITEMS FOR THE SAMPLE

Since a sample should reflect the characteristics of the population from which it is drawn, the selection of items for the sample has an important bearing on the results obtained. The principal methods of selection to be discussed are:

1. Judgmental selection.
2. Block samples.
3. Random selection.
4. Systematic selection.
5. Stratified samples.

**Judgmental selection.** As an auditor is usually interested in knowing the worst about a population, the practice has become quite widespread of selecting those items that have about them a suggestion of inaccuracy or doubt. For instance, inventory extensions that seem too large or small in relation to the quantities or prices involved would ordinarily be selected for tests of inventory extensions, and accounts receivable that are delin-quent or have unusual entries posted to them would be selected in tests of accounts receivable. There are, however, various drawbacks to the seem-ingly satisfactory process of judgmental selection. Often, the judgment exer-cised is less efficacious than the person exercising the judgment is inclined to believe.

▶ EXAMPLE: An experiment was conducted on the judgmental selection of bank depositors' accounts for written confirmation. Four experienced auditors were given the same criteria for selecting accounts from a ledger tray containing some 300 accounts, and each auditor made his own selec-tion from the complete tray of ledger cards. Ideally, each auditor should have selected the same accounts, but there was actually agreement on only 10% of the total accounts selected by the four. At the other extreme, 60% of the accounts selected were selected by only one of the four auditors.

Another difficulty with judgmental selection is that it is dependent upon the training of the auditor involved, which may be limited since sample selection is frequently delegated to young assistants. Other selection methods may be used that are independent of the ability of the person making the selection and that offer better control over the delegation of this responsibility. Particularly important is elimination of the possibility that complete freedom of selection may result in selecting those items that are most convenient or that strike some particular fancy of the person making the selection.

**Block samples.** The ease of selecting block samples has made them quite popular in auditing work. The block may be all cards in one of fifty ledger trays, all transactions occurring during one week of the year, or all accounts for customers' names beginning with one or more letters of the alphabet. The statistician's objection to block sampling stems from the purpose of sampling as he sees it: to reflect the characteristics of an entire population in a small number of items. The drawbacks of block sampling are particularly obvious when applied on a chronological basis: the fact that vendors' invoices have been properly processed and entered in the voucher register from February 2 through February 7 offers little assurance that the work in July or November was performed on a similar basis. Likewise, the fact that account balances were confirmed without exception for the accounts in the Sn–Sz ledger is not necessarily reliable evidence that the accounts in the Da–Dh ledger are equally correct.

**Random selection.** The preceding comments suggest the preference of the statistician for random samples that give each item in the population an equal opportunity of being chosen. Haphazard selection is sometimes presumed to be the equivalent of random selection, but the possibility of various forms of bias creeping into haphazard selection departs from the ideal of an equal chance of selection for each item in the population.

Random selection may be demonstrated with the bowl of black and white balls previously referred to. If the sample is taken by stirring the contents of the bowl, selecting a ball, stirring the contents again, selecting another ball, and repeating the process until the sample is completed, a random selection can be obtained. Such an approach is not readily applicable, however, to the selection of inventory extensions, accounts receivable, or cash disbursement items in the typical audit situation. Instead, if each item in the population can be numbered, random selection can be accomplished by using a random number table such as is illustrated in Figure 2. The numbers in a table of this type are arranged in completely random sequence, and the tables are even tested for randomness. In such tables, an item may appear more than once since the tables are based on sampling with replacement, thereby approximating sampling from an infinite population.

▶ EXAMPLE: To illustrate the use of a random number table, assume that 5,000 inventory items are listed 40 per page on 125 inventory pages. Starting in column 3 of Figure 2 and moving down the column (movement may also be up, across, or diagonally), the first figure is 01536, which would call for the selection of the 1,536th inventory item. Assuming that the items are not numbered consecutively (although they may be if pre-numbered inventory count tags were carried to the inventory sheets), the desired item would be the 16th item on page 38 of the inventory sheets (1536 ÷ 40). Since there are only 5,000 items in the inventory, only the last 4 digits of each random number in the table would be used, which would be 5,595 for the next number. As there is no item number that high in the inventory, the second number is simply ignored, making the next number 2,527, or item 7 on page 63, and so on.

**Systematic selection.** Although the use of random number tables is quite convenient and fast, the auditor would properly rebel at having to first take time to number a population, as would be necessary in selecting accounts receivable that are filed alphabetically in a ledger tray. When the population is unnumbered, a close approximation of random selection can be obtained by systematic selection, at a considerable saving in time. This method, familiar to most auditors, involves the selection of every Nth item in the population, with the value of N being determined by dividing the total number of items in the population by the number desired in the sample. Preferably, the starting number should be chosen on a random basis and care should be exercised that the population does not evidence a periodicity corresponding with the interval between the items selected for the sample. Under such circumstances, one type of item might have no chance of being selected, or conversely, only one type of item might be covered by the sample.

If accounts are being chosen from a ledger tray by systematic sampling, the accounts for the sample can be located by measuring a desired interval between accounts instead of counting the intervening accounts. Under either approach, however, the opportunities to control the work are as effective as in random selection based on a table of random numbers.

**Stratified samples.** Auditors have long used stratified samples, a sampling technique fully acceptable from a statistical standpoint. Stratification is particularly desirable when the population is composed of items that

| Line | Column | | | | | |
|------|--------|--------|--------|--------|--------|--------|
| | *(1)* | *(2)* | *(3)* | *(4)* | *(5)* | *(6)* |
| 1 | 10480 | 15011 | 01536 | 02011 | 81647 | 91646 |
| 2 | 22368 | 46573 | 25595 | 85393 | 30995 | 89198 |
| 3 | 24130 | 48360 | 22527 | 97265 | 76393 | 64809 |
| 4 | 42167 | 93093 | 06243 | 61680 | 07856 | 16376 |
| 5 | 37570 | 39975 | 81837 | 16656 | 06121 | 91782 |
| 6 | 77921 | 06907 | 11008 | 42751 | 27756 | 53498 |
| 7 | 99562 | 72905 | 56420 | 69994 | 98872 | 31016 |
| 8 | 96301 | 91977 | 05463 | 07972 | 18876 | 20922 |
| 9 | 89579 | 14342 | 63661 | 10281 | 17453 | 18103 |
| 10 | 85475 | 36857 | 53342 | 53988 | 53060 | 59533 |
| 11 | 28918 | 69578 | 88231 | 33276 | 70997 | 79936 |
| 12 | 63553 | 40961 | 48235 | 03427 | 49626 | 69445 |
| 13 | 09429 | 93969 | 52636 | 92737 | 88974 | 33488 |
| 14 | 10365 | 61129 | 87529 | 85689 | 48237 | 52267 |
| 15 | 07119 | 97336 | 71048 | 08178 | 77233 | 13916 |
| 16 | 51085 | 12765 | 51821 | 51259 | 77452 | 16308 |
| 17 | 02368 | 21382 | 52404 | 60268 | 89368 | 19885 |
| 18 | 01011 | 54092 | 33362 | 94904 | 31273 | 04146 |
| 19 | 52162 | 53916 | 46369 | 58586 | 23216 | 14513 |
| 20 | 07056 | 97628 | 33787 | 09998 | 42698 | 06691 |
| 21 | 48663 | 91245 | 85828 | 14346 | 09172 | 30168 |
| 22 | 54164 | 58492 | 22421 | 74103 | 47070 | 25306 |
| 23 | 32639 | 32363 | 05597 | 24200 | 13363 | 38005 |
| 24 | 29334 | 27001 | 87637 | 87308 | 58731 | 00256 |
| 25 | 02488 | 33062 | 28834 | 07351 | 19731 | 92420 |
| 26 | 81525 | 72295 | 04839 | 96423 | 24878 | 82651 |
| 27 | 29676 | 20591 | 68086 | 26432 | 46901 | 20849 |
| 28 | 00742 | 57392 | 39064 | 66432 | 84673 | 40027 |
| 29 | 05366 | 04213 | 25669 | 26422 | 44407 | 44048 |
| 30 | 91921 | 26418 | 64117 | 94305 | 26766 | 25940 |
| 31 | 00582 | 04711 | 87917 | 77341 | 42206 | 35126 |
| 32 | 00725 | 69884 | 62797 | 56170 | 86324 | 88072 |
| 33 | 69011 | 65795 | 95876 | 55293 | 18988 | 27354 |
| 34 | 25976 | 57948 | 29888 | 88604 | 67917 | 48708 |
| 35 | 09763 | 83473 | 73577 | 12908 | 30883 | 18317 |
| 36 | 91567 | 42595 | 27958 | 30134 | 04024 | 86385 |
| 37 | 17955 | 56349 | 90999 | 49127 | 20044 | 59931 |
| 38 | 46503 | 18584 | 18845 | 49618 | 02304 | 51038 |
| 39 | 92157 | 89634 | 94824 | 78171 | 84610 | 82834 |
| 40 | 14577 | 62765 | 35605 | 81263 | 39667 | 47358 |
| 41 | 98427 | 07523 | 33362 | 64270 | 01638 | 92477 |
| 42 | 34914 | 63976 | 88720 | 82765 | 34476 | 17032 |
| 43 | 70060 | 28377 | 39475 | 46473 | 23219 | 53416 |
| 44 | 53976 | 54914 | 06990 | 67245 | 68350 | 82948 |
| 45 | 76072 | 29515 | 40980 | 07391 | 58745 | 25774 |
| 46 | 90725 | 52210 | 83974 | 29992 | 65831 | 38857 |
| 47 | 64364 | 67412 | 33339 | 31926 | 14883 | 24413 |
| 48 | 08962 | 00358 | 31662 | 25388 | 61642 | 34072 |
| 49 | 95012 | 68379 | 93526 | 70765 | 10592 | 04542 |
| 50 | 15664 | 10493 | 20492 | 38391 | 91132 | 21999 |

**Fig. 2. Table of Random Digits.**

*Source:* Interstate Commerce Commission, Bureau of Transport Economics and Statistics, *Table of 105,000 Random Decimal Digits,* Washington, D.C., 1949.

vary greatly in value or importance. Thus, to assure himself that no major inventory items have been mis-counted, the auditor might make independent counts of all items whose value is likely to exceed, say, $1,000, and limit his sampling to those items estimated to be less than $1,000 in total value. It should be noted that stratification offers full opportunity of control when selection is delegated to a person other than the one responsible for designing the sample and supervising the work.

## EVALUATION OF SAMPLING RESULTS

Although the heading of this section refers only to the end result of sampling, the evaluation of the information revealed by the sample, this must be preceded by the selection of a sampling plan and the determination of the sample size in accordance with the plan that has been chosen. Each of these topics is covered under each of the following sampling plans to be presented:

1. Judgmental evaluation.
2. Acceptance sampling based on Poisson's distribution.
3. Sequential sampling.
4. Discovery sampling.
5. Estimation sampling.

**Judgmental evaluation.** Traditionally, the auditor has evaluated the results of the samples that he has taken on a judgmental basis. The results of such efforts have been reasonably satisfactory, and most auditors have acquired a sound sense of judgment that is usually in close correspondence with statistical principles. Nevertheless the approach is relatively crude and inexact, and the possibility is always strong that a misleading inference may be reached. Also, the sample chosen may be larger than necessary, or too small to support a meaningful inference, and the inference itself may be questionable.

▶ EXAMPLE: Assume that an auditor is seeking to ascertain the accuracy of an accounts receivable aging analysis prepared by a client. If 100 accounts are selected for the test, and errors are found in the aging of 3 of them, the natural inclination would be to assume that errors exist in approximately the same proportion in the remainder of the accounts in the analysis. Yet statistically, it can be shown that a sample of 100 containing 3 errors has some probability of being chosen from a population containing as few as 1% errors or as many as 10% errors. Stated another way, if exactly 3% of the accounts in the aging analysis were, in fact, aged incorrectly, and repeated random samples of 100 were selected from the aging, only about 23% of those samples would evidence the same 3% error rate present in the client's work.

In view of these facts, there is little wonder that the precision afforded through the statistical interpretation of audit samples has attracted considerable interest in auditing circles.

**Acceptance sampling based on Poisson's distribution.** The statistician Poisson derived mathematical approximations of the probabilities of occurrence of an event or characteristic in samples drawn from a population. This author has, in turn, developed a table based on Poisson's calculations that is usable in audit situations where the auditor is concerned with the rate of occurrence of errors or some other attribute of a given population.[1]

This table is used in an area closely related to "acceptance sampling," although the table offers more flexibility than most acceptance sampling plans. In acceptance sampling, which is a mainstay of *statistical quality control*, some particular attribute is tested and the entire population is accepted or rejected based on the results of the sample.

▶ EXAMPLE: A manufacturer of television receivers is concerned about the life expectancy of tubes that he purchases. Assume that 1,000 hours should be the minimum life expectancy for such tubes, although some will have a shorter life. The manufacturer wishes to be 95% confident that only 4% or less of the tubes in any one lot will fail to meet the 1,000 hour minimum. Lots failing to meet these standards will be returned to the manufacturer, but our purchaser also knows that even acceptable lots may give rise to samples that call for rejection of the lot. He wants to be 95% confident that lots actually containing less than 2% unsatisfactory tubes will not be rejected by his inspection plan. These are the factors that must be determined for any complete acceptance sampling plan.

Returning to the earlier example of the auditor testing for errors in a client's accounts receivable aging analysis, we may see how the situation

---

[1] The Poisson distribution represents a simplified approach to the binomial distribution, and closely approximates the binomial, which is based on sampling from an infinite population. An infinite population can be simulated in sampling from a finite population by returning each sampled item to the population after its characteristics have been noted. This retains a constant relationship between defective and non-defective items in the population. Most audit sampling, of course, is concerned with a finite population, and is likely to be conducted without replacing the items sampled. Under these circumstances, the technically correct approach is through the hypergeometric distribution. However, the simplicity of using the Poisson distribution under these circumstances outweighs the slight inaccuracy of the results as compared with using the hypergeometric distribution. The differences in results are nominal, provided that defectives do not exceed 10% of the population and that the sample size does not exceed 10% of the population.

can be approached through the use of the tables developed by the author and presented in Figure 3. Assume that the auditor desires 90% confidence that the rate of error in the aging analysis does not exceed 5%. He must first determine the minimum sample size he will take. This figure can be readily determined from Figure 3.

Since he seeks assurance that not more than 5% of the agings are in error, the column of figures headed by that figure is used. The first figure in that column, 72, means that if a sample of 25 items is selected and no errors occur, the auditor would be justified 72 times in 100 in assuming that the error rate does not exceed 5%. In other words, he would have 72% confidence in accepting the population as containing no more than 5% errors. The auditor has, however, specified 90% confidence, and by moving down the table to sample size 50, we observe that the reliability of a sample increases with an increase in the sample size. A sample of 50 with no errors appearing would, therefore, justify accepting the client's work under the specifications set, and would become the minimum sample size.

Assume, however, that one error is found in the sample of 50, which reduces the confidence to 71%. Although this sample does not justify accepting the client's work, neither does it justify rejecting the client's work as unsatisfactory, for the sample offers only 29% confidence that the error rate is greater than 5%. The auditor would, therefore, proceed to select additional items, and as noted earlier, by the time the sample reached 100, a total of 3 errors had been found. This sample would afford 73% confidence in accepting the sample—only slightly more confidence than was offered by the sample of 50.

Three errors in a sample of 100 represents only 3% errors, which is less than the maximum that the auditor is willing to tolerate in the population, but the variability that may appear in small samples gives little assurance that a sample evidencing only 3% errors did not actually come from a population containing a higher percentage of errors. The significance of the stability that a sample acquires as its size increases is demonstrated by subsequent values listed in Figure 3. For example, although 3 errors in a sample of 100 affords an inadequate basis for accepting the client's work, a sample of 300 with 9 errors present (the same percentage) would permit accepting the population as containing less than 5% errors with 93% confidence, which is acceptable under the specifications initially determined for accepting the population.

Acceptance sampling using the table in Figure 3, or on any other basis, presents difficulty when the percentage of errors in the population is actually very close to the percentage specified as acceptable. Thus, if the client's aging work actually contained 5% errors, the samples would tend

| Number of items test checked | Number of errors disclosed | Number of times in 100 that the auditor will be justified in deciding that the actual error rate is less than: | | | | |
|---|---|---|---|---|---|---|
| | | 0.5% | 1% | 2% | 5% | 10% |
| 25 | 0 | 12 | 22 | 39 | 72 | 92 |
| 25 | 1 | 1 | 3 | 9 | 36 | 71 |
| 25 | 2 | 0 | 0 | 1 | 13 | 46 |
| 25 | 3 | | | 0 | 4 | 24 |
| 25 | 4 | | | | 1 | 11 |
| 25 | 5 | | | | 0 | 4 |
| 25 | 6 | | | | | 1 |
| 25 | 7 | | | | | 0 |
| 50 | 0 | 22 | 39 | 63 | 92 | 99 |
| 50 | 1 | 3 | 9 | 26 | 71 | 96 |
| 50 | 2 | 0 | 1 | 8 | 46 | 87 |
| 50 | 3 | | 0 | 2 | 24 | 73 |
| 50 | 4 | | | 0 | 11 | 56 |
| 50 | 5 | | | | 4 | 38 |
| 50 | 6 | | | | 1 | 24 |
| 50 | 7 | | | | 0 | 13 |

The table is developed from Poisson's distribution as follows:

$C'$ = Average number of occurrences of a given event
$C$ = Number of times in 1,000 that $C$ or fewer occurrences can be expected under the conditions of $C'$

Thus, if a sample of 100 is drawn from a series of data that has an average of 2 per cent errors, $C'$ is 2, and the values for $C$ are

| | |
|---|---|
| 0 = 135 | 5 = 983 |
| 1 = 406 | 6 = 995 |
| 2 = 677 | 7 = 999 |
| 3 = 857 | 8 = 1,000 |
| 4 = 947 | |

In turn, when an average error of 2 per cent is present, a sample of 100 will reveal one error or less 406 times in 1,000. The auditor may therefore conclude that the probability of finding more than one error is 594 (the complement of 406) and that, in accepting a sample of 100 showing one error as coming from a population that must have contained less than 2 per cent errors, the probability of being correct is 59.4 per cent.

The value indicated in the previous example is found on the line of this table showing sample size 100, one error; under the 2 per cent column, the figure 59 appears.

All probabilities less than ½ are shown in the table as 0.

All probabilities greater than 99½ are shown in the table as 100.

This table covers only the sample sizes and maximum allowable rates of error that are most likely to be needed. Values not shown can be derived readily by using a table of the Poisson distribution as described above.

* This table, developed by the author, first appeared in the January, 1954, issue of *The Journal of Accountancy*, and is reprinted by permission.

**Fig. 3. Implications of Accepting Data Based on the Number of Errors Disclosed by the Auditor's Test Checks.**

| Number of items test checked | Number of errors disclosed | Number of times in 100 that the auditor will be justified in deciding that the actual error rate is less than: | | | | |
|---|---|---|---|---|---|---|
| | | 0.5% | 1% | 2% | 5% | 10% |
| 50 | 8 | | | | | 7 |
| 50 | 9 | | | | | 3 |
| 50 | 10 | | | | | 1 |
| 100 | 0 | 39 | 63 | 86 | 99 | 100 |
| 100 | 1 | 9 | 26 | 59 | 96 | 100 |
| 100 | 2 | 1 | 8 | 32 | 87 | 100 |
| 100 | 3 | 0 | 2 | 14 | 73 | 99 |
| 100 | 4 | | 0 | 5 | 56 | 97 |
| 100 | 5 | | | 2 | 38 | 93 |
| 100 | 6 | | | 0 | 24 | 87 |
| 100 | 7 | | | | 13 | 78 |
| 100 | 8 | | | | 7 | 67 |
| 100 | 9 | | | | 3 | 54 |
| 100 | 10 | | | | 1 | 42 |
| 150 | 0 | 53 | 78 | 95 | 100 | 100 |
| 150 | 1 | 17 | 44 | 80 | 100 | 100 |
| 150 | 2 | 4 | 19 | 58 | 98 | 100 |
| 150 | 3 | 1 | 7 | 35 | 94 | 100 |
| 150 | 4 | 0 | 2 | 18 | 87 | 100 |
| 150 | 5 | | 0 | 8 | 76 | 100 |
| 150 | 6 | | | 3 | 62 | 99 |
| 150 | 7 | | | 1 | 48 | 98 |
| 150 | 8 | | | 0 | 34 | 96 |
| 150 | 9 | | | | 22 | 93 |
| 150 | 10 | | | | 14 | 88 |
| 200 | 0 | 63 | 86 | 98 | 100 | 100 |
| 200 | 1 | 26 | 59 | 91 | 100 | 100 |
| 200 | 2 | 8 | 32 | 76 | 100 | 100 |
| 200 | 3 | 2 | 14 | 57 | 99 | 100 |
| 200 | 4 | 0 | 5 | 37 | 97 | 100 |
| 200 | 5 | | 2 | 21 | 93 | 100 |
| 200 | 6 | | 0 | 11 | 87 | 100 |
| 200 | 7 | | | 5 | 78 | 100 |
| 200 | 8 | | | 2 | 67 | 100 |
| 200 | 9 | | | 1 | 54 | 99 |
| 200 | 10 | | | 0 | 42 | 99 |
| 300 | 0 | 78 | 95 | 100 | 100 | 100 |
| 300 | 1 | 44 | 80 | 98 | 100 | 100 |
| 300 | 2 | 19 | 58 | 94 | 100 | 100 |
| 300 | 3 | 7 | 35 | 85 | 100 | 100 |
| 300 | 4 | 2 | 18 | 71 | 100 | 100 |
| 300 | 5 | 0 | 8 | 55 | 100 | 100 |
| 300 | 6 | | 3 | 39 | 99 | 100 |
| 300 | 7 | | 1 | 26 | 98 | 100 |
| 300 | 8 | | 0 | 15 | 96 | 100 |

**Fig. 3. Implications of Accepting Data Based on the Number of Errors Disclosed by the Auditor's Test Checks. (Continued.)**

| Number of items test checked | Number of errors dis- closed | Number of times in 100 that the auditor will be justified in deciding that the actual error rate is less than: | | | | |
|---|---|---|---|---|---|---|
| | | 0.5% | 1% | 2% | 5% | 10% |
| 300 | 9 | | | 8 | 93 | 100 |
| 300 | 10 | | | 4 | 88 | 100 |
| 300 | 11 | | | 2 | 81 | 100 |
| 300 | 12 | | | 1 | 73 | 100 |
| 300 | 13 | | | 0 | 64 | 100 |
| 300 | 14 | | | | 53 | 100 |
| 300 | 15 | | | | 43 | 100 |
| 400 | 0 | 86 | 98 | 100 | 100 | 100 |
| 400 | 1 | 59 | 91 | 100 | 100 | 100 |
| 400 | 2 | 32 | 76 | 99 | 100 | 100 |
| 400 | 3 | 14 | 57 | 96 | 100 | 100 |
| 400 | 4 | 5 | 37 | 90 | 100 | 100 |
| 400 | 5 | 2 | 21 | 81 | 100 | 100 |
| 400 | 6 | 0 | 11 | 69 | 100 | 100 |
| 400 | 7 | | 5 | 55 | 100 | 100 |
| 400 | 8 | | 2 | 41 | 100 | 100 |
| 400 | 9 | | 1 | 28 | 99 | 100 |
| 400 | 10 | | 0 | 18 | 99 | 100 |
| 400 | 11 | | | 11 | 98 | 100 |
| 400 | 12 | | | 6 | 96 | 100 |
| 400 | 13 | | | 3 | 93 | 100 |
| 400 | 14 | | | 2 | 89 | 100 |
| 400 | 15 | | | 1 | 84 | 100 |
| 400 | 16 | | | 0 | 78 | 100 |
| 400 | 17 | | | | 70 | 100 |
| 400 | 18 | | | | 62 | 100 |
| 400 | 19 | | | | 53 | 100 |
| 400 | 20 | | | | 44 | 100 |
| 500 | 0 | 92 | 99 | 100 | 100 | 100 |
| 500 | 1 | 71 | 96 | 100 | 100 | 100 |
| 500 | 2 | 46 | 87 | 100 | 100 | 100 |
| 500 | 3 | 24 | 73 | 99 | 100 | 100 |
| 500 | 4 | 11 | 56 | 97 | 100 | 100 |
| 500 | 5 | 4 | 38 | 93 | 100 | 100 |
| 500 | 6 | 1 | 24 | 87 | 100 | 100 |
| 500 | 7 | 0 | 13 | 78 | 100 | 100 |
| 500 | 8 | | 7 | 67 | 100 | 100 |
| 500 | 9 | | 3 | 54 | 100 | 100 |
| 500 | 10 | | 1 | 42 | 100 | 100 |
| 500 | 11 | | 0 | 30 | 100 | 100 |
| 500 | 12 | | | 21 | 100 | 100 |
| 500 | 13 | | | 14 | 99 | 100 |
| 500 | 14 | | | 8 | 99 | 100 |

**Fig. 3. Implications of Accepting Data Based on the Number of Errors Disclosed by the Auditor's Test Checks. (Continued.)**

| Number of items test checked | Number of errors dis- closed | Number of times in 100 that the auditor will be justified in deciding that the actual error rate is less than: | | | | |
|---|---|---|---|---|---|---|
| | | 0.5% | 1% | 2% | 5% | 10% |
| 500 | 15 | | | 5 | 98 | 100 |
| 500 | 16 | | | 3 | 96 | 100 |
| 500 | 17 | | | 1 | 94 | 100 |
| 500 | 18 | | | 1 | 91 | 100 |
| 500 | 19 | | | 0 | 87 | 100 |
| 500 | 20 | | | | 81 | 100 |
| 500 | 21 | | | | 75 | 100 |
| 500 | 22 | | | | 68 | 100 |
| 500 | 23 | | | | 61 | 100 |
| 500 | 24 | | | | 53 | 100 |
| 500 | 25 | | | | 45 | 100 |

**Fig. 3. Implications of Accepting Data Based on the Number of Errors Disclosed by the Auditor's Test Checks. (Continued.)**

to show about that percentage of error, and even a sample of 500, if it pro‹ duced 25 errors, would give only 45% confidence in accepting the popula‹ tion, and only 55% confidence in rejecting the population. Under such circumstances, the auditor has little choice but to examine the remaining items in the population himself in order to determine the true percentage of errors, or to request that the client re-check the work and correct all errors found. Under the latter circumstances, the auditor should take a new sample from the corrected population to assure himself that the population does in fact meet his standards.

One word of caution should be given concerning the use of Figure 3. The values are based on sampling from populations that are infinite in size, and, of course, the auditor works with finite populations. The effect of this difference may be ignored, however, since it will be negligible provided that the sample used is less than 10% of the total population. Should the sample exceed this limitation, the violation of the requirement will simply give the auditor greater confidence than is stated in the table, or alternatively, the minimum sample size determined from the table will be larger than is actually necessary.

**Sequential sampling.** Although the sampling approach based on Figure 3 in effect operates as a sequential sampling plan, since additional items can be selected in sequence until a decision is possible, the term "sequential sampling" is customarily reserved for a single specific plan, which is discussed below.

Sequential sampling necessitates that the following factors be determined in advance:

1. The percentage of errors in the population that would be unacceptable.

2. The risk (stated as a percentage that is the complement of the per-

centage of confidence) that will be tolerated of accepting a population that is unacceptable.

3. The percentage of errors in the population that would be acceptable.

4. The risk that will be tolerated of rejecting a population that is actually acceptable.

By a rather complicated formula, available in almost any textbook on statistical quality control, the values set for the above factors can be used to calculate "accept" and "reject" numbers for various sample sizes. For any calculated sample size, a number of errors equal to or greater than the "reject" number results in rejection of the population, and a number of errors equal to or less than the "accept" number results in acceptance of the population. If the number of errors falls between the accept and reject numbers, sampling is continued until the cumulative sample results permit an acceptance or rejection decision based on the calculated values for the sample size involved. Minimum sample sizes are determined that must be satisfied before a decision is permissible.

The calculated values may be reduced to the form of a graph, or a graph can be constructed from nomographs that have been developed, and the desired decision can be reached by plotting the sample results on the graph. Figure 4 illustrates such a graph for the factor values stated on the graph. Note from the graph that the sample line will plot in the "reject" area if the first two items contain errors, and the population may be rejected immediately. On the other hand, the sample line will not plot in the "accept"

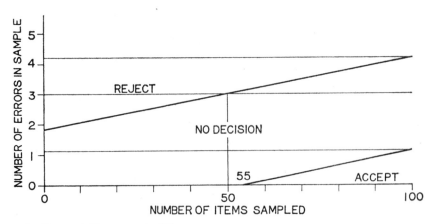

1. Unacceptable error rate, 5%.
2. Risk of accepting an unacceptable population, 10%.
3. Acceptable error rate, 1%.
4. Risk of rejecting an acceptable population, 5%.

**Fig. 4. Sequential Sampling Graph.**

area until 55 items have been chosen, none of which contain errors. This point represents the minimum sample size for acceptance of the population tested.

The space between the accept and reject lines is the area of "no decision." Therefore, additional items must be drawn until the line plotted from the sample results falls into either the accept or reject area. Note that the lines defining the accept and reject areas are parallel, however. It is thus possible that, if a sample is drawn from a population with an actual error rate about midway between the acceptable and unacceptable values originally established, the sample line will never move out of the "no decision" area. Under such circumstances, the auditor might decide to cease sampling and inspect the entire population. Or he can resort to *truncation*, which permits a decision after a specified sample size has been reached, even though the sample line has not moved outside the accept and reject lines.

**Discovery sampling.** A type of sampling referred to as "discovery sampling" has been developed for use in auditing situations; but essentially, discovery sampling is merely a variation of acceptance sampling.

Discovery sampling is usually considered to be directed primarily toward the discovery of the "rare" item. Actually, however, no form of sampling is satisfactory for detecting the truly rare item. If, for example, a population of 1,000 disbursement vouchers contains one fraudulent item, the only reasonable approach to uncovering such an item is to examine every voucher until the fraudulent item is detected.

On the other hand, if more widespread fraud is suspected, or if the auditor is seeking to satisfy himself with reasonable confidence that fairly widespread fraud does not exist, then discovery sampling can be of some assistance. The underlying basis for discovery sampling is that the auditor seeks assurance that a certain condition does not exist, and the discovery of a single example of the undesirable condition is, of course, evidence that the condition actually does exist. Most frequently, the condition involved will be some form of fraud or an indication that established procedures are not being consistently followed.

To illustrate, we can use the case of a large group of disbursement vouchers. Established procedures require that each voucher be supported by a purchase order, an invoice, a receiving report, and certain approvals. Assume that an auditor is interested in ascertaining that the established procedures are being followed, and is seeking 95% confidence that the procedures have not broken down to the extent that 2% of the vouchers are improperly supported or approved. Given these conditions, the table in Figure 3 can be used to devise a sampling plan. In the column headed

2%, we see that a sample of 150 disclosing no errors affords 95% confidence that the error rate is less than 2%. In other words, if the population does contain 2% or more errors, 95 times in 100 a sample of 150 will disclose one or more errors.

The discovery of an error before the sample of 150 is completed signals that the population cannot be accepted as meeting the specified criteria. It does not, however, justify a conclusion that 2% or more of the vouchers are improperly supported or approved. If the error is detected on the 100th voucher, the auditor would have only 41% confidence in concluding that more than 2% of the vouchers have been incorrectly handled. Under such circumstances, the auditor might either continue his testing until he can reach an inference about the population with adequate confidence, or re-examine his criteria in the light of the sampling results achieved to that point.

On the other hand, a sample showing no deviation from the established procedures does not give any useful assurance that no deviations have occurred. These results merely give the specified confidence that deviations have not occurred at a rate in excess of that originally specified.

**Estimation sampling.** Although the original interest in statistical sampling for audit purposes represented a transfer of techniques developed in statistical quality control—namely, acceptance sampling—subsequent research disclosed that other statistical techniques are also useful. Of these, estimation sampling, or survey sampling as it is also called, has offered the greatest promise. It has two particular advantages. First, it is not limited to dealing with errors and rates of error. Second, when dealing with errors by means of estimation sampling, it is possible to ascertain the probable influence of such errors on the dollar total of the population.

For instance, if 1% of the items in a client's physical inventory count are in error, the total inventory value may or may not be 1% in error. First of all, the counting errors would seldom involve a 100% misstatement, but rather, minor errors of only a few items. Secondly, the errors would ordinarily tend to be more frequent in counting items of small value, where less care might be taken, and such errors would consequently have a smaller effect on the total than would errors in counting items of greater value. Estimation sampling automatically takes care of such problems.

Estimation sampling can be particularly useful in the auditor's work on accounts receivable. Hence, that area is chosen to demonstrate the theory and methods involved in estimation sampling. The general approach is to determine the average account balance from a sample, and then project this figure by multiplying it by the total number of accounts in the population. Related calculations, involving a relatively simple formula, are used to develop a sample size that will give a stated amount of confidence that the true value of the population is within a stated amount from the figure determined by projecting the sample results. This latter range of values represents, of course, the precision of the estimate. An important factor affecting sample size in the calculations is the standard deviation of the population, which can usually be approximated from the sample. In general, the greater the variability of the population, the less precise will be the estimate based on the sample, or in turn, the larger must be the sample to assure a given amount of precision.

**Theory underlying estimation sampling.** Certain characteristics of a normally distributed population can be described statistically, and these statistical measures are the foundation of estimation sampling. Consider, for instance, a group of accounts receivable whose arithmetic mean (amount of the average balance) is $50. The standard deviation of the population of accounts would be calculated by determining the difference between $50 and the balance of each account, squaring each of these differences, computing the sum of these squared differences, dividing the sum by the number of accounts in the population, and calculating the square root of the quotient. Assume that the standard deviation of this population of accounts is $10. It is known (through statistical proofs that need not concern us here) that 68.3% of the accounts in the population will lie within plus or minus one standard deviation from the mean, or within the range of $40 to $60. Similarly, 95.4% of the accounts will lie within two standard deviations from the mean [$30–70 range], and 99.7% of the accounts will lie within three standard deviations from the mean [$20–80 range]. Graphically, these indications may be shown as in Figure 5.

Also important to estimation sampling is the known fact that if repeated samples of a given size are selected from a population, the means of those samples (average account balance for each sample, continuing with the previous illustration) will form a normal distribution (even if the population is not normally distributed). Also, the mean of those sample means will equal the mean of the population, and the standard deviation of the sample means will vary inversely with sample size. The latter phenomenon is explained by the fact that in larger samples, if an atypical account that is very large or very small should appear in the sample, the effect on the mean of the sample will be diminished by the larger number of typical accounts that are likely to appear in the sample. Similarly, as sample size increases, there is less probability that an undue proportion of the accounts selected will be either smaller or larger than the mean balance. Hence the sample means are less likely to deviate substantially from the true mean.

Another indication of the behavior of sample means in relation to sam-

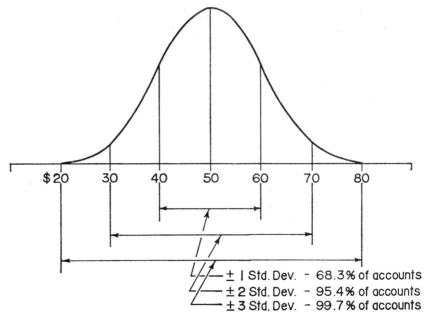

**Fig. 5. Graphic Representation of Normally Distributed Population with Indication of Percentage of Items Falling Within One, Two, and Three Standard Deviations of the Mean.**

ple size is suggested by the fact that the sample mean of a 100% sample will be identical with the true mean of the population. Hence the standard deviation of the means of repeated 100% samples would be zero.

The deviation of the means of repeated samples from the mean of the population from which they are drawn will also be influenced by the dispersion of the items in the population; i.e., the larger the standard deviation of the population, the greater will be the deviation of the means of repeated samples from the true mean of the population. Thus it is apparent that the standard deviation of the means of repeated samples varies directly with the standard deviation of the population from which the samples are drawn, and inversely with the size of the samples.

The effect of sample size and the standard deviation of the population on the standard deviation of repeated samples drawn from the population can be expressed mathematically. This being true, if the standard deviation of a population is known, the standard deviation of the means of repeated samples of a given size can be calculated. In turn, it is evident that 68.3% of the sample means will be within plus or minus one standard deviation of the population mean, 95.4% will be within plus or minus two standard deviations, and 99.7% will be within plus or minus three standard deviations. Thus, if the standard deviation of a population is known, and if a sample of appropriate size is selected from the population, it is apparent that there are 95.4 chances in a hundred that the mean of the sample will be within plus or minus two standard deviations of the mean of the population. Conversely, if the population mean is not known, it can be estimated with 95.4% confidence that the population mean does not differ from the sample mean by more than two standard deviations. In general, however, the desired confidence is expressed in whole numbers. Figure 6 shows the exact proportion of standard deviations involved for typical whole number expressions of the confidence that may be desired. The application of these concepts to a typical problem of estimation sampling is explained in the next section.

| Desired Confidence (Percentage of Sample Means Falling Within Indicated Number of Standard Deviations) | Number of Standard Deviations Necessary to Include Specified Percentage of Sample Means |
|---|---|
| 68.3% | ±1.00 |
| 90% | ±1.64 |
| 95% | ±1.96 |
| 99% | ±2.58 |

**Fig. 6. Percentage of Sample Means in a Population Encompassed by One or More Standard Deviations.**

**An example of estimation sampling.** Assume that it is desired to estimate whether the total of a client's accounts receivable is stated with sufficient accuracy to justify use of the client's figure for financial statement purposes. A sample of the accounts must be selected, and the correct balances of these accounts determined through positive confirmation procedures. The determination of the size of the sample to be taken and the determination of whether the sample justifies acceptance of the client's accounts receivable figure necessitates the following steps:

1. Determine the desired precision of the estimate to be made. This factor will depend on the auditor's opinion as to how much the actual amount of receivables might vary from the figure shown in the client's financial statements for receivables without materially affecting the client's financial position or results of operations as portrayed by the statements. In our example, the receivables are assumed to be $100,000, and it is assumed that the true figure could vary from $100,000 as much as plus or minus $7,000 without materially affecting the financial statements.

2. Set the confidence level desired in the estimate to be made. For this example assume it is 95%. The confidence chosen indicates, in effect, that

the auditor is willing to take the chance that 5 times in 100 the true value of the receivables might actually lie outside the precision limits that have been set. Other levels of confidence can, of course, be used.

3. Determine the sample size to be used for the confirmation process by the following formula:

$$\text{Sample size} = \frac{(\text{Standard deviation of population})^2}{(\text{Standard deviation of sample means})^2}$$

The standard deviation of the population may be estimated as follows:

a. Select 49 accounts on a random basis (these accounts may also be used as the first 49 accounts for the confirmation sample).

b. Divide the accounts into 7 groups of 7 each, taking the accounts in the same order in which they were drawn.

c. Calculate the range for each group (the difference between the highest and lowest balance in the group).

d. Calculate the arithmetic mean of the 7 ranges.

e. Divide the arithmetic mean of the averages by 2.704. The quotient will be a close approximation of the standard deviation of the population, which we shall assume is $3.15.

The desired standard deviation of the means of samples that would satisfy the specified precision and risk is calculated as follows:

$$\begin{array}{l}\text{Standard deviation of} \\ \text{sample means}\end{array} = \frac{\text{Precision}}{\begin{array}{l}\text{Number of items} \\ \text{in the population}\end{array}} \div \begin{array}{l}\text{Number of standard} \\ \text{deviations necessary} \\ \text{to assure desired} \\ \text{confidence.}\end{array}$$

Inserting the appropriate figures in this formula, including the population size which is assumed to be 20,000 accounts, and the figure 1.96 from Figure 6, representing the number of standard deviations within which 95% of the sample means should occur, we have:

$$\begin{array}{l}\text{Standard deviation of} \\ \text{sample means}\end{array} = \frac{\$\,7,000}{20,000} \div 1.96 = \$.179$$

Substituting this value and the standard deviation of the population in the formula for sample size, we have:

$$\text{Sample size} = \frac{(3.15\ )^2}{(\ .179)^2} = 310$$

4. Sufficient confirmation requests (randomly selected) should be sent out to assure at least 310 usable replies. From these replies, the average account balance would be computed, and when multiplied by 20,000, the total number of accounts in the population, would give an estimate of the

total receivables that would be accurate within ±$7,000 with 95% confidence. If the estimated receivables total, in turn, did not vary by more than ±$7,000 from the client's figure, the client's figure would be accepted at its stated amount. If the estimated receivables figure should fall outside the range of ±$7,000, the auditor would be entitled to 95% confidence that the true value of the population is within $7,000 of the estimate based on the sample.

As was also the case with the earlier discussion of acceptance sampling, the approach to estimation sampling has been based on an assumed infinite population. A correction factor can be applied to adjust for the actual size of the population, but such adjustment is nominal provided that the sample does not exceed 10% of the population. Furthermore, the error resulting from ignoring the correction factor is in the auditor's favor, since the actual confidence will be slightly greater than the figure used in the calculations.

Attention is called to the fact that the greater the variability of the items being sampled, the greater will be the standard deviation of the population, and the larger will be the required sample size necessary to yield the desired precision and risk. In cases of extreme variability, the advantages of stratification become evident. By selecting all major items and examining them on a 100% basis, and then adding such figures to the estimate of the remainder of the population, the auditor can not only gain greater assurance in accepting or rejecting the client's figures, but the combined samples may actually be smaller than if stratification is not employed.

### WORKING PAPERS

General considerations concerning audit working papers are equally applicable to the auditor's work with statistical sampling. Not only are the working papers a means of developing desired information, but they provide a record of the sample results that the auditor can produce as evidence in connection with litigation or for any other reason.

Particularly important is a clear record of the calculations or references to tables used in determining sample size, and the values assigned to the factors of precision and confidence should be noted in that connection, possibly with a brief statement of why the particular values were chosen. Equally important would be a description of the method used in selecting the items for the sample.

If random number tables are used, it is desirable to identify the exact table involved and to list the numbers used. It will ordinarily be more convenient to work from such a list of numbers rather than directly from a table when selecting the items. The amounts, details, or identifying information about the items selected can then be shown alongside the related numbers. The random numbers drawn from a table appear, of course, in random order. They may be recorded in the working papers, however, in numerical sequence.

## SPECIAL PROBLEMS

There are many problems in adapting any statistical technique to auditing, and several of the more important problems are discussed briefly at this point.

**Discovery of fraud.** As has already been indicated, sampling is of relatively little value in the discovery of fraud, particularly if the instances of fraud that have occurred are relatively few. On the other hand, the typical independent audit is not ordinarily concerned with isolated fraudulent items since they would be unlikely to have a material bearing on the financial or operating results.

By the same token, should fraud or errors be so widespread in the accounts that the statements would be materially affected, a properly designed sample should give whatever assurance the auditor desires that the situation will be revealed by his sample—provided, of course, that all items sampled are reviewed with due professional care.

**Testing internal control.** If, in the review of internal control, records are tested for violations of established procedures not exceeding some specified percentage, statistical techniques are obviously applicable. In many situations, however, the auditor may be satisfied with merely some very general assurance that a particular procedure is in effect. Often, the desired assurance can be obtained by examining only a very few items—a number not an adequate basis for a useful statistical inference.

Such a condition is most likely to occur when there is also other evidence that bears on the situation in question. For instance, there may be a requirement that the treasurer must approve every request to write off an uncollectible account. Assume it is known that the treasurer pays close attention to the monthly aging of accounts receivable and to the charges against the bad debt provision shown in the financial statements. Assume also that the general ledger bookkeeper understands that the treasurer's approval must appear on a request before the write-off can be journalized. In such case, the examination of a very few write-offs, together with the other information, should be adequate to assure the auditor that the required procedure has been followed.

At the present level of development, statistical techniques are of no help to the auditor in deciding how many items to examine under the above circumstances. It is the contention of this author, however, that the problem is best resolved by either taking a sample that can be justified statistically, or limiting the sample to the irreducible figure of one. Given the likelihood that a procedure is either in effect or not in effect at all, the examination of one item should reveal just as much as an examination of 10 or 20. There is, then, no opening for a subsequent question as to why, as long as several items were examined, a sufficient number was not selected to justify a useful statistical inference about the items being tested.

**Definition of the population.** Under some circumstances, the definition of the population may have a decided effect on the amount of sampling that is done. For example, if three inventory crews do all of the counting for the client's physical inventory, a decision must be made whether to consider the work of each crew as a separate population or to consider the entire inventory as the population. The decision is important since three populations would require roughly three times as much sampling as a single population.

If the sample is intended to reveal the accuracy of the counting by each of the crews, three populations must be assumed to exist. An internal auditor might be interested in such information, but as a rule the independent auditor is interested only in the overall accuracy of the inventory and hence may consider the entire inventory as the population and use a smaller total sample.

**Definition of an error.** Another problem of definition exists in terms of an error, in spite of the fact that, seemingly, "an error is an error." In the first place, there are both procedural and substantive errors, and a decision must be made whether the two types are of equal importance. A procedural error would be represented by the absence of a required approval on a document, whereas a substantive error would be represented by an actual mistake in the amount shown on the document. If the auditor is seeking to ascertain that a certain account balance is stated with reasonable accuracy, he will likely be more interested in substantive errors, but if he is testing internal control, both types would be important. A substantive error ordinarily indicates a breakdown in procedures.

A second problem the auditor must often face is whether to distinguish between major and minor substantive errors. Since ordinarily it is the overall accuracy of an amount that is of interest, minor errors (after being carefully defined and the definition noted in the working papers) may often be ignored. On the other hand, of course, even though the minor errors may have little effect on the total amount being tested, the presence of an excessive number of minor errors might well suggest the possibility that major errors also have occurred. Such a possibility would, in turn, point to the desirability of increasing the confidence factor to give the auditor greater protection in accepting the population.

Procedural errors may also be of varying importance, and the situation is further complicated by the fact that a given document may evidence more than one procedural error. One approach to these problems that has been used with a fair degree of success is to weight various types of errors. Such weights may range from a weight of less than one to a weight of more than one. The fractional weights of errors detected can simply be added arithmetically and the total treated as the number of errors entering into the decision to accept or reject the population.

**Standards of confidence and precision.** There are no single values for confidence and precision that can be used for all auditing situations. If there were, auditing would hardly warrant classification as a professional activity. Some guides can, however, be offered for setting these factors. In most auditing situations, confidence in the range of 90% to 99% would seem to be appropriate. There would be little reason to go beyond 99% since any reason for desiring greater confidence would probably suggest that 100% inspection should be made. On the other hand, less than 90% confidence would appear to involve more risk than is warranted in view of public reliance upon the independent auditor's opinions on his client's financial statements. Between these two extremes, the importance of the figure being verified, the internal control surrounding the development of the figure, and the auditor's general evaluation of the client's personnel and their attitudes would all properly enter into the determination of the confidence to be specified for each sample taken.

Somewhat similar considerations apply to the precision factor. Of perhaps major importance to the setting of precision is the question of materiality, which is itself in need of considerable further study by the auditing profession. A more precise identification of the factors bearing on materiality is needed as well as a means of weighing the factors and bringing their combined influence to bear on the problem. For the present, it may be said that materiality is generally considered to be a matter of the relationship of one figure to one or more other figures. As a rule, an amount is not likely to become material until it exceeds a 10% relationship to another figure. This contention is based in part on the fact that most decisions related to financial data involve subjective interpretations, and the human mind is seldom able to deal with variations of less than 10%.

Other factors that have a bearing on the matter of precision include whether there is a potential for fraud in a situation, or whether the only concern is for random differences. In the case of acceptance sampling, the percentage of errors that might be tolerated would depend on similar factors, plus the possible seriousness of the type of error under consideration.

## CONCLUSIONS

The reader should keep firmly in mind that the application of statistical techniques to auditing is still essentially in the experimental stage, and is likely to remain at that point for some time to come. During this period problems are being worked out, new techniques introduced, and tables worked out to simplify typical applications. Where applications have proven to be feasible and sound, they are being used on a regular basis. Nevertheless the general presumption is likely to remain valid for a considerable period of time that statistical techniques are permissible, rather than required, under generally accepted auditing standards.

The progressive practitioner who carries the load of experimentation will realize the benefits of having a sounder basis for determining the size of samples to be taken and a more precise and reliable interpretation of the sampling results obtained. A further reason for becoming familiar with the techniques is to enable the auditor to deal with them when he encounters them in the operations conducted by his clients.

# 28

# Auditing Electronically Processed Data

**CLIFFORD E. GRAESE**

*Certified Public Accountant; Partner, Peat, Marwick, Mitchell & Co., New York*

**946**

CHAPTER TWENTY-EIGHT

# Auditing Electronically Processed Data

The initial application of electronic computers to data processing caused many auditors to be concerned about what effect such equipment would have on auditing procedures; in fact, many questioned whether electronically maintained records could be audited at all. Most of the fears expressed have proved unwarranted. However, the auditor has had to expand his technical knowledge and to exercise more ingenuity to cope with the circumstances resulting from the installation of electronic data processing systems.

This chapter discusses the more important differences between electronic and manual data processing systems as they affect the auditor, what the auditor should know about electronic data processing systems, and how the auditor can evaluate internal control in such systems. It also offers various techniques for auditing electronically processed data and suggestions to systems designers for facilitating such audits.

▶ NOTE: The reader who has had little contact with electronic data processing systems can gain a deeper insight into their operations by referring to Chapter 23, *Electronic Data Processing*.

## ELECTRONIC COMPUTERS—A CHALLENGE FOR THE AUDITOR

Each new data processing system has brought with it many changes in basic approach, type of record and extent of information maintained. Certain of these have been of little particular concern to the auditor because they have not directly affected his auditing procedures. The complex capabilities of electronic computers, however, have posed some new problems to the auditor.

**Machine language.** Most computer installations use punched cards or punched paper tape as an input medium. Where there is a need to read such cards or tape, they can be, and frequently are, interpreted directly on

948

the face of such medium. The basic computer processing language, however, is recorded in code form as magnetic bits or spots on magnetic tape, or within the computer on various types of storage devices. Magnetic tape or magnetic storage cannot be interpreted as directly or readily as punched cards or paper tape. They can be made visually intelligible only by transcribing the magnetic data into separate printed listings (*hard copy*). Thus, the language barrier poses a handicap to the auditor in carrying out his conventional auditing procedures.

**Sequential processing.** Prior to electronic computers, all data processing systems, including punched card systems, could perform only one, or a very few, sequential operations without manual intervention. Usually the data were taken out of one machine in hard copy or punched card form and manually introduced into another. These records of the intermediate results made it possible for the auditor to trace transactions step by step through their entire processing. Electronic computers, however, are capable of performing a complete sequence of operations without any manual intervention or without writing out interim processing results. As a result, the auditor may find available only the input and output data, with no record of the intermediate steps of the processing of such data.

**Random access.** These electronic computers have the ability to refer to each of their internal data storage locations at random; consequently, it is frequently not necessary that data be sorted into account number or other logical sequence before processing. Even though a hard copy record is made of the data being processed, the random sequence of the data makes such record difficult for the auditor to use as part of the audit trail.

**Speed.** Computers process data at fantastic speeds. This, in itself, does not pose a problem to the auditor. However, directly as a result of this speed, the minimum batch size for economically processing data has also increased. Therefore, if the auditor selects a given batch or block of data for check, he is confronted with several thousand rather than one or two hundred items. Thus, for example, even the smallest possible test of footings may involve several thousand items.

**Elimination of hard copy.** In previous data processing systems, including punched card equipment, the auditor invariably found adequate printed details (*hard copy*) to enable him to follow the transactions through the system. Hard copy listings can also be produced in computer systems, but they are very time consuming by computer standards. Increasing awareness of the marginal utility of various conventional hard copy records and the relatively high cost of their preparation is causing many of such records to be discontinued. The absence of any one particular type or format of record should not pose a major problem to the auditor. The elimination of virtually all intermediate journals, registers, and ledgers under a computer system does, however, pose an audit problem. Computer applications to date have, as a matter of caution, included substantial amounts of hard copy. However, the trend is definitely to eliminate as much hard copy as possible.

**Wire transmission.** In an increasing number of computer installations, accounting information is being transmitted from point of transaction to a centralized computer center by wire or by other means of machine language transmission. These methods, which replace physical transmission of the source documents themselves, have the obvious advantage of reducing paper handling costs. They make it difficult, however, for the auditor at the central accounting office to obtain for his inspection *sufficient competent evidential material*, because such material may be located at scattered points many miles away. Of course, the auditor may request such selected data to be sent to the central point. However, in addition to the inconvenience caused, it is doubtful whether this procedure provides the best evidence of the true condition of the records.

**Direct input.** The use of direct input devices makes possible the recording of transactions directly into the computer system without creating a source document. This is a most desirable procedure from the point of view of efficiency. However, as a result, the only record of a transaction, hard copy or otherwise, is one that has been generated by the computer system. The auditor is, therefore, confronted with almost complete reliance upon the controls established over operation of the input device. He cannot, in many cases, check to conventional underlying *competent evidential material* since it may not exist. The determination of compliance with *generally accepted auditing standards,* of necessity, will require acceptance of auditing procedures that place even greater reliance upon existing controls than is now being done.

### WHAT THE AUDITOR SHOULD KNOW
### ABOUT COMPUTERS

It has been suggested that the auditor must become a skilled computer programmer and operator in order to audit computer installations. Certainly, the more knowledge the auditor has of computer technicalities, the better he is able to cope with any audit problems that may arise. However, the work of the auditor obviously involves too much judgment and is too broad in scope to suggest that his function can ever be limited merely to a technical evaluation of a computer program. Actually, the auditor's knowledge of computers does not need to be extensive to enable him to perform an effective audit. He must, however, have knowledge of certain basics. As was mentioned at the beginning of this chapter, Chapter 23 contains a thorough exposition of these computer basics that can be referred to in conjunction with this chapter.

**General computer operating principles.** The auditor must understand the basic operating principles of a computer. This involves the *reading, writing, arithmetic,* and *storage* functions; the manner in which computers are *programmed;* the function of the *console;* and the various *control features* (built-in, external, or programmed) that may exist in a computer system.

**Accuracy and reliability.** The auditor must have a general knowledge of computer *accuracy* and *reliability.* Without this, he may lose the proper perspective in determining the scope of his audit procedures and the extent of his audit tests. Generally, computer accuracy is far superior to manual accuracy. In fact, human errors give rise to most problems usually attributed to computer inaccuracy.

**Weaknesses.** Although computers do have many advantages in accuracy and control over manual systems, they are also subject to certain weaknesses of which the auditor should be aware. These include the possible loss of stored data through accidental erasing, overwriting, or, in some cases, power failure; and the possible jumbling of information that exceeds a certain number of digits or specified word length. Knowledge of these types of weaknesses will enable the auditor to evaluate the controls necessary to overcome the deficiencies.

**Electronic systems approach.** The auditor of electronically processed data must adjust himself to the electronic systems approach. A business transaction is frequently processed by electronics in an entirely different manner than that used in conventional manual methods. For example, it may be expedient in a manual system to compile aggregate dollar amounts (such as required reserves) by classifying the variables, accumulating the units in each class, and then making calculations for each class of variables in total; however, using a computer it may be *more expedient* to make separate calculations for each item, rather than to go through the classification routines. Also, although it may be desirable in a manual or punched card system to have a series of journals, each designed to record a specific type of transaction, it may be even more expedient under a computer system to have a single detailed journal-ledger.

**Sources of information.** There are many sources from which an auditor can acquire the necessary knowledge of computers. Mostly originating with computer manufacturers, these sources include operator handbooks, general information manuals, operator and programming training courses, and management training programs. In addition, seminars dealing with this subject are conducted from time to time by various management organizations.

### INTERNAL CONTROL IN A COMPUTER SYSTEM

It has previously been stated that the auditor will find it desirable, if not necessary, to place increasing reliance upon internal control in auditing electronically processed data. Thus, the design of specific audit procedures by the auditor is largely dependent upon his determining what controls exist and how effectively they are functioning.

**Internal control features of computer installations.** The internal control features of a computer installation can be classified into four general categories:

1. Built-in controls.
2. Programmed controls.
3. Operation controls.
4. Input-output controls.

**Built-in controls.** Within the electronic circuitry of the different computers, the manufactures have provided certain control or checking features. These *built-in controls* are largely to check on the proper functioning of the computer itself. Perhaps the most significant benefit resulting from these controls is the detection of machine failures before the faulty data is processed further in the system. In most cases, such failures would be detected ultimately through failure of the output to balance, or otherwise. However, considerably larger amounts of computer and personnel time might then be required to correct the erroneous processing. While certainly it would be wrong to say the auditor has no interest in built-in controls, such interest is secondary. The functioning of the built-in controls cannot be readily tested except by electronic engineers. The auditor must rely, to a large extent, on input and output controls to check on the overall functional reliability of the equipment.

It is not the purpose of this chapter to discuss the technical aspects of built-in controls. However, the general principles of certain of the types of built-in controls are discussed below:

*Parity bit check.* The magnetic code language of the computer uses a combination of electro-magnetic spots (*bits*) to designate a numeric or alphabetic character. The failure of the computer to detect one of these bits would cause an erroneous reading or transfer. By use of an additional channel, a *check bit* may or may not be added as necessary to make each character code contain an even number of magnetic bits. By checking that each code character read or transferred contains an even number of bits, the computer can detect a partial loss of code characters. (See Figure 1.)

ILLUSTRATION OF PARITY BIT CHECK

| Character | Magnetic Coding | | |
|---|---|---|---|
| | Check Bit | Character Coding | |
| A | 1 | 1 1 0 0 0 0 1 | |
| B | 1 | 1 1 0 0 0 1 0 | |
| C | 0 | 1 1 0 0 0 1 1 | |
| D | 1 | 1 1 0 0 1 0 0 | |
| E | 0 | 1 1 0 0 1 0 1 | |

**Fig. 1. Parity Bit Check.**

*Dual circuitry.* In some computers there exists at least a partial duplication of circuitry, so that operations of the computer are performed in parallel. The results of these dual operations are compared at intervals as a check on the operation.

*Echo checks.* Used in a broad sense, this term includes various controls that pertain to the reading, writing, transfer, and storage functions. Whenever one of these operations has been completed, the data written, stored, etc., are read back and compared with the source to insure that they agree before processing continues.

**Program controls.** One of the very significant aspects of internal control in a computer system is the ability to program the computer to perform various checking and limiting routines upon the data as it is being processed. In fact, the capabilities of the computer are such that many test calculations or comparisons can be programmed in the regular processing procedure that, for practical reasons, could not be undertaken manually. Some of the *programmed controls* are discussed below:

*Limit check.* The computer can be programmed to test all data processed against predetermined maximum or minimum limits. Thus, for example, the computer may be instructed to write out, as exceptions, any payroll checks in excess of a specified amount. Such exceptions can then be subjected to special investigations to determine their propriety.

*Hash totals.* The computer can be programmed to accumulate an arithmetic total of any data it is processing. By comparison with a predetermined total, it is possible to ascertain that all data have been processed. It is not necessary that the data total have any significance for other purposes. For example, a control total can be developed by adding employee clock numbers. Such control totals, having no other significance, are called *hash totals*. (See Figure 2.)

ILLUSTRATION OF
RECORD COUNT, HASH TOTAL, AND CONTROL TOTAL

Payroll Time Summary

| Employee | Clock No. | Hours Worked |
|----------|-----------|--------------|
| 1. J. Doe | 4563 | 37 |
| 2. M. Frank | 5086 | 35 |
| 3. P. Adler | 5194 | 35 |
| 4. M. Murray | 5198 | 40 |
| 5. P. Shepherd | 6071 | 40 |
| Total | 26112 | 187 |
| Record Count | Hash Total | Control Total |

Fig. 2. Record Count, Hash Total and Control Total.

*Record count.* The computer may be programmed to count the number of items processed. This total count can be used in the same manner as the hash total to assure that all items have been processed.

*Proof figures.* Because of the speed and capacity of the computer, it is practical to compute *proof figures* through the use of reciprocals or cumulative calculations. For example, in a multiplication operation an arbitrary number greater than the largest multiplier may be selected. Every multiplication is then made twice, first by the multiplier and second by the difference between the multiplier and the arbitrary number. The accumulated total of both sets of multiplications should equal the total of the original data multiplied by the arbitrary number. Another method that might be applied in a billing procedure, for example, involves accumulating units by item number, extending total units billed by standard billing price, and comparing these totals with the total of billings as originally processed. (See Figure 3.)

*Sequence check.* The computer can be programmed to check that data processed are in consecutive sequence and whether such sequence is complete.

*Labels.* To prevent the possibility that a wrong reel of magnetic tape may be used accidentally in a computer run, thereby erasing or jumbling valuable data, it is possible to code in computer language a label at the beginning of each reel. The computer can then be programmed to check the identity of each reel before proceeding with the processing run.

*Double arithmetic.* In a manner somewhat similar to that used to

ILLUSTRATION OF PROOF FIGURE

| Employee | Hours | Rate | Gross Wages | Proof Arithmetic Multiplier ($2.50 less rate) | Extension |
|---|---|---|---|---|---|
| J. Doe | 37 | $1.50 | $ 55.50 | $1.00 | $ 37.00 |
| M. Frank | 35 | 1.50 | 52.50 | 1.00 | 35.00 |
| P. Adler | 35 | 1.75 | 61.25 | .75 | 26.25 |
| M. Murray | 40 | 1.75 | 70.00 | .75 | 30.00 |
| P. Shepherd | 40 | 2.00 | 80.00 | .50 | 20.00 |
| | 187 | | $319.25 | | $148.25 |

Proof:

|  |  |
|---|---|
| Gross wages extended | $319.25 |
| Proof extension | 148.25 |
| Total | $467.50 = 187 hrs. × $2.50 |

**Fig. 3. Proof Figure.**

develop proof totals, the computer can be programmed to perform calculations in duplicate, preferably reversing sequence or multiplier and multiplicand, and comparing results.

*Identification checks.* In a manner similar to the label check of reels, it is also possible to check the identification of a specific item of data before processing it. For example, if an inventory quantity is to be updated, it is possible to make a comparison of item numbers before applying the current transaction against the present balance. It is also possible in this manner to detect unauthorized account numbers, thus providing an editing of the coding of input data.

**Operation controls.** Once a satisfactory program has been developed for the computer, the proper processing of data should be routine. It is, of course, possible for the computer to fail, but maintenance engineers make frequent and regular tests of the proper functioning of equipment, thus minimizing computer failure. There can be failures in the program area also. If the program is stored on punched cards rather than tape, it is possible that cards may be misplaced. It is also possible for the wrong program to be used. A standard operating check for detecting these various types of failure is the use of a *test-deck* or a series of simulated problems for which the correct results have been predetermined. The use of this approach is discussed later in this chapter in connection with the auditor's tests of computer programs.

*Console control.* The console operator can modify any of the programmed operations of the computer or any of the data being processed or stored in the computer. It is important, therefore, that as much control as is practicable exists over the possibility of intervention through the console.

A frequent deterrent to unauthorized intervention will be the lack of intimate familiarity of the console operator with the detailed program. In addition, the computer can be programmed, within limits, to record or print out any such intervention. This record can subsequently be analyzed for propriety of operation.

**Input-output controls.** Although the computer can be programmed to exercise considerable control over its own operations, some of the most effective controls over the computer system as a whole are exercised by controlling the data before it gets into the computer system and after it has been processed.

*Source document controls.* The need for adequate controls over the creation of the source documents that record consummated transactions is important under any system, whether computer or manual. In some respects, however, source document control assumes a greater degree of importance in a computer system, because the source document and individual transaction will be subjected to less subsequent review, and because the simultaneous updating of numerous records by one computer processing run may make subsequent error correction more involved. While weaknesses in source document control can be offset to some extent by program controls, good internal control in any system must begin with the initial recording data.

*Machine language conversion.* A major source of error in any automated data processing system is the conversion from source documents to machine language. Direct input and character sensing devices will minimize this problem, although it probably never can be eliminated. In most of the computer installations, data are first converted to punched cards and then into magnetic tape. In such cases, conventional punched card verification techniques should be employed in checking the conversion from source documents to punched cards.

*Control totals.* The use of *hash totals, predetermined amounts,* and *record counts* as control features (as previously discussed) begins before the input of data into the computer system. Such totals can be used to compare input and output, check conversion to machine language, and control source documents until properly entered.

*Reconciliations to standards.* In many cases in which predetermined totals are not available, the output of a computer system can be reconciled to *precomputed standards.* For example, on a salary payroll application, record counts and hash totals may be used to provide processing controls, but it may not be practicable to obtain a predetermined calculation of gross or net pay. Since changes in a salary payroll are usually quite limited from period to period, it may be feasible in many cases to reconcile the total gross or net pay with that of a *precomputed standard,* and in this way obtain controls over payroll dollars. (See Figure 4.)

ILLUSTRATION OF RECONCILIATION TO STANDARD

Monthly Payroll Reconciliation

| | Per Month | This Month |
|---|---|---|
| Standard Salary Payroll, beginning of month | $400,850.00 | $400,850.00 |
| Additions approved by control group: | | |
| New employees added to payroll | 8,650.00 | 5,150.00 |
| Salary increases effective this month | 1,500.00 | 1,500.00 |
| Bonus payments | — | 10,000.00 |
| _____ | | |
| _____ | | |
| | 411,000.00 | 417,500.00 |
| Deductions: | | |
| Employees severed from payroll | 6,000.00 | — |
| _____ | | |
| _____ | | |
| Adjusted Standard Payroll, end of month | $405,000.00 | 417,500.00 |
| Actual payroll, this month | | 417,500.00 |
| Difference (must be explained) | | $   — |

**Fig. 4. Reconciliation to Standard.**

*Reasonableness checks.* It is not always practicable to check the output of a computer to exact control totals or standards. However, it may be possible to check such output for reasonableness. For example, the crediting of interest to individual savings accounts could be checked in the aggregate for reasonableness by fairly simple manual calculations.

**Control unit.** A separate control group should be established to insure that the input and output controls, and certain of the programmed controls do actually provide the control expected.

*Independence.* The control group should be independent of the computer programmers, computer operators, and anyone else who is involved in the processing of data. Without this independence, controls can easily be bypassed. At the same time, the control group must be vested with sufficient authority, perhaps indirectly, to insure that it can bring about corrections when it detects improper situations. Ordinarily it would not have the responsibility, for example, of making the actual corrections of erroneous data, but it should exercise control over correction procedures.

*Maintenance of control registers.* The control group should have the primary responsibility for maintaining control totals over input and output data, and seeing that such totals are in balance. While ideally it would be desirable to require the computer operators to work to a blind total (without knowledge of the control total), such is frequently not practicable. Therefore, the control information probably will be available to the operator for check before output totals are released to the control group. Nevertheless, the primary control function responsibility must rest with the independent control group. (See Figure 5.)

ILLUSTRATION OF CONTROL REGISTER

Accounts Receivable Control Register

| Date | Balance | Invoices Billed | Total Credited | Cash Received | Discounts Allowed | Credit Memos | Other Adjustments |
|---|---|---|---|---|---|---|---|
| 12–30 | $345,678.00 | | | | | | |
| 1–1 | 350,836.91 | 50,701.07 | 45,542.16 | 44,608.12 | 934.04 | | |
| 1–2 | 363,748.11 | 48,672.36 | 35,761.16 | 35,018.16 | 743.00 | | |

**Fig. 5. Control Register.**

*Control over master files.* The independent control group should maintain control over all changes in the master files. The manner in which this is carried out will depend to a large extent on the number of changes that occur, and the nature or source of such changes. In the absence of actually controlling master files, the control group or internal auditors may print out selected master files from time to time and compare them with official source documents. In addition to controlling changes, the control group should also maintain a record of changes effected.

*Control over program changes.* A computer program is, in effect, a master file. The independent control group should also have control over any changes in programs. A record of program changes is of particular importance to the auditor in the event that it is necessary or desirable to reconstruct data developed under a previous program.

**Segregation of functional responsibility.** One of the basic principles of internal control is to segregate duties so that no individual is solely responsible for the accountability of any transaction or type of transactions. The reduction of clerical personnel and the concentration of data processing responsibility under a computer system, therefore, would appear to have an adverse effect on control. However, a much more effective functional segregation of duties may be accomplished under a computer system. The people recording the transaction initially are removed from the processing of such data. The computer operator seldom has any direct interest in the data he is processing, he usually has no access to cash or any other assets of the company that he might be tempted to appropriate, and he usually will not know enough of the detailed program to effect manipulating changes easily. The programmers are familiar with the detailed program, but they are not involved in the origination, processing, or ultimate use of processed data. Thus, the functional segregation of duties in a computer operation is usually beneficial from a control point of view.

▶ WARNING: The auditor must be alert, however, to situations in which the computer operator may have a direct interest in the data processed (such as employee's personal accounts), and must concentrate special audit procedures in such areas.

**Internal audit department.** The computer installation poses the same basic problems to the internal auditor as it does to the independent auditor. As a result, the approaches followed by both in auditing a computer system will be more similar to each other than in a manual system, even though the specific objectives of the internal and independent auditor may remain somewhat different. This is true in part because of limitations in approach imposed by the computer, and in part because of the shift in emphasis to controls over input to the system. Insofar as the processing of data within the computer system is concerned, the human element has been largely replaced by a series of electronic devices having extremely high degrees of reliability. Once a satisfactory program has been established, the reliability of computer processed data is primarily dependent on controlling the input to the computer. Because of the resulting similarity of approach, a high degree of cooperation may be expected between the independent and the internal auditors.

### EVALUATION OF INTERNAL CONTROL

The evaluation of existing internal control is a major factor in the audit of a computer system. This is true, of course, in any audit, but with the adoption of the more completely integrated and automated systems made feasible by computers, control becomes *all important*.

**Participation in installation.** The best way for the auditor to be sure that the controls are adequate is to participate in the installation of the computer system. As a practical matter, however, direct participation may not be as expendient as it would appear. The auditor's knowledge of control principles probably can be utilized to better advantage by a more limited participation at critical stages of the procedure design and installation. These stages include:

1. After the basic computer system concept has been established.
2. After the concept has been formalized to the block diagram stage.
3. After the detailed programming has been completed.

In this way, the auditor's time will not be spent unnecessarily on preliminary approaches that are rejected in the early stages of system design, but his know-how will be utilized before the system is so final that control changes are difficult to make.

**Review of block diagrams.** If the auditor has not been consulted in the design of the system or the establishment of controls, he is faced with the problem of evaluating the effectiveness of controls after the system has been finalized. Although suggested improvements in controls can still be incorporated in subsequent system revisions, his basic purpose at this point is to determine the extent of various audit procedures he must follow.

In order to evaluate the existing control, the auditor must first become familiar with the system. He can take the approach of checking out the program in detail, or of reviewing the block diagram with someone familiar with the system. The latter approach will usually disclose all the significant controls and give the auditor a better overall understanding of the nature of such controls than if he were to become enmeshed in the great detail of checking out the entire program. This is particularly true because at this point the auditor is only interested in establishing what controls have been provided for in the system. He will, at a subsequent time, have to satisfy himself that the controls actually function as indicated, and, in fact, that the system in operation actually conforms to the block diagram he has studied. Figure 6 illustrates a portion of a typical flow chart showing computer instructions.

**Program evaluation.** The determination of whether the system processes transactions in accordance with *generally accepted accounting principles* parallels the problem of determining whether the computer system incorporates adequate controls. Basically, the auditor has two approaches he may follow.

*1. Detailed program review.* If the auditor possesses sufficient technical computer knowledge, he can review each computer program step in detail to satisfy himself that the program is designed properly to accomplish what

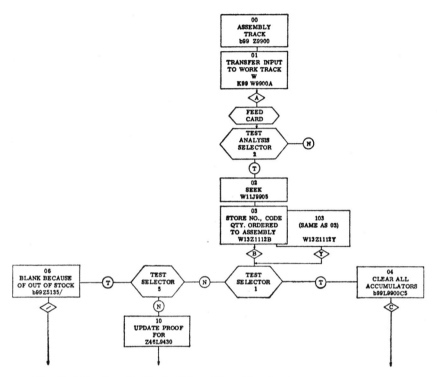

**Fig. 6. A Portion of a Typical Flow Chart Showing Computer Instructions—Grocery Billing Application.**

it is supposed to do. (See Figure 7, illustrating a typical program instruction sheet.) This is not a very practical approach, however, for the following reasons:

a. As has already been stated, the auditing profession as a whole does not have, and probably never can have, sufficient knowledge of technical programming to undertake this approach.

b. The time required to accomplish such a review would make this approach so costly that it would be prohibitive, even if the auditing profession could acquire the necessary technical knowledge.

c. The auditor would have to expend considerable effort in order to evaluate the effect of optimization and other changes made in computer programs from time to time.

d. Many computer programs are so complex that even after a detailed review it is doubtful that anyone, regardless of his technical competence, could actually state with a high degree of assurance that the program contained no flaws. Even the original programmers, who

**IBM**

### 305 RAMAC PROGRAM INSTRUCTION SHEET

Application: _GROCERY BILLING_ _____ Program Steps: ____ To ____

Routine: _____ Date: ____ Page __1__ of __20__

#### PROGRAM LOADING INSTRUCTIONS

| ONE | | | | TWO | | | | THREE | | | |
|---|---|---|---|---|---|---|---|---|---|---|---|
| FROM | TO | NO. CHAR. | CONTROL | FROM | TO | NO. CHAR. | CONTROL | FROM | TO | NO. CHAR. | CONTROL |

| PROG. STEP | FROM TR. | POS. | TO TR. | POS. | NO. CHAR. | CONTROL | | DESCRIPTION | TO PROG. STEP |
|---|---|---|---|---|---|---|---|---|---|
| 00 | b | 9 9 | Z | 9 9 | 0 0 | | | CLEAR ASSEMBLY | 01 |
| Restart: | | | | | | | | | |
| | | | | | | | | | |
| | | | | | | | | | |
| | | | | Check Reset Program Start ☑ | | | | |
| 01 | K | 9 9 | W | 9 9 | 0 0 | A | | TRF. INPUT TO WORK AREA / A- FEED A CARD AND TEST | |
| Restart: | | | | | | | | ANALYSIS SELECTOR 2 T. | 02 |
| | | | | | | | | | |
| | | | | Check Reset Program Start ☑ | | | | |
| 02 | W | 1 1 | J | 9 9 | 0 5 | | | SEEK | 03 |
| Restart: | | | | | | | | | |
| | | | | | | | | | |
| | | | | Check Reset Program Start ☑ | | | | |
| 03 | W | 1 3 | Z | 1 1 | 1 2 | B | | ASSEMBLE STORE #, CODE & QTY. / B- TEST SELECTOR 1 | |
| Restart: | | | | | | | | T- | 04 |
| | | | | | | | | N- TEST SELECTOR 5 | |
| | | | | | | | | T- | 06 |
| | | | | Check Reset Program Start ☑ | | | N- | 09 |
| 04 | b | 9 9 | L | 9 9 | 0 0 | C | 5 | RESET ALL ACCUMULATORS / C | 10 |
| Restart: | | | | | | | | | |
| | | | | | | | | | |
| | | | | | | | | | |
| | | | | Check Reset Program Start ☐ | | | | |

**Fig. 7. A Portion of a Typical Program Instruction Sheet.**

have a more intimate knowledge of the program than the auditor, use debugging routines to eliminate flaws in the program as originally conceived.

*2. Simulated problem approach.* An alternative is the *simulated problem approach.* This has also been referred to, at times, as a *test deck approach.*

This reference is confusing, however, because this term has a somewhat different connotation in punched card accounting terminology. The *simulated problem approach* consists of creating a series of transactions covering as many possible situations as can be anticipated to occur and pre-computing the correct processing results of such problems manually. The simulated transactions are then processed through the computer and the results compared with those predetermined. The sequence in which a simulated problem file is developed is given below.

▶ SUGGESTION: In addition to the typical problems, there should also be included a number of atypical situations designed to test the programmed controls. Such problems would include amounts exceeding established limits, unauthorized account numbers, redundant data, etc.

### STEPS IN DEVELOPMENT OF SIMULATED PROBLEM FILE

1. Determine possible variables in transaction data by analyzing computer input.
   a. List different fields comprising each complete input record.
   b. List different alternatives possible in each field.
   c. Determine which fields have interrelated effect upon data processing routines.
2. Permutate data established in "1" above to obtain at least one situation for each possible variable and combination of interrelated variables.
3. Create two or more problems for each situation established in "2" above. These may be hypothetical or actual transactions which conform to requirements.
4. Manually compute results which should be obtained in computer processing run of simulated transactions.
5. Ascertain control features included in computer program and create simulated transactions which violate acceptable data requirements.
6. Determine likely possibilities of error in input data and create simulated transactions containing such errors.

The following three limitations to this general approach must be recognized:

   a. *Fraud programming.* Special manipulation steps might be inserted in a program by the computer operator or a programmer for the purpose of effecting fraud. Such program steps would be followed only upon a special signal either from the computer operator or from a special code inserted in the data being processed. These steps would not necessarily be detected by the simulated problem approach. However, in order for such fraud to accomplish any benefit to either the computer operator or the programmer, there would usually have to be collusion. Such collusion would be necessary because of the functional separation of these individuals from each other and from the origination of transactions and custody of assets. If other controls are good, the auditor can rely on them for reasonable protection against such collusion. It should be mentioned here that no audit test is necessarily conclusive by itself in the detection of collusion.

b. *Incomplete scope of problems.* The simulated problem approach can never be better than the ability of the auditor to visualize the different possible types of transactions. In other words, the simulated problem deck may not contain all possible types of problems. Of course, the detailed review of program approach is equally, if not more, subject to the limits of the reviewer's knowledge of the possible variety of business transactions. Furthermore, there is no assurance in any of the more conventional auditing tests that all types of situations will occur in the sample chosen. Experience has shown that the simulated problem approach gives a more comprehensive coverage of possible situations than the post audit of selected actual transactions on a limited test basis.

c. *Peculiar computer operating characteristics.* Occasionally, peculiar combinations of input data, such as data exceeding a specified word length, may cause a malfunction of the computer system. It is, of course, not possible to include every possible type of data and data combinations in any simulated problem approach. However, this situation would probably be even more difficult to detect under a detailed program review. Again, the other controls must be relied upon to provide at least partial coverage in this area.

▶ CONCLUSION: Thus, on balance, the *simulated problem approach* would definitely appear the best audit approach in most cases.

**Testing of control registers.** The testing of the program procedures and programmed controls are a significant part of the overall evaluation of control in a computer system. Perhaps equally important, however, are the determination of what input and output controls exist, what external control totals are developed, and whether these controls are functioning effectively. Fortunately, the evaluation and testing of these controls does not require any special technical computer knowledge. The auditor, therefore, will find familiar the techniques of test comparison of entries in the control registers with input and output. Particular emphasis should be placed on seeing that the independence in maintaining these controls is present, and that situations of imbalance are promptly detected and corrected. Although it should be obvious, the auditor should also check that control registers are balanced periodically to the general ledger.

## CARRYING OUT THE AUDIT PROCEDURES

In addition to a general evaluation of the system of control, the auditor must make other appropriate tests to enable him to obtain *sufficient competent evidential material* in support of transactions and to satisfy himself as to the continued effective operation of the system. In some computer installations, the auditor may find it expedient to "go around" rather than to "go through" the computer in carrying out these tests.

**Going around the computer.** Going around the computer is usually possible in those installations that are not highly integrated, or in which the computer applications are restricted to areas involving primarily the development of management control or daily operating information. It is also possible in those installations in which a very complete, hard copy audit trail exists.

Going around the computer may have several advantages:

1. *Less technical knowledge required.* Going around the computer does not imply that the auditor can disregard the computer completely and therefore needs no knowledge of its operations. Obviously, however, going around requires less technical knowledge of the computer than going through.

2. *Time savings.* Going around may require less of the auditor's time to accomplish the audit. The review of computer programs is relatively time consuming when considered in relation to the extent of detail testing usually required by the auditor. The development of special audit computer programs (discussed later in this chapter) is likewise not a small undertaking. This is particularly true if, as is usually the case, at least minor changes are made in the system between audits. Therefore, the less glamorous approach of going around may be the most economical.

3. *Computer time availability.* Another problem that is avoided by going around the computer is that of obtaining processing time on the computer itself. Pressure of the regular work processed by the computer and the required engineering maintenance may make little computer time available for audit purposes.

4. *Retention of data.* The retention, in machine language form, of data, including master files, programs, etc., is costly. By going around, the need to retain this data in machine language form is eliminated. To some extent, the data retention problem could also be met by more frequent

periodic audits, but audit scheduling problems usually are increased thereby.

**Going through the computer.** There are some cases, usually highly integrated systems, where going through the computer is the only possible approach. In other cases, although it is possible to go around the computer, the advantages of going through the computer are greater:

1. *Time savings.* Whenever the auditor's detail checks involve a sizeable number of tranactions, it may be possible to save considerable time through utilizing the speed of the computer. This may be particularly true of clerical tests of footings and extensions.

2. *Reliability.* The auditor can also take advantage of the inherent reliability of the computer in performing clerical operations, such as comparing or checking footings and extensions.

3. *Broader coverage.* The speed and other capabilities of the computer may make possible correlation tests that would not be practicable by manual methods. Also, more refined calculations, such as determining estimates of reserve requirements, may be made practicable by the computer. Thus, going through the computer may offer the auditor an opportunity to get broader and more direct substantiation than would otherwise be possible.

**Techniques of going through.** Going through the computer requires the use of special techniques not ordinarily a part of the auditor's usual routines. It should be emphasized that these new techniques must meet the requirements of generally accepted auditing standards.

1. **Special audit programs.** Perhaps the most glamorous special audit technique is use of a special computer program designed to accomplish auditing procedures; in effect, to automate auditing in the same manner as the original processing of data was automated. Although the computer cannot substitute for the professional judgment of the auditor, the computer can perform the clerical verification, and the data classification and handling aspects of auditing procedures.

*Development of program by auditor.* Ideally, the auditor should develop his own computer program to audit the client's data accumulation. However, the staffing requirements of such an approach impose a practical limitation on the extent to which this technique will ever be used. Even if it were practical for the auditing profession to ultimately acquire adequate programming staffs, the cost of this approach to the client would be prohibitive in all but a limited number of cases.

*Development of program by client.* Use of the company's regular programming staff to develop special audit computer programs offers a means of reducing programming cost, since such programmers already have intimate knowledge of the system and the data processing programs in use.

This may offer a particularly attractive possibility to the internal auditor. However, use of this approach by the independent auditor might be subject to criticism because of the possible loss of a really independent check of the processing system. Unless the auditor checks out in considerable detail the program developed by his client's personnel, he may not fully comprehend "his own" audit tests. Though this detracts from the above approach, it does not necessarily rule it out under all circumstances.

*General limitation.* Perhaps the most serious limitation to the use of a special audit computer program is the flexibility of the system. Frequent changes in the processing program to optimize operations, to provide additional information, to accommodate more data, etc., may be very slight, but even the smallest change in a processing program ordinarily would require a corresponding change in the special audit computer program as well. Unless the audit program involved was very simple or basic, it probably would require modification each time used. This might be a more serious problem to the independent auditor, who would use such a program far less frequently than the internal auditor and, therefore, might not keep up as closely with all of the changes made. For both, however, the cost of changes in a special audit computer program could be high in relation to the usefulness of the program. In many cases, therefore, the use of a special audit computer program will prove far more glamorous than practical.

**2. Simulated problem approach.** The simulated problem approach, as previously discussed, probably offers the most practical approach to the auditor who wishes to use the computer in carrying out specific auditing procedures. Using this approach, the auditor can establish, subject to limitations also previously mentioned, that the regular data processing program satisfactorily accomplishes both the accounting and control it was designed to accomplish. Such an approach also gives the auditor, to a marginal extent, a test of the satisfactory functioning of the computer hardware, although this is not a prime purpose of the simulated problem approach. The auditor, having established that the client's program is satisfactory, can proceed to use it to reconstruct the processing of selected blocks or periods of data.

**3. Back-to-front approach.** As a part of his tests, the auditor customarily traces certain ledger postings back to their source documents and certain source documents through to their final posting. The purpose of this dual approach is to satisfy himself by test that all entries are supported by proper source documents and that all transactions have been recorded. This procedure is not necessarily invalidated by the installation of a computer system. However, the approach is modified somewhat.

The auditor probably will find that the *back-to-front step approach* will conform closely with his present orientation to audit tests. For example, if several sequential computer runs comprise a complete data processing procedure, the auditor may prefer to select certain portions of the final output data for test verification. He would then reprocess the corresponding blocks of data through the last computer run. The results would be compared with the previously selected output data. In turn, a portion of the input to this last computer run, which the auditor has just reprocessed, would be selected as a test segment of the output of the preceding computer run, and verified in the same manner. This back-to-front step approach would continue until selected final results have, in effect, been traced back to the machine language input. At this point, the auditor can list the machine language input in hard copy form and visually compare such input with source documents. If all input of a particular class is included in this test, then the auditor can check not only that the recorded transactions of this class are supported by proper source documents, but he can also check that all of the source documents falling in this class were recorded. A case study illustration of this technique is presented later in this chapter.

An alternate to the above discussed procedure of preparing hard copy listings and comparing them with source documents is the procedure of reconverting significant source document information into machine language and utilizing the computer, or other equipment, to make comparison with the original machine language input. Since, to maintain proper control, the auditor's staff would usually have to perform the burdensome conversion by the use of manual key-driven equipment, the visual comparison may instead offer the most practical approach.

**4. Conversion to punched cards.** On many occasions the auditor may find that it will be more economical for him to convert the electronic data into punched cards and to carry out many audit procedures through the use of punched-card equipment. The auditor may possess sufficient knowledge of punched-card equipment so that the programming and wiring (or checking thereof) of such equipment poses a relatively small problem when compared with using computers. Further, because the auditor will usually limit his work to tests involving small percentages of the total data processed, processing speed and other capabilities of computers may have little impact on time requirements.

### FACILITATING THE AUDIT

Although electronic computers have posed no insurmountable audit problems, there are, nevertheless, many things that can be done to minimize such problems as do arise and to facilitate the audit of computer systems. Generally, these are directly involved with adequate advance planning.

**Consultation with auditors.** To insure that controls and audit trails are adequate, the proposed computer procedure should be reviewed with the auditors in advance of installation. This is an excellent means of avoiding costly procedure changes and data reruns at a later date.

**Predetermined data analysis requirements.** Internal, independent, government contract, insurance, tax, and regulatory agency auditors, as well as management, all have certain data analysis requirements. When such requirements are recognized at the outset, it frequently does not detract greatly from the efficiency of the system to include a provision for such data. Care should be taken, however, not to create numerous analyses merely because someone may sometime happen to request it.

**Record retention schedule.** A record retention schedule, particularly of source documents, machine language input, and intermediate results, should be discussed with the auditors. Many hours of reconstruction time can be saved if all audit requirements are met before such data are destroyed.

**Retention of output copy.** Because the generation of hard copy is usually a relatively inefficient or slow procedure in a computer system, retention of extra copies of hard copy output, such as customers' statements, may serve as an adequate hard copy record for subsequent account analysis. While the format of such copy is not always the best for supplemental uses, the resulting inconvenience may be small compared with the cost of a special account analysis.

**Periodic storage listing.** The periodic print-out to hard copy of trial balances, or other stored data, is a sound operating procedure in establishing a backstop in the event of failure of the processing system. Such hard copy is also helpful from an audit analysis point of view.

**Conversion proof listing.** The generation of hard copy is not to be confused with the establishment of controls. However, to the extent that such hard copy may facilitate a visual review of transactions or the tracing of data back to source documents, at least an indirect control feature results. Thus, a conversion proof listing in the same sequence as source documents are filed is desirable. It might also be noted that it is at the point of conversion to machine language that the human error element is substantially removed from the computer processing system.

**Computer time allocation.** In scheduling machine work loads, the advance recognition of internal and independent audit computer time requirements will minimize hardships in this regard at a later date. The allocation of available computer time should, of course, be made so as to get the maximum advantage from the equipment. This does not suggest, therefore, that any predetermined amount or percentage of time should be set aside for audit, but rather that potential audit applications be considered with all others competing for computer time.

## CASE STUDIES

Each computer data processing procedure is designed to meet the particular requirements of the company involved; however, some benefit may be gained from reviewing cases illustrating certain segments of actual computer applications and the effect of computer characteristics as applied therein upon the audit procedures used.

### Case 1. Random Access, Internal Distribution and Accumulation

The case involves the maintenance of a ledger of approximately 200,000 savings accounts on magnetic tape in account number sequence. Account numbers are assigned in chronological sequence as accounts are opened. The accounts are segregated into subcontrols of about 3,000 accounts each.

One of the schedules included in the audited statements analyzes the year-end balances according to several different classifications. This classification analysis is prepared by the company in a single run of the computer that accumulates internally a total for each classification, for each subcontrol. The only hard copy created is a summary of the totals by analysis classification for each subcontrol and a grand total for all subcontrols.

*Audit technique used.* In this case it was considered most practical to convert two selected subcontrols from magnetic tape to punched cards. These cards were then sorted by classification, and listed and totalled on conventional punched card equipment. The resulting totals were compared with the data previously developed by the computer. The verification of two subcontrols in this manner was considered an adequate test of the computer procedure and, therefore, the other subcontrols were accepted without detail check. (See Figure 8.)

*Other factors and considerations.*

1. The reliability of the data on the account balance ledger tape had previously been established by other means.

2. The use of conventional punched card equipment was selected rather than the method of going directly through the computer, because of the small amount of time involved on punched card equipment. Then too, this equipment was readily available in comparison to the low availability of computer time.

### Case 2. Back-to-Front Simulated Problem Approach

The case involves the maintenance of mortgage loan accounts on magnetic tape. In addition to payments on principal and interest (charged on balance at beginning of payment period), monthly payments received on

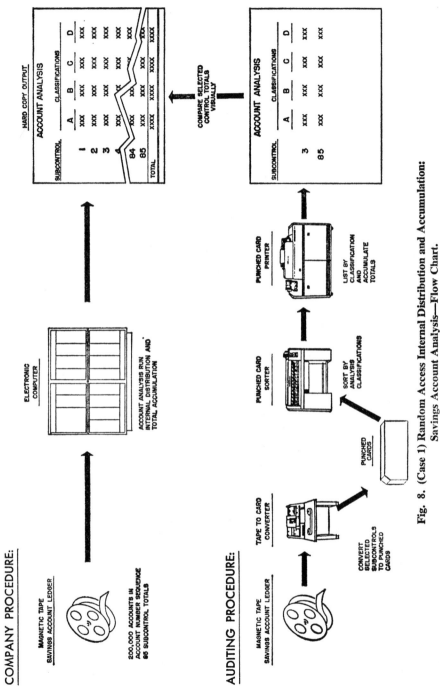

Fig. 8. (Case 1) Random Access Internal Distribution and Accumulation: Savings Account Analysis—Flow Chart.

the accounts may include life insurance premiums under several alternative programs, as well as payments to escrow funds for insurance, taxes, etc. Payments when received are batched, sorted into mortgage number sequence, and processed against the balance tape. As a result, a new updated balance tape is created and the distribution of payments as between interest, principal, escrow payments, and insurance is obtained in total. The updated balance tape includes the date and amount of the last payment applied.

*Audit technique used.* A simulated problem deck of cash payments was created in which were included all possible variables as to principal, interest insurance, escrow, etc. In addition, a separate deck containing exceptions was also prepared. These two decks were used to test the client's regular program for processing payments. As of an interim audit date, various subcontrols of the mortgage balance tape were selected for test. All account balances that were credited with payments on a selected date were transcribed to a separate tape and converted to punched cards for subsequent comparison purposes. The input data tape for the selected date was then processed against the trial balance tape for the preceding cut off period for the selected block. The resulting updated balance tape was converted into punched cards. These cards were compared on a punched card collator with the cards created previously and the exceptions investigated. (There should not ordinarily be any exceptions since all error corrections should have been made at the time of original processing.)

Following this procedure, selected blocks of the input tape were listed on hard copy and visually compared with remittance advices on file. All items in the selected block were accounted for both as to items on input tape and remittance advices on file. (See Figure 9.)

*Other factors and considerations.*

1. Usual reconciliations of deposits to daily cash distributions were also made.

2. The distribution totals obtained from the reprocessing of selected days transactions were also traced into general ledger posting summaries.

## CONCLUSIONS

New equipment developments undoubtedly will continue to present the auditor with new challenges in adapting his auditing techniques. It is likely, however, that in the long run, better systems, better controls, and more efficient audit procedures will be the result.

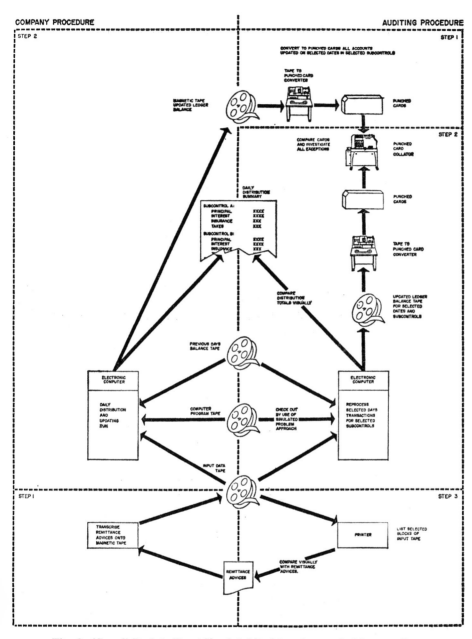

**Fig. 9. (Case 2) Back-to-Front Simulated Problem Approach: Mortgage Loan Cash Application Procedure Flow Chart.**

# 29

# Reporting on Audit Findings

## MAURICE A. WEBSTER, JR.

*Certified Public Accountant; Partner, Peat, Marwick, Mitchell & Co., Philadelphia*

# CHAPTER TWENTY-NINE

# Reporting on Audit Findings

This chapter explores the important area of audit reports together with the applicable standards of auditing and rules of conduct promulgated by the American Institute of Certified Public Accountants. Short-form, long-form and special types of reports are discussed in conjunction with representative samples of variations of the accountant's report.

In addition to these formal audit reports, the preparation of the auditor's report on internal control is explained and illustrated. The mechanics of report preparation, the auditor's legal liability and self-protection, and the interpretation of audit reports are each discussed in turn.

## PURPOSE AND CONTENT OF THE AUDIT REPORT

**Purpose of the audit report.** Management, stockholders and interested third parties can little rely on financial data and information of an unknown or doubtful quality. The principal advantage of the independent audit report is that it contains, in addition to the usual necessary financial information, an independent expert's evaluation of the reliability of the data presented and a description of the scope of the examination supporting the evaluation or opinion.

The type and extent of financial information supplied by the audit report depend largely on the purpose for which it is to be used. Thus, short-form reports are traditionally issued to stockholders of publicly held corporations, while long-form reports are supplied to parties requiring additional or special kinds of information.

**Contents of the audit report.** The audit report basically consists of:

*1. Financial statements and supplementary information.* Financial statements contained in the report usually consist of a balance sheet and statements of earnings and retained earnings for a period ending with the date of the balance sheet. Additional informative disclosure in a *short-form report* is usually limited to notes to the financial statements, and, possibly,

976

an application of funds statement, while the *long-form report* may contain a wide assortment of related information and analyses.

It is important to recognize that the statements incorporated in the audit report are those of the client, not of the auditor. Hence, while it is the auditor's responsibility to exercise due diligence and reasonable care in carrying out the audit engagement, it is the board of directors, partners or sole proprietors who are primarily responsible for any misleading information contained in these statements.

▶ OBSERVATION: As a practical procedure, the auditor frequently drafts the financial statements and discusses them with the client. The client thereupon accepts the statements and adopts them as his own.

*2. The accountant's report.* In his report, sometimes called a *certificate* or *opinion,* the independent accountant states the scope of his examination and expresses his professional opinion on the client's financial statements and related information. He may issue an unqualified or qualified opinion, or completely disclaim an opinion; occasionally he may find it necessary to issue an adverse opinion.

The following illustration is typical of an unqualified short-form accountant's report. Further on in the chapter, there will be a detailed explanation and analysis of the meanings of each of the highly technical, highly stylized phrases contained in this concise report.

| | |
|---|---|
| *Scope of Examination* | We have examined the balance sheet of Smith Manufacturing Company as of December 31, 19___ and the related statements of earnings and retained earnings for the year then ended. Our examination was made in accordance with generally accepted auditing standards, and accordingly included such tests of the accounting records and such other auditing procedures as we considered necessary in the circumstances. |
| *Unqualified Opinion* | In our opinion, the accompanying balance sheet and statements of earnings and retained earnings present fairly the financial position of Smith Manufacturing Company at December 31, 19___ and the results of its operations for the year then ended, in conformity with generally accepted accounting principles applied on a basis consistent with that of the preceding year. |

## AUDITING STANDARDS

As *generally accepted auditing standards* are the bedrock upon which the accountant's report rests, inquiry will be made into the nature of these standards and their effect upon the auditor's conduct of the examination and his report. The standards considered in this discussion are those approved by the members of the American Institute of Certified Public Accountants. These standards, in turn, are supplemented by the *Code of Professional Ethics,* which is quoted in the Appendix to Chapter 38 (for ready reference, some of the rules are also quoted in this chapter). In summary form, the auditing standards are:

*General Standards*

1. The examination is to be performed by a person or persons having adequate technical training and proficiency as an auditor.

2. In all matters relating to the assignment an independence in mental attitude is to be maintained by the auditor or auditors.

3. Due professional care is to be exercised in the performance of the examination and the preparation of the report.

*Standards of Field Work*

1. The work is to be adequately planned and assistants, if any, are to be properly supervised.

2. There is to be a proper study and evaluation of the existing internal control as a basis for reliance thereon and for the determination of the resultant extent of the tests to which auditing procedures are to be restricted.

3. Sufficient competent evidential matter is to be obtained through inspection, observation, inquiries and confirmations to afford a reasonable basis for an opinion regarding the financial statements under examination.

*Standards of Reporting*

1. The report shall state whether the financial statements are presented in accordance with generally accepted principles of accounting.

2. The report shall state whether such principles have been consistently observed in the current period in relation to the preceding period.

3. Informative disclosures in the financial statements are to be regarded as reasonably adequate unless otherwise stated in the report.

4. The report shall either contain an expression of opinion regarding the financial statements, taken as a whole, or an assertion to the effect that an opinion cannot be expressed. When an over-all opinion cannot be expressed, the reasons therefor should be stated. In all cases where an auditor's name is associated with financial statements the report should contain a clear-cut indication of the character of the auditor's examination, if any, and the degree of responsibility he is taking.

**General Standards:**

1. *Training and proficiency.* As previously stated, the widespread reliance on audit reports is based on the recognition that the report contains an *independent expert's* opinion on the financial information presented.

It goes without saying that an expert must have adequate formal training and proficiency in his field. Additionally, he must maintain a continuous program for keeping up with new developments in the profession.

There is no precise way to define an auditor's expertness. One of the oldest standards is the passing of the uniform CPA examination, and the meeting of the educational and experience requirements of the state that grants the certificate. Although there are some expert auditors who have never fully satisfied all the necessary requirements for certification, the title of CPA is, nevertheless, a sign of substantial compliance with the training and proficiency requirements of the first general standard.

It is also incumbent that an auditor maintain his competence by keeping abreast of new and changing accounting principles and auditing procedures. One way to do this is through membership and active participation in professional accounting organizations. A formal or informal study and reading program is also indispensable in maintaining and increasing professional competence. By being alert to new ideas and knowledge, the auditor gives recognition to the importance of this standard of training and proficiency.

2. *Independence.* Independence is the single most important attribute that the auditor must possess. Without it, all other attributes are of little importance. To achieve true impartiality, the auditor must be both mentally and financially independent of the client.

*Mental independence.* This all important quality, which cannot be precisely defined, is an attitude or state of mind involving objectivity, honesty and a kind of courageous impartiality. Although the accountant should develop a cordial, cooperative and understanding association with the client, he should never fail to maintain a professional aloofness that serves to remind the client of his independent and unbiased status.

*Financial independence.* Not only must the accountant *be* impartial, but he must also avoid giving any impression to the contrary. For this reason, the American Institute of Certified Public Accountants and many state societies have imposed certain restrictions on the rights of the accountant or members of his immediate family to acquire interests in client enterprises. These rules are becoming increasingly more stringent.

Rule 2-01 of the Securities and Exchange Commission's Regulation *S-X,* quoted below, embodies the most rigid requirements as to financial and other aspects of independence:

(a) The Commission will not recognize any person as a certified public accountant who is not duly registered and in good standing as such under the laws of the place of his residence or principal office. The Commission will not recognize any person as a public accountant who is not in good standing and entitled to practice as such under the laws of the place of his residence or principal office.

(b) The Commission will not recognize any certified public accountant or public accountant as independent who is not in fact independent. For example, an accountant will be considered not independent with respect to any person or any of its parents or subsidiaries in whom he has, or had during the period of report, any direct financial interest or any material indirect financial interest; or with whom he is, or was during such period, connected as a promoter, underwriter, voting trustee, director, officer, or employee.

(c) In determining whether an accountant may in fact be not independent with respect to a particular person, the Commission will give appropriate consideration to all relevant circumstances, including evidence bearing on all relationships between the accountant and that person or any affiliate thereof, and will not confine itself to the relationships existing in connection with the filing of reports with the Commission.

3. *Professional care.* It is useless to belabor the obvious point that an auditor's skill and training are worthless if used carelessly or negligently in the performance of the examination or the preparation of the report. The legal aspects of negligent or careless performance are treated in this Chapter on pages 1004 to 1012.

### Standards of Field Work:

1. *Planning and supervision.* In order that the audit work may be properly organized, a program should be carefully devised outlining in reasonable detail the nature and extent of the various audit operations that appear to be required in the light of the client's internal control. As the examination progresses, this program is necessarily subject to modification or expansion depending on the audit findings. Another phase of planning is the assignment of the proper number of persons, each possessing the necessary technical skills demanded for the engagement. These planning techniques are further detailed in Chapter 24, *Planning the Audit Program.*

Adequate supervision is also essential, both in the conduct of the field work and in the post audit review. Although the senior in charge of the audit is normally entrusted with supervising most of the field work, the responsible partner or supervisor should keep in touch with the progress of the audit. He may accomplish this by periodic review of the work papers and by conferences with staff members and representatives of the client. He should also be available for consultation with members of the field staff on extraordinary problems that may arise.

At the conclusion of the field work, the partner or supervisor should thoughtfully review the working papers and draft of the audit report, satisfying himself that all problems are properly resolved.

2. *Internal control.* To paraphrase the *standard* itself, the auditor's study and evaluation of the client's internal control is a vital source of evidence in judging the reliability of the data produced by the accounting system, and thus, in effect, in determining the character and extent of the audit tests that are necessary. This matter is further pursued in pages 998 to 1002 of this Chapter and in Chapter 24.

3. *Evidential matter.* The reference to "sufficient competent evidential matter" in this standard of field work envisions a broad range of procedures beyond inspection of the books of account. Depending on the circumstances, it may encompass such procedures as obtaining direct confirmation from banks, customers and creditors; witnessing the physical inventory count; counting cash and securities; examining customers' and vendors' invoices, shipping documents, notes receivable, contracts, correspondence and minute books; and making inquiries of officers or other principals and their employees (see Chapter 25).

**Standards of reporting.** Reporting standards concerning (1) generally accepted accounting principles, (2) consistency, (3) informative disclosures, and (4) expressing an opinion, will be treated in the discussion of *short-form, long-form,* and *no opinion* reports in the following sections of the chapter.

### THE SHORT-FORM REPORT

The short-form audit report normally consists of a balance sheet, statements of earnings and retained earnings, notes to the financial statements and the accountant's report or opinion. An application of funds statement is sometimes also included as supplemental information.

This type of report is customarily furnished to stockholders as their essential need is for basic financial statements accompanied by an independent accountant's opinion. Management is normally furnished with copies of all reports rendered by the auditor; however, where both kinds of reports are submitted, management prefers the long-form report containing supplementary information, comments and schedules.

The following types of accountant's short-form reports or certificates will be discussed:

1. Unqualified opinion.
2. Qualified opinion.
3. Disclaimer or no opinion report.

4. Adverse opinion.

5. Modifications of standard reports.

**Unqualified opinion.** Where the examination has met generally accepted auditing standards and the financial statements are in conformity with generally accepted accounting principles consistently applied, the independent accountant is usually in a position to give an unqualified opinion. The following is a standard form of short-form accountant's report containing an unqualified opinion:

*salutation*   The Board of Directors
Smith Manufacturing Company:

*scope*   We have examined the balance sheet of Smith Manufacturing Company as of December 31, 19___ and the related statements of earnings and retained earnings for the year then ended. Our examination was made in accordance with generally accepted auditing standards, and accordingly included such tests of the accounting records and such other auditing procedures as we considered necessary in the circumstances.

*opinion*   In our opinion, the accompanying balance sheet and statements of earnings and retained earnings present fairly the financial position of Smith Manufacturing Company at December 31, 19___ and the results of its operations for the year then ended, in conformity with generally accepted accounting principles applied on a basis consistent with that of the preceding year.

*signature*                                                       John Jones & Company

*dating*   New York, N. Y.
February 21, 19___

*Salutation.* The report should be addressed to the board of directors of the corporation, unless the auditor is elected by the stockholders. Then, of course, the report should be addressed to them. As to other than corporations, the report should be addressed to the sole proprietor, partnership, board of trustees, or the like, as may be specified by the client or bylaws.

*Scope paragraph.* Dictionary definitions indicate that the opening phrase "we have examined" is synonymous with "we have audited." However, the American Institute of Certified Public Accountants considers the word "audit" to imply a more detailed inquiry than is usually made and, therefore, has chosen the word "examine."

It will be observed that the scope paragraph refers to the examination of the financial statements and not to the books or accounts. This is because the purpose of the examination is to enable the accountant to offer an opinion on the statements. The books or accounts are merely linkage in the chain of evidence supporting the financial statements, as attested by the phrase "and accordingly included such tests of the *accounting records and such other auditing procedures as we considered necessary in the circumstances.*" *Accounting records* include all kinds of accounting records, not just ledgers. Under modern accounting systems, every invoice, voucher, check, contract, etc., becomes part of the books of account.

The language "our examination was made in accordance with generally accepted auditing standards" represents an unqualified statement of fact and, as such, implies that the auditor is fully cognizant of the auditing standards that are generally accepted by the profession. The second part of this sentence, quoted in the preceding paragraph, indicates that the auditor has no reservations as to the adequacy of the scope of his examination. It also indicates that he has done everything that is, in his judgment, necessary to warrant an expression of opinion as to the statements examined.

*Opinion paragraph.* The expression of a professional opinion is a serious matter and carries definite legal responsibilities. The auditor has the duty to make a reasonable examination and one of sufficient scope so that he has reason to believe in the substantial accuracy of the accounts. In addition to the *Auditing Standards of Reporting* listed on page 978, *Articles 2.02* and *2.03* of the American Institute of Certified Public Accountants' *Code of Professional Ethics* are here applicable:

*Article 2.02.* In expressing an opinion on representations in financial statements which he has examined, a member or associate may be held guilty of an act discreditable to the profession if

(a) he fails to disclose a material fact known to him which is not disclosed in the financial statements but disclosure of which is necessary to make the financial statements not misleading; or

(b) he fails to report any material misstatement known to him to appear in the financial statement; or

(c) he is materially negligent in the conduct of his examination or in making his report thereon; or

(d) he fails to acquire sufficient information to warrant expression of an opinion, or his exceptions are sufficiently material to negative the expression of an opinion; or

(e) he fails to direct attention to any material departure from generally accepted accounting principles or to disclose any material omission of generally accepted auditing procedure applicable in the circumstances.

*Article 2.03.* A member or associate shall not permit his name to be associated with statements purporting to show financial position or results of operations in such a manner as to imply that he is acting as an independent public accountant unless he shall:

(a) express an unqualified opinion; or

(b) express a qualified opinion; or

(c) disclaim an opinion on the statements taken as a whole and indicate clearly his reasons therefor; or

(d) when unaudited financial statements are presented on his stationery without his comments, disclose prominently on each page of the financial statements that they were not audited.

The words *present fairly* in the opinion paragraph are used to indicate that the statements are not exact, but that they are fair and not misleading. Perhaps, the only completely exact statement is one in which there are no assets except cash, no liabilities, and one capital account. Thus, it follows that the auditor's opinion has equal limitations and no greater weight should be attached to it.

The scope paragraph states that the examination was made in accordance with generally accepted *auditing standards*. Now, it is stated that, in the opinion of the auditor, the accounts conform with generally accepted *accounting principles*. Since the auditor previously was charged with the full knowledge of what are generally accepted auditing standards, he is now committed to knowing the nature and appropriate applications of accounting principles that are recognized as generally accepted. (See Chapter 1.)

One more facet of the opinion remains, that having to do with the matter of consistency, expressed in the words, "applied on a basis consistent with that of the preceding year." This phrase gives the reader assurance that the comparability of the statements between one year and the next has not been impaired by a change in the accounting principles employed or the manner of their application.

▶ EXAMPLE: At the beginning and end of the preceding year, inventory was stated at *first-in, first-out cost,* not in excess of market. This year, the *last-in, first-out* method was adopted with the result that the closing inventory is carried at substantially less than it would be under the previous method. Quite obviously, the earnings for these two periods are not comparable.

*Signature.* The report is signed in the firm name as it appears on the letterhead.

*Dating.* The report should be dated as of the time the field work was completed. To use a later date, such as the time the report is released for typing, can expose the auditor to unnecessary risk. He may be charged, for example, with the knowledge and disclosure of material events occurring subsequent to the completion of his examination, of which he could not reasonably be expected to be aware. For example, the client may have become a defendant in a law suit involving a substantial amount of money, or a large receivable may suddenly be in jeopardy because of the insolvency of the customer.

▶ OBSERVATION: Although dating the report at the time the field work is completed relieves the accountant of the responsibility of being aware of and reporting subsequent events, he is nevertheless responsible for full disclosure of adverse occurrences if, by chance, he finds out about them before the report is issued.

**Qualified opinion.** The following types of qualifications will be discussed:

1. Limitation on the scope of examination.
2. Departure from generally accepted accounting principles.
3. Lack of consistency.
4. Inadequate disclosure.

1. *Limitation on the scope of examination.* If in one or more respects the auditor finds that usual procedures cannot be readily carried out, he should determine whether any practicable alternative procedures would be satisfactory. To illustrate, it may not be practicable to confirm receivables, such as from the U. S. Government, chain stores, etc., by communication with the debtors. Although direct confirmation of receivables is required by generally accepted auditing standards, the auditor may use alternate procedures to satisfy himself as to the genuineness of the particular receivable. He may, in this case, examine all or some of the following records: related invoices and shipping documents, remittance advices from customers, and related cash book and accounts receivable entries.

When the auditor has been able to satisfy himself by other means, he need not qualify his opinion. He should, however, extend the scope paragraph of the standard audit report somewhat as follows:

> It was not practicable to confirm accounts receivable from U. S. Government departments and agencies by communication with them but we satisfied ourselves as to such accounts by means of other auditing procedures.

When the auditor has been unable to make an examination sufficiently complete to warrant the expression of an unqualified opinion, the standard accountant's report should be revised along the following lines:

(a) The first paragraph would contain only the standard introductory sentence specifying the statements examined.

(b) The second paragraph would set forth the exception to scope and would conclude with the following: "With this exception our examination was made in accordance with generally accepted auditing standards and included such tests. . . ."

(c) The opinion paragraph would contain the following introductory language: "In our opinion, except for possible adjustment not disclosed because of the limitation in scope of our examination. . . ."

The limitations on the scope of the examination may be such as to destroy the significance of the auditor's opinion on the statements taken as a whole. In such case, the auditor is obliged to indicate that he is not in a position to express an opinion on the overall fairness of the financial statements and to give his reasons. He may, if he considers it appropriate, express an opinion limited to those parts of the financial statements with which he is satisfied; but if he does so, he should make it clear that he is not expressing an opinion on the overall fairness of the financial statements.

2. *Departure from generally accepted accounting principles.* If the client is unwilling to correct material departures from generally accepted accounting principles, the accountant must decide whether to qualify his opinion or to express an adverse opinion. This will depend on the significance of the departure. An opinion may be qualified rather than adverse if the statements read in conjunction with the qualification would permit a reasonable appraisal of the financial position and operating results.

If he concludes that he may properly express a qualified opinion, his report should generally contain an intermediate paragraph outlining the exceptions. The opinion paragraph is then appropriately qualified with a reference to the preceding paragraph. In the unusual case, where he issues an adverse opinion, he must set forth the reasons which require it.

3. *Lack of consistency.* The auditor should be alert to any accounting inconsistencies with the preceding year and should determine the effect of the change on operating results. Changes from one accepted accounting principle to another, or in the application of an accepted principle, may have significant effect on financial position and operating results, destroying comparability with financial statements for the preceding year.

Where the effect of the change is found to be significant, the change should be described together with its effect on net earnings and possibly pretax earnings. This disclosure is required only in the year of change. Depending on whether the change is explained in the accountant's report or in a note to the financial statements, the treatments may be:

> . . . in conformity with generally accepted accounting principles which, except for the change mentioned in the preceding paragraph, have been applied on a basis consistent with that of the preceding year.

or

. . . in conformity with generally accepted accounting principles which, except for the change (of which we approve) in the method of providing for depreciation as set forth in note ___ to the financial statements, have been applied on a basis consistent with that of the preceding year.

▶ OBSERVATION: Sometimes a change in accounting principles or in the manner of their application may not have a significant effect on the financial statements for the current year, but may be expected to substantially affect future years. Here again, appropriate disclosure should be made in a note to the financial statements in the year of change. If so disclosed, no mention is required in the accountant's report.

4. *Inadequate disclosure.* As provided in the *Standards of Reporting No. 3,* informative disclosures are to be regarded as reasonably adequate unless otherwise stated in the accountant's report. If disclosure is deemed to be inadequate, the deficiency can be cured by an intermediate explanatory paragraph in the accountant's report. It is far better, however, to persuade the client to incorporate the additional disclosure in the financial statements and related notes, as this material should contain all the necessary information required for reasonable disclosure.

▶ WARNING: Where certain informative disclosures are included in the accountant's report, they become the auditor's representations. This may impose greater responsibility on the auditor as to the fairness of the disclosures than if they were the client's representations.

**Disclaimer or no opinion report.** A no opinion report or disclaimer is issued in situations in which the auditor does not attempt a formal examination and, therefore, is not in a position to express an opinion. In such cases, the auditor nevertheless has a duty to satisfy himself that the financial statements incorporated in the report are in agreement with the underlying records. Further, he should compare the current statements with those for the preceding period and, possibly, other prior periods, obtaining explanation for any significant variations. *Rule 4* of the *Standards of Reporting* (page 978) and *Article 2.03* of the AICPA *Code of Professional Conduct* (page 1403) are particularly relevant to this discussion.

The two instances to be considered in further detail are:

1. Interim statements.
2. Statements prepared from the books without audit.

1. *Interim statements.* In addition to making a year-end examination of sufficient scope for the expression of an opinion, the auditor may assist in the preparation of quarterly or monthly financial statements. While such

interim statements may be prepared principally for the use of management, the auditor cannot be sure that they will be so restricted. If his name appears in connection with interim unaudited statements, he should make it clear that he is not expressing an opinion.

> We submit herewith financial statements of XYZ Company for the three months ended March 31, 19___. Under the terms of our engagement, certain phases of our annual examinations are conducted on an interim basis throughout the year but it is only at the close of the company's fiscal year, December 31, that our examination is sufficient in scope to permit us to express an opinion on the financial statements of the company. We are not, therefore, in a position to express an opinion on the accompanying financial statements.

*2. Statements prepared from the books without audit.* Where the auditor has made no formal examination and, by arrangement with the client, has done little or no audit work, he may prepare the financial statements on his stationery with just a prominent notation on each page, such as "Prepared from the Books Without Audit." However, he may include a report as follows:

> The accompanying balance sheet of the XYZ Company at December 31, 19___ and related statement of earnings for the year then ended were prepared by us from the financial records of the company and are in agreement therewith. However, as we did not audit the accounts, we are precluded from expressing an independent accountant's opinion on the representations contained in the statements.

**Adverse opinion.** If the auditor believes the financial statements to be false and misleading, it is not sufficient for him to disclaim an opinion or state that they have been "prepared from the books without audit." In such cases his report should clearly set forth his disagreement with the financial statements. The position to be taken in this situation is well stated in *Opinion No. 8* of the AICPA Committee on Professional Ethics, as now quoted:

> In a circumstance where a member believes the financial statements are false or misleading as a whole or in any significant respect, it is the opinion of the committee that he should require adjustments of the accounts or adequate disclosure of the facts, as the case may be, and failing this the independent accountant should refuse to permit his name to be associated with the statements *in any way.* (italics added)

**Modifications of standard reports.** In some instances, primarily because of the nature of the client entity, the standard form of accountant's report must be modified to conform to the particular circumstances. These will be treated under the following groupings:

1. Regulated industries.
2. Sole proprietorships.
3. Partnerships.
4. Non-profit institutions.
5. S.E.C. reports.
6. Cash basis statements.

1. *Regulated industries.* The problem of expressing an opinion on financial statements of regulated companies, where there is a material variance between accounting practices prescribed by the regulatory body and generally accepted accounting principles, is one of the most difficult facing auditors today. Examples of such differences in accounting practices are:

a. The Interstate Commerce Commission prohibits the recognition by carriers of the deferred income tax applicable to the excess of accelerated depreciation deducted for tax purposes over book depreciation.
b. State regulatory laws prescribe that certain assets (called "non-admitted" assets) must be eliminated from the balance sheets of insurance companies. Excluded are equipment, furniture and supplies, receivables outstanding over 90 days, and many other items.

The accounting profession has dealt with this dilemma in two ways. The first has been to state that the financial position and results of operations are fairly presented *in conformity with accounting practices prescribed by the regulatory body,* without reference to conformity with generally accepted accounting principles; the second has been to set forth the departures from generally accepted accounting principles with appropriate qualification of the auditor's opinion.

It is evident that the profession as a whole is moving in the direction of the second position. Therefore, as a minimum, it is generally desirable to explain in a footnote to the financial statements the principal differences between prescribed and generally accepted principles, and to refer to this footnote in the opinion paragraph of the accountant's report.

2. *Sole proprietorships.* The assets employed in a sole proprietor's business activity are generally available for his personal liabilities. Sometimes, particularly when the business is small, the individual proprietor may commingle personal assets, liabilities and transactions with those of the business.

When records are adequate, auditable, and relate to one or more specific enterprises, an opinion report may be appropriate. In this case, there should be disclosure, both in the scope paragraph of the accountant's report as well as in the financial statements, of the specific enterprise(s) involved and their ownership by a sole proprietor.

If there is a mingling of personal and business assets and liabilities, and the auditor cannot isolate those pertaining to the business, he may describe his examination and state that he is unable to express an opinion.

▶ WARNING: Disclosure must be made if the auditor ascertains that business assets of a material amount are to be used for the payment of personal liabilities or vice versa.

As income taxes payable by a sole proprietor are based on his taxable income from all sources, after allowing for all permitted deductions, the auditor may not know the amount of income tax, if any, that is payable for the current year. When the amount of the taxes or the amount that will be withdrawn for their payment is known, disclosure should be made. If the amount is not known, it should be disclosed that the statements do not include provision for income taxes that may be payable on the earnings of the enterprise. In neither case is a qualification required when full disclosure is made in the statements. If the report embraces all income producing activities of the proprietor, it would usually be appropriate to provide for income taxes in the financial statements in substantially the same manner as for corporate enterprises.

Frequently a sole proprietor is paid a so-called salary that is actually a drawing against profits. The inclusion or exclusion of such payments is not a cause for qualification so long as proper disclosure is made.

3. *Partnerships.* The existence of a partnership agreement and the separate interests of the individual partners usually make for more precise accounting and better control than generally exist in a sole proprietorship.

The rules of disclosure with respect to income taxes, which are payable by the individual partners, and partners' salaries are essentially the same as those applicable in the case of sole proprietorships, as set forth in the previous section.

Personal assets and liabilities of the partners not applicable to partnership operations should be excluded from partnership financial statements. If it is known that partnership assets are to be used for the payment of a material amount of personal liabilities of any of the partners, disclosure should be made, preferably in the financial statements.

4. *Non-profit institutions.* Following is a partial discussion of some of the special problems involved in reporting on non-profit institutions. See Chapters 31 and 32 for a detailed exposition of the principles of governmental and institutional accounting.

There are inherent difficulties in adequately safeguarding funds received as contributions. In many cases, no system of control or detailed examination could fully satisfy the auditor that all contributions received have been recorded. When voluntary contributions are material and the auditor is unable to substantially satisfy himself as to their recording, some reference to this should be made in the scope paragraph. Also, the financial statements should contain the word *recorded* in describing receipts.

Some organizations on the accrual basis of accounting carry pledges as assets, after deducting allowance for uncollectible pledges or, possibly, an allowance in the full amount of the pledges. Organizations on a cash basis may make footnote reference to expected receipts from pledges or may omit reference thereto. Usually the auditor need not qualify his opinion when disclosure of pledges is not made. When disclosure is made, the usual audit confirmation procedures should be carried out.

Non-profit institutions frequently receive gifts of property. It is desirable to record such property in the accounts and, when the property is income producing, to provide regularly for depreciation. If not carried on the books, disclosure should be made except for minor items. Sometimes disbursements for equipment are charged to expense. This also requires disclosure in the report if the amounts are material in the current year or on a cumulative basis.

Certain types of non-profit organizations, particularly colleges and universities, municipalities and hospitals, may follow accounting principles and practices differing somewhat from, and not as clearly defined as, those followed by business enterprises. In such a situation, the auditor should carefully consider whether it is appropriate to express an opinion as to conformity of the financial statements with (1) generally accepted accounting principles, or (2) accounting practices for non-profit organizations in the particular field. The second alternative may be used only when the auditor has satisfied himself that the accounting principles and practices reflected in the financial statements being examined are, in fact, supported by authoritative literature and have been adopted by a large majority of organizations in the particular field. In any event, the principles and practices followed should result in a fair presentation of financial position and results of operations; otherwise, the auditor should state his exceptions.

Deviations from generally accepted accounting principles and practices by organizations referred to in the preceding paragraph frequently relate to depreciation, profits and losses on sales of securities, and the use of a modified accrual basis.

5. *Securities and Exchange Commission reports.* In reporting on financial statements included in filings with Securities and Exchange Commission, the auditor must observe the requirements set forth in *Rule 2-02 of Regulation S-X.* This rule specifies the representations to be made and opinions to be expressed by the auditor. In essence, these requirements are similar to

those discussed in connection with the standard short-form report. S.E.C. reporting requirements will be further detailed in Chapter 34.

6. *Cash basis statements.* Statements prepared on a cash basis are not intended to present the financial position of an enterprise or the operating results for a particular period because, by their nature, they exclude such items as inventories, receivables, payables and accruals. Sometimes such statements are footnoted to inform the reader of the amount of receivables, payables, inventories, and the like, that are not reflected in the statements, particularly where such amounts are material. Despite their limitations, cash basis statements are often prepared by smaller business enterprises—especially sole proprietorships and partnerships—and by some non-profit organizations.

In expressing an opinion on cash basis statements, it is inappropriate for the independent accountant to refer to generally accepted accounting principles; rather, the opinion should be directed to the fairness with which they present the cash transactions.

Titles of cash basis statements should be sufficiently descriptive to avoid misleading inferences as to what the statements are presenting. Basically, such statements may embrace *all* cash receipts and disbursements for a period, or there may be a Statement of Assets and Liabilities Resulting From Cash Transactions and a Statement of Cash Receipts and Disbursements on Account of Income and Expenses.

A representative form of unqualified accountant's report that would be appropriate in connection with cash basis statements appears as follows:

We have examined the accompanying statement of assets and liabilities, resulting from cash transactions, of _____ as of December 31, 19___, and the related statement of cash receipts and disbursements on account of income and expenses for the year then ended. Our examination was made in accordance with generally accepted auditing standards, and accordingly included such tests of the accounting records and such other auditing procedures as we considered necessary in the circumstances.

In our opinion, the accompanying statements present fairly the assets and liabilities of _____ at December 31, 19___ resulting from cash transactions, and the income collected and expenses disbursed during the year then ended, on a basis consistent with that of the preceding year.

**LONG-FORM REPORTS**

While the short-form report is generally issued in connection with financial statements intended for general publication, auditors frequently issue long-form reports either in conjunction with or in place of the short-form. Long-form reports are frequently demanded by management and/or interested third parties because of the additional or special kinds of information they furnish.

Where the client is indebted to banks, insurance companies, or other investors, there is often a requirement that the creditor be furnished a copy of the long-form report. Where funded debt exists, such a report may have to be furnished to the trustee.

Another important use of the long-form report is to supply information to the prospective purchaser of an enterprise or, where there are merger negotiations, copies would be supplied to the several negotiating companies. In the area of business combinations, the information submitted by the independent accountant may extend well beyond the content of the regular long-form report; for example, a contract for the purchase of a company's capital stock may contain a formula for determining the purchase price based upon data audited by a designated independent accountant.

▶ WARNING: Copies of reports, or any other related information, must not be released to third parties without first obtaining the client's written approval. Often it is preferable to furnish the client with extra copies of a report for transmittal to third parties.

**Contents of the long-form report.** The following is a listing of some of the material included in a representative long-form report, in addition to the basic financial statements:

1. Comparative summary of earnings for current and preceding years with percentage of gross profit, operating expenses and net earnings in terms of net sales.

2. Brief, pertinent comments on why net earnings increased or decreased for the current year.

3. Summary of source and application of funds for the current year.

4. Comparative summary of financial position.

5. Comparative aged summary of accounts receivable at year-end.

6. Comparative summary of closing inventories with brief comments on how the quantities were determined, significant changes in group values compared with preceding year, etc.

7. Summary of changes in plant and equipment and allowance for depreciation for the current year with brief comments on the more important plant and equipment additions and retirements.

8. Comparative schedules of such items as cost of sales, selling expenses, and administrative and general expenses.

9. Statement of the percentage of allowance for depreciation to gross

amount of depreciable properties at year-end; also percentage of current year's provision for depreciation to gross amount of depreciable properties at beginning of year.

10. Maturity dates and respective amounts of bank loans payable at year-end. Maximum and minimum amounts of short-term borrowings during current year.

11. Comment on Federal income tax status, indicating year to which returns were examined by the *United States Treasury Department* and whether all additional assessments have been paid or provided for.

12. Comment on whether purchase contracts unfilled at the year-end appear to be usual and normal in the light of operating requirements.

13. General information on insurance coverage and comments on coverage that appears to be inadequate.

14. Scope of work performed by the accountant.

▶ COMMENT: To many readers of long-form reports, the detailed scope of the auditor's work is of little interest. Usually, it is of special interest only to the credit departments of banks or other credit grantors. Where explanation of scope is omitted, it may be advisable, nevertheless, to state the result of the confirmation of receivables and to indicate that a physical test of inventories was made.

**Opinion on supplementary data.** In addition to stating his opinion on the basic financial statements, the auditor has the obligation to set forth clearly his responsibility with regard to comments, schedules, and other supplementary data contained in the long-form report. If he fails to do so, is ambiguous, or vague, the reader has a right to assume that the auditor's opinion on the basic statements is equally applicable to the supplementary information.

▶ WARNING: The auditor must particularly avoid creating the impression that his opinion relates to supplementary data on which he is incapable of rendering a valid judgment. For example, earnings forecasts, being dependent on future transactions, are not susceptible to audit. *Article 2.04* of the AICPA *Code of Professional Ethics* expressly states, "A member or associate shall not permit his name to be used in conjunction with an estimate of earnings contingent upon future transactions in a manner which may lead to the belief that the member or associate vouches for the accuracy of the forecast."

Figure 1 is an illustration of the accountant's report that might accompany a long-form report. The final paragraph of the report, in satisfaction of the requirement for adequate disclosure of the auditor's position on the supplementary information, states that (1) the supplementary information is not considered necessary for a fair presentation of the financial position and results of operations, (2) the additional material is furnished for supplementary analysis purposes, (3) the examination was made primarily to formulate an opinion on the current year's basic financial statements, (4) the additional material was subjected to the same audit procedures as the basic financial statements, and (5) in his opinion, it is fairly presented when considered together with the basic financial statements.

*Other variations.* Variations that may be applicable in selected instances are:

1. At times, the financial statements in the detailed report may differ in detail rather than in substance from the formal statements previously issued; e.g., details of fixed assets or other accounts may be shown. Although it is preferable to present both sets of statements in exactly the same way (giving additional detail in the comments), if for some good reason the two sets of statements do differ as to the amount of detail, then the final paragraph of the accountant's report should be amended to read:

> Under date of February 21, 19___, we have reported as above on the formal statements (or the statements issued to the stockholders or some other descriptive title). Certain details contained in the accompanying financial statements were not included in the formal statements (or the statements issued to stockholders) and these details and the accompanying comments and schedules, though not considered necessary. . . .

2. The report may contain detailed data supplied by the company for which the auditor would not wish to take responsibility. In this case, the auditor should state:

> While our examination was made primarily for the purpose of formulating our opinion on the current year's basic financial statements, the additional data, *except where otherwise stated in the accompanying comments and schedules,* have been subjected to the same audit procedures and, in our opinion, are stated fairly in all material respects when considered in conjunction with the financial statements taken as a whole.
>
> Examples of these exceptions are:
>
> (a) Details of sales by product and type of customer have been obtained from the company's statistical department and have not been checked.
>
> (b) Statistical figures as to ton miles have been taken from monthly reports to the Interstate Commerce Commission and have not been audited.

3. Where the prior year's figures are submitted for comparative purposes and the auditor has not examined them, or where there are significant exceptions or reservations in the prior report, appropriate disclosure should be made to that effect.

The Board of Directors
  Smith Manufacturing Company:

We have examined the balance sheet of Smith Manufacturing Company as of December 31, 19___ and the related statements of earnings and retained earnings for the year then ended. Our examination was made in accordance with generally accepted auditing standards, and accordingly included such tests of the accounting records and such other auditing procedures as we considered necessary in the circumstances.

In our opinion, the accompanying balance sheet and statements of earnings and retained earnings present fairly the financial position of Smith Manufacturing Company at December 31, 19___ and the results of its operations for the year then ended, in conformity with generally accepted accounting principles applied on a basis consistent with that of the preceding year.

Under date of February 21, 19___ we have reported as above on the appended financial statements (Exhibits A, B and C). The accompanying comments and schedules, though not considered necessary for a fair presentation of the financial position and results of operations, are now presented mainly for supplementary analysis purposes and to give information as to the scope of work. While our examination was made primarily for the purpose of formulating our opinion on the current year's basic financial statements, the additional data have been subjected to the same audit procedures and, in our opinion, are stated fairly in all material respects when considered in conjunction with the financial statements taken as a whole.

John Jones & Company

New York, N. Y.
  February 21, 19___

**Fig. 1. Long-Form Accountant's Report.**

4. When there are no accompanying comments and the supplementary data is limited to schedules of such items as manufacturing expenses, selling expenses, and administrative and general expenses, the third paragraph of the accountant's long-form report may be omitted and, in lieu, the following sentence added at the end of the opinion (second) paragraph:

> Also, in our opinion, the accompanying schedules are stated fairly in all material respects when considered in conjunction with the financial statements taken as a whole.

**REPORTS ON FRAGMENTARY MATTERS**

It is not uncommon for the auditor to be called upon to make an examination of a limited nature pursuant to the provisions of a contract to which the client is a party. These special examinations are often made as a supplement to the auditor's regular examination, and the report is prepared in letter form.

**Bond indentures and loan agreements.** Many bond indentures and long-term agreements require submission of some or all of the following at stated intervals: (1) financial statements, possibly at quarterly intervals but to be audited annually; (2) representations of the borrowing company that it has complied with the provisions of the agreement up to a specified date; and (3) a report from an independent accountant as to the borrower's compliance with the agreement's provisions to a specified date. A sample form of the accountant's report on such an engagement appears in Figure 2.

Smith Manufacturing Company *
    New York, N. Y.

We have examined the balance sheet of Smith Manufacturing Company as of December 31, 19___ and the related statements of earnings and retained earnings for the year then ended, as reported to you on February 21, 19___. Our examination was made in accordance with generally accepted auditing standards, and accordingly included such tests of the accounting records and such other auditing procedures as we considered necessary in the circumstances.

In making our examination we obtained no knowledge of any default by the company in the observation, performance or fulfillment of any of the terms, convenants, provisions or conditions contained in the loan agreement with the _____ Insurance Company dated _____ 19___ and in the note executed thereunder. However, it should be understood that our examination was not directed primarily toward obtaining such knowledge.

John Jones & Company

New York, N. Y.
    (Date)

**Fig. 2. Accountant's Report on Bond Indenture or Loan Agreement.**

* Adapted with permission from *Special Reports—Application of Statement on Audit Procedure #28,* published by the American Institute of Certified Public Accountants.

**Other agreements.** There are innumerable other kinds of agreements that may require examinations of a limited nature, including those pertaining to the determination of the amounts of profit-sharing bonuses, royalties and rentals.

An accountant's report that is concerned with the determination of a specified amount or with other specific financial representations should state the nature of the information presented, the basis on which it is prepared and whether in the auditor's opinion it is presented fairly on that basis. In the usual case where financial position or operating results are not involved, it would be inappropriate to include a statement regarding conformity with generally accepted accounting principles. However, where there is an incomplete financial presentation, such as a company's working capital, a statement regarding conformity with accepted principles should be included.

▶ CAUTION: At times, the indenture's definition of working capital, or other required financial data, may be in conflict with generally accepted accounting principles. Where this situation exists, the accountant's report should point out these exceptions.

## THE AUDITOR'S REPORT ON INTERNAL CONTROL

Fundamental to the auditor's examination of the financial statements is his review of the company's system of internal control. His observations and comments on internal control and other procedural matters are generally *not included* with the financial statements or in the accountant's formal report. This communication, being more intimate in nature and having limited distribution, is a form of management service, distinct from the financial statements.

▶ CAUTION: Comments expressed by the auditor in this report should not contradict the opinion he has expressed on the financial statements. If there are serious flaws in internal control, the auditor should be sure that he has extended his tests sufficiently to justify the opinion he has expressed.

▶ NOTE: A detailed treatment of the auditor's review of internal control, together with actual specimen internal control questionnaires, are furnished in Chapter 24.

### Advantages of preparing this report:
1. *Benefit to client.* At the completion of an examination, the auditor probably has a better insight into the operations of a company's accounting system and procedures than anyone except company personnel directly involved in accounting matters. Being impartial, he is in an excellent position to evaluate the effectiveness, the strengths and the limitations of the internal control system. Unless he gives management the benefit of his observations, he misses a golden opportunity to be of constructive service by providing management with impartial views and recommendations that can result in corrective action and cost savings.
2. *Benefit to the auditor.* Besides the intangible but valuable fostering of client gratitude and goodwill, the auditor's comments often stimulate systems revisions requiring the auditor's professional assistance.
3. *Fraud prevention.* Because of the importance of internal control in

reducing the client's exposure to fraud, it behooves the auditor to inform his client of the areas in which his accounting system and control procedures can be strengthened. Because the usual type of examination is not primarily designed to detect fraud, such a warning not only aids the client but also protects the auditor if a defalcation is subsequently discovered.

**Contents and form of report.** Figure 3 reproduces a typical internal control report to management.

Mr. John Smith, President
Smith Manufacturing Company
New York 14, N. Y.

Dear Mr. Smith:

In connection with our examination of the financial statements of your company for the year ended September 30, 19___, we present for your consideration certain suggestions and recommendations relating in general to the company's accounting procedures and system of internal control. The matters discussed do not affect the validity of the financial statements on which we rendered our report under date of November 30, 19___, or the overall adequacy of your present accounting methods and records.

Since our examination is based on a sampling and test-checking of the company's transactions, we are not in a position to detect all irregularities which could possibly occur. Adequate internal control affords protection of the company's assets and a check on the accuracy and reliability of accounting data. Accounting records, procedures, and related operations should, where practicable, be organized in such a way that no part thereof is under the absolute and independent control of one person, but rather that the individual duties are interdependent so that a continuous check on day-to-day transactions is provided.

*Cash*

Checks submitted to officers for signature are not accompanied by invoices or other suppporting documents, nor are the supporting documents approved for payment or subsequently marked to prevent their reuse. We suggest that a rubber stamp imprint, providing for check number, date paid, account charged, approval of prices, receipt of goods or services, approval of footings and extensions, and final approval for payment by an officer be stamped on the supporting documents. The supporting documents bearing the appropriate approvals and other information should then accompany the checks submitted for signature. After the check is signed the underlying documents should be marked "PAID" or otherwise cancelled by a perforating machine or rubber stamp.

Internal control is most effective when the bank reconciliation is prepared by someone who is not responsible for entries in the receipts and disbursements records. Inasmuch as this is difficult with a small number of office employees, it is suggested that reconciliations be made by one of the officers at least occasionally.

**Fig. 3. Auditor's Internal Control Report to Management.**

*Accounts Receivable*

| Comment | Action Suggested |
|---|---|
| (1) One person handles cash, posts accounts receivable, prepares and mails monthly statements of accounts. | (1) The employee handling cash should not also post accounts receivable. Furthermore, monthly statements to customers should be examined and mailed by a second person. |
| (2) During the past year, the accounts receivable detail ledger was never balanced to the general ledger control account. | (2) To provide proper control and to assure accurate posting, the detail balances should be balanced monthly to the general ledger control. |
| (3) Presently, there is no systematic accounting for shipper and invoice numbers. | (3) To assure prompt and proper billing, this should be done regularly. |

Bad debt write-offs are authorized in writing by the office manager. We recommend that all such write-offs over a given amount, say $50.00 or $100.00, be further approved by an officer by signing or initialing the voucher.

*General*

It was noted that purchases for employees are charged to inventory accounts and the cash, when received, is credited to inventory. These purchases should be charged directly to an employees' receivable account, so that accounting control is established over subsequent collections.

During October, 19___, we visited the company's safe deposit box accompanied by the Secretary, who has individual access to the box. At that time the box contained $1,750,000 in negotiable securities. Other officers also have individual access. For the protection of these persons, it is recommended that the presence of two individuals be required for access to the box.

The present general ledger chart of accounts has been used for many years. As the company has grown and new types of operations have been undertaken, additional accounts have been added on a haphazard basis. The result is that the chart has become very detailed and certain classifications of expenses are difficult to obtain. We believe that a new chart should be developed to provide readily the data required for administrative reports, as well as for more formal quarterly reports. This matter has been discussed with the Treasurer who agrees that the chart of accounts should be completely revised.

* * * * * * * * *

We should like to acknowledge the courtesy and assistance extended to us by personnel of the company during our examination.

Should you have any questions concerning the matters presented herein, we shall be pleased to discuss them with you at your convenience.

Very truly yours,

John Jones & Company

**Fig. 3. Auditor's Internal Control Report to Management. (Continued.)**

*Reporting negative findings.* In setting forth deficiencies observed in a company's system or procedures, the auditor must be certain that his facts and conclusions are correct. It can be very embarrassing if it turns out that the auditor's criticism was based on misinformation.

▶ SUGGESTION: Before actually issuing a report, review the criticisms and suggestions with company personnel who are in a position to know the facts.

Regardless of the size of a company, there are areas where, because the controls are less than ideal, the opportunity for fraud exists. The auditor should acquaint management with the risks that are involved and suggest ways of reducing them. Occasionally, management will prefer to take a calculated risk of loss or theft because the exposure does not appear to warrant the cost of corrective action. As a matter of record and for his own protection, the auditor may wish to cover such a situation in his letter.

In detailing negative findings the auditor should avoid items of little or no consequence and matters of purely individual preference. Generally the auditor should be able to present a reasonable solution to the weakness he has observed, but his recommendations for correction should be practical in relation to the size and operating conditions of his client. Little is accomplished by suggesting that certain duties be reassigned to other clerks when the size of the operation requires only one such employee.

▶ WARNING: Remember that a procedure that makes the records easier to audit may not necessarily be the most economical for the client.

*Reporting positive findings.* When substantial improvements have been made in the accounting procedures or system of internal control, the auditor may express his approval in his letter to management. This is good public relations. When a weakness is disclosed in the course of the audit and the controller immediately takes corrective action, it is also good public relations to emphasize the prompt response rather than the former weakness.

It is sometimes customary to conclude such a letter by acknowledging the cooperation and assistance shown by client personnel during the course of the auditor's examination. Remarks of this nature are completely gratuitous and should be included only when the appreciation is genuine.

*Oral and written reports.* During the examination most of the internal control matters will have been discussed orally with personnel responsible for the accounting records. This oral communication may be sufficient for routine items of relatively minor importance, but all significant matters should be summarized in a letter so that they become a matter of permanent record.

Generally, the letter should be addressed to the president or the chairman of the board with a copy to the controller and/or treasurer. The objective is to bring the comments to the attention of the officials administratively responsible for, but not functionally contributing to, the deficiency under consideration. When these deficiencies relate to outside branch activities of a relatively minor nature, it is appropriate to address the letter to the chief accounting officer.

*Style.* The formal *accountant's report* and related financial statements tend to become stereotyped and often do not tax the writing ability of the auditor. On the other hand, internal control reports are difficult to standardize and, therefore, require the auditor to organize his thoughts clearly and grammatically. Because senior management officers are often too busy to analyze the minute details of a problem and may not understand all of the technical accounting terms, the auditor should train himself to present the problem and suggested solution in concise language, expressed in simple and direct terms. More often than he imagines, his skill as an auditor is judged by the effectiveness of this type of communication.

**File copies and follow-up.** Since the internal control letter has importance to the auditor as a matter of record, a copy should be preserved in the same manner as copies of audit reports. At the beginning of the succeeding year's examination, the auditor should ascertain what corrective action has been taken with respect to his comments. As an extension of his audit work may be required, he should particularly investigate the areas in which no action was taken.

▶ SUGGESTION: When management repeatedly fails to act upon a significant deficiency, the auditor can protect himself by reporting this to the board of directors.

### MECHANICS OF REPORT PREPARATION

**Format.** The report that the auditor delivers to his client is usually contained in a small package. Its size bears no relationship to the hours of work and thought that have gone into its preparation. However, since it is the only tangible evidence of his efforts, the auditor should design the appearance of his report so that it will make a favorable impression on the client.

No one format is necessarily better than another, and each auditor (or firm) may develop a style of reporting that has individuality and becomes identified with all his work. In any event, neatness and precise arrangement of data, as well as accuracy, are essential to the professional appearance of a report.

▶ SUGGESTION: A financial statement is more attractive if it is uncluttered. Omit unnecessary dollar marks and underscorings, and limit the use of capitals to the first letter of captions.

**Review of the report draft with client.** Although the financial statements and footnotes are the representations of the client, in a majority of audit engagements the auditor, because of his experience and skills, plays a leading part in drafting these statements. Furthermore, the accountant's opinion section of the report may contain qualifications and explanations. In order to prevent the contents of the final report from coming as a surprise to the client, it is prudent to submit the report draft to one or more top officials of the client for review and discussion. Often this review and subsequent conference will clear up misconceptions that the auditor may have had, thus relieving him of the embarrassment of correcting a report that has been issued.

**Recording adjusting entries.** Although auditor-prepared adjusting entries are not part of the body of the report, it is important that they be properly recorded by the client. Otherwise, the accountant will be in the anomalous position of expressing an opinion on financial statements not in agreement with the books of account.

Journal entries prepared by the auditor fall into two categories: (1) reclassification of book accounts for statement purposes; e.g., segregation of credit balances in accounts receivable and debit balances in accounts payable; and (2) entries representing actual adjustments that often affect operating results. Although reclassification entries are not usually reflected in the client's books, both types of entries should be discussed with and copies furnished to the client.

**Proofreading and review.** Accurate audit reports demand careful proofreading and review of the typed material. The reader in the proofreading team should be a person other than the typist, so that he or she will be able to detect misinterpretations of the original material. The person who checks the typed copy should be familiar with the proper forms of presentations and should be capable of detecting errors in grammar and punctuation, as well as typographical errors.

The independent verification of all footings (including crossfooting of final totals) is also an important checking feature. This operation should be performed after the proofreading has been completed, so that all figures on the typed copy are presumed to agree with the draft. Tick marks should be made on the copy to provide permanent visual evidence of the footing of all columns.

Finally, the typed report should be slowly and carefully reread by a knowledgeable person who is responsible for cross-referencing all figures appearing in the statements, schedules, notes and comments. This person should consider the overall clarity of the report and question any disclosure that appears unclear or inconsistent. Following this review, the typed report is ready for signature.

**Distribution.** A sufficient number of report copies should be delivered directly to the president or chief financial officer of the client for distribution to banks or other third parties. If the auditor is requested to make distribution to outside parties, he should furnish his client with copies of transmittal letters or otherwise inform him of the persons to whom delivery has been made.

It is desirable that the auditor prepare at least three copies of each report for his own files—one, a record copy for permanent retention; two, a copy to be filed with the working papers; and three, a spare copy for use as a draft in preparing the report for the succeeding year.

**Client's printed reports.** Publicly owned companies generally issue printed annual reports to their stockholders containing financial statements (usually including comparative figures for the preceding year) and the accountant's report. Also, there is an increasing tendency for annual reports to include charts, statistical comparisons of major operating and balance sheet items for five, ten or more years, and pictures of products, plants or other subjects of interest.

*Check of printer's proof.* As a matter of protection, the auditor should arrange to check the printer's proof of the client's annual report. First, the auditor should assure himself that the printed financial statements, related notes and accountant's report are in complete agreement with his audit report. It is desirable, also, to proofread the narrative and to check financial figures to the financial statements, related notes or possibly the audit working papers. Likewise, figures appearing in the statistical summary and represented by charts should be checked to the statements or other source material. The broad purpose of this check is to determine whether the various kinds of information are consistently presented in the several sections of the printed report.

*Signing printed report in lieu of typed report.* Occasionally, by agreement with the client, no typed audit report is rendered. Instead, the auditor manually signs a number of copies of the printed report. The signature in this case should be affixed above the auditor's printed name at the bottom of the accountant's report. This practice saves the cost of typing an audit report and is entirely acceptable. Obviously, before signing, the auditor should carefully compare the printer's proof, and then the printed report, with his drafts of financial statements, related notes and accountant's report.

## THE AUDITOR'S LIABILITY AND SELF-PROTECTION

This topic is divided into the following subtopics:

1. Auditor's liability to clients.
2. Auditor's liability to third parties.
3. Disciplinary action.

4. Auditor's work papers.
5. Insurance.

**Auditor's liability to clients.** Because public accountancy is a relatively new learned profession, legal guide lines are few. However, the factors involved in the accountant's liability to clients can be effectively outlined under the following headings:

1. General extent of liability at common law.
2. Contractual obligations for services.
3. Responsibility for uncovering fraud or defalcations.
4. Legal responsibility for acts of employees.

*1. General extent of liability at common law.* Basically, at common law, the auditor must be qualified for the task he undertakes. He is expected to possess a special professional skill and is, therefore, required to perform his work with a high degree of competence and care. He must measure up to the other members of his profession in both learning and skill. Generally accepted auditing standards are the yardstick.

▶ SUGGESTION: Keep up with current developments in the profession; it can help if you are called upon to justify your position in court.

*2. Contractual obligations for services.* Accounting service is rendered to a client under a contractual arrangement. The contract may be oral or written. It is a good policy to obtain written contracts for new engagements, but oral contracts may often serve as the basis of the continued relationship. The nature of the engagement, whether covered by oral or written contract, should be clearly understood by the parties. An auditor's liability to his client will be determined in great measure by what he contracted to do, the work actually performed, and the manner of the performance. Liability to clients will be based upon failure to live up to contractual requirements and negligent performance of work done.

▶ WARNING: If for some reason the scope of your work is limited, make sure there is a clear understanding between you and your client.

Contractual language should be explicit; avoid vague terms such as "detailed audit," "complete audit," or other generalizations of this nature. In *Maryland Casualty Company v. Cook,* decided in 1940, the court held that where an auditor contracted to perform a "complete audit," the words had to be interpreted in accordance with the plain language used.

▶ SUGGESTION: The auditor can avoid possible misinterpretation of the contractual obligations if he uses technical terms, such as "in accordance with generally accepted auditing standards."

*3. Responsibility for uncovering fraud or defalcations.* The most common legal action by clients is the assertion of civil liability for the failure to uncover shortages, defalcations or other similar irregularities. Where the service performed by the auditor is in the nature of an examination in accordance with generally accepted auditing standards rather than a special examination for the purpose of determining a specific shortcoming, the auditor, if he has used due care and was not negligent, will *not* be held responsible for uncovering peculations. However, he does retain responsibility for discovering irregularities that he should have uncovered using average professional competence and reasonable care in the normal course of the work contracted for.

Clients' suits on the grounds that the auditor has been negligent can be defended by establishing that the client has contributed to such negligence (*Craig v. Anyon*). Where losses have occurred and the client has not exercised reasonable care, he cannot expect to recover such losses from the auditor.

In *Statement on Auditing Procedure No. 30,* the Committee on Auditing Procedure of the American Institute of Certified Public Accountants sets forth the responsibilities and functions of the independent auditor in the examination of financial statements, especially as related to the area of responsibility for discovery of fraud (including defalcations and other similar irregularities). The committee states:

> The ordinary examination incident to the expression of an opinion on financial statements is not primarily or specifically designed, and cannot be relied upon, to disclose defalcations and other similar irregularities, although their discovery may result. Similarly, although the discovery of deliberate misrepresentation by management is usually more closely associated with the objective of the ordinary examination, such examination cannot be relied upon to assure its discovery. . . . The subsequent discovery that fraud existed during the period covered by the independent auditor's examination does not of itself indicate negligence on his part. . . . He is not an insurer or guarantor and, if his examination was made with due professional skill and care, in accordance with generally accepted auditing standards, he has fulfilled all of the obligations implicit in his undertaking.

> If an objective of an independent auditor's examination were the discovery of all fraud, he would have to extend his work to a point where its cost would be prohibitive. Even then he could not give assurance that all types of fraud had been detected. . . . It is generally recognized that good internal control and fidelity bonds provide protection more economically and effectively.

The Committee also notes that fidelity bonds, in addition to offering the obvious advantage of indemnification for discovered defalcations, also have a possible deterrent effect upon employees. However, the presence of these bonds should not affect the scope of the ordinary examination.

*4. Legal responsibility for acts of employees.* In addition to liability for incompetence, negligence and fraud, the auditor is also responsible for acts of employees within the scope and in the course of their employment.

**Auditor's liability to third parties.** While an auditor's services are performed for his client, the report may be used by the client to inform or to influence third parties. This type of auditor's liability is delineated as follows:

1. General extent of liability at common law.
2. Liability under statutes.

*1. General extent of liability at common law.* Generally, no contractual relationship exists between the auditor and third parties. In *Landell v. Lybrand* the court held that a claim by a third party against an auditor for negligence was not valid. There was no contractual relationship between the parties and therefore no breach of duty on the part of the auditor. Where there is no intent to deceive on the part of the auditor, a third party cannot bring suit at common law on the grounds of negligence (failure to exercise reasonable care).

▶ WARNING: Where you know that the work is being performed for the specific use of a third party or where the third party is paying all or part of the fee, *Landell v. Lybrand* will not apply.

The landmark case of *Ultramares Corp. v. Touche* established certain additional responsibilities of auditors to third parties at common law. When the auditor knows with sufficient exactness that his report will be used for the primary benefit of a third party, there may be a liability for either negligence or fraud. If there has been neither reckless misstatement nor insincere profession of an opinion, but only an honest mistake, the liability is for negligence. Where the audit has been so deficient that it could not support a genuine belief in its adequacy, watch out—this could be construed as fraud.

At common law, a third party in addition to proving negligent misrepresentation must also be able to show that the misrepresentation was material, that it was the direct cause of his damage and that he had relied upon the misrepresentation. All factors must be present.

*2. Liability under statutes.* The common law liability of the auditor to third parties has been substantially affected by the enactment of the Federal Securities Act of 1933 and the Federal Securities Exchange Act of 1934. These acts impose additional responsibilities in connection with reporting on financial data for inclusion in registration statements or annual reports filed with the Securities and Exchange Commission.

*Federal Securities Act of 1933.* This Act deals with the offering of securities for sale to the public in interstate commerce. The Act permits the security purchaser to sue the certifying auditor in the event the financial statements included in the registration statement contain, on the effective date, an untrue statement of a material fact or an omission of a material fact required to be stated or necessary to make the statements not misleading. The auditor must not only believe that the statements were true and did not omit material facts, but must be able to prove that he had performed a reasonable investigation to support this belief.

▶ WARNING: The auditor must satisfy himself, *as of the effective date,* that there have been no changes in the client's affairs since completion of his examination that would have a material adverse effect on the financial statements, unless disclosed in the registration statement. Under the 1933 Act, the third party need only show there is a false statement or misleading omission in order to recover damages from the auditor; he does not have to prove that his loss resulted therefrom. The burden, therefore, lies with the auditor to show that he was not negligent or guilty of fraud. This differs from common law where the burden of proof as to negligence or fraud is upon the third party. Action under the Act must be brought within one year after discovery of the cause of action and, in any event, within three years after the security was offered to the public.

*Federal Securities Exchange Act of 1934.* This Act regulates securities exchanges and the securities traded and listed thereon. Provisions include filing of periodic reports with the SEC, including financial statements certified by independent public accountants. Under the 1934 Act, the auditor's responsibility for the financial statements does not appear to extend in time beyond the completion of his audit work, even though the report is filed with the Commission at a subsequent date. This does not relieve the auditor of the responsibility for full disclosure of post balance sheet events occurring up to the date of his report.

▶ COMMENT: Whereas under the 1933 Act the auditor must prove that after a reasonable investigation he had grounds to believe and did believe the statements to be true and free of material omission, the 1934 Act requires the auditor to prove only that he acted in good faith and had no knowledge that the statements were false and misleading.

**Disciplinary action.** The auditor can be found criminally liable, or he may be disciplined by government and private bodies, under some circumstances.

*Criminal liability.* The auditor is subject to criminal liability under

Federal law—principally under the Federal Securities Act of 1933, the Securities Exchange Act of 1934, and under the provisions of the United States Internal Revenue Code. Although the provisions of the Acts and the Code do not necessarily identify the auditor, they are clearly applicable to him. Generally, the statutes provide for fines in amounts up to $10,000 or imprisonment for not more than five years, or both, upon conviction thereunder.

State laws that apply to auditors are those principally concerned with regulating the practice of accountancy within the state. Usually, the state boards of accountancy police compliance with state law.

*Professional societies and other.* The by-laws of the American Institute of Certified Public Accountants and of the various state accounting societies provide for disciplinary action against a member who violates the ethical rules of the profession or is adjudged to have committed a fraud. Suspension or expulsion is particularly damaging to an individual's professional reputation.

In addition to the criminal liability under Federal statutes, government agencies, such as the Securities and Exchange Commission and the Internal Revenue Service, are empowered to enforce disciplinary proceedings, usually by suspension or withdrawal of the right to practice before such agency.

**The auditor's working papers.** It is important that the auditor know the following essentials about working papers.

*Ownership.* It is well established at law that the auditor owns his working papers. The first case involving this point was *Ipswich Mills v. Dillon, et al.,* decided in Massachusetts in 1927. Here the court found that the auditor held title to the working papers in the absence of any specific agreement to the contrary.

▶ NOTE: No right of privileged communication exists between auditor and client under common law. However, statutes granting privilege have been enacted in several states including Florida, Illinois, Kentucky, Louisiana and New Mexico.

*Working papers can defend or weaken your position.* The audit working papers will almost inevitably play a crucial role in any situation where audit work is attacked. Practically every case brought against an auditor is supported by evidence secured from working papers or evidence developed through leads provided by the working papers. On the other hand, the auditor's working papers often serve as evidence in defense of his work.

▶ WARNING: Make sure that audit working papers are reviewed carefully and completely. Guard against hindsight criticism. The final review should resolve anything that might have excited suspicion during the course of the audit or that was questioned and not satisfactorily explained.

*Client's representation letter.* A client's representation letter is an important part of the auditor's working papers. Even though the auditor diligently performs an examination in accordance with generally accepted auditing standards, the examination cannot be relied on to reveal any or all spurious entries or information deliberately withheld by management. The representation letter, drafted by the auditor and addressed to him by the client, should contain various assurances as to (1) the full and proper recording of assets and liabilities, and disclosure of all contingent liabilities, (2) recognition that the auditor's test examination would not necessarily disclose all or any irregularities, (3) the fact that no shortages or other irregularities were discovered that had not been brought to the attention of the auditor, and (4) that there have been no developments since the balance sheet date that would cause the financial statements to be inaccurate or misleading in a material respect. Figure 4 illustrates a specimen representation letter.

SMITH MANUFACTURING COMPANY
New York 14, N. Y.

February 21, 19___

John Jones and Company
   Certified Public Accountants

In connection with your examination of our financial statements for the year ended December 31, 19___, we submit, at your request, the following representations, according to the best of our knowledge and belief:

ASSETS

The company had satisfactory title to all recorded assets, and there are no liens or encumbrances thereon not recorded on the books.

No asset owned by the company at December 31, 19___, was, or is now, pledged or deposited in escrow as security for liabilities, performance of contracts, etc., except that real estate located at 717 No. Third St. is pledged as security for the mortgage payable to First National Bank.

The notes and accounts receivable at December 31, 19___ aggregating $1,751,-649 represent valid claims against customers and other debtors, and do not include amounts in respect to goods shipped on consignment or approval. Adequate provision has been made to cover losses which may be sustained in the collection of the receivables.

The inventories of raw materials, work in process, finished goods and supplies at December 31, 19___ amounting to $2,143,721, are based on physical quantities determined as of December 31, 19___ by actual count, weight or measurement by competent employees under proper supervision. The inventories do not include any items billed to customers but not shipped, nor any items returned by customers for which credits had not been recorded. No obsolete, damaged or unusable items are included in the inventories except at net realizable values. The inventories are stated on the same basis and were determined

**Fig. 4. Client's Representation Letter.**

generally in the same manner as inventories at the end of the preceding year.

All important items of property, plant and equipment sold, destroyed, abandoned or otherwise disposed of or considered to be obsolete, have been removed from the accounts.

### LIABILITIES

All direct liabilities of the company at December 31, 19___ were recorded on the books as of that date.

Our Federal income tax returns have been examined by the Internal Revenue Service through December 31, 19___.

At December 31, 19___ the company had no unfilled purchase commitments in excess of normal requirements or at prices materially in excess of prevailing market prices, and had no sales contracts at prices materially below current sales prices or inventory prices.

Contractual obligations for plant construction and purchases of plant property and equipment amounted to approximately $575,000 at December 31, 19___.

There were no contingent liabilities at December 31, 19___ not provided for in the accounts.

### GENERAL

We understand you have examined or tested accounting records of the company and other supporting evidence by methods and to the extent you deemed appropriate for the purpose of expressing an opinion on the financial statements, but that such test examination would not necessarily disclose irregularities should any exist. No shortages or other irregularities have been discovered that have not been disclosed to you.

No events have occurred or matters been discovered since the date of the balance sheet which would render the financial statements inaccurate or misleading in any material respect.

/s/      *John Doe*

Treasurer

/s/      *Ralph Roe*

Controller

**Fig. 4. Client's Representation Letter. (Continued.)**

While this letter cannot relieve the auditor of his professional and legal responsibilities, it may be of protection to him in some cases where the financial statements are later found to be deficient. Furthermore, the letter serves as a specific reminder to management of its responsibilities for maintaining proper accounting records and making adequate disclosure to the auditor.

**Liability insurance.** Liability insurance coverage is available to the auditor. In general, it covers liability imposed by law for damages caused, or alleged to have been caused, by the insured in the performance of professional services, and arising out of:

1. Any negligent act, error or omission.

2. Dishonesty, misrepresentation or fraud, except if made or committed by the insured or any partner of the insured with affirmative dishonesty or actual intent to deceive or defraud.

3. Breach of contract.

4. Libel or slander.

In addition, the policies usually state that the insurance company will defend the insured against any action alleging such negligent act, error or omission, even if such action is unjustified.

Most policies exclude liability for claims under the Federal Securities Act of 1933, but not the Federal Securities Exchange Act of 1934. This exclusion may be removed by payment of an additional premium varying from 10% to 33⅓% of the base premium.

Coverage under item 1 may be eliminated from the policy, usually at a substantial reduction of premium, but this is not recommended as third party liability suits against the auditor will generally be brought on the grounds of fraud, constructive fraud (legal fraud), misrepresentations and deceit.

The approximate cost of accountant's liability insurance is summarized in the schedule below. These premiums are based upon policies containing the Federal Securities Act of 1933 exclusion, but including coverage for legal fraud. Policies written on a three-year basis usually provide for a reduced premium. The inclusion of a deductible clause whereby the insured pays the first $500 or $1,000 of loss serves to further reduce the annual premium.

RATE SCHEDULE FOR ACCOUNTANT'S LIABILITY INSURANCE

| Number of Persons on Staff | Amount of Coverage | | | | |
|---|---|---|---|---|---|
| | $20,000 | $60,000 | $100,000 | $200,000 | $250,000 |
| 1 | $ 50.00 | $100.00 | $ 125.00 | $ 150.00 | $ 162.50 |
| 5 | 70.00 | 140.00 | 175.00 | 210.00 | 227.50 |
| 10 | 93.50 | 186.50 | 233.50 | 280.00 | 304.00 |
| 15 | 116.50 | 233.50 | 291.50 | 350.00 | 278.50 |
| 20 | 140.00 | 280.00 | 350.00 | 420.00 | 455.00 |
| 25 | 163.50 | 326.50 | 408.50 | 490.00 | 531.00 |

## INTERPRETATION OF AUDIT REPORTS

When the responsible auditor releases a report that contains his unqualified opinion on the fairness of the presentation of financial position and operating results, he is satisfied that it will stand the scrutiny of the credit grantor and investor, as well as management. The type of analysis given to the report varies greatly from reader to reader. The casual stockholder may look only at earnings and dividends; the banker will study the company's current position and its ability to repay its loans; the sophisticate may carefully peruse the notes to the financial statements, because these might give special insight into the company's affairs, and he will read the accountant's report to make sure there are no qualifications. In a few pages, the audit report serves these differing interests.

Management, for whom the report is directly prepared, may study it the least. In the very large company, a battery of talent has already analyzed the financial statements in every conceivable way and compared every ratio with that of competitors; in this case, the audit report is a formal conclusion to a historical period.

At the other end of the scale is the small business man who has no accounting officer competent to interpret financial data and who is himself almost too busy to read the audit report. The auditor may be of great assistance to him in explaining the significance of the financial statements and the actions that they indicate. Often, the client must be educated to understand what the auditor has done and why. In this area, the auditor is a business counselor. He should be able to apply the general rules of economics and the business practices of successful companies to the particular circumstances and problems of his client.

**What should the auditor explain to management about the financial statements?** This question must be answered in a different way for each client, but there are certain general areas that the auditor should usually consider.

 1. *As to the balance sheet.*
 a. Has the company sufficient working capital?
 b. Are surplus funds being used to maximum advantage?
 c. What is the collection experience? Is a trend indicated?
 d. Are inventories excessive? Slow-moving?
 e. Should the client consider adopting LIFO?
 f. If new equipment is needed, how will it be financed?
 g. Should consideration be given to leasing rather than owning plant and equipment? Or vice-versa?
 h. Is the capital structure appropriate?

 2. *As to the earnings statement.*
 a. How is profit in relation to sales? To capital employed? To others in the industry?
 b. How much is the profit by product lines? What trends are indicated?

c. How is the customer mix? Is the company dependent on one customer or one industry?

d. Were there any unusual items of income or expense in the past year?
Expected for coming year?

e. Is the cost system producing the best information? Should *direct
costing* be considered?

f. Are dividends appropriate in relation to profits? Are they so high as
to limit growth?

3. *General considerations.*

a. Should key-man life insurance be considered?

b. Does a "buy-sell" agreement between the owners appear appropriate?

c. How about pension and profit-sharing plans? Or a combination of
the two?

d. Is the company adequately staffed in the accounting area?

*Part VII*

# SPECIAL FIELDS
# OF ACCOUNTING

# 30

# Fiduciary Accounting— Estates and Trusts

**LEWIS L. TANGUY**

*Certified Public Accountant; Assistant Professor of Business Administration, Pennsylvania Military College; Retired Member of the Staff, Lybrand, Ross Bros. & Montgomery, Philadelphia*

**THOMAS J. GAFFNEY, Esq.**

*Member of the Philadelphia Bar*

CHAPTER THIRTY

# Fiduciary Accounting—
# Estates and Trusts

This chapter is designed to provide an accountant in public or private practice with a perspective of the several fields of fiduciary accounting. Within these fields, we will try to supply sufficient detail for the accountant with reasonable experience and accounting sense to carry out an engagement in a manner satisfactory to his client and himself. The legal aspects of estates and trusts are covered only to the extent necessary to explain the accounting material. In fiduciary accounting, the public accountant usually works under the guidance of, or in close association with, legal counsel, so that a complete technical knowledge of the law is not needed. Incidentally, this brings out one of the important advantages of engaging in this type of work —the opportunity for professional referrals, which is discussed in Chapter 38, *Obtaining New Business*. Another advantage is the fact that the work can frequently be done during the summer season, as we will explain in the second section of this chapter.

The chapter will begin with an introduction to basic terminology and procedures that are essential to an understanding of the subject matter in general. Then we will consider the role of the public accountant in fiduciary accounting, with emphasis on the types of engagements and on working arrangements. Special accounting and tax problems will be examined next, followed by the final section, which will describe the accounting system.

## TERMINOLOGY AND PROCEDURES

Some well-known accounting terms have special meaning when applied to fiduciary accounting. Other terms that will be explained are found only in the field of estates and trusts. The definitions of those terms that are necessary for an understanding of fiduciary accounting will be approached through an exposition of procedures for estates and trusts, under the following headings:

1. The court.
2. Decedents' estates.
3. Trusts.
4. Wards' estates.
5. Limitations on the fiduciary.

**The court.** The court that has jurisdiction over estates and trusts is known by different names in the various states—for example, Probate Court (Maine), Orphans' Court (Pennsylvania), Superior Court (California), and Surrogate's Court (New York). The *account* (Pennsylvania), *account current* (California), and *account of proceedings* (New York) each refers to the financial statements and report made to the court in the form prescribed by the court rules or local legal precedent. The fiduciary who is responsible for preparing the account is the *accountant.* The court reviews the account and makes such tests of the transactions as it deems appropriate. It also holds a hearing, known as the *audit,* at which parties at interest may present objections and exceptions to the account.

**Decedents' estates.** If a decedent left a will, he died *testate;* if he left no will, he died *intestate.* The decedent leaving the will, if a man, is the *testator;* if a woman, the *testatrix.* The will names a man or a trust company as the *executor* to carry out its provisions. A woman, so named, would be the *executrix.*

Within a few days after the death, the will is presented at the office of the Register of Wills, or similar county office, where it is *probated* (proved valid), and the named executor, if able and willing, is issued *letters testamentary,* authorizing him to settle the estate. If the named executor refuses the appointment, or if there is no will, the parties at interest present a petition for appointment of an administrator and suggest a suitable person. If the suggested person is appointed and qualifies, he becomes *administrator c. t. a.* (*cum testamento annexo*—that is, with the will attached) to carry out the provisions of the will. If there is no will, he is appointed *administrator* to settle the estate in accordance with the *state intestate laws*—the laws of descent.

The term *personal representative* is used to refer to either the executor(-trix) or administrator(-trix). *Fiduciary* is a still more general term that refers not only to executors and administrators but also to trustees and guardians, whose duties will be described later.

The personal representative advertises his appointment, as required by law. He also proceeds to search out and take possession of the decedent's assets. These he lists and values in an *inventory and appraisement,* or a document with a similar title. The inventory and appraisement is filed with the county officer (or the court) and becomes the starting point of the personal representative's accountability and of his accounting records. The total of these assets becomes the *principal* or *corpus* (body) of the estate.

If real estate or the rights to real estate are listed in the inventory, the aggregate value becomes the *principal of real estate*. All other assets comprise the *principal of personal estate*.

▶ OBSERVATION: There is only one inventory and appraisement, which is at the date of death. Thereafter, the assets remaining at any date comprise the *balance* at that date.

If the will makes a gift of real estate, the gift is a *devise* and the recipient is the *devisee*. The title passes directly to the devisee—subject, however, to any debts, expenses, and taxes that the proceeds of the assets of the personal estate are insufficient to pay.

During the period that the personal representative is assembling the assets and paying the debts, expenses, and taxes, the assets should be producing income. The income from assets of the personal estate becomes *income of personal estate*. Income from real estate or from assets into which it has been converted becomes *income of real estate*.

*Distribution* of the estate consists of distributing in accordance with the will—or, if no will, the intestate laws—the assets remaining after paying the obligations of the estate. The gifts of personal property are known as *bequests* or *legacies* and the recipients are *legatees*. The will may direct that specific items, such as a desk, a portrait, or items of jewelry shall be given to designated persons—these gifts are *specific bequests*. A gift of cash in a specified amount is a *general bequest,* while a gift of cash from a specified fund is a *demonstrative bequest.* When the directions concerning the foregoing bequests have been carried out, "all the rest, residue, and remainder" of the personal estate is the *residuary bequest* and is distributed to the *residuary legatee(s).*

If a fiduciary fails in his trust and the estate suffers losses through his neglect, failure to use reasonable care, or by wilful acts, the court may *surcharge* him—that is, make him personally liable for the losses.

If the estate, when ready for distribution, is too small to meet the bequests in full, they are *abated*. This means that the bequests are reduced by classes in the following order, unless the will makes other provision: (1) residuary, (2) general, (3) demonstrative, and (4) specific. As we have already indicated, when the personal property has been exhausted the court may approve leasing, placing a mortgage on, or sale of real estate devised.

**Trusts.** Trusts are usually classified both according to the means of their creation and the purposes for which they are created. The means of creating a trust are:

1. By will, creating a *testamentary trust* after decedent's death.

2. By deed or agreement made by a living person, creating an *inter vivos trust.*

3. By deed or agreement made by a corporation, creating a *corporate trust.*

The purposes for which trusts are created are numerous. The more common ones are:

1. To provide an income for relatives or friends through an *individual trust,* frequently called a *personal* or a *private trust.*

2. To provide an income, usually in perpetuity, for some charitable, educational or similar purpose, or for support of a hospital, a college, a church or a similar organization specified in the creating instrument. Such trusts, in general, are known as *perpetual, charitable* or *public trusts.*

3. To take possession of the assets of a financially-distressed debtor for protection of the creditors. The person, living or corporate, that takes possession is a *receiver* or a *trustee in bankruptcy.*

4. To provide benefits for employees, such as pensions, pay while ill or unemployed, sharing of profits, and the like. These trusts are known, in general, as *employee trusts* and, specifically, as *pension benefit trusts* and *health and welfare benefit trusts.*

▶ NOTE: Employee trusts are considered in detail in Chapter 33.

*Testamentary trusts.* Trusts, in general, and testamentary trusts, in particular, are explained by the following simple example.

A man is making his "last will and testament." He wishes (1) to provide for his wife during her lifetime and (2) to give his property outright to his son upon the death of the wife. His property consists of cash and marketable securities that yield sufficient income to provide amply for the wife. In his will he directs that, after payment of his debts, taxes, and the expenses of settling his estate, all his remaining assets are to be distributed to a trust company (or to an individual) *in trust,* to be kept invested in suitable securities. The income from the securities is to be paid monthly to his wife during her lifetime. At the death of the wife, the trust is to cease and the assets comprising the trust are to be distributed outright to the son.

In this example, the trust company is the *trustee,* the wife is the *life tenant,* and the son is the *remainderman.* The executor may be, and frequently is, named in the will as trustee, also.

It would be customary for the testator to provide for disposition of the trust assets in the event the son died first. The testator might direct that, in such case, the assets, at the death of the mother, should continue in trust for the son's children until they reach the age of twenty-one years. As each reaches that age, he is to receive his one-half share, if he is one of two children; or a one-third share, if one of three children; and so on. In the example, the children of the remainderman (grandchildren of the testator) are *contingent remaindermen.*

*Inter vivos trusts.* An individual, while still living, may wish to provide an income for a relative, create a scholarship fund, or endow a bed in a hospital. By a deed of trust, he could give cash or securities in trust to a trust company or to the college or the hospital, to be kept invested, with the income used for the purpose specified in the deed. Such a trust created during the life of the *grantor* is known as an *inter vivos* trust (a trust between living persons).

If the deed creating an *inter vivos* trust allows the grantor to change, directly or indirectly, the provisions of the deed, the trust is *revocable.* If the grantor loses all control over the assets of the trust, the trust is *irrevocable.*

▶ COMMENT: A corporate trust is similar to an *inter vivos* trust, except that the deed or agreement is made by a corporation rather than by an individual.

*Individual trusts versus perpetual trusts.* Trusts, as we have already pointed out, are classified not only according to the means of their creation but also according to the purposes for which they were created. Thus, a trust, whether it be testamentary or *inter vivos,* can be either individual (sometimes called personal or private) or perpetual (sometimes called charitable or public). The different purposes for which each type of trust is created were given on the previous page.

As to time, the duration of a trust for individuals is limited to a period prescribed by individual state statute. The pertinent law is called the *Rule Against Perpetuities.* The period is based upon a *life in being* at the time the trust is created, which means that a living person or persons must be named in the trust agreement against whose life-span the duration of the trust will be measured. The rule differs in various states—it might read "twenty-one years after a life in being," or "twenty-one years after two lives in being," with other variations also possible. A perpetual trust, as the name implies, has a duration not limited by statute or the common law. However, its life may be limited by a provision in the instrument creating it.

Individual, personal, or private trusts operate under specific instructions of the will or the deed of trust. If properly drawn, the instrument clearly designates the beneficiaries who are to receive the income and eventually the principal. By way of contrast, the instrument that creates a perpetual trust states the purpose(s) for which the principal and income are to be used. The purpose may be simple to carry out, such as when the income can be used only to assist in the operation of the designated hospital, church, or college, or it may be more difficult to implement. Examples of the latter would be a scholarship trust requiring the trustee to select a qualified recipient each year, and a trust providing that a part of the principal be used to construct an engineering school, with the income from the remaining principal subsequently channeled to the operation and maintenance of the completed school.

Sometimes it becomes impossible or impractical for the fiduciary to follow literally the instructions in the creating instrument for a perpetual trust. In such cases, the courts apply the *doctrine of cy pres*—that is, they authorize changes that comply with the instructions as nearly as is practicable.

▶ EXAMPLE: The trust created by the will of Benjamin Franklin in 1790 presents an interesting illustration of the application of the doctrine of *cy pres*. The principal was "to be loaned to an amount not exceeding sixty pounds sterling to Young Married Artificers" who had "faithfully" served indentured apprenticeships in Philadelphia and who "furnished two satisfactory sureties" for the return of the money. When the practice of becoming an indentured apprentice ceased late in the 1800's, there were soon no applicants who could qualify. In 1949, the court decreed (in part) that loans up to $6,000 could be made to workers, preferably those trained in Philadelphia, upon well-secured first mortgages on real estate in Philadelphia.

*Receiverships and trusts in bankruptcy—the Federal Bankruptcy Act.* To become subject, involuntarily, to the Federal Bankruptcy Act, a debtor —either an individual, a partnership, or a corporation—must be found *insolvent* under one of two definitions: (1) his liabilities exceed his assets, or (2) he is unable to pay his debts as they become due, and he has committed an *act of bankruptcy* at some time during a four month period prior to the filing of a petition by his creditors. He commits an act of bankruptcy under the Act when he does any one of the following:

1. Makes a fraudulent conveyance or concealment.
2. Makes a preferential transfer.
3. Allows a creditor to obtain a lien through legal proceedings.
4. Makes a general assignment for the benefit of creditors.
5. Permits the appointment of a receiver or a trustee.
6. Admits in writing his inability to pay debts.

▶ NOTE: Numbers 4 and 5 are actions under state law, as explained under the next heading.

After receipt of the creditors' petition and assuming that the debtor is legally insolvent, the Federal court appoints a *receiver,* who takes possession of the debtor's assets, which are valued by court-appointed appraisers. The receiver's primary duty is to safeguard the assets until a trustee is appointed by the court and has qualified. Where delay will cause losses, the receiver can sell perishable inventory, or if the occupancy costs are high, he may petition the court for leave to sell all the assets. Real estate is excepted, for the receiver does not have title.

In a voluntary bankruptcy, the bankrupt must file with his petition (1) a detailed schedule of all his property, (2) a detailed schedule of all creditors and the amount due each, and (3) a questionnaire disclosing details of his financial affairs. This questionnaire is called a *statement of affairs.*

▶ OBSERVATION: This should not be confused with the special form of balance sheet traditionally known as the statement of affairs, which is explained on page 1062 and illustrated in Figure 5.

Any liability not included in the schedule of creditors survives the bankrupt's discharge if the omitted creditor was not notified of the bankruptcy proceeding. When the trustee is appointed and qualifies, the receiver makes an accounting to the court (the judge or a *referee in bankruptcy* to whom the judge has assigned the case) and turns over to the trustee the proceeds of the assets sold plus the remaining assets. The two schedules and the questionnaire filed by the bankrupt become the basis for the trustee's accounting. In an involuntary proceeding, the debtor must file the two schedules and the statement of affairs within ten days after the court has declared him a bankrupt.

Two actions are possible after a debtor has been declared bankrupt: (1) his business may be kept in operation with a view toward rehabilitating it, or (2) the assets of the business may be sold and the proceeds distributed to creditors. Whether the bankrupt goes out of business or is allowed to continue operations depends largely on his ability and that of his counsel to work out a plan with the creditors for an extension of time in which to make payment of the debts in full or in a reduced amount. The plan, if accepted by the creditors, may become effective either in an out-of-court settlement, or under an *arrangement proceeding.* When there is a chance of restoring the bankrupt's business, an out-of-court settlement or an arrangement proceeding will usually be less expensive and will normally produce higher dividends for the creditors than straight bankruptcy and liquidation.

*Assignments and receiverships under state law.* The usual legal actions under state law are (1) the debtor's assignment of his assets to an *assignee,* who sells the assets and distributes the proceeds *pro rata* to the creditors, or (2) the appointment of a receiver or trustee to handle the assets or the business of the debtor. Taking either action under state law constitutes, respectively, the fourth or the fifth act of bankruptcy under the Federal Act, which means that the debtor can be brought before the Federal district court sitting as a bankruptcy court. Therefore, an insolvent debtor usually goes or is brought before the Federal court.

▶ COMMENT: If action under state law has been brought less than four months prior to filing the bankruptcy petition in the Federal court, the state action is superseded and the assignee or nonbankruptcy receiver must account to the Federal court for the debtor's property. If more than four months have elapsed, the state proceeding is superseded only if it is regarded as an insolvency proceeding.

**Wards' estates.** The procedures in wards' estates are similar to those in decedents' estates and testamentary trusts. In the example of a testamentary trust on page 1022 let us assume that the testator and later his widow (the life tenant) die. The son (remainderman) survives but is less than twenty-one years of age. Under the law, he is a *minor* and not considered competent to handle financial matters. Upon the death of the widow, the trustee files his account with the court. But the trustee cannot make distribution of the assets until the court appoints a *guardian* to receive and manage the estate for the minor son, who becomes the *ward.* When the son attains the age of twenty-one, the guardian files his account with the court and, upon approval by the court, distributes the assets to the son.

Similarly, either the relatives or creditors, or both, of an adult who has become mentally incompetent can petition the court for appointment of a guardian. The guardian, if appointed, takes possession of the assets of the ward (the *ward's estate*), prepares an inventory and appraisement, and arranges and pays for the maintenance of the ward. If the ward subsequently recovers his mental faculties, the guardian files an account with the court and turns over to the ward the remaining assets. If the ward dies without recovering his mental faculties, the guardian files an account with the court upon the ward's death and turns the remaining assets over to the personal representative of the deceased.

▶ COMMENT: Any will made by the ward during the period of his incompetency is not valid. If he dies while still incompetent, the intestate laws apply unless he had prepared a valid will prior to losing his mental faculties.

**Limitations on the fiduciary.** A fiduciary must follow certain broad rules in his handling of an estate or trust. The most important of these limitations are:

1. He must not commingle assets.
2. He should avoid nonlegal investments.
3. He should avoid transactions between the estate or trust and himself.
4. He must use reasonable care.

*No commingling of assets.* The fiduciary must keep assets of the estate or trust separate from his personal assets and from those of other estates and trusts of which he is fiduciary. He must have one or more bank accounts for fiduciary purposes only. A trust company is permitted to commingle the cash of its trusts but it must keep separate cash accounts for each.

A fiduciary must keep his personal investment portfolio separate from any fiduciary portfolios, each of which should be clearly identified.

*Legal investments.* Although the will or other instrument may allow the fiduciary to make nonlegal investments, if they result in losses he may be surcharged. In most states, legal investments include government and high-quality corporation bonds, well-secured mortgages on real estate, and preferred and common stocks of companies that have a long record of profitable operations and continuous dividend payments. The seasoned common stocks may provide a hedge, or protection, against inflation.

Some states have a government department that issues a list of the principal stocks that meet the legal requirements. In others, an organization, such as the state bankers' association, issues a list of some stocks that, in the opinion of the organization's counsel, meet the requirements.

*Fiduciary-trust transactions.* A fiduciary should avoid transactions not approved by the court between the estate or trust and himself. Where such transactions have been consummated without court approval, full disclosure must be made in the next account filed with the court. If the transaction is under consideration, court approval should be obtained before completing it.

▶ EXAMPLE: Without court approval, the executor of an estate invested cash belonging to the estate in a mortgage on real property that the executor owned personally. In this case, the court did not surcharge the executor because the investment did not result in a loss to the estate.

One necessary type of transaction of this kind relates to a *fiduciary's compensation,* which is usually requested at the audit of an account. The amount allowed is stated in the *adjudication,* or decree of the court. Some states have rates of commission based on graduated scales that decrease with increased income, and separate scales for changes in principal resulting from changes in indicated market values of the investments. The rates of commission are sometimes set in the will or deed of trust. They may be increased by consent of the beneficiaries.

*Reasonable care.* A fiduciary is required to exercise reasonable care in his handling of the estate or trust. The rule as to investments is frequently the care that a prudent man would use (the *prudent man rule*).

*Actions for failure.* If the fiduciary fails in his trust through negligence, lack of ability, bad faith, dishonesty, or similar reasons, parties at interest may bring action against him for *breach of trust,* present a petition to the court for his *removal,* seek an *injunction* against him, or take such other legal action as may be appropriate.

## THE PUBLIC ACCOUNTANT AND FIDUCIARY ACCOUNTING

There are a number of functions that the public accountant can perform in fiduciary accounting. These are best explained through a discussion of the various types of engagements, as follows:

1. Stating an account.
2. Examining an account.
3. Testifying before a court.
4. Preparing tax returns.
5. Other engagements.

In addition, we will outline the situation with regard to fees for and scheduling of fiduciary work, and we will discuss the independent accountant's report and opinion as it pertains to fiduciary work.

**Stating an account.** This is the preparation of the detailed financial report that is to be filed with the court (see Figure 4, page 1056). The report is usually prepared from the books of account without verification of the transactions.

▶ SUGGESTION: Before the draft of the account is typed, you should count or otherwise verify the assets owned at the closing date of the account to make sure that the assets are shown correctly on the draft. Frequently, an exchange of bonds, a stock split, or some other noncash transaction has not been recorded on the books of account.

Since the *form* of the account is prescribed by court rules or follows local legal precedent, it varies from state to state and even from county to county. The best guide is a copy of a similar account that legal counsel can supply. The *period* of the account may be short, say six months, or it may be for a year or a number of years. The *paper* required is usually 8½" x 13". Wider sheets that require folding are seldom acceptable.

The accounts to be stated may be any of the following:

1. Those of decedents' estates, testamentary and *inter vivos* trusts, and wards' estates, prepared for filing with county probate courts.

2. Those of receivers in equity to be filed with county courts of equity.

3. Those of receivers and of trustees in bankruptcy to be filed with Federal district courts sitting as bankruptcy courts.

▶ OBSERVATION: Stating an acount for an employee trust may be required as a provision of the trust agreement. Ordinarily, the account would not be filed with a court unless it was needed in connection with a proceeding in the court. If the account is filed, its form might be either (1) that of a testamentary trust account, frequently without classification as to principal and income, or (2) the court might accept statements in the form regularly submitted to the employer and employees.

**Examining an account.** After an account has been filed, it is audited by the court at a public hearing. Some accounts, however, are not filed. Whether an account is filed or not, the fiduciary may engage an independent public accountant to examine the account. This independent examination may be either necessary or advisable for any of the following reasons:

1. *Assurance to the fiduciary.* The fiduciary, because of regular business or professional duties, may find it necessary to delegate many of his fiduciary duties to responsible subordinates. He desires the examination as assurance that the account to be filed is complete and fairly stated before he signs it.

2. *Assurance to beneficiaries.* In some states, the accounts of testamentary and *inter vivos* trusts are filed with the court only when there is some occurrence such as the resignation or death of the trustee. At that time, the account filed is for the period from the previous account filed, if any, to the current date. If no account has been filed, the period starts from the inception of the trust. Obviously, then, the beneficiaries could remain uninformed as to the status of the account for a long period of time, if their only source of information were a court proceeding.

To avoid this situation, the trustee frequently will send each beneficiary a copy of an informal annual account. Often, the account is examined each year by an independent public accountant, and a copy of the accountant's report and opinion is also sent.

▶ COMMENT: Sometimes the trustee obtains a waiver from each beneficiary, indicating agreement with the account as forwarded to them. When the time comes for the trustee to state the account for the court, he is allowed in some jurisdictions to omit the income account for the periods for which he has obtained waivers.

▶ NOTE: In an employee trust, the employees are the beneficiaries, and should be informed about the status of the trust. Usually, the trustee is legally required to make proper disclosure, as explained in Chapter 33.

3. *Omission of details.* It is not the established practice of the courts to accept reports of independent public accountants in lieu of the detailed accounts required by the court rules. However, in an increasing number of cases involving charitable trusts, where there is voluminous detail, some courts have accepted accounts in which summary figures for frequently recurring transactions have been used. An account in this form may have attached to it a report of an independent public accountant covering annual examinations for the period of the account.

4. *One part of the examination of an institution.* Examination of the accounts of charitable trusts is often a necessary part of the examination of the financial statements of the institution that receives the income. For example, the trusts may be endowment, building, scholarship and special purpose funds for a college, university, or other educational institution. If the institution maintains one or more common trust funds, they too must be included in the overall examination (see Chapter 32 for a discussion of institutional accounting).

**Testifying before a court.** A fiduciary takes many cases to court to obtain judicial rulings in situations where previous rulings conflict or there is no previous ruling, or where the situation is not of normal administrative character. Assume, for example, that a tenant has a long-term lease at a high rental on real estate owned by a trust. The tenant now considers the rentals burdensome and convinces the trustee that the change in local economic factors justifies a reduction. The trustee and the tenant may join in a petition to the court for a modification of the lease.

Before joining in the petition, the trustee might have his independent accountant make a study and prepare a report concerning the tenant's financial statements and other relevant data. The report could be presented in evidence, with the public accountant called as a witness to supplement the report with oral explanations and replies to specific questions of the court.

Sometimes, at an audit by the court, parties at interest contest the account for any one of a variety of reasons, with the result that the hearing is postponed, or *continued,* to a later date. The fiduciary might then retain an independent accountant to review the account and, if necessary, to testify. The fiduciary, the fiduciary's counsel, and the accountant usually meet to discuss the matters at issue and decide what position the fiduciary should take. They also agree concerning the areas that the fiduciary and the accountant, respectively, will be expected to cover when they testify. At a later meeting, counsel will usually outline the questions that he plans to ask.

▶ SUGGESTIONS: In making a review, try to construct a clear mental picture of the account as a whole. Explaining the account and important transactions to an associate often speeds the process. Have your working papers carefully indexed and make notes of important items for reference while on the witness stand. When testifying give clear, simple answers and avoid pronouncements on theory.

**Preparing tax returns.** Following is a brief summary of the various tax requirements for estates and trusts, which often lead to an engagement for the public accountant. More detail concerning the preparation of these returns is given on pages 1039 to 1047.

1. *Federal estate tax.* If a decedent's estate has total assets of less than $60,000 at fair market value, it is not subject to the Federal estate tax and no return need be filed. If the total assets exceed $60,000, a return must be filed. But deductions, exemptions, and credits may so reduce the taxable estate that no tax will be payable.

The return is due 15 months after the date of death.

2. *State inheritance and estate taxes.* The provisions of the inheritance tax laws vary greatly among the states. However, all states have a death tax that may be taken as a credit in computing the Federal estate tax. This special state tax is frequently called an estate tax.

The filing date depends on the provisions of the law in the particular state. In some states, a discount is allowed for early filing.

3. *Income taxes.* In connection with the preparation of a death tax return, the public accountant's engagement would normally include preparation of the individual income tax return (Federal and, if any, state) of the decedent for the short tax year ending on the date of death. As a result, the public accountant might be engaged to prepare the annual fiduciary income tax return. He might also receive the personal tax business of beneficiaries whose principal source of income is the estate or trust.

▶ OBSERVATION: Not only individual fiduciaries, but also the trust departments of a number of the smaller banks depend on independent accountants to prepare the required fiduciary and individual returns. In addition to fiduciary returns for decedents' estates and for trusts, the public accountant might be called on to prepare individual returns for wards, and for decedents to the date of death.

If he is retained by a receiver or a trustee in bankruptcy, an independent accountant should be aware of these provisions of the Internal Revenue Code: (a) the receiver for a corporation, or the trustee in bankruptcy, must file the corporation income tax return if he has possession of or title to all, or substantially all, the business or property of the corporation; (b) in similar circumstances, the receiver for an individual must file the individual's income tax return; (c) if the receiver for a corporation or an individual is in charge of only a portion of the taxpayer's property, he does not have to file the return for the corporation or the individual; (d) a trustee in bankruptcy for an individual must file a fiduciary income tax return if the income is sufficient to require it (the bankrupt himself files his personal return).

▶ INFORMATION RETURNS: Trusts for charitable and similar purposes and certain employee trusts are normally exempt from Federal income tax. The trusts in the first group must file an application for exemption which, with the required supporting papers, is open to public inspection. The ruling on the application will inform the trustee if he must file an annual information return as evidence of the trust's right to continued exemption. The tax law as it pertains to employee trusts is discussed in Chapter 33.

**Other engagements.** Frequently, a public accountant retained by a receiver or a trustee in bankruptcy will find that the most important part of his work is an examination of the bankrupt's financial condition. The results of this examination usually determine whether the creditors will allow the debtor to remain in business or insist that his assets be sold and distributed. Too often, the examination discloses such adverse elements as uncollectible accounts receivable, obsolete and slow-moving inventory, unrecorded accounts payable, and contingent liabilities. However, the examination may disclose, or merely indicate, hidden assets, fraudulent conveyances, and unjust claims. In the latter case, the accountant should obtain authorization to ferret out additional facts necessary for the trustee to proceed to recover the assets or to reject the claims. This type of examination requires a high degree of auditing ability.

Other services that a public accountant might perform for a fiduciary are:

1. Install the accounting system and maintain the records for the estate or trust.

2. Examine the financial statements of (a) a business controlled or operated by the estate or trust, or (b) operating companies holding land containing natural resources that has been leased from the estate or trust on a royalty basis.

3. Examine the statements of sales of any tenants who rent under a percentage-of-sales lease.

**Fees and working arrangements.** Fees ordinarily are comparable with those for similar skills on other engagements. However, the public accountant may have to justify the amount to the court. Failure to do so to the satisfaction of the court can result in an arbitrary reduction. Fees in Federal bankruptcy cases are determined by the court.

▶ IMPORTANT: Some engagements last several months. Therefore, in arranging for your fee, make sure you have a clear, court-approved agreement with the fiduciary. Otherwise, you will run the risk of receiving an inadequate fee for the time you must spend. Remember that a bill rendered at the completion of this type of engagement does not have the same effect as one rendered at the completion of an ordinary tax or audit engagement— unless there has been *prior* court approval of the amount, you may have difficulty collecting what you consider an equitable fee. It might be better, in some cases, to refuse the engagement if you cannot obtain this court approval.

The public accountant will often find that he can arrange his fiduciary engagements so that they will occur during the off-season for auditing and tax work. The stating of an account can usually be done during the summer, with the account then filed in September, after the court's summer recess. The trustees of many testamentary and *inter vivos* trusts select fiscal years that permit the public accountant to perform his examination and prepare the fiduciary tax returns after the normal busy season.

**Independent accountant's report and opinion.** The Technical Services Department of the American Institute of Certified Public Accountants has compiled a set of forms of auditor's reports and opinions that may be used in special circumstances. An example of a short-form report for a trust on a cash basis, as quoted from an Institute publication on the subject,[1] follows:

> We have examined the statement of assets, liabilities and principal, on a cash basis, at December 31, 19___ of the trustees under a Trust Fund estab-

---

[1] *Special Reports: Application of Statement on Auditing Procedure No. 28*, page 27. New York: American Institute of Certified Public Accountants, 1960.

lished by _____, deceased, for _____, and the related statement of cash receipts of income and disbursements of expenses of the Trust for the year then ended. Our examination was made in accordance with generally accepted auditing standards, and accordingly included such tests of the accounting records and such other auditing procedures as we considered necessary in the circumstances.

In our opinion, these statements present fairly the assets, liabilities, and principal of the Trust, on a cash basis, at December 31, 19___, and the cash receipts of income and disbursements of expenses for the year then ended, on a basis consistent with that of the preceding year.

## SPECIAL ACCOUNTING PROBLEMS

There are, in addition to the terminology and procedures already mentioned, other areas of special knowledge that distinguish fiduciary accounting from commercial, industrial, and financial accounting. This section will consider those special accounting problems that must be recognized by the public accountant in a fiduciary engagement. (The next section will cover the related tax problems.)

The two basic accounting problems that exist and which will be discussed are:

1. Principal versus income.
2. Real estate versus personal estate.

Certain special problems in connection with perpetual trusts will also be considered.

**Principal versus income.** The will or deed of trust provides, in many cases, that different individuals have the right to the principal and the income, respectively. For example, the life tenant will receive the income until he dies, but the remainderman is entitled to the principal and the income upon the death of the life tenant. Therefore, it is essential for the fiduciary to be able to distinguish between principal and income. If the will or deed of trust sets forth how certain items are to be classified, such provisions must be respected unless they violate some broad rule as to income and principal. Thus, the court would not allow an unreasonable accumulation of income. If there are no pertinent provisions in the will or deed of trust, applicable statutes or precedents are the basis for the determination.

▶ NOTE: In receiverships and bankruptcies, there may be no need to separate principal and income. If the business is liquidated, the proceeds are used to pay the creditors. If the business continues in operation under an arrangement, the proceeds of any assets that are sold, less fiduciary expenses, are either distributed as an initial payment to creditors or are returned to the debtor. In any case, a distinction between principal and income seldom has significance.

**General rules regarding principal and income.** Income consists of the earnings or return on investments and other assets owned by an estate or trust. Principal (or corpus) can be defined, in general, as follows:

1. *Decedent's estate.* The assets owned by the decedent when he dies. However, real estate is excepted if it passes directly to the devisee (see page 1021).

2. *Testamentary trust.* The assets distributable by the executor to the trustee according to the provisions of the will, together with any real estate that the trustee receives directly.

3. *Inter vivos trust.* The assets given by the donor to establish the trust. Any subsequent gifts increase the principal.

4. *Ward's estate.* The assets that the guardian takes possession of or receives for his ward.

**Determination of principal and income in specific cases.** Statutes and legal precedents concerning the classification of an item as principal or income are not standardized among the states. Some states have adopted, in whole or in part, the Uniform Principal and Income Act, and this Act will be referred to where appropriate. But in the following discussions, recognition should be given to the fact that differences might exist in individual states.

1. *Premiums and discounts on bonds.* The Uniform Principal and Income Act provides that a premium paid when purchasing bonds should be amortized over the period until the date of the bonds' maturity or redemption, against the interest received on the bonds. In other words, the premium is considered to be a reduction of the effective interest rate. Similarly, when bonds are purchased at a discount, the discount is considered to be an increase of the effective interest rate. However, under the cash basis of probate court accounting (see page 1048), the discount is recorded as income only when it is actually realized—at the sale or redemption of the bonds.

Some obligations are issued at a discount and without a stated interest rate; for example, U.S. Savings Bonds, Series E, and short-term U.S. Treasury Notes. The amount paid for these obligations is principal, and the difference between principal and redemption value, when collected, is income.

2. *Rents and royalties.* Rents from real estate are income. Under com-

mon law, royalties for the extraction of coal, ores, petroleum, and similar resources are also income. But the Uniform Principal and Income Act treats such royalties as principal, on the theory that the lease represents the sale of assets in place.

▶ COMMENT: Either treatment of royalties may cause hardship. Pennsylvania, in its modification of the Act, apportions two-thirds to principal and one-third to income.

3. *Dividends.* The Uniform Principal and Income Act considers cash or other property dividends as income, and stock dividends as principal. In practice, regular cash dividends are normally treated as income. However, the treatment of stock dividends varies among the states. In some states, stock dividends paid in shares of the same kind and rank as the shares on which they are issued are principal, while all others are income. Other states use different methods of apportionment. A description of the frequently used *intact value* method of apportionment appears under the next heading.

Liquidating dividends are ordinarily principal. But dividends declared by a corporation prior to the start of its liquidation or dissolution, and cumulative or guaranteed dividends in arrears declared after the start of such procedure are usually income.

4. *Dividends, intact value.* Extraordinary (extra) dividends, whether paid in stock or cash, are apportioned in some states between principal and income on the basis of intact value, which is the value required to be kept intact for the remaindermen. If the security was received from the grantor or decedent, the intact value is usually presumed to be a value determined from the issuing corporation's books (but the true value must be shown on the books of the estate or trust). This corporate book value consists of the capital, surplus, and reserves for contingencies (at date of valuation) after giving effect to any adjustments made in subsequent years that are applicable prior to the date of valuation. Surplus includes the income or loss for the period to the date of valuation, as determined by apportionment of the income or loss for the fiscal year in which the valuation date falls. If the fiduciary has purchased the security, courts have frequently held that the purchase price is the intact value.

When the extraordinary dividend reduces the corporation's book value of the stock below the intact value, the portion of the dividend necessary to restore the intact value must be considered principal. The remainder of the dividend would be income.

▶ EXAMPLE: The following computation illustrates the apportionment of an extraordinary dividend, based on the intact value at the date the trust began:

PER CORPORATION'S BOOKS

|  | No. of Shares Out- standing | Book Value | | Fiduciary's Ledger Value Per Share |
|---|---|---|---|---|
|  |  | Total | Per Share |  |
| Value at date trust began | 1,000 | $105,270 | $105.27 | $92.00 |
| Value after extraordinary dividend of $15 per share | 1,000 | 97,530 | 97.53 |  |
| Intact value impaired |  | $ 7,740 | $ 7.74 |  |
| Amount of dividend to be apportioned to principal in reduction of fiduciary's ledger value per share |  |  |  | 7.74 |
| Fiduciary's remaining ledger value per share |  |  |  | $84.26 |

5. *Operation of a business.* If an estate or trust owns a business, the equity of the testator (at death) or the grantor becomes principal. If the fiduciary obtains authorization to continue the operations instead of liquidating, the net income becomes income of the estate or trust. A loss from the operations in any year after the income from the business has been exhausted reduces the principal.

▶ OBSERVATION: Incorporation of the business may facilitate its sale as a going concern or permit its capital stock to be distributed in kind. If the operations prove unprofitable, the limited liability of a corporation would free the other assets of the estate or trust from the claims of creditors and reduce the fiduciary's liability to surcharge.

6. *Animals for breeding.* If one of the assets of an estate or trust is a herd of livestock held for breeding, those of the offspring necessary to replace any lost or sold from the original herd become principal; the remaining offspring are income.

7. *Interest-bearing obligations in default.* Aside from the treatment of premiums and discounts on bonds, which has already been explained, interest-bearing obligations seldom present any problem as to principal and income unless they go into default. The subsequent settlement might be for less than the full amount of principal and uncollected interest on the obliga-

tion. Usually a statute or a precedent-setting local case provides a basis for apportioning the proceeds between principal and income.

8. *Expenses.* The duties of an executor or administrator in settling a decedent's estate are primarily in connection with principal—assembling the assets, paying the debts, converting some assets into cash, and distributing the assets. Collection and distribution of the income are secondary. The expenses, therefore, are paid from principal unless they are directly related to income.

The duties of a trustee, by contrast, are primarily related to the production of income; changes in investments are made to increase income or to protect principal. Consequently, expenses are paid from income unless they are directly related to principal. An example of an expense directly related to principal would be the Federal income tax on a capital gain.

**Real estate versus personal estate.** In some jurisdictions, the courts do not require any separation of real estate from personal estate unless the interests of the involved parties require the separation. But in other jurisdictions, the separation of both principal and income into real estate and personal estate is required.

There is no real estate in many instances, for title has passed directly to the heirs, or to the trustee if it was left in trust. In some estates, the will may direct or allow the executor to sell the real estate, or the court may order it sold, mortgaged, or leased to pay debts and expenses. But when the fiduciary does have title to real estate and has not acquired this title through foreclosure of a mortgage, he should open an account for Principal of Real Estate and one for Income of Real Estate, unless counsel advises that one, or both, are unnecessary in the circumstances.

An explanation of principal and income of both real estate and personal estate follows:

1. *Principal of real estate.* The appraisement figure for real estate in the inventory becomes the principal of real estate. If the real estate is sold, the principal is adjusted to the amount of the proceeds. Thereafter, the principal is increased by gains or reduced by losses from disposition of securities in which the original proceeds were invested and reinvested. The fiduciary at his option may pay from principal the expenses of unproductive real estate.

2. *Income of real estate.* The rents of real estate and the income from securities in which the proceeds of sale of real estate have been invested become the income of real estate. Expenses of real estate and of investments of the real estate account are paid from the income.

3. *Principal of personal estate.* All assets of a decedent at date of death except real estate comprise the principal of personal estate. Investment and reinvestment of proceeds of sale of the assets together with gains and net of losses on their disposition continue to be principal. Included in the assets may be a mortgage. If it is necessary to foreclose on the mortgage and take title to the real estate securing it, the acquired real estate remains an asset of personal estate.

4. *Income of personal estate.* The interest, dividends, and other income received on the assets comprising the principal of personal estate are the income of personal estate. The expenses not properly payable from the principal of personal estate or from the real estate accounts are payable from the income of personal estate (see *expenses,* page 1038).

**Special accounting problems of perpetual trusts.** A perpetual trust that operates an institution may have special problems similar to those of institutions. These problems are discussed in Chapter 32, *Fund Accounting for Institutions.* Two problems that fall within the scope of this chapter are:

1. *Conversion from a cash to an accrual basis.* The fiduciary of a perpetual trust that operates an institution necessarily keeps his accounts on a cash basis for court purposes (see page 1048). When it becomes desirable to convert these to an accrual basis, he may do so on an approximate basis by setting up the assets and liabilities unrecorded on the cash basis at the beginning and at the end of the year. These, together with the contra entries to income and expense, or to principal, when applied to the cash basis statements will give a satisfactory set of financial statements on the accrual basis.

2. *Accumulation of income.* The courts recognize that institutions cannot readily expand and contract their operations to meet fluctuations in income and expenses. Therefore, they permit a *reasonable* accumulation of income to carry the operations over loss years.

### SPECIAL TAX PROBLEMS

The tax problems of an estate or trust relate primarily to the Federal taxes to which it is subject. These taxes were referred to on pages 1031 and 1032, where they were considered in the light of engagments for the public accountant. We will now deal with the tax requirements for an estate or trust from a substantive viewpoint. However, the purpose of the following coverage is not to provide complete detail regarding the applicable provisions of the Internal Revenue Code, but rather to either offer suggestions as to approach, to outline a procedure to be followed, to point out differences in the tax and accounting treatment, or to warn that no short explanation is adequate and that the instructions require careful study.

▶ NOTE: Any comments concerning state taxes are included in the discussion of the similar Federal tax.

**Estate tax.** Some of the problems arising under the estate tax relate to:

1. Valuation of the assets in general.
2. Stock of a close corporation.
3. Estates in low estate tax brackets.
4. Employee death benefits.
5. Requirements of state probate laws.
6. Discharge of the fiduciary from personal liability.

*Valuation of the assets in general.* The date of valuation may be that of the decedent's death or an optional date one year later. At either date, the methods of valuation given below are used. When items have been sold within the year, they are valued at their sales price.

1. Bonds and stocks should be priced at the mean of the price for the day. If no published price is available for an unlisted security, the price can usually be obtained from the decedent's broker.

2. Valuations of annuities should be obtained in writing from the issuing corporation.

3. Real estate should be valued at the average of the appraisals of three independent realtors who are familiar with the property and the area in which it is located.

4. Valuable pieces of jewelry should be appraised in writing by a reputable jeweler.

*Stock of a close corporation.* There are a number of factors to be considered when attempting to establish and sustain the fair market value of a substantial block of stock in a closely-held corporation. Some of these factors are:

1. Book value usually has little relationship to fair market value. Earnings and their trend are generally more important.

2. If the stock is unlisted and a sale has occurred within recent years, the selling price as adjusted for changes in the interim may be accepted.

3. If the stock is unlisted but that of competitors is listed, a range of values within which the fair market value should fall can be established through comparative analyses of such data as (a) financial statements, (b) capitalized earnings, (c) published market prices, and (d) financial ratios.

4. If the shares represent control, offering the block might either improve or depress the market, depending to a great extent on the desire of the company's competitors to take over the business.

5. If the decedent was the "brains" of the company and had no competent understudy, the company might be unable to continue operating efficiently.

Unless all the significant factors are considered, the valuation may prove excessive as shown by later events. Since the amount involved is usually substantial—often the largest in the return—it deserves careful study. Skillful negotiation with the Revenue Agent and his superiors is often necessary to keep the valuation at a fair figure.

*Estates in low estate tax brackets.* In preparing an estate tax return for an estate in the low tax brackets, it may be possible to effect an overall saving to the distributees. The method is to use the *higher* of the values at the date of death or at the optional date in order to effect a higher basis for the related assets for income tax purposes. The saving occurs if the estate or the distributees would have to pay a higher effective rate of income tax on capital gains than the estate tax rates are on the higher valuation.

*Employee death benefits.* Many death benefits are exempt from estate tax when received from an employer by beneficiaries of a decedent-employee under a plan to which the employee has not contributed. Under contributory plans, the portion of the benefits based on the employee's contributions is taxable, while the remainder is usually exempt.

When the estate or executor receives the death benefits, they frequently are taxable.

*Requirements of state probate law.* Occasionally a decedent and spouse may have held title to substantially all their property in joint name with right of survivorship. As a result the estate may not be subject to state inheritance tax and there may be no need to make an accounting to the local probate court. Nevertheless, a review of the estate assets could disclose that the estate is sufficiently large to require the filing of a Federal and a state estate tax return and perhaps payment of a substantial tax.

*Discharge of fiduciary from personal liability.* The fiduciary, by written request to the District Director of Internal Revenue, can obtain a determination of the tax within one year after the return is filed or the request is made, whichever is later. This request does not extend the limitation period for assessment. Upon payment of any deficiency shown by the determination letter, the fiduciary is discharged from any personal liability.

**Income taxes.** A fiduciary usually has the duty of filing income tax returns for the decedent, the estate, or the trust for which he acts. The returns may be one or more of the following:

1. Individual.
2. Fiduciary.
3. Corporation.
4. Information.

Each return should show the name of the fiduciary, the fiduciary capacity, and the name of the person or persons for whom the fiduciary is acting.

**Individual income tax returns.** The fiduciary will file the individual return form appropriate for the amount and nature of income for:

1. A decedent; it will be either a separate return or the joint return of the decedent and surviving spouse.
2. A ward.
3. An individual whose property is held by the fiduciary as receiver (see page 1032).

*Return for decedent.* The executor or administrator of a decedent's estate usually has the duty of filing any income tax returns of the decedent required for the period prior to his death. For the short period, no annualization of income is required and, even though the decedent was on an accrual basis, no accruals by reason of death are necessary; also, the personal exemption is not reduced or prorated.

*Joint return of decedent and surviving spouse.* If the decedent was married at the time of death and his tax year had been the same as that of the surviving spouse, his income for the period to his death and that of the spouse for the entire year may be included in a joint return. This applies if the spouse has not remarried before the end of the taxable year.

*Due date of decedent's last return.* The return for the decedent only or a joint return for the decedent and surviving spouse is due on the same date as if the decedent had lived.

*Medical expenses of decedent in last return.* A provision of the Code allows as a deduction in his last return the medical expenses of a decedent paid from his estate within one year after death. These are treated as though paid when the services were rendered. If the fiduciary claims the deduction in the decedent's income tax return, he must waive the deduction for the estate tax return.

*Declarations of estimated tax.* The surviving spouse may file any declarations of estimated tax required after the date of death for the tax year in which death occurred. The estimated tax may be based on the combined taxable incomes. Frequently, a reduced estimated tax is payable by reason of the income taxable to the decedent ceasing at the date of death. Therefore, an amended declaration may be in order.

*Guardian's returns.* The guardian must file the individual income tax returns of his ward unless the ward is a minor who files for himself. The income, deductions, and credits to be included in the return are subject to the same provisions of the Code as those of any other individual. The return may be a joint return if the ward was married at the close of the taxable year and neither he nor his wife was the dependent of another.

*Basis of ward's capital gains and losses.* Although the guardian of a ward's estate appraises at fair market value the inventory of assets for which he becomes accountable, he must use the cost or other basis required by the Code in computing capital gains and losses for his ward's returns.

**Fiduciary income tax returns.** A fiduciary income tax return differs from other returns in the deductions allowed. One such deduction is the income properly distributed or distributable to the beneficiaries of the estate or trust. In many trusts, therefore, the only income taxable to the trust is its net capital gains.

▶ COMMENT: The income distributed or distributable to the beneficiaries retains the nature of the income to the estate or trust. For example, the dividends received by the trust remain dividends when distributed to the beneficiaries.

Another difference in the deductions allowed in a fiduciary return relates to contributions. Those for charitable, educational, religious, scientific, and similar purposes ordinarily are deductible to the extent of the gross income, if under the terms of the will or deed of trust the amount claimed is paid, permanently set aside for, or is to be used for the purposes stated above.

The tax rates for estates and trusts are the same as for individuals. The standard deduction and the optional tax tables are *not* available to estates and trusts.

The fiduciary files a fiduciary income tax return:

1. For a decedent's estate in process of administration.
2. For a trust, whether testamentary or *inter vivos,* provided there are individual beneficiaries.
3. As trustee in bankruptcy for an individual.

▶ NOTE: In general, a decedent's estate, a testamentary trust, and an *inter vivos* trust are taxable entities separate and distinct from the person who created any one of them. An exception is a revocable trust, the income of which is taxable to the grantor.

*Fiduciary return for a decedent's estate.* During the period of settling an estate, the personal representative must file fiduciary income tax returns annually. The income and some expenses accrued at death are included in the fiduciary return as well as in the estate tax return. As a result of this duplication, the Code allows a deduction in the fiduciary return of a proportion of the estate tax resulting from the duplication.

The other items of income subject to tax are the same as for individuals. Some of them, such as capital gains and losses, will be items of principal.

The deductions allowed an estate are also, in general, the same as for individuals. But in addition to the differences already mentioned, there are differences as to the handling of depreciation and depletion and the computation of the net operating loss deduction. Reasonable administrative expenses are allowed as deductions. Those taken as deductions for income tax must be waived as deductions for estate tax.

The personal exemption of an estate is the same as for an individual.

The tax credits are the same as for an individual to the extent that they are not allocable to beneficiaries.

*Distributions to beneficiaries.* The estate has been described as a conduit through which income flows to the beneficiaries. Based on this principle, the personal representative of an estate may take as a deduction the amounts that the beneficiaries are required to include in gross income in their respective returns. However, the deduction may not exceed the distributable net income of the estate. In determining this distributable net income, the return form and the instructions must be followed closely.

*Capital gains and losses of a decedent's estate.* The capital gains and losses included in the fiduciary income tax return for a decedent's estate frequently differ from those shown on the fiduciary's books of account. The differences result from differing bases for the two purposes. Some of these bases are shown in the following chart:

| | *Federal Tax Basis* | *Probate Court Basis* |
|---|---|---|
| Assets in inventory | (a) At date of death—probate court values. | At date of death—values set by appraisers selected by fiduciary. |
| | (b) At optional date (one year later)—valued by fiduciary. | |
| | Both (a) and (b) are subject to Government examination and adjustment. | |

|  | *Federal Tax Basis* | *Probate Court Basis* |
|---|---|---|
| Stock dividends received | In general, not valued. Under special provisions of Code, may be taxable, thus are valued. | Not valued. |
| Exchange of assets with no cash received | Gain or loss recognized in some cases. | No gain or loss recognized. |
| Exchange of assets with cash received | Gain recognized, not in excess of cash received. | Cash applied in reduction of book value. |
| Sale of an asset (in general) | Value as determined for estate tax, or subsequent cost. | Inventory value, or subsequent cost. |
| Sale of stock rights | Zero in special cases. Otherwise, apportion basis for the stock between the stock and the rights. | Proceeds applied in reduction of book value. |
| Sale of decedent's real estate | Value as determined for estate tax. | Inventory value. If not valued in inventory, entire proceeds are applied as increase in principal of real estate. |
| Assets received in distribution—basis for subsequent sale | Values as determined for estate tax, or subsequent cost. | Reappraised values (usually quoted market values if available) as of date of distribution. |

*Fiduciary return for a trust.* The trustee of a testamentary trust or an irrevocable *inter vivos* trust must file a fiduciary income tax return for the trust if the beneficiary is an individual or a trust for an individual. Trusts are classified for income tax purposes as follows:

1. A *simple trust* is one that distributes current income only, distributes no corpus, must distribute all its income, and makes no charitable contributions.

2. A *complex trust* is one that does not meet the requirements of a simple trust.

▶ OBSERVATION: A trust may be a simple trust in some years and a complex trust in other years.

The gross income of a trust is determined in the same manner as that of an individual. In general, a trust is allowed the same deductions as an individual, but is not allowed the standard deduction. The following deductions allowed to trusts have the same modifications as for estates: (1) contributions, (2) depreciation, (3) depletion, (4) net operating loss, and (5) the expenses of administration. Tax credits allowed to trusts are limited to the portions not allocated to beneficiaries.

The distribution to beneficiaries from a simple trust requires that the beneficiaries include in their gross income all taxable trust income that must be distributed to them as long as it does not exceed the trust's distributable net income. If the income required to be distributed exceeds the distributable net income, each beneficiary is taxed only on his proportionate share of the distributable net income.

If the trust is a complex trust, the requirements are the same as for estates. The form of the return and the instructions must be followed with extreme care.

The personal exemptions are less than those of an individual or an estate.

*Capital gains and losses for a trust.* The differences in basis for capital gains and losses for a trust's income tax return and for the trustee's accounting are the same as those shown for estates on pages 1044 and 1045 for the following assets:

1. Stock dividends received.
2. Exchange of assets with no cash received.
3. Exchange of assets with cash received.
4. Sale of stock rights.
5. Sale of decedent's real estate.

In addition, the bases differ for assets acquired in trust as follows:

| | *Federal Tax Basis* | *Probate Court Basis* |
|---|---|---|
| In testamentary trust: | | |
| Personal property received from estate | Values as determined for estate tax, or subsequent cost. | Values shown by schedule of distribution. |
| Real estate received under will | Value as determined for estate tax. | Value in inventory, or not valued. |
| In *inter vivos* trust: | | |
| Transfer in trust after Dec. 31, 1920, by gift | As to gains—Cost to the donor or the last preceding purchaser. | At quoted market values at date of transfer, or at cost. |

| Federal Tax Basis | Probate Court Basis |
|---|---|
| As to losses— | |
| The lower of: | |
| 1. Cost to the donor or the last preceding purchaser, | |
| or | |
| 2. Fair market value at time of the gift. | |

| | Federal Tax Basis | Probate Court Basis |
|---|---|---|
| Transfer in trust before Jan. 1, 1921, by gift | At fair market value on date of transfer. | At quoted market values at date of transfer, or at cost. |

*Fiduciary return of trustee in bankruptcy for an individual.* A trustee in bankruptcy for an individual uses the return as a means of reporting his fiduciary transactions for the year, and of showing the resulting income or loss to be reported by the bankrupt in gross income in his individual return. If the conditions requiring a return are present, an individual is not relieved of filing an individual return by reason of his bankruptcy.

**Corporation income tax returns.** A receiver who has possession of all or substantially all the business or property of a corporation and a trustee in bankruptcy for a corporation have the duty of filing the corporation income tax returns of the respective corporations. Each would use the regular corporation form.

There are special provisions of the Code that should be taken into account when plans for reorganization or liquidation are under consideration. Tax relief provisions, such as for the forgiveness of debt and for tax-free reorganizations and liquidations, frequently operate to postpone the tax.

**Information returns.** A trust claiming exemption as a charitable trust must file an information return for each year it makes this claim. Financial statements and information regarding contributions paid or permanently set aside must be furnished.

Information returns for employee trusts are discussed in Chapter 33.

## THE ACCOUNTING SYSTEM FOR ESTATES AND TRUSTS

The accounting systems for perpetual trusts and for employee trusts are covered in Chapters 32 and 33, respectively. This section, then, will confine its discussion to estates and the other types of trusts. We will consider:

1. Basis of probate court accounting.
2. Accounting by an individual fiduciary.

3. Accounting by a corporate fiduciary.
4. Form of accountings to the court.
5. Accounting by a receiver.
6. Accounting by a trustee in bankruptcy.

**Basis of probate court accounting.** Probate court accounting requires the use of the cash basis whenever it is reasonable to do so. The fiduciary records the purchase of an investment at cost and a sale at the net proceeds. If the cost has been increased or reduced by intervening exchanges, in which cash was paid or received, or by stock rights sold for cash, the fiduciary uses the cost thus adjusted to determine the increase or decrease (the gain or loss) in principal. A stock dividend, if principal, is included in the account value of the shares on which it is received. If the stock dividend is income, it is not valued. It may be distributed in kind, or if sold, the net proceeds are added to income.

Debts and expenses normally are not recorded until paid. If a mortgage is placed on real estate by a fiduciary, usually with court approval, the cash received is sometimes treated as increasing principal and the payments as decreasing principal. If local precedent permits, it is preferable to treat the item as neither increasing nor decreasing principal, for the cash received is offset by the liability assumed.

Upon the death of a life tenant, income subsequently received, such as bond interest, is apportioned, unless the controlling instrument provides otherwise, between the deceased life tenant's estate and the succeeding life tenant or remainderman on the basis of the number of days before and after the date of death. Expenses are similarly apportioned at payment, or subsequently if the expense was paid in advance.

If an estate or trust has suffered a heavy potential loss on an investment it still holds, the courts occasionally permit the fiduciary to take the loss and reduce the asset to a realistic value. In some instances, where the property is of no value to the trust, the fiduciary is allowed to abandon it.

**Accounting by an individual fiduciary.** Following is a summary of the usual transactions to be recorded by the fiduciary for a decedent's estate, an individual trust, and a ward's estate:

| | *Decedent's Estate* | *Individual Trust* | *Ward's Estate* |
|---|---|---|---|
| Principal: | 1. The inventory in detail at appraised values. | Receipt of bequest of decedent or gift of donor in cash or in kind. | The inventory in detail at appraised values. |
| | 2. After-discovered assets. | | After-discovered assets. |

| *Decedent's Estate* | *Individual Trust* | *Ward's Estate* |
|---|---|---|
| 3. Gains or losses on sales or other disposition of assets. | Gains or losses on sales or other disposition of assets. | Gains or losses on sales or other disposition of assets. |
| 4. Payment of funeral expenses and expenses of last illness. | | |
| 5. Payment of decedent's debts. | | Payment of ward's debts. |
| 6. Payment of death and other taxes on estate. | Payment of income taxes on capital gains. | |
| 7. Payment of expenses of administration. | | |
| 8. Temporary investment of excess principal cash, pending payment of death taxes and making distribution. | Reinvestment of proceeds of sales and other dispositions. | Reinvestment of proceeds of sales and other dispositions. |
| 9. Distributions, in cash or in kind. | Distributions as required by will or deed, in cash or in kind. | Payment for support and maintenance of ward if income is not sufficient (with court approval). |

| Income: | | | |
|---|---|---|---|
| | 1. Collection of interest on bonds, dividends, other interest, and other income. | Collection of interest on bonds, dividends, other interest, and other income. | Collection of interest on bonds, dividends, other interest, and other income. |
| | 2. Payment of expenses directly related to income. | Payment of expenses and taxes of the trust. | Payment of expenses and taxes of the ward. |

| *Decedent's Estate* | *Individual Trust* | *Ward's Estate* |
| --- | --- | --- |
| 3. Distributions to beneficiaries. | Distribution of income to beneficiaries. | Distribution of income for support and maintenance of the ward. |

*Books of account—individual fiduciary.* The books of account of an estate or trust in which to record the transactions outlined above are usually simple and should be based on double-entry bookkeeping. They ordinarily consist of a cashbook, a journal (or a combined cashbook-journal), a general ledger, and an asset (or investment) ledger. For many trusts it is satisfactory to keep individual investment accounts in the general ledger and omit the investment ledger.

Figure 1 is a combined cashbook-journal sheet showing a series of transactions. Figures 2 and 3 illustrate the two sides of a sheet from the asset or investment ledger. The general ledger follows the standard accounting form, so it is not illustrated.

**Accounting by a corporate fiduciary.** The formal accountings by a trust company or other corporate fiduciary must necessarily comply with court rules and precedents in the jurisdiction where the accounting is filed, just as must those of an individual fiduciary. Their bookkeeping, too, must record the same types of transactions as those of an individual fiduciary, but in wider variety. Therefore, the accounting objective of a trust company is one of processing numerous transactions promptly, accurately, and in a manner easy to assemble in the prescribed court form.

To accomplish this objective, a trust company keeps several separate controls for its trusts and estates. The controls customarily are for (1) income cash, (2) principal cash, (3) other assets (or investments), and (4) principal. Instead of one investment control, the company may have controls for (a) bonds, (b) stocks, (c) mortgages, and (d) other investments.

▶ NOTE: In the states that use ground rents or notes secured by trust deeds for home financing, the control account would be labeled *ground rents* or *trust deeds* instead of *mortgages*.

*Accounting procedures and books of account—corporate fiduciary.* The arrangement of controls shown above can be used in the small trust department that continues to use handwritten records, and it is also effective with systems that incorporate bookkeeping machines, punched cards, and electronic data processing equipment. Basically, the procedure is as follows:

1. The original entries showing complete details are prepared on debit and credit tickets, which are classified as to controls. These tickets are sorted by controls and at the end of the day are posted in total to the trust department control accounts, at which time the latter must balance.

2. On the following morning, the tickets are sorted by trust numbers, and then entered on the combined cashbook-journal cards for the respective trusts. These cards have headings corresponding with the controls, in addition to date and explanation columns. The headings are: (a) date, (b) explanation, (c) ledger account, (d) income cash, (e) principal cash, (f) other assets (or investments), and (g) principal. The cards could have the same arrangement as that shown in Figure 1.

Column (d), income cash, has no contra account on the card; its implied contra is *income*. To prove the income cash, its control must agree daily with the department's actual income cash, and the entries made on the respective trust cards must agree daily with the control. Periodically, at least once each month, the bookkeeper runs a machine tape trial balance of the income cash per the trust cards. The total must agree with the income cash control, or the difference must be located and corrected.

The same procedure is followed to prove each of columns (e), (f), and (g). For these columns, there is also a cross check—the totals of columns (e), principal cash, and (f), other assets, must always equal column (g), principal (or corpus).

Any tickets that represent journal entries, such as for gains and losses on sales or redemptions of investments, are also entered on the cashbook-journal cards. The tickets for amortization of bond premiums represent a transfer from income cash (and an implied contra reduction of income) and a transfer to principal cash with a like reduction in the book value of the investment; the reverse transactions would be required for amortization of discounts.

In this procedure, no ledger is required except for other assets. The ledger may have separate controls for bonds, stocks, mortgages, and other assets, with separate accounts for the individual investments in the respective controls. These must balance within the trust and together with those in the other trusts must balance with the overall controls of the trust department.

▶ COLUMNAR CASHBOOK: The trustees of a large trust for individual beneficiaries—for example, one with assets of ten million dollars—might prefer a columnar cashbook with numerous columns, and a separate journal. By using the cashbook columns to classify the receipts and disbursements

ESTATE of HENRY JAMES

CASHBOOK-

*Income Account*

*Cash*

| Date | Received from or Paid to and Description | Account | Dr. | Cr. |
|------|------------------------------------------|---------|-----|-----|

19___

as of

May 10  Per inventory and appraisement **as**
of this date, filed May 15:
   *Bonds:*
     $25 000  City of Philadelphia, Pa.,
       (Loan of 6/1/50) 3s,
       1/1/66 @ $105.40     Investments
       Interest accrued 1/2 to
       4/29, 3 mos. 28 days     Investments
   On deposit in Security National Bank
   Total inventory

Jun 15  George C. Mark, funeral director     Funeral expenses

15  Nieder Bros., meats and groceries     Debts of decedent

15  Temple & Grove, brokers, proceeds of
sale of $25,000 City of Philadelphia,     Investments, gain
3s, 1/1/66 @ $106     or loss
Accrued interest 1/2 to 4/29,
  included in inventory     Investments
Accrued interest 4/30 to 6/15,
  1 mo. 16 days     Interest received     $95.83

Sep 15  A. M. Barr, Esq., legal services     Administration

15  Register of Wills, state inheritance tax     Taxes

Nov 30  A. M. Barr, Esq., probate costs, filing
fees, etc., advanced

                                         95.83

Nov 30  Balances per First Account (Filed Dec 2, 19___)     95.83

Feb 3  Distribution to Eleanor Marshall Smith, widow     —     95.83

                                         $95.83    $95.83

\* If there are a number of investments, the fiduciary may desire two additional col-
number of shares of investments.

**Fig. 1.**

largely in accordance with classifications on the fiduciary income tax return,
controls are developed that expedite the preparation of the fiduciary return
and the submission of data that the beneficiaries must include in their individual returns.

   **Form of accountings to the court.** There are, in general, two basic forms
of accountings to the court, as follows:

   1. The first, and apparently the earlier form is essentially that of a
*cashbook,* except that all the assets are treated as a group. The gain on the

SMITH, DECEASED
JOURNAL

| | | | Principal Account | | | | |
|---|---|---|---|---|---|---|---|
| | Cash | | * | Other Assets | | Principal | |
| Dr. | | Cr. | Dr. | | Cr. | Dr. | | Cr. |

| Cash Dr. | Cash Cr. | Other Assets Dr. | Other Assets Cr. | Principal Dr. | Principal Cr. |
|---|---|---|---|---|---|
| | | $26 350.00 | | | |
| | | 245.83 | | | |
| $ 3 027.46 | | | | | |
| 3 027.46 | | 26 595.83 | | | $29 623.29 |
| | $ 1 085.00 | | | $1 085.00 | |
| | 63.71 | | | 63.71 | |
| 26 500.00 | | | $26 350.00 | | 150.00 |
| 245.83 | | | 245.83 | | |
| | 1 000.00 | | | 1 000.00 | |
| | 551.48 | | | 551.48 | |
| | 50.47 | | | 50.47 | |
| 29 773.29 | $ 2 750.66 | $26 595.83 | $26 595.83 | $ 2 750.66 | 29 773.29 |
| 2 750.66 | | | | | 2 750.66 |
| 27 022.63 | | | | | 27 022.63 |
| — | 27 022.63 | | | 27 022.63 | — |
| $27 022.63 | $27 022.63 | | | $27 022.63 | $27 022.63 |

umns for other assets (debit and credit) as control columns for the par values and

**Cashbook-Journal.**

sale of an asset increases the total of the assets and is therefore a debit, just as the receipt of cash increases the total cash and is a debit. After-discovered assets in an estate or an additional gift by the donor of a trust increase the total assets of the estate or trust and are also debits.

A loss on the sale of an asset or the payment of income tax on capital gains decreases the total assets, just as a disbursement of cash decreases the total cash, and is therefore a credit.

The conversion of an asset into cash at the asset's book value neither

City of Philadelphia (Loan of June 1, 19__) 3s, Jan 1, 19__

SECURITY    RATE AND MATURITY    CLASS AND PAR    J & J 1 INT. OR DIV. PERIOD

CERTIFICATE NOS. M23, 732, M23, 937-23960 ($1,000 ea.)

| DATES 19— | PAR OR SHARES | DESCRIPTION | PRICE | AMOUNT | | TAX BASIS* |
|---|---|---|---|---|---|---|
| | | | | DR. | CR. | |
| Apr 29 | 25,000 | Per inventory and appraisement filed May 15. | $105 40 | $26 350 00 | | |
| | | Interest accd. Jan 2 to Apr 29, per invty. & app. | | 245 83 | | |
| Jun 15 | (25,000) | Sale through Temple & Grove | 106 | | $26 500 00 | |
| | | Accd. interest collected | | | 245 83 | |
| | | Gain transferred to principal | | 150 00 | | |
| | | | | $26 745 83 | $26 745 83 | |

*Fill in only when tax basis differs from accounting basis.

Fig. 2. Asset (or Investment) Ledger.

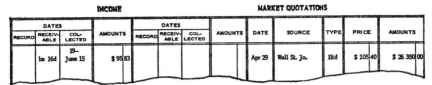

| | INCOME | | | | | | MARKET QUOTATIONS | | | | |
|---|---|---|---|---|---|---|---|---|---|---|---|
| | DATES | | AMOUNTS | | DATES | | AMOUNTS | DATE | SOURCE | TYPE | PRICE | AMOUNTS |
| RECORD | RECEIV-ABLE | COL-LECTED | | RECORD | RECEIV-ABLE | COL-LECTED | | | | | | |
| | 1m 16d | 19—June 15 | $ 95 83 | | | | | Apr 29 | Wall St. Jo. | Bid | $ 105 40 | $ 26 350 00 |

Fig. 3. Asset (or Investment) Ledger—Reverse Side of Fig. 2.

increases nor decreases the total of the assets; and the reverse situation, the purchase of an investment for cash, neither decreases nor increases the total assets. Comparable situations in a cashbook would be transfers of cash between a company's deposit accounts or between a deposit account and a working fund—the total cash is unchanged. The device used in formal accountings of this form to report transactions that neither increase nor decrease the total assets is to show them *short,* that is, as a memorandum only.

Where this first type of formal accounting is used, the classification of accounts in the general ledger may be as simple or as elaborate as the fiduciary desires for administrative purposes. The respective asset balances shown by the ledger as of the date of the accounting comprise the details of the balance shown by the formal accounting.

This cashbook form, or modifications of it, is used in a number of jurisdictions, including Philadelphia County (Philadelphia), other counties in Pennsylvania, and some counties of Maine.

Figure 4 shows a very simple example in the Philadelphia form, which reports the transactions recorded in Figure 1.

▶ NOTE: A simpler form than that used in Philadelphia is acceptable in the Cook County (Chicago), Illinois, court.

2. The second form of probate court account uses the pattern of a *ledger,* and permits the same type of books of original entry as the cashbook form. To avoid unnecessary work in preparing the court accounting, it is most important that the classifications required in the formal accounting are used in setting up the ledger accounts. From the very beginning the professional accountant must plan carefully how he will present each kind of transaction in the formal accounting. For that accounting New York uses elaborate sets of printed forms with meticulous wording on each form; Los Angeles, California, has another method of classification and summary; Camden County (New Jersey) and Montgomery County (Pennsylvania), both adjacent to Philadelphia, have still others.

▶ SUGGESTION: A suggestion earlier in the chapter bears repeating here. Obtain from counsel of the estate or trust a copy of an accounting

IN the ORPHANS' COURT of PHILADELPHIA COUNTY
ESTATE of HENRY JAMES SMITH, DECEASED
FIRST ACCOUNT
of
WALTER SMITH, EXECUTOR

Decedent died April 29, 19___
Letters Testamentary granted May 10, 19___
First complete advertising May 11, 19___
Will No. 1485 of 19___

Account stated from May 10, 19___ to November 30, 19___

RECAPITULATION AND INDEX

*Principal—Personalty:*

|  | Pages |  |  |
|---|---|---|---|
| Receipts | 79–80 | $29,773.29 | |
| Disbursements | 80–81 | 2,750.66 | |
| Balance | 81 | | $27,022.63 |

*Income—Personalty:*

| Receipts | 81 | 95.83 | |
|---|---|---|---|
| Disbursements | 82 | — | |
| Balance | 82 | | 95.83 |

| Combined balances consisting of cash | | | $27,118.46 |
|---|---|---|---|

PRINCIPAL—PERSONALTY

*Receipts*

The Accountant charges himself with Principal received as follows:

Goods, Chattels and Credits of the decedent, as per inventory and appraisement filed May 15, 19___:

*Bonds:*

| $25 000 | City of Philadelphia, Penna. (Loan of Jun 1, 19___) 3s, due Jan 1, 19___ @ $105.40 | $26,350.00 | |
|---|---|---|---|
| | Accrued interest from Jan 2 to Apr 29, 3 mos. 28 days | 245.83 | |
| | | | $26,595.83 |
| Cash, on deposit in Security National Bank | | | 3,027.46 |
| | Forward | | 29,623.29 |

**Fig. 4. Report to Court—Philadelphia Method.**

PRINCIPAL—PERSONALTY

| | | |
|---|---|---|
| *Receipts*, forward | | $29,623.29 |

And items since received:

*19___*

Jun 15  Excess of amount received over book value on sale of $25,000 City of Philadelphia 3s, Jan 1, 19___:

| | | |
|---|---|---|
| Proceeds of sale @ 106 | $26,500.00 | |
| Value included in inventory | 26,350.00 | |
| | | 150.00 |

Changes in the corpus of the estate not increasing its book value:

*19___*

Jun 15  Interest accrued from Jan 2, to Apr 29, 3 mos. 28 days on

| | | |
|---|---|---|
| $25,000 City of Philadelphia 3s due Jan 1, 19___, sold this day | $  245.83 | |
| Value included in inventory | 245.83 | |

| | | |
|---|---|---|
| Total | | $29,773.29 |

*Disbursements*

The Accountant claims credit for the following:

*19___*

| | | |
|---|---|---|
| Jun 15  George C. Mark, funeral director | | $ 1,085.00 |
| 15  Nieder Bros., meats and groceries, debts of decedent | | 63.71 |
| Sep 15  Register of Wills, inheritance tax | | 551.48 |

*Administration expenses:*

| | | |
|---|---|---|
| Sep 15  A. M. Barr, Esq., legal services | $ 1,000.00 | |
| Nov 30  A. M. Barr, Esq., probate fee, filing fee, etc., advanced | 50.47 | |
| | | 1,050.47 |

| | | |
|---|---|---|
| Total | | 2,750.66 |
| Balance of principal, cash in bank | | 27,022.63 |
| | | $29,773.29 |

**Fig. 4. Report to Court—Philadelphia Method. (Continued.)**

INCOME—PERSONALTY

*Receipts*

The Accountant charges himself with income collected as follows:

*19___*

| | |
|---|---|
| Jun 15 Interest for 1 mo. 16 days from **Apr** 30 to Jun 15 accrued on $25,000 City of Philadelphia 3s, Jan 1, 19___, sold this day | $   95.83 |
| Total | $   95.83 |

*Disbursements:*

The Accountant claims credit for disbursements of income, as follows:

| | |
|---|---|
| | None |
| Balance of income, cash in bank | $   95.83 |
| | $   95.83 |

(If the balances include assets other than cash, the account must show, in parallel columns, (1) the market value of each asset as of the close of the account and (2) the asset's value in the account. These would be included in a recapitulation section normally appearing at this point in the account.)

*S/Walter Smith*

Walter Smith, Executor of the Estate of Henry James Smith, Deceased.

(Followed by affidavit of executor)

(Subsequent to adjudication of the account by the Court, the Executor would distribute the balance of principal and of income in accordance with the adjudication.)

**Fig. 4. Report to Court—Philadelphia Method. (Continued.)**

approved by the court, for use as a guide in your engagement. A copy of the local court's rules should be available to you, too.

▶ No FORMAL ACCOUNTING: If a decedent's estate is of nominal size, or if the spouse and/or the children of the decedent are the sole beneficiaries and are all of full age, a formal accounting with the court may not be required or may be waived by all the parties in interest. But even if no formal accounting is required, the personal representative must keep accurate accounts and be able to satisfy the parties in interest.

**Accounting by a receiver.** Receiverships may be either (1) those in equity under state law, or (2) those under the Federal Bankruptcy Act for the period from filing of the petition in bankruptcy and the receiver's appointment until the trustee is selected and qualifies. This period is usually brief, and the receiver is a temporary appointee of the court.

*Receiver in equity under state law.* A receiver in equity must account for the assets of which he has taken possession from the distressed debtor under the court order. The receiver debits the assets and credits respective valuation allowances, such as for bad debts, shown by the debtor's books; the net of these entries, representing their net book value to the debtor, becomes a credit to the debtor on the receiver's books. On the books of the debtor, the asset and allowance accounts, representing assets taken over by the receiver, are closed out and their net book value charged to the receiver.

The receiver should maintain detailed records of sales of assets and of debts paid, distinguishing clearly between the old debts and those incurred by the receiver, which are entitled to priority of payment. The old debts paid are charged to the debtor, for the receiver does not record such debtor liabilities on his books. The receiver must also distinguish clearly between accounts receivable taken over from the debtor and additional accounts receivable, for he is responsible for granting credit on the latter accounts. In recording the payments of debtor liabilities, the charges should be to the debtor, classified according to the debtor's general ledger code of accounts, thus:

*Debtor—notes payable paid*
*Debtor—accounts payable paid*
*Debtor—mortgage installments paid*

The receiver must notify the debtor of any debits or credits to him, so that the debtor may record the transactions in his accounts. If debtor liabilities are paid, the entry is:

| | | |
|---|---|---|
| Notes payable | 2,500 | |
| Accounts payable | 1,275 | |
| Mortgage installments payable | 5,000 | |
| Receiver | | 8,775 |
| For liabilities paid by receiver. | | |

If the receiver is liquidating the business, a cashbook, a journal, and a ledger are usually sufficient for his requirements.

To prepare financial statements of the debtor's business during a receivership in which the receiver maintains separate books of account, it is necessary to:

1. Adjust the debtor's books for the net income or, more commonly, loss for the period shown by the receiver.

2. If after the adjustment the balance due from (or to) the receiver on the debtor's books does not agree with the balance due to (or from) the debtor on the receiver's books, the difference must be located and the missing entry or entries made.

3. Prepare a trial balance of the debtor's and the receiver's books.

4. Eliminate the reciprocal accounts from the two trial balances. After the income or loss adjustment, the net balance due to the debtor on the receiver's books should equal the balance due from the receiver on the debtor's books.

5. Combine the trial balances after eliminating the reciprocal accounts.

6. Prepare the debtor's financial statements from the combined trial balances.

If the receiver continues the operation of the business and the accounting records are at all adequate, it is less expensive and entirely satisfactory to close the books of account in the conventional manner as of the date the receiver takes over. The asset, liability, and owner's equity accounts should be ruled also and the balances brought down, so that there is a clear break in the records.

The receiver will then have the accounting records continued with this change—he should have new accounts opened for customers to whom he grants credit and for the receiver's certificates (or notes) issued for loans obtained from banks. New accounts should be opened for other new assets and liabilities for which he is responsible.

*Receiver under the Federal Act.* The duties of a receiver under the Federal Bankruptcy Act, as they relate to accounting, consist of (1) taking an immediate inventory, (2) petitioning the court for leave to retain accountants if he desires an examination of the bankrupt's records and books of account, (3) petitioning the court for appointment of appraisers to value the inventory, (4) accounting for the proceeds of any sale of assets, and (5) accounting for disbursements made. The Act prescribes no particular forms for the accounting.

The court audits the accounting at a public hearing, about which all creditors are notified. At the hearing, the court also hears requests for commissions and counsel fees.

**Accounting by a trustee in bankruptcy.** The accounting of a trustee under the Federal Bankruptcy Act has as its basis (1) the schedule of the bankrupt's property, (2) the schedule of amounts due creditors, and (3) the questionnaire (statement of affairs) submitted by the bankrupt. The detailed examination of the bankrupt's books of account may disclose inaccuracies in the schedules and questionnaire; it may disclose voidable transfers and concealed property that can be recovered; and there may be unjust claims by creditors to which the trustee should object.

Depending on the circumstances (see page 1025), the trustee will face one of these situations:

1. A liquidation.
2. An arrangement.

*A liquidation.* In accounting for a liquidation, the property shown by the bankrupt's schedule becomes the starting point. The appraisers' report will supply values. The records should also show (1) errors and omissions in the bankrupt's schedule, adjusted as discovered, (2) assets recovered by legal action, (3) assets sold by receiver, (4) proceeds of sales by receiver, (5) assets sold by trustee and gains or losses thereon, (6) claims having priority allowed by the court and payments thereof, and (7) allowed claims of unsecured creditors and dividends paid thereon.

Secured creditors recover amounts owed them by sale of the collateral. If the proceeds of sale exceed the debt, the creditor must pay over the excess to the trustee. If the proceeds are less than the debt, the creditor has an unsecured claim for the balance.

Before the trustee makes any payments to unsecured creditors, he must pay the priority claims. These claims have priority in the following order, subject to the effect of statutory liens described below in Item 6:

1. Administrative costs, such as for preserving the assets, filing fees, recovering concealed and fraudulently transferred assets, fees of counsel, commissions of receiver and trustee.
2. Wage claims, not exceeding $600 to each claimant, earned within three months prior to bankruptcy. The claimants may not be managerial or supervisory employees.
3. Costs of creditors in opposing discharge of a bankrupt and procuring convictions for offenses under the Act.
4. Taxes legally due and owing to the United States, to any state, or to any subdivision thereof.
5. Debts due the Federal government, its sureties, and agencies given

priority under Federal law. Also, rent claims under state law, if they are for actual use and occupancy, within three months of bankruptcy. Rent under acceleration clauses in the lease is excluded.

6. Effect of statutory liens:

a. Liens on real property and liens on personal property accompanied by possession have preference and are paid *before* priority claims.

b. Liens on personal property without possession and distraints for rents *follow* administration costs and wage claims in priority.

c. A distress for rent gives the landlord priority over taxes and other obligations owed the United States for which liens were not filed.

After provision for payment in full of liens and priority claims, the trustee upon instruction of the court pays the unsecured creditors *pro rata*. The unsecured or general creditors include, as to the balance of their claims, partially secured creditors, and claimants for wages, rent, and the like in excess of their priorities.

The Act provides that the court shall declare a first dividend within 30 days after the first meeting of creditors if the money of the estate, after provision for debts having priority, equals 5% or more of the unsecured claims. The first dividend may not exceed 50% of such available money.

Subsequent dividends are to be declared upon like terms whenever the amount available equals 10% or more of the unsecured claims. A final dividend may not be declared sooner than three months after the first dividend unless the 6-month period for filing claims has expired.

*An arrangement.* Under arrangement proceedings, no special accounting is required. A public accountant's services would be primarily those of a consultant to the receiver or trustee.

**Financial statements—receiver and trustee in bankruptcy.** The financial statements that may be useful in the management and liquidation of a bankrupt's estate are:

1. *Statement of affairs and deficiency account.* In the traditional statement of affairs (not the questionnaire required by the Federal Bankruptcy Act and mentioned on page 1025), estimated realizable values of the assets become the basis for estimating the loss, if any, to creditors in liquidation of the business. An example of the statement of affairs and related deficiency account is presented in Figure 5.

2. *Balance sheet and pro forma balance sheet.* A balance sheet and pro forma balance sheet giving effect to an arrangement with creditors under the Federal Act are useful in showing the improved financial position in a postponement arrangement if the postponement permits moving at least a part of current liabilities into a noncurrent position. A scaling-down of un-

# The Lucas Manufacturing Company
## Statement of Affairs—August 31, 19___

### Assets

| Book Value | | | Expected to Realize |
|---|---|---|---|
| | Assets pledged with fully secured creditors: | | |
| $ 5,000 | Land—estimated value | | $ 5,350 |
| 21,000 | Buildings—estimated value | | 16,000 |
| | $27,500 Cost | | |
| | 6,500 Reserve for depreciation | | |
| | $21,000 Book value | | |
| 12,500 | Sinking fund | 12,250 | |
| | Total security for bonds payable | $33,600 | |
| | Deduct: Bonds payable $25,000 | | |
| | Accrued interest 500 | 25,500 | $ 8,100 |
| | Assets pledged with partially secured creditors: | | |
| 5,000 | Bonds of Fairview Company—estimated value | $ 4,850 | |
| 100 | Accrued interest on bonds | 100 | |
| 2,350 | Finished goods | 1,200 | |
| | Total security for $10,000 of notes payable—deducted contra | $ 6,150 | |
| | Free assets: | | |
| 495 | Cash | $ 495 | |
| | Less worthless checks held | 210 | 285 |
| 32,375 | Accounts receivable | 19,800 | |
| 1,200 | Notes receivable | 800 | |

### Liabilities

| Book Value | | | Expected to Rank |
|---|---|---|---|
| | Liabilities having priority: | | |
| $ 225 | Accrued taxes—deducted contra | | |
| 425 | Reserve for federal income tax—deducted contra | | |
| | Fully secured liabilities: | | |
| 25,000 | Bonds payable—deducted contra | | |
| 500 | Accrued bond interest—deducted contra | | |
| | Partially secured liabilities: | | |
| 10,000 | Notes payable | $10,000 | |
| 120 | Accrued interest on notes payable | 120 | |
| | Total | $10,120 | |
| | Deduct security—detailed contra | 6,150 | $ 3,970 |
| | Unsecured liabilities: | | |
| 25,000 | Notes payable | | 25,000 |
| 355 | Accrued interest on notes payable | | 355 |
| 32,350 | Accounts payable | | 32,350 |
| | Contingent liabilities: | | |
| 400 | Notes receivable discounted | | 400 |
| 3,000 | Reserve for damage suit | | |

Fig. 5. Statement of Affairs and Related Deficiency Account. (Continues on next page.)

## The Lucas Manufacturing Company
### Statement of Affairs—August 31, 19___

| Book Value | Expected to Realize | | Book Value | Expected to Rank |
|---|---|---|---|---|
| 18 | 18 | Accrued interest on notes receivable | | |
| 5,900 | | Goods in process | | |
| | | Estimated value when completed $ 6,000 | | |
| | | Less cost to complete: | | |
| | | Raw materials worth $ 500 | | |
| | | Other expenditures 200  700 | | |
| | 5,300 | | | |
| 7,000 | | Raw materials | | |
| | 500 | $ 1,000 to be used in finishing goods in process | | |
| | 3,000 | $ 6,000 to be sold | | |
| 5,000 | 4,850 | Bonds of Fairview Company | | |
| 100 | 100 | Accrued interest on bonds | | |
| 23,700 | 18,500 | Machinery—estimated value | | |
| | | $31,000 Appraised value | | |
| | | 7,300 Reserve for depreciation | | |
| | | $23,700 Book value | | |
| 10,000 | | Goodwill—No value | | |
| 125 | | Unexpired insurance | | |
| 500 | 300 | Discount on capital stock | | |
| | $61,553 | Total free assets | | |
| | 650 | Deduct liabilities having priority—per contra | | |
| | $60,903 | Net free assets | | |
| | 2,172 | Estimated deficiency to unsecured creditors | | |
| $132,363 | $63,075 | | $132,363 | $63,075 |

Right-side detail:

| Book Value | | Expected to Rank |
|---|---|---|
| | Possible liability for nondelivery of merchandise | 1,000 |
| | Reserves: | |
| 1,500 | Reserve for doubtful receivables | |
| | Stockholders' equity per books: | |
| 25,000 | Capital stock | |
| 12,500 | Sinking fund reserve | |
| 9,012 * | Deficit | |
| 5,000 | Unrealized gain on appraisal of machinery | |

* Deduction.

Fig. 5. Statement of Affairs and Related Deficiency Account. (Continued.)

THE LUCAS MANUFACTURING COMPANY

Deficiency Account—August 31, 19___

| | | | | |
|---|---|---|---:|---:|
| Deficit | | | | $ 9,012 |
| Estimated loss on: | | | | |
| Buildings | | | | 5,000 |
| Sinking fund | | | | 250 |
| Bonds of Fairview Company | | | | 300 |
| Finished goods | | | | 1,150 |
| Cash | | | | 210 |
| Receivables: | | | | |
| Accounts receivable | $12,575 | | | |
| Notes receivable | 400 | | | |
| Total | $12,975 | | | |
| Less reserve for doubtful receivables | 1,500 | 11,475 | | |
| Goods in process | | 600 | | |
| Raw materials | | 3,500 | | |
| Machinery: | | | | |
| Net book value | $23,700 | | | |
| Less unrealized gain on appraisal | 5,000 | | | |
| Cost less depreciation | $18,700 | | | |
| Less estimated realizable value | 18,500 | 200 | | |
| Goodwill | | 10,000 | | |
| Unexpired insurance | | 125 | | |
| Discount on capital stock | | 200 | | |
| Possible liability for nondelivery of merchandise | | 1,000 | | |
| | | $43,022 | | |

| | |
|---|---:|
| Estimated gain on land | $ 350 |
| Reserve for damaged suit—not required | 3,000 |
| Capital stock | 25,000 |
| Sinking fund reserve | 12,500 |
| Estimated deficiency to unsecured creditors | 2,172 |
| | $43,022 |

**Fig. 5. Statement of Affairs and Related Deficiency Account. (Continued.)** [From Finney and Miller's *Principles of Accounting, Advanced*, Fifth Edition, pages 70–172. Englewood Cliffs, N. J.: Prentice-Hall, Inc., 1960.]

## C COMPANY—IN RECEIVERSHIP—F. C. WHITE, RECEIVER
### Realization and Liquidation Account
#### July 1, 19___ to June 30, 19___

**Assets to be realized:**

| | | | |
|---|---|---:|---:|
| (a) | Accounts receivable—Old | $50,000 | |
| (a) | Less allowance for doubtful accounts | 1,500 | $ 48,500 |
| (a) | Notes receivable—Old | | 15,000 |
| (a) | Inventory | | 60,000 |
| (a) | Unexpired insurance | | 900 |
| (a) | Marketable securities | | 7,500 |
| (a) | Land | | 10,000 |
| (a) | Building | $80,000 | |
| (a) | Less accumulated depreciation | 15,000 | 65,000 |
| (a) | Furniture and fixtures | $10,000 | |
| (a) | Less accumulated depreciation | 3,000 | 7,000 | $213,900 |

**Assets acquired:**

| | | |
|---|---|---:|
| (c) | Accounts receivable—New | 200,000 |

**Supplementary charges:**

| | | | |
|---|---|---:|---:|
| (b) | Purchases | $120,000 | |
| (g) | Sales discounts | 2,300 | |
| (k) | Mortgage interest—June 30, 19___ to June 30, 19___ | 2,950 | |
| (n) | Salaries and wages | 17,000 | |
| (n) | Freight in | 350 | |
| (n) | Delivery expense | 1,000 | |
| (n) | Taxes | 1,200 | |
| (n) | General expense | 7,500 | 152,300 |

**Liabilities to be liquidated:**

| | | | |
|---|---|---:|---:|
| (a) | Accounts payable—Old | $ 95,000 | |
| (a) | Notes payable—Old | 25,000 | |
| (a) | Accrued mortgage interest | 500 | |
| (a) | Mortgage payable | 50,000 | $170,500 |

**Liabilities assumed:**

| | | | |
|---|---|---:|---:|
| (b) | Accounts payable—New | $120,000 | |
| (k) | Accrued mortgage interest—from June 30, 19___ to June 30, 19___ | 2,950 | 122,950 |

**Supplementary credits:**

| | | | |
|---|---|---:|---:|
| (c) | Sales | $200,000 | |
| (f) | Interest on notes receivable | 300 | |
| (h) | Interest on securities | 120 | |
| (m) | Purchase discounts | 1,400 | 201,820 |

**Realization proceeds:**

| | | | |
|---|---|---:|---:|
| (d) | Accounts receivable—Old | $ 47,500 | |
| (e) | Notes receivable—Old | 15,000 | |
| (g) | Accounts receivable—New | 160,000 | |
| (i) | Marketable securities | 7,350 | 229,850 |

**Assets not realized:**

| | | | |
|---|---|---:|---:|
| | Accounts receivable—New | $40,000 | |
| | Less allowance for doubtful accounts | 1,200 | $ 38,800 |
| | Inventory | | 23,000 |
| | Unexpired insurance | | 350 |
| | Land | | 10,000 |

**Liabilities liquidated:**

| | | | |
|---|---:|---:|---:|
| (j) Accounts payable—Old | $ 95,000 | | |
| (j) Notes payable—Old | 25,000 | | |
| (j) Accrued mortgage interest—June 30, 19___ | 500 | | |
| (j) Mortgage installment | 5,000 | | |
| (l) Accrued mortgage interest from June 30, 19___ to April 30, 19___ | 2,500 | | |
| (m) Accounts payable—New | 75,000 | 203,000 | |

**Liabilities not liquidated:**

| | | | |
|---|---:|---:|---:|
| Accounts payable—New | $ 45,000 | | |
| Mortgage payable | 45,000 | | |
| Accrued mortgage interest | 450 | 90,450 | |
| Net income | | 5,420 | |
| | | $865,070 | |

| | | | |
|---|---:|---:|---:|
| Building | $80,000 | | |
| Less accumulated depreciation | 18,200 | 61,800 | |
| Furniture and fixtures | $10,000 | | |
| Less accumulated depreciation | 4,000 | 6,000 | 139,950 |
| | | | $865,070 |

**CASH ACCOUNT—JULY 1, 19___**

| | | |
|---|---:|---|
| (a) Balance—June 30, 19___ | $ 1,800 | |
| (d) Accounts receivable—Old | 47,500 | |
| (e) Notes receivable—Old | 15,000 | |
| (f) Interest on notes receivable | 300 | |
| (g) Accounts receivable—New | 157,700 | |
| (h) Interest on securities | 120 | |
| (i) Marketable securities | 7,350 | |
| | $229,770 | |

**TO JUNE 30, 19___**

| | |
|---|---:|
| (j) Accounts payable—Old | $ 95,000 |
| (j) Notes payable—Old | 25,000 |
| (j) Mortgage installment | 5,000 |
| (j) Accrued mortgage interest—June 30, 19___ | 500 |
| (l) Mortgage interest—June 30, 19___ to Apr 30, 19___ | 2,500 |
| (m) Accounts payable—New | 73,600 |
| (n) Salaries and wages | 17,000 |
| (n) Freight in | 350 |
| (n) Delivery expense | 1,000 |
| (n) Taxes | 1,200 |
| (n) General expense | 7,500 |
| Balance—June 30, 19___ | 1,120 |
| | $229,770 |

**MEMORANDUM CAPITAL ACCOUNT**

| | | | |
|---|---:|---|---:|
| (a) Deficit—June 30, 19___ | $ 4,800 | (a) Capital stock | $ 50,000 |
| Stockholders' equity—June 30, 19___ | 50,620 | Net income | 5,420 |
| | $ 55,420 | | $ 55,420 |

Fig. 6. **Realization and Liquidation Account Supplemented by Cash Account and Memorandum Capital Account.** [From Finney and Miller's *Principles of Accounting, Advanced,* Fifth Edition, pages 202, 203. Englewood Cliffs, N. J.: Prentice-Hall, Inc., 1960.]

C COMPANY—IN RECEIVERSHIP—F. C. WHITE, RECEIVER

COMPARATIVE BALANCE SHEET

June 30, 19__ and 19__

| | June 30 | | |
|---|---|---|---|
| *Assets* | *19__* | *19__* | *Increase (Decrease)* |
| Cash on hand and in bank | $ 1,120 | $ 1,800 | ($ 680) |
| Marketable securities | | 7,500 | (7,500) |
| Accounts receivable, net of allowances (19__—$1,200; 19__—$1,500): | | | |
| Prior to receivership | | 48,500 | (48,500) |
| During receivership | 38,800 | | 38,800 |
| Note receivable, prior | | 15,000 | (15,000) |
| Inventory | 23,000 | 60,000 | (37,000) |
| Unexpired insurance | 350 | 900 | (550) |
| Total current assets | 63,270 | 133,700 | (70,430) |
| Land | 10,000 | 10,000 | |
| Buildings, net of accumulated depreciation (19__—$18,200; 19__—$15,000) | 61,800 | 65,000 | (3,200) |
| Furniture and fixtures, net of accumulated depreciation (19__—$4,000; 19__—$3,000) | 6,000 | 7,000 | (1,000) |
| | $141,070 | $215,700 | ($74,630) |

| *Liabilities* | | | |
|---|---|---|---|
| Accounts payable: | | | |
| Prior to receivership | | 95,000 | (95,000) |
| During receivership | 45,000 | | 45,000 |
| Notes payable, prior | | 25,000 | (25,000) |
| Accrued mortgage interest | 450 | 500 | (50) |
| Total current liabilities | 45,450 | 120,500 | (75,050) |
| Mortgage payable | 45,000 | 50,000 | (5,000) |
| *Stockholders' Equity:* | | | |
| Capital stock | 50,000 | 50,000 | |
| Retained earnings (deficit) | 620 | (4,800) | 5,420 |
| | $141,070 | $215,700 | ($74,630) |

**Fig. 7. Comparative Balance Sheet.**

C COMPANY—IN RECEIVERSHIP—F. C. WHITE, RECEIVER

Statement of Income and Retained Income
for the Year Ended June 30, 19___

| | | |
|---|---:|---:|
| Sales, net of $2,300 discounts | | $197,700 |
| Cost of sales: | | |
| Inventory, July 1, 19___ | $ 60,000 | |
| Purchases, net of $1,400 discounts | 118,600 | |
| Freight in | 350 | |
| | 178,950 | |
| Less, inventory, June 30, 19___ | 23,000 | |
| | | 155,950 |
| | | 41,750 |
| Selling, administrative and | | |
| general expenses: | | |
| Salaries and wages | 17,000 | |
| Delivery expense | 1,000 | |
| Insurance | 550 | |
| Taxes | 1,200 | |
| Depreciation | 4,200 | |
| Bad debts (receiver's accounts | | |
| receivable) | 1,200 | |
| General | 7,500 | |
| | | 32,650 |
| | | 9,100 |
| Interest: | | |
| Interest expense on mortgage | 2,950 | |
| Interest earned on securities | | |
| and notes | 420 | |
| | | 2,530 |
| | | 6,570 |
| Losses on liquidation: | | |
| On accounts receivable, prior | 1,000 | |
| On marketable securities | 150 | |
| | | 1,150 |
| Net income | | 5,420 |
| Deficit, July 1, 19___ | | 4,800 |
| Retained income, June 30, 19___ | | $    620 |

**Fig. 8. Statement of Income and Retained Income.**

secured liabilities will reduce the current liabilities and sometimes non-current liabilities.

3. *Realization and liquidation account.* The purpose of this statement is to report the realization of assets and the liquidation of liabilities. It is generally supplemented by a *cash account* and a *memorandum capital account,* as illustrated in Figure 6.

4. *Comparative balance sheet and statement of income and retained income.* These statements, shown in Figures 7 and 8, have the advantage of closely following the conventional form of financial statements, which makes them familiar to lawyers, creditors, and accountants. The dollar amounts on the illustrated comparative balance sheet and statement of income and retained income tie in to those on the realization and liquidation account (Figure 6).

# 31

# Fund Accounting for Governments

**JAMES W. BAKER**

*Certified Public Accountant; Professor of Accounting, University of Georgia*

# CHAPTER THIRTY-ONE

# Fund Accounting
# for Governments

This chapter deals with governmental accounting involving the use of funds. Although the material as presented refers specifically to municipalities, it is also applicable to the Federal government, state governments, and local governments other than municipalities, such as counties, townships, and school districts.

Accounting principles and standard procedures will be discussed along with fund concepts and definitions. Then the accounting system will be explained in general, followed by an examination of the operations of the various funds and groups of accounts. Finally, there will be a description of the special features of governmental audits.

▶ ADDITIONAL APPLICATION: Much of the material in this chapter is pertinent to the next chapter, *Fund Accounting for Institutions,* which will, therefore, cover only those points of differences between governmental and institutional accounting.

## ESSENTIALS OF GOVERNMENTAL ACCOUNTING [1]

As a necessary introduction to the subject of governmental accounting, the following will be considered:

1. Principles of governmental accounting.
2. Standard governmental accounting procedures.
3. Fund concepts and definitions.

**Principles of governmental accounting.** Following are the basic premises that support governmental accounting theory and practice:

1. A municipal accounting system must make it possible (a) to show that legal provisions have been complied with, and (b) to reflect the financial condition and financial operations of the municipality.

---

[1] This section adapted from: National Committee on Governmental Accounting, *Municipal Accounting and Auditing,* Part I. Municipal Finance Officers Association of the United States and Canada, 1951.

2. If there is a conflict between legal requirements and sound accounting practices, the legal requirements must take precedence. In such cases, the financial officer has a duty to seek statutory changes that will effect a harmony with sound accounting principles.

3. The general accounting system should be on a double-entry basis with a general ledger in which all financial transactions are recorded in detail or in summary. Additional subsidiary records should be kept where necessary.

4. Every municipality should establish the funds called for either by law or by sound financial administration. It should be recognized, however, that funds introduce an element of inflexibility in the financial system. Accordingly, consistent with legal provisions and the requirements of sound financial administration, as few funds as possible should be established.

5. Depending on the legal and financial requirements mentioned immediately above, the following types of funds are recognized: (a) *General,* (b) *Special Revenue,* (c) *Working Capital,* (d) *Special Assessment,* (e) *Bond,* (f) *Sinking,* (g) *Trust and Agency,* and (h) *Utility or Other Enterprise.* This classification of funds should be followed, to the extent required, in the budget document and in the municipality's financial reports.

6. A complete balancing group of accounts should be established for each fund. This group should include all of the accounts needed to set forth the financial condition and financial operations of the fund and to reflect compliance with legal provisions.

7. A clear segregation should be made between those accounts relating to current assets or liabilities and those relating to fixed assets or liabilities. Fixed assets should not be carried in the same fund with current assets (except in the case of a Working Capital Fund, a Utility or other Enterprise Fund, or a Trust Fund), but should be set up in a self-balancing group of accounts known as *General Fixed Assets.* Similarly, except in a Special Assessment Fund or a Utility Fund, long-term liabilities should be shown in the *General Bonded Debt and Interest* group of accounts.

▶ NOTE: The General Fixed Assets group of accounts and the General Bonded Debt and Interest group of accounts are discussed on pages 1113 to 1115.

8. The fixed asset accounts should be maintained on the basis of original cost, or the estimated cost if the original cost is not available, or, in the case of gifts, the appraised value at the time received.

9. Depreciation on general municipal fixed assets should not be reflected in the accounts unless cash for replacements can legally be set aside. If cash for replacements cannot legally be set aside, depreciation charges may be computed for memorandum purposes only.

10. The accounting system should provide for budgetary control for both revenues and expenditures, and the financial statements should reflect, among other things, budgetary information.

11. The use of the accrual basis in accounting for revenues and expenditures is recommended to the extent applicable. Revenues, partially offset by provisions for estimated losses, should be taken into consideration when earned, even though not received in cash. Expenditures should be recorded as soon as liabilities are incurred.

12. Revenues should be classified by fund and source; and expenditures by fund, function, department, activity, character, and by main classes of objects, in accordance with standard classifications.

▶ NOTE: Classification of expenditures by function, activity, character, and object is explained in detail on page 1087.

13. Cost accounting systems should be established wherever costs can be measured. Each cost accounting system should provide for the recording of all the elements of cost incurred to accomplish a purpose, to carry on an activity or operation, or to complete a unit of work or a specific job. Although depreciation on general municipal fixed assets may be omitted in the general accounts and reports (see Principle 9), it should always be considered in determining unit costs, by means of separate memorandum records if necessary.

14. A common terminology and classification should be used consistently throughout the budget, the accounts, and the financial reports.

**Standard governmental accounting procedures.** Certain procedures are generally accepted as standard in connection with the administration and operation of a municipality's accounting system. These procedures are:

1. The accounts are centralized under the direction of one officer, who is responsible for keeping or supervising *all* accounts and for preparing and issuing *all* financial reports.

2. A budget is prepared even if not required by law because such budgets are essential to the proper management of financial affairs. A distinction between the different funds is made in the budget.

3. When purchase orders or contracts are signed, the resulting obligations are recorded *at once* as encumbrances of the chargeable funds and appropriations.

4. Inventories of both consumable and permanent property are kept in subsidiary records controlled by accounts in the general accounting system. Physical inventories are taken at least annually, and the accounts and records are made to agree with such inventories.

5. The accounting for municipal business enterprises follows the stand-

ard classifications employed by similar private enterprises. Each college, hospital, library, or other public institution follows the standard classification for such institutions.

6. Financial reports are prepared monthly or oftener, to show the current condition of the budgetary accounts and other information necessary to control operations. At least once each year a general financial report is prepared and published.

7. A general uniformity is maintained with the financial reports of other municipalities of similar size and type.

8. A periodic audit is performed by independent accountants.

**Fund concepts and definitions.** Some of the basic concepts and definitions relating to funds and fund accounting are as follows:

1. *Fund defined.* A fund is a sum of money or other resources segregated for the purpose of carrying on specific activities or attaining certain objectives in accordance with special regulations, restrictions, or limitations. It constitutes an independent fiscal and accounting entity.

2. *Uses of fund accounting.* Fund accounting provides a means by which an organization can control its disbursements of cash or use of other resources in accordance with the laws or regulations that govern its operation. A primary function of governmental accounting is, therefore, to report on the adherence by officials to these legal provisions. Another important purpose of fund accounting is to provide the necessary data for sound financial administration.

3. *Establishment and abolition of funds.* There are various legal bases for the establishment of governmental funds: (a) state statutes, (b) municipal charter requirements, and (c) ordinance provisions. In addition, funds may be created by order of the executive branch for the purpose of financial administration only. Funds can be abolished only by action of the proper legal authority having that power; generally such authority must come from the creating agency or sources higher in the legal hierarchy of government.

4. *Classification and purposes of funds.* Classification of funds must take into account both the sources of revenue or receipts and the various types of activities that are financed. Such classification also has value from the standpoint of: (a) accounting, (b) auditing and reporting, (c) financial administration and control, (d) compiling uniform financial statistics, and (e) preparing statements to show compliance with legal provisions.

▶ Note: The different types of funds were listed on page 1074. The purpose and function of each are discussed in the sections on the operation of specific funds, pages 1082 to 1113.

## THE ACCOUNTING SYSTEM FOR GOVERNMENTAL UNITS [2]

The purpose of this section is to provide the accountant with an understanding of the governmental accounting system through an enumeration of the accounts used as they apply to individual funds. Also, certain general characteristics of a governmental accounting system will be discussed as a prelude to a consideration of the detailed operation of specific funds.

**Classification of accounts.** There are four main purposes in classifying accounts: (1) to insure compliance with budgetary provisions, (2) to provide a basis for financial and administrative control, (3) to furnish data required for financial statements, and (4) to provide a basis for comparison with similar data for other periods or for other governmental units.

A listing of the general ledger accounts for governmental units must take into consideration the funds in which each account could be found. The following chart of accounts has been prepared with this in mind. Of course, because of variances in organization and activities performed, it may be necessary to make some modifications when adapting this master chart to the requirements of a particular governmental unit. As we have previously pointed out, any organization should use only those funds and accounts required by legal provisions and sound financial administration.

### LIST OF GENERAL LEDGER ACCOUNTS

| | General Fund | Special Revenue Funds | Bond Funds | Special Assessment Funds | Sinking Funds | Trust and Agency Funds | Working Capital Funds | Utility or Other Enterprise Funds | General Fixed Assets | General Bonded Debt and Interest |
|---|---|---|---|---|---|---|---|---|---|---|
| **ASSETS AND OTHER DEBITS.** | | | | | | | | | | |
| *Assets—other than Fixed* | | | | | | | | | | |
| Cash | x | x | x | | x | x | x | x | | |
| Cash for Construction | | | | x | | | | | | |
| Cash for Bond Payments | | | | x | | | | | | |
| Cash for Interest Payments | | | | x | | | | | | |
| Cash for Note and Interest Payments | | | | x | | | | | | |
| Cash with Fiscal Agents | x | | | | x | | | | | x |
| Petty Cash | x | x | x | x | x | x | x | x | | |
| Taxes Receivable—Current | x | x | | | x | | | | | |

[2] This section adapted from: National Committee on Governmental Accounting, *Municipal Accounting and Auditing* (1951), Part I, and *A Standard Classification of Municipal Accounts* (1953). Municipal Finance Officers Association of the United States and Canada.

LIST OF GENERAL LEDGER ACCOUNTS—CONTINUED

| | General Fund | Special Revenue Funds | Bond Funds | Special Assessment Funds | Sinking Funds | Trust and Agency Funds | Working Capital Funds | Utility or Other Enterprise Funds | General Fixed Assets | General Bonded Debt and Interest |
|---|---|---|---|---|---|---|---|---|---|---|
| *Assets—other than Fixed (cont.)* | | | | | | | | | | |
| Estimated Uncollectible Current Taxes (Credit) | x | x | | | x | | | | | |
| Taxes Receivable—Delinquent | x | x | | | x | | | | | |
| Estimated Uncollectible Delinquent Taxes (Credit) | x | x | | | x | | | | | |
| Interest and Penalties Receivable on Taxes | x | x | | | x | | | | | |
| Estimated Uncollectible Interest and Penalties Receivable on Taxes (Credit) | x | x | | | x | | | | | |
| Tax Liens Receivable | x | x | | | x | | | | | |
| Estimated Uncollectible Tax Liens (Credit) | x | x | | | x | | | | | |
| Accounts Receivable | x | x | x | | | | x | x | | |
| Estimated Uncollectible Accounts Receivable (Credit) | x | x | x | | | | | x | | |
| Special Assessments—Receivable Current: | | | | | | | | | | |
|     For Construction | | | | x | | | | | | |
|     For Bond Payments | | | | x | | | | | | |
| Special Assessments—Receivable Delinquent: | | | | | | | | | | |
|     For Construction | | | | x | | | | | | |
|     For Bond Payments | | | | x | | | | | | |
| Special Assessments—Receivable Deferred: | | | | | | | | | | |
|     For Construction | | | | x | | | | | | |
|     For Bond Payments | | | | x | | | | | | |
| Special Assessment Liens Receivable: | | | | | | | | | | |
|     For Construction | | | | x | | | | | | |
|     For Bond Payments | | | | x | | | | | | |
| Municipality's Share of Assessment Improvement Costs (Specify fund from which these costs are receivable) | | | | x | | | | | | |
| Due from Other Funds | x | x | x | x | | x | x | x | | |
| Notes Receivable | | | | | | | | x | | |
| Loans Receivable | | | | | | | x | | | |
| Interest Receivable on Assessments | | | | x | | | | | | |

| | General Fund | Special Revenue Funds | Bond Funds | Special Assessment Funds | Sinking Funds | Trust and Agency Funds | Working Capital Funds | Utility or Other Enterprise Funds | General Fixed Assets | General Bonded Debt and Interest |
|---|---|---|---|---|---|---|---|---|---|---|
| Interest Receivable on Investments | x | x | x | | x | x | | x | | |
| Accrued Interest on Investments Purchased | x | x | x | | x | x | | x | | |
| Due from Other Governmental Units | x | | | | | | | | | |
| Taxes Levied for Other Governmental Units | | | | | | x | | | | |
| Unbilled Accounts Receivable | | | | | | | | x | | |
| Inventory of Materials and Supplies | x | x | | | | | x | x | | |
| Inventory of Stores Purchased for Resale | | | | | | | | x | | |
| Investments | x | x | x | | x | x | | x | | |
| Unamortized Premiums on Investments | | | | | x | x | | x | | |
| Unamortized Discounts on Investments (Credit) | | | | | x | x | | x | | |
| Prepaid Expenses | | | | | | | | x | | |
| Engineering Development Expense | | | | | | | | x | | |
| Unamortized Discounts on Bonds Sold | | | | | | | | x | | |
| *Fixed Assets* | | | | | | | | | | |
| Land | | | | | | | x | x | x | |
| Buildings | | | | | | | x | x | x | |
| Allowance for Depreciation—Buildings (Credit) | | | | | | | x | x | | |
| Improvements Other Than Buildings | | | | | | | x | x | x | |
| Allowance for Depreciation—Improvements Other Than Buildings (Credit) | | | | | | | x | x | | |
| Machinery and Equipment | | | | | | | x | x | x | |
| Allowance for Depreciation—Machinery and Equipment (Credit) | | | | | | | x | x | | |
| Construction Work in Progress | | | | | | | | x | x | |
| *Other Debits* | | | | | | | | | | |
| Estimated Revenues | x | x | | | | | | | | |
| Revenues (Credit) | x | x | | | | | | | | |
| Bonds Authorized—Unissued | | | x | | | | | | | |
| Bonds Eligible to be Sold (Credit) | | | | x | | | | | | |
| Improvements Authorized | | | x | x | | | | | | |
| Required Sinking Fund Contribution | | | | | x | | | | | |

## LIST OF GENERAL LEDGER ACCOUNTS—CONTINUED

| | General Fund | Special Revenue Funds | Bond Funds | Special Assessment Funds | Sinking Funds | Trust and Agency Funds | Working Capital Funds | Utility or Other Enterprise Funds | General Fixed Assets | General Bonded Debt and Interest |
|---|---|---|---|---|---|---|---|---|---|---|
| **Other Debits (cont.)** | | | | | | | | | | |
| Contribution Revenues (Credit) | | | | | x | | | | | |
| Required Sinking Fund Earnings | | | | | x | | | | | |
| Interest Earnings (Credit) | | | | | x | x | | | | |
| Required Pension Fund Contribution from Municipality | | | | | | x | | | | |
| Contribution—Municipality (Credit) | | | | | | x | | | | |
| Required Pension Fund Contribution from Employees | | | | | | x | | | | |
| Contribution—Employees (Credit) | | | | | | x | | | | |
| Required Pension Fund Earnings | | | | | | x | | | | |
| Amount Available in Sinking Fund | | | | | | | | | | x |
| Amount to be Provided for Payment of Bonds | | | | | | | | | | x |
| Amount to be Provided for Payment of Interest | | | | | | | | | | x |
| **LIABILITIES, OTHER CREDITS, AND SURPLUS.** | | | | | | | | | | |
| *Liabilities—other than Long-Term* | | | | | | | | | | |
| Vouchers Payable | x | x | x | x | | x | x | x | | |
| Unaudited Accounts Payable | x | x | x | x | | | x | x | | |
| Judgments Payable | x | x | x | x | | | | | | |
| Pensions Payable | | | | | | x | | | | |
| Contracts Payable—Uncompleted Contracts | x | x | x | x | | | | x | | |
| Contracts Payable—Retained Percentage | | | x | x | | | | x | | |
| Due to Other Funds | x | x | x | | | x | x | x | | |
| Due to Other Governmental Units | x | | | | | | | | | |
| Matured Bonds Payable | x | | | | x | | | x | | |
| Matured Interest Payable | x | | | | | | | x | | |
| Interest Payable on Customers' Deposits | | | | | | | | x | | |
| Accrued Interest Payable | | | | | x | | | x | | |
| Accrued Wages Payable | | | | | | | | x | | |
| Accrued Taxes Payable | | | | | | | | x | | |
| Customers' Deposits Payable | | | | | | | | x | | |
| Taxes Collected in Advance | x | x | | | | | | | | |
| Revenues Collected in Advance | | | | | | | | x | | |
| Unamortized Premiums on Bonds Sold | | | | | | | | x | | |

| | General Fund | Special Revenue Funds | Bond Funds | Special Assessment Funds | Sinking Funds | Trust and Agency Funds | Working Capital Funds | Utility or Other Enterprise Funds | General Fixed Assets | General Bonded Debt and Interest |
|---|---|---|---|---|---|---|---|---|---|---|
| *Long-Term Liabilities* | | | | | | | | | | |
| Bonds Payable | | | | x | | | | x | | x |
| Interest Payable on Bonds in Future Years | | | | | | | | | | x |
| *Other Credits* | | | | | | | | | | |
| Appropriations | x | x | x | x | | | | | | |
| Appropriation Expenditures (Debit) | x | x | | | | | | | | |
| Expenditures (Debit) | | | x | x | | | | | | |
| Encumbrances (Debit) | x | x | x | x | | | | | | |
| Reserve for Encumbrances | x | x | x | x | | | | | | |
| Reserve for Encumbrances—Prior Years | x | x | | | | | | | | |
| Expenditures Chargeable Against Reserve for Encumbrances (Debit) | x | x | | | | | | | | |
| Contributions from Other Funds | | | | | | | x | | | |
| Municipality's Contribution | | | | | | | | x | | |
| Reserve for Retirement of Sinking Fund Bonds | | | | | x | | | x· | | |
| Reserve for Retirements | | | | | | x | | | | |
| Reserve for Rebates | | | | x | | | | | | |
| Trust and Agency Fund Balances | | | | | | x | | | | |
| *Surplus* | | | | | | | | | | |
| Unappropriated Surplus | x | x | x | | x | x | x | | | |
| Unappropriated Surplus—Construction | | | | x | | | | | | |
| Unappropriated Surplus—Interest | | | | x | | | | | | |
| Unappropriated Budget Surplus | x | x | | | | | | | | |
| Earned Surplus | | | | | | | | x | | |
| Reserve for Inventories | x | x | | | | | | | | |
| Investment in General Fixed Assets | | | | | | | | | x | |

**Recording budgetary provisions.** Governmental units formally record the provisions of the budget in their books of account. This explains the inclusion, in the above listing, of the following accounts:

1. Estimated revenues (debit).
2. Appropriations (credit).
3. Encumbrances (debit).
4. Reserve for encumbrances (credit).

In addition to these general ledger accounts, subsidiary accounts are set up to categorically control actual revenue and expenditures by comparing them with the appropriate budgeted amount. Thus, each estimated revenue and corresponding actual revenue are set up in the same subsidiary account. Similarly, each appropriation and related expenditure and encumbrance account are set up in a single subsidiary account.

The reserve for encumbrances, however, is shown only in the general ledger. Under the encumbrance system, which is in general use in governmental units, purchase obligations or other commitments chargeable against an appropriation are entered on the books as soon as incurred, with a reserve for encumbrances being set up to provide a self-balancing account. But only the encumbrance, not the reserve, is entered in the appropriate subsidiary account. When the goods or services encumbered are received, the encumbrances entry originally set up for these goods or services is reversed.

**Bases of accounting.** There are three bases of accounting used by governmental units:

1. *Cash basis.* Revenues and expenditures are recorded only when cash is collected or paid out.

2. *Accrual basis.* Revenues are recorded when earned or entered in the tax roll, while expenditures are reflected on the books when the liability is incurred.

3. *Modified cash (or accrual) basis.* Revenues are recorded on the cash basis, but expenditures are recorded on the accrual basis.

▶ OBSERVATION: Due to the fact that certain revenues are not billed, many governmental units that record most of their revenues on an accrual basis will record some when collected. Likewise, even though a municipality may record most charges as soon as incurred, it will not record some expenses that are payable in the next year. These exceptions do not preclude a governmental unit being considered on the accrual basis—it is generally considered sufficient if the more important items are accrued.

▶ NOTE: All the journal entries and financial statements illustrated in this chapter are based upon the accrual method.

### OPERATION OF THE GENERAL FUND [3]

The general fund is the most important fund of the governmental unit, since it deals with the basic services supplied by general governmental

[3] This section adapted from: National Committee on Government Accounting, *Municipal Accounting and Auditing,* Part II, pages 19 to 35. Municipal Finance Officers Association of the United States and Canada, 1951.

activities. All revenues and activities not provided for in other funds are accounted for in the general fund. Therefore, the general fund receives a much greater variety of revenues and covers a much wider range of activities than do other funds. The following will be discussed and illustrated:

1. The relation of the general fund to other funds.
2. The relation of the general fund to the budget.
3. The accounting cycle for the general fund.
4. General fund financial statements.

**The relation of the general fund to other funds.** The general fund has dealings with all of the other funds in operation. Following is a summary of the transactions that affect both the general fund and another fund, as indicated:

1. *Special revenue fund.* The general fund may collect certain taxes for the special revenue fund. The amounts collected are subsequently transferred to the special revenue fund.

2. *Bond fund.* Premiums on bond issues in the bond fund are usually transferred to the general fund at once, while the general fund makes transfers to the bond fund to compensate for bond discounts.

▶ EXCEPTION: In some cases, the bond discount and premium are handled through a special revenue fund instead of through the general fund (see page 1098).

3. *Special assessment fund.* When it is necessary to finance special assessment projects, the required cash is collected in the general fund and then transferred to a special assessment fund.

4. *Sinking fund.* Sinking fund contributions are frequently appropriated for in the general fund and subsequently transferred to the sinking fund. Debt retirement payments are sometimes made through the general fund by transferring the required amount of cash from the sinking fund to the general fund. Also, as with a special revenue fund, certain taxes may be collected by the general fund and transferred to the sinking fund.

5. *Trust and agency funds.* The governmental unit's required contributions to a trust fund, such as a pension fund, are made through the general fund, then transferred to the trust fund.

6. *Working capital fund and utility or other enterprise fund.* Both a working capital and a utility or other enterprise fund are usually set up by original contributions of capital from the general fund. Charges by either of these funds to the governmental unit for services rendered are paid by the general fund.

▶ TRANSFER OF SURPLUS: Another transaction that could arise would be the transfer of the unappropriated surplus of any of the other funds to the general fund. However, legislative action is necessary before this can be done.

**The relation of the general fund to the budget.** The estimates for operating expenses and revenues apply primarily to the general fund. There are two reasons for this. First, all of the expenditures of the general fund must be made pursuant to appropriations that lapse annually. Second, as has been already pointed out, the general fund embraces many more activities than any other fund. The recording of budgetary provisions was discussed in general on pages 1081 and 1082. Specific entries are illustrated and explained in the following delineation of the accounting cycle.

**The accounting cycle for the general fund.** *Recording the budget.* The initial step in accounting for general fund operation is to record the adoption of the budget. The entry, if we assume that estimated revenues exceed appropriations, is as follows:

| | | |
|---|---|---|
| Estimated revenues | 1,350,000 | |
| Appropriations | | 1,300,000 |
| Unappropriated surplus | | 50,000 |
| To record adoption of budget. | | |

The above entry is reflected only in the general ledger, with postings made to the subsidiary accounts for the various revenues and appropriations. If appropriations exceed estimated revenues, there would be a debit entry in the unappropriated surplus account. Increases or decreases in estimated revenues or appropriations require the appropriate debit or credit entry to unappropriated surplus.

*Handling general property taxes.* The operation of the general fund actually begins when revenue is accrued or received and expenditures are made. The first step is generally the recording of the levy of general property taxes:

| | | |
|---|---|---|
| Taxes receivable—Current | 884,300 | |
| Estimated uncollectible current taxes | | 8,800 |
| Revenues | | 875,500 |
| To record levy of taxes. | | |

When current taxes are collected, the following entry is made:

| | | |
|---|---|---|
| Cash | 840,000 | |
| Taxes receivable—Current | | 840,000 |
| To record collection of current taxes. | | |

Other entries involving tax transactions are as follows:

| | | |
|---|---|---|
| Taxes receivable—Delinquent | 44,300 | |
| Estimated uncollectible current taxes | 8,800 | |
|   Taxes receivable—Current | | 44,300 |
|   Estimated uncollectible delinquent taxes | | 8,800 |

To record taxes becoming delinquent.

| | | |
|---|---|---|
| Cash | 20,000 | |
|   Taxes receivable—Delinquent | | 20,000 |

To record collection of delinquent taxes.

| | | |
|---|---|---|
| Interest and penalties receivable on taxes | 3,500 | |
|   Estimated uncollectible interest and penalties | | 700 |
|   Revenues | | 2,800 |

To record interest and penalties on delinquent
taxes and to provide for uncollectible interest
and penalties.

| | | |
|---|---|---|
| Cash | 1,400 | |
|   Interest and penalties receivable on taxes | | 1,400 |

To record collection of interest and penalties
on taxes previously set up as receivable.

| | | |
|---|---|---|
| Tax liens receivable | 17,100 | |
|   Taxes receivable—Delinquent | | 15,000 |
|   Interest and penalties receivable on taxes | | 2,100 |

To record conversion of delinquent taxes
and interest and penalties thereon into
tax liens.

| | | |
|---|---|---|
| Tax liens receivable | 300 | |
|   Cash | | 300 |

To record cost of conversion of delinquent
taxes and interest and penalties thereon
into tax liens.

| | | |
|---|---|---|
| Estimated uncollectible delinquent taxes | 4,000 | |
| Estimated uncollectible interest and penalties | 500 | |
|   Estimated uncollectible tax liens | | 4,500 |

To transfer estimated uncollectible
taxes and interest and penalties to
estimated uncollectible tax liens.

| | | |
|---|---|---|
| Cash | 4,100 | |
| Estimated uncollectible tax liens | 1,100 | |
|   Tax liens receivable | | 5,200 |

To record collection of tax liens and
to write off uncollectible tax liens.

| | | |
|---|---:|---:|
| Cash | 15,000 | |
|     Taxes collected in advance | | 15,000 |

To record taxes collected in advance
of their levy.

| | | |
|---|---:|---:|
| Taxes collected in advance | 3,000 | |
|     Revenues | | 3,000 |

To record taxes collected in advance
that have become due.

*Recording other revenues.* There are eight main groups of general fund revenues other than general property taxes. These groups are:

1. Other taxes.
2. Licenses and permits.
3. Fines, forfeits, and other penalties.
4. Revenue from use of money or property.
5. Revenue from other agencies.
6. Charges for current services.
7. Sales of fixed assets and compensation for loss of fixed assets.
8. Transfers from other funds.

▶ REVENUES DEFINED: Revenues are (1) additions to assets that do not increase any liability or represent the recovery of an expenditure, and (2) the cancellation of liabilities without a corresponding increase in other liabilities or a decrease in assets.

Other taxes are handled in the same manner as general property taxes. The following journal entries illustrate how revenues from the other sources listed above are recorded:

| | | |
|---|---:|---:|
| Accounts receivable | 15,000 | |
|     Estimated uncollectible accounts | | 1,300 |
|     Revenues | | 13,700 |

To record billings for services rendered
and to provide for uncollectible
accounts.

| | | |
|---|---:|---:|
| Due from other governmental units | 186,500 | |
|     Revenues | | 186,500 |

To record grants-in-aid due from
other governmental units.

| | | |
|---|---:|---:|
| Cash | 202,000 | |
|     Due from other governmental units | | 172,000 |
|     Accounts receivable | | 30,000 |

To record collection of various
receivables,

If the revenues collected had not been accrued, the entry is as follows:

| | | |
|---|---|---|
| Cash | 233,000 | |
|   Revenues | | 233,000 |

To record collection of revenues not
  previously accrued.

Postings are also made to the individual revenue accounts involved.

*Accounting for expenditures.* Expenditures by the general fund have a broader meaning than in commercial accounting or in the commercial-type governmental funds. This is due to the fact that no fixed assets or long-term debt are carried in the general fund. As a result, general fund expenditures are classified by *character,* i.e., on the basis of the fiscal period that they are presumed to benefit. The chief character classes are:

1. *Current expenses,* which can be further classified by *object* into (a) personal services, (b) contractual services, (c) materials and supplies, and (d) financial charges, including retirement of serial bonds.

2. *Retirement of term bonds.*

3. *Capital outlays,* which can be further classified by *object* into (a) land, (b) buildings, (c) improvements other than buildings, such as sidewalks, highways, drives, tunnels, drains, and sewers, and (d) machinery and equipment.

Expenditure accounts such as those listed above are grouped together under broader classifications known as *functions* and *activities.* *Function* relates to the purpose to be accomplished by expenditures, and *activity* to a specific line of work carried on to accomplish a function. For example, the collection of vital statistics and the regulation and inspection of milk and dairy products are activities performed in connection with the health function.

▶ OBSERVATION: Since a clear-cut distinction between functions and activities is not always practicable, the classification often is referred to as a classification of expenditures by activities rather than by functions *and* activities. However, since the account for any function reflects the sum total of accounts for all the activities making up that function, there is no need in such cases to have *special* functional accounts in addition to the regular activities accounts.

*Handling encumbrances.* Under the encumbrance system, when an order is placed the following entry is made:

| | | |
|---|---|---|
| Encumbrances | 300,000 | |
|   Reserve for encumbrances—Current year | | 300,000 |

To record encumbrances in the form of
  purchase orders and open market contracts.

Postings are also made to the individual appropriation accounts charging them with the amount of the encumbrances applicable to them, thereby reducing the amount of the appropriation available for additional expenditures or encumbrances. When the materials and the invoice relating to the order are received, so that the actual liability is determined, the encumbrance is cancelled by reversing the above entry for the amount of the encumbrance involved. In addition, credit postings are made to the proper subsidiary appropriation accounts, along with debit postings to expenditures in the same accounts. Assuming that orders representing a recorded encumbrance of $262,000 are delivered, and that these purchase orders actually cost only $260,000, the entries are:

| | | |
|---|---|---|
| Reserve for encumbrances—Current year | 262,000 | |
|   Encumbrances | | 262,000 |
| To record cancellation of encumbrances. | | |
| | | |
| Appropriation expenditures | 260,000 | |
|   Vouchers Payable | | 260,000 |
| To record actual expenditures. | | |

Certain types of appropriations, however, are not charged until the actual liability is incurred. These appropriations are for (1) salaries and wages that have been fixed by law or regulation for the entire fiscal period, (2) bond and interest payments, which are made in compliance with contractual terms under pertinent laws, and (3) judgments and other payments made pursuant to legal requirements. No useful purpose would be served by encumbering such expenditures. The entry to record expenditures for which no encumbrances have previously been set up is as follows:

| | | |
|---|---|---|
| Appropriation expenditures | 940,000 | |
|   Vouchers payable | | 767,850 |
|   Judgments payable | | 20,000 |
|   Contracts payable | | 62,600 |
|   Due to other funds | | 10,000 |
|   Matured bonds payable | | 42,500 |
|   Matured interest payable | | 37,050 |
| To record expenditures for which no encumbrances<br>  have been previously set up. | | |

▶ OBSERVATION: Some of the smaller governmental units do not record encumbrances in the accounts. They maintain a file of unfilled orders that is checked to determine whether there are any encumbrances chargeable against the appropriation to which a proposed purchase is to be charged.

*Recording cash disbursements.* Following are representative entries reflecting cash disbursements:

| | | |
|---|---:|---:|
| Cash with fiscal agents for payment of bonds and interest | 77,750 | |
|     Cash | | 77,750 |
| To record transmittal of cash to fiscal agent for payment of bonds and interest. | | |
| | | |
| Temporary investments | 65,000 | |
| Accrued interest on investments purchased | 50 | |
|     Cash | | 65,050 |
| To record purchase of temporary investments and accrued interest thereon. | | |
| | | |
| Due from other funds | 24,000 | |
|     Cash | | 24,000 |
| To record loans to other funds. | | |
| | | |
| Matured interest payable | 34,550 | |
| Matured bonds payable | 40,000 | |
|     Cash with fiscal agents for payment of bonds and interest | | 74,550 |
| To record payment of bonds and interest by fiscal agent. | | |
| | | |
| Judgments payable | 25,000 | |
| Contracts payable | 27,000 | |
| Due to other funds | 3,000 | |
| Vouchers payable | 800,000 | |
|     Cash | | 855,000 |
| To record payment of various liabilities. | | |

*Closing the accounts.* At the end of the fiscal period, the budgetary and operating accounts are closed out. Assuming that actual revenues are less than estimated revenues, the entry to close out revenues is as follows:

| | | |
|---|---:|---:|
| Revenues | 1,314,500 | |
| Unappropriated surplus | 35,500 | |
|     Estimated revenues | | 1,350,000 |
| To close out the revenue accounts. | | |

Postings would be also made to the subsidiary revenue accounts for the net difference between estimated and actual revenues.

If not all of the appropriations were used or obligated, the entry to close out appropriations, expenditures, and encumbrances is:

| | | |
|---|---:|---:|
| Appropriations | 1,300,000 | |
|     Appropriation expenditures | | 1,200,000 |
|     Encumbrances | | 38,000 |
|     Unappropriated surplus | | 62,000 |
| To close out appropriations, expenditures, and encumbrances. | | |

Postings would also be made to the subsidiary appropriation accounts to close out the net difference between (1) the appropriations and (2) expenditures plus encumbrances. It should be noted that the above entry does not close out the reserve for encumbrances. Instead, this reserve is carried forward into the following year and is charged, by means of an expenditures account, with the actual expenditures when they are determined. The following entry is made at the beginning of the next year:

| | | |
|---|---|---|
| Reserve for encumbrances—Current year | 38,000 | |
|   Reserve for encumbrances—Preceding year | | 38,000 |
| To set up the reserve for encumbrances | | |
|   carried forward from preceding year. | | |

Now, assuming that during the following year purchase orders representing the above encumbrances were received and that the actual cost was only $37,500, this entry would be made:

| | | |
|---|---|---|
| Expenditures chargeable against reserve | | |
|     for encumbrances—Preceding year | 37,500 | |
|   Vouchers payable | | 37,500 |
| To record expenditures resulting from | | |
|   encumbrances set up during preceding year. | | |

At the end of the year an entry to close out the accounts pertaining to the preceding year is required:

| | | |
|---|---|---|
| Reserve for encumbrances—Preceding year | 38,000 | |
|   Expenditures chargeable against reserve | | |
|     for encumbrances—Preceding year | | 37,500 |
|   Unappropriated surplus | | 500 |
| To close out the expenditures chargeable | | |
|   against the reserve for encumbrances | | |
|   carried forward from preceding year. | | |

▶ ANOTHER METHOD: Some governmental units close out both the encumbrances and the reserve for encumbrances at the end of the year. In such instances, recognition must be given in the budget to purchase orders outstanding at the close of the year. When the new budget is approved, an entry must be made debiting the encumbrances account and crediting the reserve for encumbrances account for the estimated cost of these purchase orders. Thereafter the procedure is the same as for other appropriations encumbered during the fiscal period. It should be remembered, however, that there must be an appropriation account available against which the encumbrance and resultant expenditures can be charged. Otherwise, such encumbrances and expenditures are invalid.

*Handling inventories.* If a governmental unit wants to reflect on the books the value of closing inventories of materials and supplies, a reserve account must be set up as follows:

| | | |
|---|---|---|
| Inventory of materials and supplies | 10,000 | |
| Reserve for inventories | | 10,000 |

To record inventories on hand at end of the year.

When there is already an inventory account on the books, an adjustment is made to show the ending inventory. Assuming a net decrease of $5,000 in inventory during the year, the following entry is required:

| | | |
|---|---|---|
| Reserve for inventories | 5,000 | |
| Inventory of materials and supplies | | 5,000 |

To record the decrease in inventory during the fiscal year.

Appropriation expenditures may be charged on a consumption basis. When this is combined with a periodic inventory, the entries are:

| | | |
|---|---|---|
| Appropriation expenditures | 5,000 | |
| Inventory of materials and supplies | | 5,000 |

To record the decrease in inventory during the fiscal year.

| | | |
|---|---|---|
| Reserve for inventories | 5,000 | |
| Unappropriated surplus | | 5,000 |

To restore to unappropriated surplus inventory reserve no longer needed.

A perpetual inventory method combined with the use of the consumption basis results in the following series of entries:

| | | |
|---|---|---|
| Inventory of materials and supplies | 90,000 | |
| Vouchers payable | | 90,000 |

To record the purchases of stores.

| | | |
|---|---|---|
| Appropriation expenditures | 95,000 | |
| Inventory of materials and supplies | | 95,000 |

To charge expenditures with stores issued.

| | | |
|---|---|---|
| Reserve for inventories | 5,000 | |
| Unappropriated surplus | | 5,000 |

To restore to unappropriated surplus inventory reserve no longer needed.

**General fund financial statements.** The four most essential types of statements for the general fund are:

1. Balance sheet.
2. Analysis of changes in unappropriated surplus.
3. Comparison of actual revenues with estimated revenues.
4. Comparison of authorizations with expenditures and encumbrances.

These statements are illustrated in Figures 1, 3, 4, and 5. In addition, an interim balance sheet is shown in Figure 2.

# A GOVERNMENTAL UNIT

### General Fund
### Balance Sheet
### June 30, 19____

| Assets | | | Liabilities, Reserves, and Surplus | | |
|---|---|---|---|---|---|
| Cash | | $ 72,750 | Liabilities: | | |
| Temporary Investments | | 65,000 | Vouchers Payable | $34,900 | |
| Taxes Receivable—Delinquent | $49,300 | | Due to Other Funds | 10,000 | |
| Less Estimated Uncollectible | | | Taxes Collected in Advance | 15,000 | $ 59,900 |
| Taxes | 12,800 | 36,500 | | | |
| | | | Reserves: | | |
| Accounts Receivable | $20,300 | | Reserve for Encumbrances | $38,000 | |
| Less Estimated Uncollectible | | | Reserve for Inventories | 5,700 | 43,700 |
| Accounts | 4,000 | 16,300 | | | |
| Due from Other Funds | | 16,000 | Unappropriated Surplus | | 108,650 |
| Materials and Supplies | | 5,700 | | | |
| | | $212,250 | | | $212,250 |

Fig. 1. General Fund Balance Sheet (End of Fiscal Year).

A GOVERNMENTAL UNIT

General Fund
Balance Sheet
March 31, 19___

| *Assets* | | | |
|---|---:|---:|---:|
| Cash | | | $ 61,850 |
| Temporary Investments | | | 65,000 |
| Taxes Receivable—Current | | $ 58,300 | |
| Less Estimated Uncollectible Taxes | | 9,800 | 48,500 |
| Taxes Receivable—Delinquent | | $ 10,000 | |
| Less Estimated Uncollectible Taxes | | 3,000 | 7,000 |
| Accounts Receivable | | $ 22,000 | |
| Less Estimated Uncollectible Accounts | | 4,000 | 18,000 |
| Due from Other Funds | | | 14,000 |
| Materials and Supplies | | | 6,500 |
| Estimated Revenues | | $900,000 | |
| Less Revenues | | 856,000 | 44,000 |
| | | | $264,850 |

| *Liabilities, Appropriations, Reserves, and Surplus* | | | |
|---|---:|---:|---:|
| Liabilities: | | | |
| Vouchers Payable | | $ 27,900 | |
| Due to Other Funds | | 12,000 | |
| Due to Other Governmental Units | | 9,000 | |
| Taxes Collected in Advance | | 15,000 | $ 63,900 |
| Appropriations | | $880,000 | |
| Less Appropriation | | | |
| Expenditures | $800,000 | | |
| Encumbrances | 42,000 | 842,000 | 38,000 |
| Reserves: | | | |
| Reserve for Encumbrances | | $ 42,000 | |
| Reserve for Inventories | | 6,500 | 48,500 |
| Unappropriated Surplus | | | 114,450 |
| | | | $264,850 |

**Fig. 2. General Fund Interim Balance Sheet.**

A GOVERNMENTAL UNIT
General Fund
Analysis of Changes in Unappropriated Surplus
For Fiscal Year Ending June 30, 19___

| | Estimated | Actual | Actual Over or (Under) |
|---|---|---|---|
| Unappropriated Surplus, July 1, 19___ | $ 43,600 | $ 43,600 | |
| Add: | | | |
| Reserve for Encumbrances, July 1, 19___ | 37,500 | 37,500 | |
| Reserve for Inventories, July 1, 19___ | 6,000 | 6,000 | |
| Revenues | 900,000 | 912,500 | $12,500 |
| Total Balances and Additions | $987,100 | $999,600 | $12,500 |
| Deduct: | | | |
| Expenditures | $880,000 | $847,250 | ($32,750) |
| Reserve for Encumbrances, June 30, 19___ | — | 38,000 | 38,000 |
| Reserve for Inventories, June 30, 19___ | — | 5,700 | 5,700 |
| Total Deductions | $880,000 | $890,950 | $10,950 |
| Unappropriated Surplus, June 30, 19___ | $107,100 | $108,650 | $ 1,550 |

**Fig. 3. Analysis of Changes in Unappropriated Surplus.**

A GOVERNMENTAL UNIT
General Fund
Statement of Revenue—Estimated and Actual
For Fiscal Year Ending June 30, 19___

| | Estimated Revenue | Actual Revenue | Actual Over or (Under) |
|---|---|---|---|
| General Property Taxes: | | | |
| Current Year's Levy | $ 880,000 | $ 878,500 | ($ 1,500) |
| Interest and Penalties on Taxes | 2,500 | 2,800 | 300 |
| Total General Property Taxes | $ 882,500 | $ 881,300 | ($ 1,200) |
| Other Local Taxes: | | | |
| Property Taxes on Other than Assessed valuation | $ 50,000 | $ 53,400 | $ 3,400 |
| Business Taxes | 105,000 | 103,600 | (1,400) |
| Sales Taxes | 200,000 | 221,000 | 21,000 |
| Poll Taxes | 15,000 | 15,050 | 50 |
| Total Other Local Taxes | $ 370,000 | $ 393,050 | $23,050 |

**Fig. 4. Statement Showing Comparison of Actual Revenues with Estimated Revenues.**

| | | | |
|---|---|---|---|
| Licenses and Permits: | | | |
| Licenses and Permits for Street Use | $ 15,500 | $ 16,000 | $ 500 |
| Business Licenses | 90,000 | 66,000 | (24,000) |
| Non-Business Licenses and Permits | 20,000 | 21,000 | 1,000 |
| Total Licenses and Permits | $ 125,500 | $ 103,000 | ($22,500) |
| Fines, Forfeits, and Penalties: | | | |
| Fines | $ 15,000 | $ 15,700 | $ 700 |
| Forfeits | 5,000 | 5,500 | 500 |
| Penalties | 12,500 | 12,000 | (500) |
| Total Fines, Forfeits, and Penalties | $ 32,500 | $ 33,200 | $ 700 |
| Revenue from Use of Money and Property: | | | |
| Interest Earnings | $ 1,500 | $ 2,000 | $ 500 |
| Rents and Concessions | 18,000 | 17,500 | (500) |
| Total Revenue from Use of Money and Property | $ 19,500 | $ 19,500 | — |
| Revenue from Other Agencies: | | | |
| Shared State Taxes | $ 95,000 | $ 92,000 | ($ 3,000) |
| State Grants-in-Aid | 50,000 | 36,000 | (14,000) |
| Grants from Federal Government | 55,000 | 58,500 | 3,500 |
| Total Revenue from Other Agencies | $ 200,000 | $ 186,500 | ($13,500) |
| Charges for Current Services: | | | |
| General Government | $ 40,000 | $ 45,000 | $ 5,000 |
| Public Safety | 10,000 | 11,000 | 1,000 |
| Highways | 8,000 | 8,500 | 500 |
| Sanitation and Waste Removal | 12,000 | 11,000 | (1,000) |
| Recreation | 20,000 | 15,500 | (4,500) |
| Total Charges for Current Services | $ 90,000 | $ 91,000 | $ 1,000 |
| Grand Total | $1,720,000 | $1,707,550 | $12,450 |

**Fig. 4. Statement Showing Comparison of Actual Revenues with Estimated Revenues. (Continued.)**

## OPERATION OF SPECIAL FUNDS [4]

The journal entries to illustrate the operation of the general fund were given in full detail. Since the other funds operate either under conditions similar to the general fund or along the customary lines of comparable commercial activities, the discussion of the operations of special funds will be more limited so as to avoid covering already familiar ground. A thorough knowledge of the handling of general fund transactions plus the accountant's private experience should, in conjunction with this limited coverage, be sufficient for an understanding of how the other funds operate.

[4] This section adapted from: National Committee on Governmental Accounting, *Municipal Accounting and Auditing,* Part II, pages 36 to 125. Municipal Finance Officers Association of the United States and Canada, 1951.

# A GOVERNMENTAL UNIT
## General Fund
### Statement of Expenditures and Encumbrances—Compared with Authorizations
### For Fiscal Year Ending June 30, 19___

| | Appropriations (after Revisions) | Reserve for Encumbrances Outstanding at Beginning of Year | Total | Expenditures | Unexpended Balance | Encumbrances Outstanding at Close of Year | Unencumbered Balance |
|---|---|---|---|---|---|---|---|
| **GENERAL GOVERNMENT:** | | | | | | | |
| Control: | | | | | | | |
| Legislative | | | | | | | |
| Personal Services | $ 15,000 | | $ 15,000 | $ 14,500 | $ 500 | $ 500 | — |
| Other Current Expenses | 5,000 | $ 400 | 5,400 | 5,400 | — | — | — |
| Total | $ 20,000 | $ 400 | $ 20,400 | $ 19,900 | $ 500 | $ 500 | — |
| Executive | | | | | | | |
| Personal Services | $ 10,000 | | $ 10,000 | $ 10,000 | | | |
| Other Current Expenses | 1,500 | $ 200 | 1,700 | 1,600 | $ 100 | — | $ 100 |
| Equipment | 750 | 300 | 1,050 | 1,030 | 20 | — | 20 |
| Total Executive | $ 12,250 | $ 500 | $ 12,750 | $ 12,630 | $ 120 | — | $ 120 |
| Judicial | | | | | | | |
| Personal Services | $ 15,000 | | $ 15,000 | $ 14,200 | $ 800 | $ 400 | $ 400 |
| Other Current Expenses | 6,000 | | 6,000 | 5,400 | 600 | 300 | 300 |
| Equipment | 1,000 | $ 800 | 1,800 | 1,600 | 200 | 200 | — |
| Total Judicial | $ 22,000 | $ 800 | $ 22,800 | $ 21,200 | $ 1,600 | $ 900 | $ 700 |
| Total Control | $ 54,250 | $ 1,700 | $ 55,950 | $ 53,730 | $ 2,220 | $ 1,400 | $ 820 |
| **Staff Agencies:** | | | | | | | |
| Total Staff Agencies | $ 84,750 | $ 1,300 | $ 86,050 | $ 79,375 | $ 6,675 | $ 2,700 | $ 3,975 |
| Total General Government | $ 139,000 | $ 3,000 | $ 142,000 | $ 133,105 | $ 8,895 | $ 4,100 | $ 4,795 |
| CONTRIBUTION TO PENSION FUND | $ 5,000 | — | $ 5,000 | $ 5,000 | — | — | — |
| INTEREST ON DEBT | 37,500 | — | 37,050 | 37,050 | — | — | — |
| REDEMPTION OF BONDS | 42,500 | — | 42,500 | 42,500 | — | — | — |
| Grand Total | $1,300,000 | $37,500 | $1,337,500 | $1,236,200 | $101,300 | $38,000 | $63,300 |

Fig. 5. Statement Showing Comparison of Authorizations with

**Special revenue funds.** A special revenue fund is used to account for revenues derived from specific taxes or other special sources, usually provided for by statute or charter to finance a particular activity. The fund may be employed for either current operating or capital outlay purposes. Its operation may encompass a limited area, such as the maintenance of some historic landmark, or a broad area, such as the support of a public school system or a school district. As additional examples, a special revenue fund could be established for the benefit of a park or a museum.

The operation of a special revenue fund is usually controlled through the general budget. The only difference, then, between a special revenue fund and the general fund is one of degree—revenues for a special revenue fund are limited to a single source or a few sources, and the activities of a special revenue fund are normally confined to a single purpose. Therefore, the journal entries and statements for a special revenue fund are similar to those for the general fund.

**Bond funds.** A bond fund is used to account for the receipt and disbursement of the proceeds of any bonds issued by the municipality except special assessment and utility or other enterprise bonds. A separate bond fund must be provided for each bond issue, and each fund must have its own self-balancing group of accounts. The bonds are usually authorized and issued for one of the following purposes:

1. Construction or purchase of improvements.
2. Funding operating deficits.
3. Refunding previous bond issues.
4. Providing a permanent revolving fund for municipal service activities or for improvements, including special assessment and utility or other enterprise improvements.

**The accounting cycle for a bond fund.** *Authorization of bonds.* The first entry in a bond fund is to record the authorization of bonds:

| | | |
|---|---:|---:|
| Bonds authorized—Unissued | 200,000 | |
| Appropriations | | 200,000 |
| To record authorization to issue bonds. | | |

*Sale of bonds.* The next step is to sell the bonds. Entries are as follows:

| | | |
|---|---:|---:|
| Cash | 202,000 | |
| Bonds authorized—Unissued | | 200,000 |
| Premium on bonds | | 2,000 |
| To record sale of bond issue at a premium. | | |
| Cash | 198,000 | |
| Discount on bonds | 2,000 | |
| Bonds authorized—Unissued | | 200,000 |
| To record sale of bond issue at a discount. | | |

At the same time, an entry is made in the general bonded debt and interest group of accounts:

| | | |
|---|---|---|
| Amount to be provided for payment of bonds | 200,000 | |
| Amount to be provided for payment of interest | 100,000 | |
| Bonds payable | | 200,000 |
| Interest payable on bonds in future years | | 100,000 |
| To record liability for bonds and interest payable | | |
| in future years. | | |

*Handling bond premium or discount.* A bond premium should be transferred to the fund that is going to pay the interest on the bonds (usually the general fund or a special revenue fund), since premiums represent an adjustment of the interest rate. The entry in the bond fund is:

| | | |
|---|---|---|
| Premium on bonds | 2,000 | |
| Cash | | 2,000 |
| To record transfer of premium to fund that | | |
| will pay the interest. | | |

Inasmuch as appropriations are made for the general fund or special revenue fund to pay the amount called for in the bond coupons, there is no object in setting up an unamortized premium account in the general ledger. Accordingly, the transfer from the bond fund is picked up as revenue in the appropriate fund, as follows:

| | | |
|---|---|---|
| Cash | 2,000 | |
| Revenues | | 2,000 |
| To record the receipt of the bond premium from bond fund. | | |

A bond discount, like a premium, represents an adjustment of the interest rate. Theoretically, then, it should be accounted for according to the same principles as a premium. In actual practice, however, this is not possible because legal provisions do not usually permit transfers from the general fund or the special revenue funds to eliminate the discount. Instead the appropriations account is reduced by the amount of the discount. The entry in the bond fund is:

| | | |
|---|---|---|
| Appropriations | 2,000 | |
| Discount on bonds | | 2,000 |
| To record closing out the bond discount into appropriations. | | |

*Accounting for operations.* Operating transactions are handled in the same manner as in the general fund. However, in funds involving construction or improvements, a certain percentage of the total contract price is frequently retained pending final inspection and acceptance of a project. This procedure is recorded as follows:

| | | |
|---|---:|---:|
| Contracts payable | 85,000 | |
| Contracts payable—Retained percentage | | 9,500 |
| Cash | | 75,500 |

To record a retention of 5% of total contract
price in making payments, pending inspection
and approval.

▶ OBSERVATION: Other funds involving construction or improvements
are special assessment funds and utility or other enterprise funds. The
above type of entry may also apply to these funds.

*Closing the accounts.* Closing entries for a bond fund are different than
those for the general fund. If the project for which the bonds were issued is
completed during the fiscal year in which the bonds were issued, the following entry is made:

| | | |
|---|---:|---:|
| Appropriations | 200,000 | |
| Appropriation expenditures | | 195,000 |
| Unappropriated surplus | | 5,000 |

To record the closing out of the appropriations and
expenditures accounts.

A corresponding entry is made in the general fixed assets group of accounts:

| | | |
|---|---:|---:|
| Appropriate fixed asset account | 195,000 | |
| Investment in general fixed assets— | | |
| From bonds | | 195,000 |

To record cost of fixed assets financed
from bond issue.

When the project is not completed during the current fiscal year, the
entry is:

| | | |
|---|---:|---:|
| Appropriations | 110,000 | |
| Appropriation expenditures | | 110,000 |

To record closing out of expenditures
for current fiscal year.

The corresponding entry in the general fixed assets group of accounts is as
follows:

| | | |
|---|---:|---:|
| Construction work in progress | 110,000 | |
| Investment in general fixed assets— | | |
| From bonds | | 110,000 |

To record cost of construction work in process
financed from bond issues.

Assuming that the project is completed during the next fiscal year, the
following entry is made at that time in the bond fund:

| | | |
|---|---|---|
| Appropriations | 90,000 | |
| Appropriation expenditures | | 85,000 |
| Unappropriated surplus | | 5,000 |

To record closing out of expenditures when project
is completed.

Again, a corresponding entry is required in the general fixed assets group
of accounts:

| | | |
|---|---|---|
| Appropriate fixed asset account | 195,000 | |
| Construction work in progress | | 110,000 |
| Investment in general fixed | | |
| assets—From bonds | | 85,000 |

To record cost of completed project and to close out
construction account.

*Dissolution of the fund.* The final step in accounting for the bond fund
is to record the dissolution of the fund when the project is completed. Any
unappropriated surplus is transferred to the fund that will make the payment at the time the bond issue is retired. In the case of serial bonds, this
is usually the general fund or a special revenue fund. In the case of term
bonds, it is usually a sinking fund, although frequently the assets of the
sinking fund are transferred to the general fund for the actual bond retirement payment. The entries are as follows:

| | | |
|---|---|---|
| Unappropriated surplus | 5,000 | |
| Cash | | 5,000 |

To record the closing out of the bond fund by
transfer of cash.

| | | |
|---|---|---|
| Cash | 5,000 | |
| Revenues (Contribution revenues) | | 5,000 |

To record receipt of cash representing transfer
of unappropriated surplus to general fund or
special revenue fund (sinking fund).

▶ HANDLING A DEFICIT: The encumbrance system is employed in the
operation of a bond fund, so no deficit should ordinarily arise. But if it
becomes apparent that a sizeable deficit will be incurred due to increased
costs of completing the project for which the bonds were issued, a supplementary bond issue is authorized and sold in order to raise the necessary
funds. The supplementary issue is accounted for in the same manner as the
original bond issue. When the deficit is small, and such action is not for-
bidden by law, the legislative body can authorize a transfer of the necessary
amount of cash from the general fund to the bond fund to cover the

anticipated deficit. Assuming there is a deficit of $1,000, the following entries would be in order:

| | | |
|---|---|---|
| Cash | 1,000 | |
|   Unappropriated surplus | | 1,000 |

To record the receipt of cash in the bond fund
  to remove deficit.

| | | |
|---|---|---|
| Appropriation expenditures | 1,000 | |
|   Cash | | 1,000 |

To record the transfer of cash in the general fund.

At any rate, provision must be made to remove the deficit from the bond fund before the fund is closed out.

**Bond fund financial statements.** The essential statements for a bond fund are:

1. Balance sheet.
2. Statement of cash receipts and disbursements.
3. Comparison of expenditures and encumbrances with appropriations.

Separate statements must be prepared for each bond fund. Figure 6 illustrates a year-end balance sheet for an uncompleted project being financed from bonds.

**Special assessment funds.** Special assessment funds are employed to finance permanent improvements or current services that benefit certain properties rather than the governmental unit as a whole. Permanent improvements include streets, sidewalks, curbs, gutters, sewers, and similar items. Current services financed by special assessments include such things as the cleaning, oiling, or lighting of streets, and the cleaning or maintenance of drainage ditches.

A separate fund must be created for each special assessment project. When a project is small and the required assessments can be collected in one or two installments, short-term borrowing may be resorted to. This is usually the case in financing current services. In the case of construction projects, however, the special assessment installments may cover a period of ten years or longer. Such extended financing is generally accomplished through long-term serial bonds. The levy of special assessments against benefited property owners, including the governmental unit itself, is generally spread out in installments over the life of the bonds. The annual collections from the taxpayers concerned are designed to cover current interest charges on the entire bond issue plus the principals of bonds being retired in that particular year. The following discussion deals with the typical long-term financing required in connection with a large construction project.

# A GOVERNMENTAL UNIT
## Bond Fund
### Balance Sheet
### June 30, 19___

| Assets | | |
|---|---:|---:|
| Cash | | $328,350 |
| Temporary Investments | | 100,000 |
| Accounts Receivable | $4,000 | |
| *Less* Estimated Uncollectible | | |
| Accounts | 500 | 3,500 |
| Due from Other Funds | | 6,000 |
| Bonds Authorized—Unissued | | 65,000 |
| | | $502,850 |

| *Liabilities, Appropriations, Reserves, and Surplus* | | | |
|---|---:|---:|---:|
| Liabilities: | | | |
| Vouchers Payable | | $17,000 | |
| Judgments Payable | | 9,100 | |
| Contracts Payable— | | | |
| Uncompleted Contracts | $78,000 | | |
| Completed Contracts— | | | |
| Retained Percentage | 15,000 | 93,000 | |
| Due to Other Funds | | 3,000 | $122,100 |
| Appropriations—Unencumbered | | | |
| Balances | | | 189,450 |
| Reserve for Encumbrances | | | 188,450 |
| Unappropriated Surplus | | | 2,850 |
| | | | $502,850 |

**Fig. 6. Bond Fund Balance Sheet.**

**The accounting cycle for a special assessment fund.** *Authorization of the project.* The accounting for a special assessment fund begins when the project is authorized. The entry is:

| | | |
|---|---|---|
| Improvements authorized | 200,000 | |
| Appropriations | | 200,000 |
| To record authorization of a | | |
| special assessment project. | | |

*Recording assessments and sale of bonds.* The next step is to record the levy and collection of assessments, and the sale of bonds. Assume that the project is to be financed by special assessments in the amount of $190,-000 plus a contribution from the general fund of $10,000, the latter to be paid at once. The first installment of special assessment collections will amount to $15,000, so only $175,000 worth of bonds has to be issued. The entries are:

| | | |
|---|---|---|
| Special assessments receivable—Deferred | 190,000 | |
| Due from general fund—Municipality's | | |
| share of assessment improvement costs | 10,000 | |
| Improvements authorized | | 200,000 |
| To record levy of special assessments | | |
| and municipality's share of cost. | | |
| | | |
| Special assessments receivable—Current | 15,000 | |
| Special assessment receivable—Deferred | | 15,000 |
| To record current special assessments. | | |
| | | |
| Cash for construction | 24,500 | |
| Due from general fund—Municipality's | | |
| share of assessment improvement costs | | 10,000 |
| Special assessment receivable—Current | | 14,500 |
| To record collections of cash. | | |
| | | |
| Bonds authorized—Unissued | 175,000 | |
| Bonds eligible to be sold | | 175,000 |
| To record unissued bonds eligible | | |
| to be sold. | | |
| | | |
| Cash for construction | 175,000 | |
| Bonds payable | | 175,000 |
| To record sale of bonds at par. | | |
| | | |
| Bonds eligible to be sold | 175,000 | |
| Bonds authorized—Unissued | | 175,000 |
| To reverse entry setting up unissued | | |
| bonds eligible to be sold. | | |

▶ NOTE: If the bonds are sold at a premium, the extra cash received is debited to Cash for Interest Payments. When bonds are sold at a discount, only the actual cash received is debited to Cash for Construction. The premium or discount accounts are handled in the same manner as in commercial accounting.

*Accounting for operations.* Any installment of special assessment collections that is not paid by a designated time becomes delinquent. The entry is:

| | | |
|---|---|---|
| Special assessments receivable—Delinquent | 500 | |
|     Special assessments receivable—Current | | 500 |
| To record delinquencies on first installment. | | |

Sometimes installments are paid in advance of their due date. A collection of payments on the second installment at the time the first installment became due would be recorded as follows:

| | | |
|---|---|---|
| Cash for bond payments | 3,000 | |
|     Special assessments receivable—Deferred | | 3,000 |
| To record collection of assessments not yet due. | | |

Construction transactions are handled through entries similar to those for the general fund. Another operating transaction of a special assessment fund arises from the fact that interest must be paid on the bonds outstanding. Consequently, special assessment taxpayers are charged interest on their unpaid installments. The entries for these interest transactions are:

| | | |
|---|---|---|
| Interest receivable on assessments | 2,500 | |
|     Interest revenues | | 2,500 |
| To record interest receivable on unpaid special assessments. | | |

| | | |
|---|---|---|
| Cash for interest payments | 2,475 | |
|     Interest receivable on assessments | | 2,475 |
| To record interest collections. | | |

| | | |
|---|---|---|
| Cash for interest payments | 20 | |
|     Interest revenues | | 20 |
| To record collection of interest revenue not set up as a receivable. | | |

| | | |
|---|---|---|
| Interest expenses | 2,400 | |
|     Accrued interest payable | | 2,400 |
| To record accrued interest on special assessment bonds | | |

*Closing the accounts.* Since the authorization to incur special assessment fund expenditures does not lapse at the end of the fiscal year, it is not necessary to close out the construction expenditures account into the appropriations account. However, it is permissible to do so. Interest accounts, on the other hand, must be closed out. Closing entries are:

| | | |
|---|---:|---:|
| Appropriations | 117,100 | |
|    Construction expenditures | | 117,100 |
| To close out expenditures for | | |
|    current fiscal year. | | |
| Interest revenues | 2,520 | |
|    Interest expenses | | 2,400 |
|    Unappropriated surplus—Interest | | 120 |
| To close out interest accounts at end of current | | |
|    fiscal year. | | |

At the same time, a corresponding entry is made in the general fixed assets group of accounts:

| | | |
|---|---:|---:|
| Construction work in progress | 117,100 | |
|    Investment in general fixed assets— | | |
|      From property owners' share of | | |
|      assessment improvement costs | | 111,245 |
|    Investment in general fixed assets— | | |
|      From municipality's share of | | |
|      assessment improvement costs | | 5,855 |
| To record work in progress at end of year. | | |

▶ EXPLANATION: In the above entry, the municipality is credited with 5% of the work completed. This is because the municipality is contributing 5% of the estimated cost of the project ($10,000 out of $200,000).

Assuming that the construction project is completed during the second year, the only distinctive entries to be recorded at that time are as follows:

| | | |
|---|---:|---:|
| Accrued interest payable | 3,500 | |
|    Cash for interest payments | | 3,500 |
| To record interest payment on bonds. | | |
| Appropriations | 82,900 | |
|    Construction expenditures | | 80,000 |
|    Unappropriated surplus—Construction | | 2,900 |
| To close out appropriation and construction | | |
|    expenditures account. | | |

A corresponding entry is made in the general fixed assets group of accounts similar to that shown for a completed bond fund project. The entry required to retire maturing serial bonds in any year is:

| | | |
|---|---:|---:|
| Bonds payable | 17,500 | |
|    Cash for bond payments | | 17,500 |
| To record retirement of bonds. | | |

*Dissolution of the fund.* A special assessment fund continues in operation until all the serial bonds have been retired. Any surplus in the fund when the final bonds are retired is transferred to the general fund or otherwise disposed of in accordance with the law. Two kinds of surplus may develop during the life of the fund:

1. *Construction surplus.* A construction surplus will generally arise at the completion of the construction project. It is usually held in the fund to make up possible interest deficits later on.

2. *Interest surplus.* When it is known that there will be an interest surplus, the special assessment installments can be reduced to conform with the lower requirements.

If construction surplus and/or prior interest surplus are insufficient to cover deficiencies developing in the later years of a fund, the interest rates on unpaid installments may be increased in order to meet interest requirements. Transfers of cash representing unappropriated surpluses at the closing out of the fund are handled like those discussed under bond funds.

**Special assessment fund financial statements.** The essential statements for a special assessment fund are:

1. Balance sheet.
2. Statement of cash receipts and disbursements.
3. Comparison of expenditures and encumbrances with appropriations.

A balance sheet at the end of a fiscal year during the construction period is illustrated in Figure 7.

**Sinking funds.** A sinking fund is set up to account for the accumulation of resources to retire the *principal only* of specified term bonds or other bonds. Each sinking fund is a separate legal entity and must be accounted for on an individual basis. However, all the sinking funds of a governmental unit may be controlled by one group of general ledger accounts, with each fund having its own self-balancing subsidiary ledger accounts.

▶ NOTE: The principles discussed below apply only to sinking funds established to retire general bonded debt. Also, only the entries that are peculiar to governmental sinking funds will be shown.

**The accounting cycle for a sinking fund.** *Recording the budget.* A sinking fund operates on an actuarial basis. Thus, a formal schedule of sinking fund requirements is prepared to determine required annual contributions and required fund earnings. Normally, the governmental unit's contributions

## A GOVERNMENTAL UNIT
### Special Assessment Fund
### Balance Sheet
### June 30, 19___

| Assets | | | Liabilities, Appropriations, Reserves, and Surplus | | | |
|---|---:|---:|---|---:|---:|---:|
| Cash: | | | Liabilities: | | | |
| For Construction | $90,500 | | Voucher's Payable | | $11,705 | |
| For Bond Payments | 4,000 | | Judgments Payable | | 9,500 | |
| For Interest Payments | 6,400 | $100,900 | Contracts Payable— | | | |
| | | | Uncompleted | $45,000 | | |
| Special Assessments Receivable: | | | Completed—Retained Percentage | 20,000 | 65,000 | |
| Current—Construction | $ 5,000 | | Interest Payable | | 1,000 | |
| Delinquent—Construction | 1,000 | | Bonds Payable | | 90,000 | $177,205 |
| Delinquent—Bond Payments | 13,000 | | | | | |
| Deferred—Construction | 65,000 | | | | | |
| Deferred—Bond Payments | 38,000 | 122,000 | Appropriations—Unencumbered Balance | | | 7,900 |
| | | | Reserve for Encumbrances | | | 40,000 |
| Due from General Fund— Governmental Unit's Share of Cost | | 5,000 | Unappropriated Surplus | | | |
| Interest Receivable | | 1,000 | Construction | | $3,000 | |
| | | | Interest | | 795 | 3,795 |
| | | $228,900 | | | | $228,900 |

Fig. 7. Special Assessment Fund Balance Sheet.

are made through the general fund, so it is necessary that the budget include data pertaining to a sinking fund. The budgetary entry in the sinking fund is:

| | | |
|---|---:|---:|
| Required contributions | 9,900 | |
| Required earnings | 700 | |
|   Reserve for retirement of | | |
|     sinking fund bonds | | 10,600 |
| To record budgetary provisions based on | | |
|   actuarial requirements. | | |

*Accounting for contribution revenues.* Required contributions can come either from the general fund or directly from a tax levy imposed for the sinking fund. If taxes are levied to provide required contributions, the entries in the sinking fund parallel those for general property taxes in the general fund. The accruing of the revenue is accomplished as follows:

| | | |
|---|---:|---:|
| Taxes receivable—Current | 10,000 | |
|   Estimated uncollectible current taxes | | 100 |
|   Contribution revenues | | 9,900 |
| To record levy of taxes. | | |

If the general fund is to provide the required contributions, the entry in the sinking fund is:

| | | |
|---|---:|---:|
| Due from general fund | 9,900 | |
|   Contribution revenues | | 9,900 |
| To set up contribution receivable from the general fund. | | |

At the same time, the following entry is made in the general fund:

| | | |
|---|---:|---:|
| Appropriation expenditures | 9,900 | |
|   Due to sinking fund | | 9,900 |
| To set up the contributions due to the sinking fund. | | |

When the actual cash is paid to the sinking fund, the entries are:

| | | |
|---|---:|---:|
| Cash | 9,900 | |
|   Due from general fund | | 9,900 |
| To record in the sinking fund the receipt of the | | |
|   contribution. | | |

| | | |
|---|---:|---:|
| Due to sinking fund | 9,900 | |
|   Cash | | 9,900 |
| To record payment by general fund to the sinking fund. | | |

*Accounting for earnings.* A sinking fund is accumulated through the earnings of its investments. The following series of entries illustrate the process:

| | | |
|---|---:|---:|
| Investments | 9,500 | |
| Unamortized premiums on investments | 100 | |

| | | |
|---|---|---|
| Accrued interest on investments purchased | 110 | |
|     Cash | | 9,710 |
| To record purchase of investments. | | |

| | | |
|---|---|---|
| Interest receivable on investments | 770 | |
|     Interest earnings | | 770 |
| To record interest earnings. | | |

| | | |
|---|---|---|
| Cash | 880 | |
|     Interest receivable on investments | | 770 |
|     Accrued interest on investments purchased | | 110 |
| To record collection of interest. | | |

| | | |
|---|---|---|
| Interest earnings | 20 | |
|     Unamortized premiums on investments | | 20 |
| To record amortization of premiums. | | |

*Closing the accounts.* At the end of the fiscal year, revenues and earnings are closed out, as follows:

| | | |
|---|---|---|
| Contribution revenues | 9,900 | |
|     Required contributions | | 9,900 |
| To close out required and actual contributions. | | |

| | | |
|---|---|---|
| Interest earnings | 750 | |
|     Required earnings | | 700 |
|     Unappropriated surplus | | 50 |
| To close out required and actual earnings. | | |

A corresponding entry is made in the general bonded debt and interest group of accounts:

| | | |
|---|---|---|
| Amount available in sinking fund | 10,650 | |
|     Amount to be provided for payment of bonds | | 10,650 |
| To adjust for amount equal to the net assets of the | | |
|     sinking fund. | | |

*Accounting for matured bonds.* When the bonds mature, payment is made either by the sinking fund itself or through the general fund. If the sinking fund is to make the payment directly, the entry is:

| | | |
|---|---|---|
| Reserve for retirement of sinking fund bonds | 500,000 | |
|     Matured bonds payable | | 500,000 |
| To set up matured bonds as a liability of the | | |
|     sinking fund. | | |

If payment is to be made by the general fund, the following entry is made in the sinking fund:

| | | |
|---|---|---|
| Reserve for retirement of bonds | 500,000 | |
|     Cash | | 500,000 |
| To transfer cash to the general fund, | | |

At the same time, an entry is made in the general fund:

| | | |
|---|---|---|
| Cash | 500,000 | |
| Matured bonds payable | | 500,000 |
| To record receipt of cash and to set up liability. | | |

In either case, the corresponding entry in the general bonded debt and interest group of accounts is:

| | | |
|---|---|---|
| Bonds payable | 500,000 | |
| Amount available in sinking fund | | 500,000 |
| To remove bond liability. | | |

The actual payment of the bonds, whether it be out of the general fund or by the sinking fund, is recorded as follows:

| | | |
|---|---|---|
| Matured bonds payable | 500,000 | |
| Cash | | 500,000 |
| To record the payment for retiring the bond issue. | | |

*Dissolution of the fund.* Any unappropriated surplus remaining in the sinking fund after the bonds have been paid is closed out and transferred to the appropriate fund, in most cases the general fund. When there is a deficit, the amount is usually made up by the general fund through a special appropriation for that purpose.

**Sinking fund financial statements.** Statements needed to exhibit the financial condition and operations of a sinking fund are:

1. Balance sheet.
2. Statement of cash receipts and disbursements.
3. Comparison of fund revenue with requirements.
4. Statement analyzing changes in the reserve for retirement of sinking fund bonds account.

A sinking fund balance sheet at the close of the fiscal period is shown in Figure 8.

**Trust and agency funds.** A trust fund or an agency fund is set up to account for money and property received and held by a governmental unit as trustee or custodian, or in the capacity of an agent for individuals, private organizations, or other governmental units. Separate accounts should be maintained for the transactions and balances of each trust or agency fund. Sometimes, however, it is more feasible to account for a trust fund as part of another fund.

The difference between a trust fund and an agency fund is one of degree only—a trust fund is usually in existence over a longer period of time than an agency fund and presents additional administrative problems, such

## A GOVERNMENTAL UNIT
### Sinking Fund
### Balance Sheet
### June 30, 19____

| Assets | | | Liabilities, Reserves, and Surplus | |
|---|---|---|---|---|
| Cash | | $ 31,878 | Matured Bonds Payable | $100,000 |
| Cash with Fiscal Agents | | 100,000 | Reserve for Retirement of Sinking | |
| Taxes Receivable—Delinquent | $8,518 | | Fund Bonds | 232,370 |
| *Less* Estimated Uncollectible Taxes | 2,200 | 6,318 | Unappropriated Surplus | 4,215 |
| Investments | | 194,000 | | |
| Unamortized Premiums | | 2,260 | | |
| Accrued Interest Receivable | | 2,129 | | |
| | | $336,585 | | $336,585 |

**Fig. 8. Sinking Fund Balance Sheet.**

as the proper investment of fund assets. But from an accounting standpoint the two funds are so similar that they may be considered as one class. Except for pension funds, no budgetary accounts are involved in the operation of trust and agency funds. In the case of a pension fund, budgetary accounts are used to show the required contributions to be made to the pension fund by both the governmental unit and its participating employees, as well as the required earnings of the fund. This procedure follows the method already described for the sinking fund. A common example of an agency fund is one established by a governmental unit to account for taxes that it collects for other governmental units. This type of fund follows the general property tax procedures outlined for the general fund. Otherwise, trust and agency funds follow the same procedures as in private accounting.

**Working capital funds.** A working capital fund is established to account for service activities performed by one department for other departments of the same governmental unit. These activities are usually of a manufacturing or service nature, such as shops and garages, cement and asphalt plants, and central purchases and stores departments. A working capital fund may also be established to provide temporary financing for construction projects in other funds, with repayment being made from the proceeds of public bond issues or bank loans. Working capital activities should be distinguished from those financed primarily from the sale of products or services to the public. These latter are handled in utility or other enterprise funds and include such operations as electric power plants, water plants, and airports. Capital for working capital funds is derived from three sources: (1) advances from the general fund, (2) sale of bonds, and (3) segregation of resources contributed by two or more funds. The fund capital is maintained intact by billings for goods or services furnished to the other funds. The activities carried on by a working capital fund are not intended to result in profits, but all costs incurred must be recovered. The accounting follows that for comparable private enterprises.

▶ COMMENT: Another name for a working capital fund is rotary or revolving fund, because it finances self-supporting operations featuring a continuous turnover of working capital.

**Utility or other enterprise funds.** A utility or other enterprise fund is established to account for the financing of self-supporting enterprises that render services primarily to the public. Examples of utilities are gas, electric, and water plants. Other enterprises include airports, docks and piers, and public housing. It should be noted, however, that services rendered for compensation by schools, libraries, highway departments, and other governmental organizations for which such services are only incidental to the performance of regular governmental functions, should be accounted for through special revenue funds. A governmental utility should be accounted for on the same basis as a similar privately owned utility, and other governmental enterprises should be accounted for in the same manner as private enterprises.

### FIXED ASSETS AND LONG-TERM DEBT [5]

This section will consider the handling of general fixed assets and long-term debt for a governmental unit. Reference should be made to *Principles of Governmental Accounting,* numbers 7 through 10 on pages 1074 and 1075, and the previous section for a better understanding of this subject.

**General ledger control accounts—fixed assets.** Fixed assets are classified into five principal groups: (1) land, (2) buildings, (3) improvements other than buildings, (4) machinery and equipment, and (5) construction work in progress. The differences between commercial enterprises and governmental units in the handling of fixed assets are:

1. Cost to the government includes all financial charges incurred in the acquisition of the fixed assets or improvements and additions thereto.

2. Assets used for general governmental purposes are not carried in the accounts of any fund, but instead are placed in a memorandum self-balancing group of accounts called *general fixed assets.*

3. No depreciation is charged unless the fixed assets are being used in a commercial-type governmental activity.

Thus, only working capital funds and utility or other enterprise funds carry property accounts and charge depreciation. Other than the differences noted above, governmental fixed assets are handled in the same manner as in private enterprise.

**Journal entries and statement—general fixed assets group of accounts.** Journal entries to record the acquisition or improvement of general fixed assets have already been illustrated under bond funds and special assessment funds. Titles used in statements of general fixed assets are self-explanatory in indicating other sources. When property is retired or otherwise disposed of, the original entry is reversed. A memorandum account is usually kept of depreciation, where appropriate, for cost analysis and budget information only. Thus, when a general fixed asset is transferred to a commercial-type governmental fund, the proper accumulated deprecia-

---

[5] This section adapted from: National Committee on Governmental Accounting, *Municipal Accounting and Auditing,* Part II, pages 126 to 140. Municipal Finance Officers Association of the United States and Canada, 1951.

tion can be set up in the transferee fund. Any cash received in disposing of general fixed assets is usually credited to the revenues account in the general fund. In some cases, however, where the general fixed asset was donated by a working capital fund or a utility or other enterprise fund, such cash receipts may be recorded in the donor fund. Cash received in disposal of general fixed assets pertaining to a special revenue fund may be credited to that fund, provided that the special revenue fund concerned is responsible for financing the replacement of the property retired. A statement of general fixed assets is shown in Figure 9, page 1116.

**General ledger control accounts—long-term debt.** As in the case of fixed assets, long-term debt is not shown in all the funds, being carried only in special assessment funds and utility or other enterprise funds. Long-term debt incurred for general governmental purposes is carried in a memorandum self-balancing group of accounts called *general bonded debt and interest.* Long-term debt in special assessment funds and utility or other enterprise funds is handled as in commercial enterprises. There are two distinctive features in the general bonded debt and interest group of accounts:

1. The debit accounts show not only the amount available in sinking funds for debt retirement, but also the amounts to be provided in future years for payment of bonds and interest.

2. The credit accounts show not only the bonds payable but also the interest payable on the bonds in future years.

**Journal entries and statement—general bonded debt and interest group of accounts.** Journal entries to record the incurring of general bonded debt have already been illustrated under bond funds, while journal entries to record the accumulation of assets in sinking funds and to record the retirement of general term bonds were shown under sinking funds. Retirement of general serial bonds and payments of interest on all types of general bonded debt are handled through the general fund. The entries in the general bonded debt and interest group of accounts are as follows:

| | | |
|---|---|---|
| Bonds payable | 57,500 | |
|   Amount to be provided for | | |
|     payment of bonds | | 57,500 |
| To remove bond liability. | | |
| | | |
| Interest payable on bonds in | | |
|     future years | 39,300 | |
|   Amount to be provided for | | |
|     payment of interest | | 39,300 |
| To reduce interest payable by amount being | | |
|   paid by general fund. | | |

At the same time, corresponding entries are made in the general fund:

| | | |
|---|---|---|
| Appropriation expenditures | 57,500 | |
| Matured bonds payable | | 57,500 |
| To set up matured bonds as a liability. | | |

| | | |
|---|---|---|
| Appropriation expenditures | 39,300 | |
| Matured interest payable | | 39,300 |
| To set up matured interest as a liability. | | |

A statement of general bonded debt and interest is shown in Figure 9.

### AUDITING GOVERNMENTAL UNITS [6]

Generally accepted auditing standards and procedures are established by the American Institute of Certified Public Accountants and disseminated through its *Statements of Auditing Procedure*. The pronouncements contained in these statements serve as a guide to the accounting profession in performing commercial audits; they are equally applicable, however, to audits of governments and institutions. General principles and suggested procedures for governmental audits have been developed by the National Committee on Governmental Accounting. These procedures pertain specifically to the audits of municipalities and other public bodies below or subordinate to the State, but they can be followed in auditing any governmental unit or institution using funds as the basis of its accounting system. This section, then, while dealing with the audit of governmental units is also applicable to the next chapter, *Fund Accounting for Institutions*.

**Application of audit procedures.** The audit procedures described apply to independent post-audits. A governmental post-audit is an audit made after the transactions to be audited have taken place and been recorded, or have been approved for recording by designated officials, if such approval is required. Independent post-audits may be performed by:

1. State audit agencies.
2. Independent private accountants.
3. Independent municipal auditors.

▶ OBSERVATION: An *independent* municipal auditor is an auditor appointed by the legislature or elected by the people, who is responsible solely to the legislative body. An *internal* municipal auditor is an auditor who is a member of the municipality's administrative organization.

[6] This section adapted from: National Committee on Governmental Accounting, *Municipal Accounting and Auditing*, Part III. Municipal Finance Officers Association of the United States and Canada, 1951.

## A GOVERNMENTAL UNIT
### Statement of General Fixed Assets
June 30, 19___

| | | Investment in General Fixed Assets: | |
|---|---|---|---|
| Land | $1,300,000 | From General Bonds | $3,304,650 |
| Buildings | 2,504,650 | From Current Revenues | 525,000 |
| Improvements Other Than Buildings | 1,027,200 | From Gifts | 400,000 |
| Machinery and Equipment | 400,000 | From Property Owners' Share of | |
| Construction Work in Progress | 697,800 | Assessment Improvement Costs | 320,000 |
| | | From Governmental Unit's Share of | |
| | | Assessment Improvement Costs | 80,000 |
| | | From State Grants | 300,000 |
| | | From Federal Grants | 1,000,000 |
| | $5,929,650 | | $5,929,650 |

## A GOVERNMENTAL UNIT
### Statement of General Bonded Debt and Interest
June 30, 19___

| | | General Bonds and Interest Payable in Future Years: | |
|---|---|---|---|
| Amount Available and to be Provided for Payment of General Bonds and Interest: | | General Bonds— | |
| Bond Principal— | | Sinking Fund Bonds Payable | $ 900,000 |
| Amount Available in Sinking Funds | $ 239,326 | Serial Bonds Payable | 800,000 |
| To be Provided in Future Years | 1,460,674 | | |
| Total Available and to be Provided for Principal | $1,700,000 | Total General Bonds Payable | $1,700,000 |
| To be Provided in Future Years for Bond Interest | 403,900 | Interest Payable in Future Years | 403,900 |
| Total Available and to be Provided | $2,103,900 | Total Bonds and Interest Payable | $2,103,900 |

Fig. 9. Statement of General Fixed Assets and Statement of General Bonded Debt and Interest.

**Classification of audits.** Governmental audits are classified as:

1. *General audits.* A general audit embraces all financial transactions and records, and it is made regularly at the close of the accounting period, which is usually a year.

2. *Special audits.* A special audit is one that is limited to some particular phase of the governmental unit's activities, such as one particular fund, or covers all of the activities for a shorter or longer period of time than the usual audit period.

Both general and special audits are in turn classified as to whether they are:

1. *Complete.* A complete audit is one in which an examination is made of the system of internal control and of the details of all the books of accounts, including subsidiary documents, as to (a) legality, (b) mathematical accuracy, (c) complete accountability, and (d) application of accepted accounting principles.

2. *Limited.* In a limited audit, only certain selected transactions are examined on a sample basis.

▶ COMMENT: The auditor should have a clear understanding of the type of audit he is to perform. Where practicable, a written contract of agreement should be prepared in duplicate, one copy to be kept by the organization and the other copy to be given to the auditor.

**Summary of recommended audit procedures.** The audit procedures that follow are offered only as a guide. They do not constitute a complete audit program, but rather reflect the principal procedures peculiar to the audit of the various funds of a governmental unit. Thus, the significant points of difference between commercial auditing and governmental auditing are emphasized. The procedures are divided into four groups:

1. General directions.
2. Revenues and receipts.
3. Expenditures and disbursements.
4. Balance sheet accounts.

**General directions.** *Legal provisions.* Study the general statutes governing municipalities in the state in which the municipality under audit is located. Examine in particular the provisions of the charter or other document by which the municipality acquired its right of existence and its powers. In other words, acquire a thorough understanding of the type of organization permitted, powers granted, and duties imposed by the charter and by state laws, together with a similar understanding of how the municipality is actually organized, what activities it is carrying on, and how these activities are being administered.

*Funds maintained.* Ascertain what funds are maintained and by what authority or under what circumstances each fund was created.

*Basis of accounting.* Ascertain what basis of accounting is being followed—cash, accrual, or a combination of both. Obtain this information for each fund, since the same basis is not always used for all funds of the same governmental unit.

*Digest of minutes or other records.* Prepare a digest of the minutes or other official records of the proceedings of the legislative body. Take particular note of expenditure authorizations and the appropriations made to cover them, by making a complete list showing the date of each and the page on which it was recorded in the minutes book. Note further whether each appropriation carries provision for financing the expenditures authorized. Such provision is sometimes omitted through oversight, especially in the case of supplemental appropriations. A properly drawn budget should always show the means of financing any appropriation authorized.

**Revenues and receipts.** *Handling of receipts.* Before beginning the actual audit of revenues, ascertain who is supposed to collect each class of revenue, who is actually collecting it, who is supposed to hold it, who is actually holding it, and exactly what the collection routine is. This is important because there is no uniformity of administrative organization for the receipt and custody of municipal revenues and other receipts. Practice runs all the way from the requirement that all payments to a municipality be made to a single officer and that all amounts collected be held by a single officer, to the requirement that different classes of revenue and other receipts be collected and held by different officers.

*General property taxes.* Check the tax levy ordinance to see that it is properly drawn. Verify the valuation of assessable property by examining the records of the assessor or corresponding agency independently of the treasurer or other tax-collecting officer. Then check the tax roll for verification of the following items: (1) the original total, (2) cash collections, (3) cancellations, (4) remissions, (5) adjustments, and (6) the delinquent tax roll. Finally, determine that the governmental unit is getting all the revenues from this source to which it is entitled. Since the general property tax is the most important single source of revenue, it requires special attention.

▶ IMPORTANT: A special precauation to be taken is the circularization of taxpayers whose taxes, according to the books of the municipality, are unpaid. The audit report should state whether or not taxpayers have been circularized. If this recommended procedure is carried out, the percentage circularized should be mentioned and the results discussed in the report.

*Other receipts.* Examine the minutes of the legislative body, sinking fund commission, and other administrative and regulatory bodies to reveal any authorizations for the issuances of bonds and notes, and sale of fixed property and equipment, temporary borrowing, and other transactions whose receipts are not properly classifiable as revenue. Verify that all such transactions were properly authorized and that the receipts have been collected and properly recorded.

**Expenditures and disbursements.** *Proper authorization.* Municipal expenditures must be authorized in the budget. So, first of all, ascertain what appropriations have been made and verify that they have been properly recorded in the appropriations accounts. The expenditures charged against these appropriation accounts can then be properly audited.

*Encumbrances.* Verify that unfilled purchase orders have been charged to the proper appropriation accounts. Also determine that all encumbrances have been recorded and that no appropriation has been over-encumbered. One of the auditor's chief duties is to see that expenditures are charged to the proper appropriations and that total expenditures in any appropriations account do not exceed the authorized amount. If encumbrances are not recorded on the municipality's books, the auditor should set them up as adjustments in his working trial balance, so that the encumbrances will be reflected in the statements.

*Purchases.* Ascertain by satisfactory tests, that (1) purchases were made in accordance with the procedures prescribed by law, (2) the goods or services were actually received, (3) the goods or services were what was ordered and paid for, (4) the prices paid for the purchases were no more than those shown in the related purchase orders, bids, and contracts, (5) all authorized discounts were taken, and (6) the municipality got the benefit of the purchase.

*Payrolls.* A number of municipalities have strict laws or regulations forbidding the use for other purposes of money appropriated for personal services, and vice versa. If such restrictions are imposed, make sure that they have not been violated. Where the employment of personnel is on a civil service basis, determine that employees have been properly certified and that pertinent civil service rules and regulations have been complied with.

*Nonexpenditure disbursements.* Not all disbursements are recorded as expenditures or are made in payment of a liability incurred as the result of an expenditure. There are five main groups of nonexpenditure disbursements: (1) making or repaying notes or loans, (2) making investments or retiring debt through sinking funds, (3) transfers of money collected for other funds or agencies, (4) payments or transfers to other funds or agencies not involving prior charges for goods or services, and (5) refunds of excess collections from taxpayers or other government agencies. Verify that all such transactions were properly authorized and the payments properly recorded.

**Balance sheet accounts.** *Assets.* Each fund is a separate legal and accounting entity, so the assets of individual funds must be separately accounted for and verified. Otherwise, the assets of a municipality are subject to verification in much the same manner as the assets of a private enterprise. Be sure to ascertain, however, that cash is on deposit only in banks designated as depositaries pursuant to legal provisions. Also, municipalities usually require their depositaries to give security for the balances carried with them. Examine the security if it is held by the municipality, or obtain a certificate from the escrow agent if it is held in escrow.

*Liabilities.* Smaller municipalities frequently do not record purchase obligations until the bill is paid, so that there is no general ledger control for accounts payable. Ascertain and prepare a list of all unpaid purchase obligations and determine if they have been recorded on the books. If they have not, make the necessary adjustments so that the audit report will reflect all the liabilities of the municipality. Generally, the liabilities of a municipality are similar to those of private enterprises. Even those that are peculiar to a municipality are of such a nature that the proper methods of verification will readily suggest themselves to the experienced auditor.

*Sinking funds.* Ascertain whether or not the balance in the reserve for retirement of sinking fund bonds represents the actuarial requirements of the sinking fund. The specifications as to how much shall be set aside for the retirement of debt will usually be found in the charter. Sometimes, however, the charter provisions as to contributions to sinking funds will be more or less general and will leave the determination of sinking fund requirements to the discretion of the municipality's lawmaking body. In either case, the ordinance by which each issue of sinking fund bonds was authorized usually contains specifications as to when contributions shall be made for the retirement of bonds and what the amount of these contributions shall be. The charter or ordinances will specify the classes of securities in which sinking fund contributions may be invested. Determine that the sinking fund securities meet these requirements.

*Surplus and surplus reserves.* There is no one surplus account in a municipality and there is no one surplus figure for a municipality. Every fund, except certain trust or agency funds, may have a surplus. The surplus accounts of the general fund and special revenue funds are the most important and warrant special attention because (1) the unappropriated surplus of these funds is designed to show the net cash position of the funds, and (2) this net cash position is of the utmost importance in preparing the budget, since the unappropriated surplus represents cash against which appropriations can be made. If the surplus accounts are not divided properly on the books, set them up correctly in the audit working papers so that the financial statements will show the true net cash position of the fund in the unappropriated surplus account.

**Submitting the audit report.** The body of the audit report should be preceded by a table of contents. The report itself is divided as follows:

1. *Letter of transmittal.* The letter of transmittal contains (a) a statement of the scope and limitations of the audit, (b) a summary of the findings of the audit, (c) recommendations for changes in the general accounting procedure, and any other suggestions deemed appropriate, and (d) the auditor's certificate. In general, the form of the auditor's certificate should follow as closely as possible the standard form, making due allowance for the special conditions under which the audit was performed.

2. *Financial section.* The financial section contains the appropriate financial statements covering the complete operations of the municipality. All funds and self-balancing groups of accounts should be included. Statements of cash receipts and disbursements are usually prepared for each fund.

3. *Statistical section.* This section contains the necessary statistical tables to supplement the financial statements. However, the preparation of the statistical tables is not a part of the auditor's ordinary work unless special arrangements are made. The inclusion of the statistical tables does make the audit report more valuable, especially for investors. It also obviates the need for a special report in this area by the municipality's chief accounting officer.

# 32

# Fund Accounting for Institutions

**JAMES W. BAKER**

*Certified Public Accountant; Professor of Accounting, University of Georgia*

CHAPTER THIRTY-TWO

# Fund Accounting
# for Institutions

Institutions have certain essential characteristics in common with governmental units, which were discussed in the previous chapter. These mutual characteristics are:

1. The object of both is to render service without profit.
2. They both use fund accounting.
3. The operations of both generally are controlled by budgets.

Therefore, in order to avoid duplication, this chapter was prepared not on a self-contained basis but as an extension of the previous chapter, and should be read accordingly. Only those areas where accounting for an institution differs from that for a governmental body will be covered. No discussion of auditing procedures is included, since the pertinent discussion in the previous chapter has application to institutions as well as to governmental bodies.

The types of institutions that will be considered are:

1. Colleges and universities.
2. Hospitals.
3. Social service organizations.
4. Religious institutions.

While these institutions are specifically covered, the information provided is also applicable to other organizations using fund accounting, such as orphanages, national and state societies, and private social groups or clubs.

## COLLEGES AND UNIVERSITIES [1]

**Types of funds.** The following fund groups are recommended for educational institutions:

1. Current funds.
2. Loan funds.
3. Endowment and other non-expendable funds.
4. Annuity funds.
5. Plant funds.
6. Agency funds.

**Current funds.** The current funds group includes (1) operating funds that are available for any purpose, and (2) current funds that are restricted by outside agencies as to their use. The accounts of these two types of funds are segregated into separately balanced groups, if practicable. If this segregation is not practicable, the assets of the two groups may be combined, provided the balance in restricted funds appearing on the liability side of the balance sheet is shown separately. The current general funds may be subdivided further into two separately balanced groups, one for general operations and one for auxiliary enterprises. This subdivision is especially desirable if there are bonds outstanding or other forms of indebtedness on the plant used for auxiliary enterprises.

**Loan funds.** The loan funds group includes only funds that are loanable to students, faculty, and staff. If just the income of a fund may be loaned, the principal should be grouped with the endowment funds and the income added to the loan funds group.

**Endowment and other non-expendable funds.** Only funds that are non-expendable at the date of reporting are included in this group. The primary purpose of these funds, then, is investment, and only the income from the investment may be used. The following principles apply to this fund group:

1. The liability side of the balance sheet section shows separately endowment funds, funds functioning as endowment, and funds held in trust by others for the benefit of the institution.

2. If practicable, each of the divisions in this group may be classified further, either on the balance sheet or in a supporting schedule, to show separately funds the income of which is unrestricted as to use and funds the income of which is designated for restricted purposes, such as professorships, scholarships, and research.

[1] This section adapted from: National Committee on the Preparation of a Manual for College and University Business Administration, *College and University Business Administration,* Volume 1. American Council on Education, 1952.

3. Assets may be pooled for investment purposes unless prohibited by statute or by the terms of the instrument of gift. If they are so pooled, only one account is maintained for each class of investments of the pool. Individual accounts, however, must be kept for the principal of each fund in the pool. Investments of different fund groups—that is, current, loan, endowment, and plant funds—should not be commingled in the same investment pool.

4. The assets of endowment funds and of funds functioning as endowment may be shown together whether or not investments are pooled, but the assets of funds held in trust by others must be shown separately from those held by the institution.

5. Funds held in trust by others include funds that are not under the control of the institution, but are held for its benefit by a trustee or other agency designated by the donor. It is desirable to include such funds on the balance sheet in order to show the total endowment resources of the institution.

6. Realized gains or losses on the sale of investments are carried to the principal of the funds involved, or to an appropriate reserve account for pooled investments. Gains from the sale of assets do not constitute income.

7. Investments purchased are recorded at cost.

8. Securities and other property donated to an institution are recorded in the accounts at market value or at an expertly appraised value as of the date of the gift.

9. The book values of investment should not be changed to reflect fluctuations in market prices.

10. In order to maintain unimpaired the principal of the funds, suitable provisions should be made for the depreciation of real property held as investments, and for the amortization of premiums paid on securities purchased.

11. If endowment funds are invested in institutional property, these investments should be limited to income-producing property. Such investments should be accompanied by a formal commitment of the governing board for the amortization of the amounts so invested, in addition to the payment of interest from earnings of the property. If such earnings are insufficient, payment should be made from current general funds, or from other unrestricted funds, so that the principal will remain intact.

**Annuity funds.** The annuity funds group includes funds acquired by an institution subject to annuity or living trust agreements. If these funds are small in amount, they may be grouped with endowment and other non-expendable funds, provided they are clearly identified.

▶ WARNING: Although annuity funds may be grouped with endowment and other non-expendable funds for convenience or for reporting purposes, the funds themselves should not be commingled. Under the Federal Internal Revenue Code, such commingling could lead to a loss of non-taxable status.

**Plant funds.** The plant funds group includes funds designated or expended for the acquisition of physical property used for institutional purposes. The following principles apply to this fund group:

1. Plant funds are subdivided into separately balanced sections so as to report *funds not yet expended* and *funds already invested in plant*.

2. Funds accumulated for the *retirement of debt* incurred for plant acquisition are also reported in a separately balanced section.

3. Plant items are carried in the accounts at cost until disposed of.

4. Gifts of property, such as land, buildings, equipment, and similar items, to be used for institutional purposes are recorded in the accounts at an expertly appraised value as of the date of the gift.

5. Reserves created for renewals and replacements of institutional property should be identified clearly in the unexpended plant funds section.

6. The total investment in physical plant assets used for institutional purposes should appear in the plant funds group. If endowment funds have been invested in institutional property, the value of that property is reported in the plant funds group, and the amount of investment of those funds is shown either as a deduction from the plant fund assets or as an account on the liability side of the balance sheet.

**Agency funds.** The agency funds group includes funds in the custody of the university but not belonging to it. Receipts and disbursements of agency funds are not institutional income and expenditures, so they should be reported separately.

**Principles of fund operations.** The principles that follow are pertinent to the operation of the various fund groups of an educational institution:

1. If money is advanced or loaned temporarily by one fund to another, that fact should be set forth on the balance sheet by showing the amount as an asset in the fund group making the advance, and as a liability in the fund group receiving the advance.

2. Receipts of cash or other property specifically designated to be added to the principal or balance of funds, or to be expended only for physical plant additions, should be accounted for separately from income expendable for current purposes. This principle provides for the exclusion from current income of all receipts that are intended to increase the assets and fund balances of loan, endowment, annuity, plant, and agency funds. Such

receipts should be reported in the statements of fund transactions support-ing the appropriate fund group on the balance sheet rather than in the current income statement.

3. The necessity for providing for renewals and replacements of prop-erty and of charging depreciation depends on the class of property under consideration, as follows:

a. *Property used specifically for educational functions.* This property is usually initially provided by gifts, grants, or legislative appropria-tions, and it is ordinarily replaced in the same manner. Therefore, it is not necessary to accumulate funds out of current income for re-newals or replacements.

b. *Service property and property used for auxiliary or other income-producing activities.* It is desirable to make provision for renewals and replacements of this property. The necessity for making such provision depends upon the financial program of the institution.

c. *Real property held as investments of endowment funds.* It is essen-tial to provide for depreciation of this property. The depreciation re-serve, to be effective, requires a periodic transfer of cash from in-come to principal. This depreciation reserve should be included in the endowment funds group as a deduction from the related asset.

▶ OBSERVATION: In any case when replacement fund reserves for in-stitutional property are created, they should be represented by cash or other liquid assets included in the plant funds group. A reserve account for replacements resulting merely from a journal entry without transfer of cash serves no useful purpose.

4. In general, accounts should be kept on the accrual basis. But since the primary purpose of accounting in educational institutions is to report on the stewardship of the funds and property entrusted to the institution rather than to determine net profits and net worth, some items of income need not be accrued and certain expenditures need not be prorated. For example, few institutions find it either necessary or desirable to report accrued interest receivable, or to allocate insurance premiums to subse-quent periods. Consequently, it may be said that the accounts generally are maintained on a *modified accrual basis.* It should be noted that this defini-tion of modified accrual basis is different from the generally accepted meaning of that term as used in governmental accounting.

5. Current restricted receipts are reported as income only to the extent expended during the year. Current funds frequently are received for re-stricted purposes with the related expenditures extending beyond the cur-rent fiscal year. Such receipts are not income of the institution until the

terms of the gift or grant have been met and the money expended in accordance with those terms. Unexpendable balances of grants are sometimes returnable to the grantors. The amount to be reported as income in any fiscal period, therefore, should be limited to the amount that has been expended in that period. The total receipts, disbursements, and the unexpended balances of such funds are shown in a subsidiary statement called *Summary of Changes in Current Restricted Funds Balances.*

6. Earnings from endowment investments are reported as current general income only to the extent distributed to the individual endowment income accounts. When endowment assets are pooled for investment purposes, it may be neither practicable nor desirable to distribute all income from the pool in the year in which it is earned. Inasmuch as this undistributed balance may include both general and restricted income, it should not be reflected in the income statement. The undistributed portion of earnings serves frequently as a reserve for stabilization of endowment income.

7. Auxiliary enterprises usually are expected to be self-supporting, so it is desirable to report their total operations separately in the current funds operating statements in order to show the extent to which this objective is achieved. Expenditures should include appropriate charges for the operation and maintenance of the physical plant, for general administration, and for other indirect costs.

**Budgetary accounting.** The budget is of such vital importance in the operation and administration of an educational institution that budgetary accounts should be made an integral part of the accounting system by being recorded in the general books of account.

*Recording the budget.* After the budget has been approved by the governing board, the total estimated income for the year is charged in the general ledger to an account entitled Unrealized (or Estimated) Income, and the total estimated expenditures are credited to an account termed Appropriations. The excess of estimated income over estimated expenditures is credited to an account that represents the free and unassigned balance of general funds available for appropriation and expenditure. The title Unappropriated Income is suggested for this account. Other possible titles are Unassigned Balance, or Unappropriated Budget Surplus.

*Recording income and expenditures.* Income as received or accrued is credited to Unrealized Income. Expenditures are charged to Appropriations. Subsidiary accounts should be maintained in which to record, under desired classifications, details of estimated and realized income and of estimated and actual expenditures. In the case of expenditures, each item as entered in the subsidiary records supporting Appropriations may be coded according to object classifications.

*Handling encumbrances.* An encumbrance system similar to that described in the previous chapter under the general fund in governmental accounting is desirable. The encumbrances set up should include not only orders and contracts for materials, equipment, and contractual service, but also unpaid salaries of members of the staff on definite appointment. The unencumbered balance in salary appropriations is the difference between the amount of such appropriations and the total salary appointments. All encumbrances should be recorded in the appropriations ledger.

*Closing budgetary accounts.* Any balance remaining in the Unrealized Income and Appropriations accounts at the end of the fiscal year, as well as in the Unappropriated Income account, should be closed into Unappropriated Surplus. Encumbrances are also closed out into Unappropriated Surplus, leaving the reserve for encumbrances on the books. If a separate surplus or reserve account is kept for unexpended income from auxiliary enterprises and organized activities, the net income or expense from these enterprises and activities for the year should be credited or debited to this separate surplus or reserve account.

**Setting up the accounts.** Each asset, liability, and fund balance should be represented by an account in the general ledger, or in a subsidiary ledger with proper control through summary accounts in the general ledger. These accounts should be classified in such a manner as to set out in separately balanced groups the assets, liabilities, and balances of each group of funds. This arrangement is followed on the balance sheet, with similar accounts being grouped under broad captions for reporting purposes. A sample balance sheet, showing such broad captions, is presented in Figure 1.

The general ledger control or subsidiary ledger accounts are broken down to show necessary or desired information. Budgetary accounts are set up as previously described. Separate statements (usually called summaries) of current income and expenditures are shown only for the current funds. All other funds include income or expenditures in their respective summary of changes in fund balances. It is necessary to set up income and expenditure accounts only to the extent required for adequate reporting. A sample summary of current income and expenditures is shown in Figure 2. This illustration gives the broad income and expense categories generally recognized for colleges and universities. Account titles should follow the illustration.

Supporting the summary of current income and expenditures are detailed statements, including statements of income and expenditures for all auxiliary enterprises. These follow accepted commercial practices in similar lines. A summary of changes in surplus for the current general fund is shown in Figure 3. A typical summary of changes in other funds is shown in Figure 4. In all instances, account titles can be set up according to the statement captions with appropriate breakdown either in the general ledger or subsidiary ledgers.

# A UNIVERSITY
Balance Sheet
June 30, 19___

## Assets

**CURRENT FUNDS:**

*General*

| | | |
|---|---:|---:|
| Cash | | $ 195,000 |
| Investments | | 275,000 |
| Accounts receivable: | | |
| United States Government | $ 150,000 | |
| Students | 10,000 | |
| Other | 2,000 | |
| Total | | $ 162,000 |
| Less allowance for doubtful accounts | | 3,000 |
| | | 159,000 |
| Inventories | | 337,500 |
| Prepaid expenses | | 2,350 |
| Due from Unexpended Plant Funds | | 5,000 |
| Total general | | $ 973,850 |

*Restricted*

| | | |
|---|---:|---:|
| Cash | $ 52,000 | |
| Investments | 230,000 | |
| Total restricted | | 282,000 |
| Total current funds | | $ 1,255,850 |

## Liabilities

**CURRENT FUNDS:**

*General*

| | | |
|---|---:|---:|
| Accounts payable | | $ 90,500 |
| Deposits | | 13,850 |
| Deferred income | | 7,500 |
| Surplus: | | |
| Reserve for encumbrances | $ 10,150 | |
| Reserve for working capital | 372,500 | |
| Other reserves (itemize) | 239,100 | |
| Unappropriated | 240,250 | |
| Total surplus | | 862,000 |
| Total general | | $ 973,850 |

*Restricted*

| | | |
|---|---:|---:|
| Accounts payable | | $ 15,500 |
| Undistributed endowment income | | 30,500 |
| Restricted Funds balances | | 236,000 |
| Total restricted | | 282,000 |
| Total current funds | | $ 1,255,850 |

**LOAN FUNDS:**

| | | |
|---|---:|---:|
| Cash | | $ 75,000 |
| Investments | | 33,000 |
| Notes receivable | | 125,000 |
| Total loan funds | | $ 233,000 |

**LOAN FUNDS:**

| | | |
|---|---:|---:|
| Loan Funds balances | | $ 233,000 |
| Total loan funds | | $ 233,000 |

**ENDOWMENT AND OTHER NON-EXPENDABLE FUNDS:**

| | | |
|---|---:|---:|
| Cash | | $ 12,200 |
| Investments: | | |
| Bonds | $3,000,000 | |
| Preferred stocks | 1,013,000 | |
| Common stocks | 3,003,000 | |
| Mortgage notes | 8,000 | |
| Real estate (less depreciation) | 1,000,000 | |
| Investment in institutional plant | 220,000 | 8,244,000 |
| Funds held in trust by others | | 225,000 |
| Total endowment and other non-expendable funds | | $ 8,481,200 |

**ENDOWMENT AND OTHER NON-EXPENDABLE FUNDS:**

| | |
|---|---:|
| Principal of Endowment Funds | $ 5,095,950 |
| Principal of Funds Functioning as Endowment | 2,920,000 |
| Reserve for Gains and Losses on Investments | 240,250 |
| Total | $ 8,256,200 |
| Funds Held in Trust by Others | 225,000 |
| Total endowment and other non-expendable funds | $ 8,481,200 |

**ANNUITY FUNDS:**

| | | |
|---|---:|---:|
| Cash | | $ 12,200 |
| Investments | | 200,000 |
| Total annuity funds | | $ 212,200 |

**ANNUITY FUNDS:**

| | |
|---|---:|
| Annuity Funds balances | $ 212,200 |
| Total annuity funds | $ 212,200 |

Fig. 1. Balance Sheet for Colleges and Universities. (Continues on next page.)

1131

# A UNIVERSITY—(Continued)
## Balance Sheet
### June 30, 19____

| Assets | | |
|---|---:|---:|
| PLANT FUNDS: | | |
| *Unexpended plant funds* | | |
| Cash | $ 128,500 | |
| Investments | 350,000 | |
| | | |
| Total unexpended plant funds | | $ 478,500 |
| | | |
| *Retirement of indebtedness funds* | | |
| Cash | $ 5,000 | |
| Investments | 185,000 | |
| | | |
| Total retirement of | | |
| indebtedness funds | | $ 190,000 |

| Liabilities | | |
|---|---:|---:|
| PLANT FUNDS: | | |
| *Unexpended plant funds* | | |
| Accounts payable | | $ 23,500 |
| Notes payable | | 100,000 |
| Due to Current General Funds | | 5,000 |
| Unexpended Plant Funds | | |
| balances: | | |
| Plant additions | $ 130,000 | |
| Renewals and replacements | 220,000 | 350,000 |
| | | |
| Total unexpended plant funds | | $ 478,500 |
| | | |
| *Retirement of indebtedness funds* | | |
| Funds balances | | $ 190,000 |
| | | |
| Total retirement of | | |
| indebtedness funds | | $ 190,000 |

**Invested in plant**

| | | |
|---|---:|---:|
| Land | | $ 250,000 |
| Improvements other than buildings | | 850,000 |
| Buildings | | 5,165,000 |
| Equipment | | 1,410,000 |
| Total | | $7,675,000 |
| Less endowment funds invested in plant | | 220,000 |
| Total invested in plant | | $ 7,455,000 |
| Total plant funds | | $ 8,123,500 |

**AGENCY FUNDS:**

| | | |
|---|---:|---:|
| Cash | | $ 75,000 |
| Investments | | 25,000 |
| Total agency funds | | $ 100,000 |
| Grand Total | | $18,405,750 |

**Invested in plant**

| | | |
|---|---:|---:|
| Bonds payable | | $ 800,000 |
| Notes payable | | 150,000 |
| Net investment in plant: | | |
| From gifts | $ 975,000 | |
| From current funds | 325,000 | |
| From governmental appropriations | 5,205,000 | 6,505,000 |
| Total invested in plant | | $ 7,455,000 |
| Total plant funds | | $ 8,123,500 |

**AGENCY FUNDS:**

| | | |
|---|---:|---:|
| Agency Funds balances | | $ 100,000 |
| Total agency funds | | $ 100,000 |
| Grand Total | | $18,405,750 |

Fig. 1. Balance Sheet for Colleges and Universities. (Continued.)

A UNIVERSITY
Summary of Current Income and Expenditures
For the Year Ended June 30, 19___

| | Total | Current General Funds | Current Restricted Funds |
|---|---|---|---|
| CURRENT INCOME: | | | |
| 1. *Educational and general* | | | |
| Student fees | $1,460,000 | $1,460,000 | |
| Governmental appropriations | 2,750,000 | 2,750,000 | |
| Endowment income | 346,000 | 140,000 | $206,000 |
| Gifts and grants | 652,900 | 225,000 | 427,900 |
| Sales and services of educational departments | 30,000 | 30,000 | |
| Organized activities relating to educational departments | 50,000 | 50,000 | |
| Other sources | 5,250 | 5,250 | |
| Total educational and general | $5,294,150 | $4,660,250 | $633,900 |
| 2. *Auxiliary enterprises* | 1,320,000 | 1,315,000 | 5,000 |
| 3. *Student Aid* | 41,100 | — | 41,100 |
| Total current income | $6,655,250 | $5,975,250 | $680,000 |
| | | | |
| CURRENT EXPENDITURES: | | | |
| 1. *Educational and general* | | | |
| General administration | $ 220,000 | $ 215,000 | $ 5,000 |
| Staff benefits | 285,000 | 285,000 | |
| General expense | 680,000 | 680,000 | |
| Instruction and departmental research | 1,700,000 | 1,480,600 | 219,400 |
| Organized activities relating to educational departments | 50,000 | 50,000 | |
| Organized research | 500,000 | 91,700 | 408,300 |
| Extension and public services | 200,000 | 200,000 | |
| Libraries | 400,000 | 400,000 | |
| Operation and maintenance of physical plant | 800,000 | 798,800 | 1,200 |
| Total educational and general | $4,835,000 | $4,201,100 | $633,900 |
| 2. *Auxiliary enterprises* | 1,320,000 | 1,315,000 | 5,000 |
| 3. *Student Aid* | 180,000 | 138,900 | 41,100 |
| Total current expenditures | $6,335,000 | $5,655,000 | $680,000 |
| Excess of current income over current expenditures | $ 320,250 | $ 320,250 | |

**Fig. 2. Summary of Current Income and Expenditures for Colleges and Universities.**

A UNIVERSITY
Summary of Changes in Surplus
For the Year Ended June 30, 19___

| | | |
|---|---:|---:|
| Balance July 1, 19___, consisting of: | | |
| Reserve for encumbrances | $ 13,000 | |
| Reserve for working capital | 256,000 | |
| Other reserves (itemize) | 177,000 | |
| Unappropriated | 40,750 | |
| Total | | $ 486,750 |
| Additions: | | |
| Excess of current income over current expenditures | $605,250 | |
| Transfers from Annuity Funds | 10,000 | |
| Total additions | | 615,250 |
| Total balance and additions | | $1,102,000 |
| Deductions: | | |
| Transfers to Unexpended Plant Funds | $200,000 | |
| Transfers to Funds for Retirement of Indebtedness | 40,000 | |
| Total deductions | | 240,000 |
| Balance, June 30, 19___ | | $ 862,000 |
| Consisting of: | | |
| Reserve for encumbrances | $ 10,150 | |
| Reserve for working capital | 372,500 | |
| Other reserves (itemize) | 239,100 | |
| Unappropriated | 240,250 | |
| Total | | $ 862,000 |

**Fig. 3. Summary of Changes in Current General Fund Surplus for Colleges and Universities.**

A UNIVERSITY
Summary of Changes in Balances of Funds for Retirement
of Indebtedness for the Year Ended June 30, 19___

| | | |
|---|---:|---:|
| Balance July 1, 19___ | | $254,850 |
| Additions: | | |
| Income from temporary investments | $ 650 | |
| Governmental appropriations | 200,000 | |
| Transfers from Current General Funds surplus | 40,000 | |
| Total additions | | 240,650 |
| Total balance and additions | | $495,500 |

**Fig. 4. Summary of Changes in Balances of Funds for Retirement of Indebtedness for Colleges and Universities. (Continues on next page.)**

A UNIVERSITY—(Continued)
Summary of Changes in Balances of Funds for Retirement
of Indebtedness for the Year Ended July 30, 19___

Deductions:

| | | |
|---|---:|---:|
| Retirement of bonds | $200,000 | |
| Payments on notes | 100,000 | |
| Interest charges | 5,000 | |
| Trustee service charges | 500 | |
| Total deductions | | 305,500 |
| Balance June 30, 19___ | | $190,000 |

**Fig. 4. Summary of Changes in Balances of Funds for Retirement of Indebtedness for Colleges and Universities. (Continued.)**

**HOSPITALS** [2]

**Types of funds.** The funds recommended for use by hospitals are:

1. *General fund.* The balance sheet accounts for the general fund are those that pertain to unrestricted cash or other assets available for general operating purposes. Agency accounts are also handled through the general fund. Liabilities resulting from agency transactions are shown in the liability section of the general fund balance sheet. There is also a set of income accounts to record general operating revenues and expenses.

2. *Temporary funds.* The principal and income of temporary funds are expendable only for specific purposes. Donations or other gifts designated for hospital assets are recorded in the plant fund rather than in a temporary fund.

3. *Endowment funds.* Endowment funds are those given to or set aside by the hospital, the principal of which is to be maintained intact—only the income is expendable for general or special activities. Net income earned on unrestricted endowment funds is transferred to the general fund, while net income earned on restricted endowment funds is transferred to a temporary fund.

4. *Plant funds.* Plant fund accounts consist of balance sheet items only. The assets are carried under two categories: (a) cash or investments restricted to improvement and replacement of plant, and (b) fixed assets used by the hospital in carrying on its operations. Plant funds are not used to account for fixed assets held as investments of endowment funds—such assets are carried in the appropriate endowment fund.

---

[2] This section adapted from: American Hospital Association, *Uniform Chart of Accounts and Definitions for Hospitals.* American Hospital Association, 1959.

**Classification of balance sheet accounts.** The accrual method is recommended in handling hospital accounts. Following is a master list of the general ledger balance sheet accounts for each fund, with the corresponding account numbers. This list can be adjusted to meet the requirements of any hospital, large or small, public or private:

| *Assets* | *General Fund* | *Temporary Funds* | *Endowment Funds* | *Plant Funds* |
|---|---|---|---|---|
| Cash | 100 | 140 | 150 | |
| Cash Imprest Funds | 101 | | | |
| Temporary Investments | 102 | | | |
| Investments | | 141 | 151 | |
| Accounts and Notes Receivable: | | | | |
| Patients in Hospital | 103 | | | |
| Patients Discharged | 104 | | | |
| Contracting Agency | 105 | | | |
| Other | 106 | | | |
| Allowance for Uncollectibles (Credit) | 107 | | | |
| Accrued Interest Receivable | 108 | 142 | | |
| Inventory—Supplies | 109 | | | |
| Prepaid Expenses | 110 | | | |
| Land | | | | 160 |
| Land Improvements | | | | 161 |
| Accumulated Depreciation—Land Improvements (Credit) | | | | 162 |
| Buildings | | | | 163 |
| Accumulated Depreciation—Buildings (Credit) | | | | 164 |
| Fixed Equipment | | | | 165 |
| Accumulated Depreciation—Fixed Equipment (Credit) | | | | 166 |
| Automobiles and Trucks | | | | 167 |
| Accumulated Depreciation—Automobiles and Trucks (Credit) | | | | 168 |
| Major Movable Equipment (Depreciable) | | | | 169 |
| Accumulated Depreciation—Major Movable Equipment (Credit) | | | | 170 |
| Minor Equipment (Nondepreciable) | | | | 171 |
| Plant Assets Under Construction | | | | 172 |
| Assets Restricted for Improvement, Replacement and Expansion of Plant | | | | 173 |
| Due from Other Funds | 111 | 143 | 152 | 174 |

| *Liabilities* | |
|---|---|
| Accounts Payable | 200 |
| Salaries, Wages and Fees Payable | 201 |
| Withholding Taxes Payable | 202 |
| Social Security Taxes Payable | 203 |
| Notes and Loans Payable | 204 |
| Accrued Expenses Payable | 205 |
| Deferred Income | 206 |
| Other General Fund Liabilities | 207 |

| Liabilities | General Fund | Temporary Funds | Endowment Funds | Plant Funds |
|---|---|---|---|---|
| Bonds Payable | | | | 260 |
| Mortgages Payable | | | 250 | 261 |
| Plant Improvement and Replacement Liabilities | | | | 262 |
| Due to Other Funds | 208 | 240 | 251 | 263 |
| *Capital Accounts* | | | | |
| General Fund Capital | 300 | | | |
| Income Summary | 331 | | | |
| Temporary Fund Balance | | 340 | | |
| Principal—Endowment Funds for General Purposes | | | 350 | |
| Principal—Endowment Funds for Restricted Purposes | | | 351 | |
| Capital—Invested in Plant | | | | 360 |
| Reserves for Plant Improvement and Expansion | | | | 361 |

**Classification of revenue and expense accounts.** Only the general fund has a separate set of income accounts. The other funds have so few types of revenues and expenses that transactions can be recorded directly in the fund balance accounts. Depreciation and other plant operating expenses are recorded in the general fund. However, the accumulated depreciation is shown in the plant fund. The net income or loss resulting from transactions recorded in the general fund revenue and expense accounts is transferred at the end of the hospital's fiscal year to the income summary in the general fund balance sheet accounts. Journal entries to illustrate these and other distinctive hospital transactions will be described on pages 1140 to 1145.

Following is a master list of general ledger revenue and expense accounts, showing the segregation of classes of accounts as well as account numbers:

REVENUE ACCOUNTS

*Revenue from Service to Patients*
511  Routine Service—Inpatients
512  Special Services—Inpatients
513  Routine Services—Outpatients
514  Special Services—Outpatients

*Deductions from Revenue*

Adjustments and Allowances—
521  Contracting Agencies
522  Noncontractual Patients
523  Contractual Patients
524  Employees
525  Provision for Uncollectibles

EXPENSE ACCOUNTS

610–619  *Administrative and General*
620–629  *Dietary*
*Household and Property*
631  Housekeeping Department
632  Laundry Department
633  Linen Service
634  Maintenance of Personnel
635  Operation of Plant
636  Motor Service
637  Repairs and Maintenance of Building, Equipment and Grounds

*Other Revenues*

531 General Contributions, Donations, Legacies, and Bequests
532 Grants from Community Chests, Foundations, and Government Agencies
533 Donated Services
534 Donated Commodities
535 Income from Investments
536 Transfers from Temporary Funds
537 School of Nursing
538 Telephone and Telegraph Service
539 Special Meals
540 Rental of Rooms to Employees
541 Supplies Sold
542 Purchase Discounts
543 Meals Sold
544 Miscellaneous Revenues

*Professional Care of Patients*

641 Nursing Service
642 Nursing Education
643 Medical and Surgical Service
644 Pharmacy Department
645 Medical Records and Library
646 Social Service Department
647 Operating Rooms
648 Delivery Rooms
649 Department of Anesthesiology
651 Department of Radiology
652 Laboratory Department
653 Basal Metabolism
654 Electrocardiology
655 Physical Therapy Department
656 Ambulance Service
657 Inhalation Therapy
658 Occupational Therapy
659 Electroencephalography
660 Blood Bank
661 Postoperative Room
662 Central Supply

*Outpatient*

671 Emergency Department
672 General Outpatient Department —For Clinic Patients

*Other Expenses*

681 Provision for Depreciation
682 Interest Expense
683 Rentals of Hospital Land and Buildings
684 Real Estate and Other Property Taxes
685 Fund-Raising Expenses
686 Miscellaneous Expenses

▶ NOTE: In order to provide a more detailed control over operations, it may be desirable to provide a set of subsidiary accounts to support the general ledger control accounts. Examples are as follows:

> 514 Revenue from Special Services—Outpatients
> 514.1 Operating Rooms
> 514.2 Anethesiology
> etc.
> 610 Administrative and General
> 610.1 Salaries and Wages
> 610.2 Supplies and Expense
> 610.2.1 Printing, Stationery, Postage and Office Supplies, etc.

**Recording distinctive hospital transactions.** Special hospital accounting transactions will be listed and their distinctive handling explained. The numbers appearing in conjunction with account titles refer to the master lists previously presented:

1. *Income Summary (331).* The balances of all income and expense accounts are transferred to this summary account at the end of the hospital's fiscal year. The balance in the income summary account should then be transferred to General Fund Capital (300).

2. *Temporary Fund Balance (340).* All income applicable to temporary funds is credited to this controlling account, and any losses are debited. Separate subaccounts are maintained for the balance of each individual temporary fund.

3. *Temporary Fund Expenditures.* The two types of temporary fund expenditures, each of which requires a different accounting treatment, are (a) expenditures chargeable as general or plant fund expense, and (b) expenditures chargeable directly against Temporary Fund Balance (340).

If charges normally recorded as general fund expense are paid from general fund cash but are to be met out of temporary funds, they should be recorded in the appropriate general fund expense account at the time they are incurred. The entries to record the transfer of temporary funds cash to cover such charges are:

TEMPORARY FUNDS:

| | | |
|---|---|---|
| Temporary fund balance (340) | 1,000 | |
|   Cash (140) | | 1,000 |
| To record transfer of cash to general fund. | | |

GENERAL FUND:

| | | |
|---|---|---|
| Cash (100) | 1,000 | |
|   Income transfers from temporary funds (536) | | 1,000 |
| To record receipt of cash from temporary fund. | | |

When similar items are paid directly from temporary fund cash, the entries are as follows:

TEMPORARY FUNDS:

| | | |
|---|---|---|
| Temporary fund balance (340) | 1,000 | |
|   Cash (140) | | 1,000 |
| To record payment of charges for general fund. | | |

GENERAL FUND:

| | | |
|---|---|---|
| Appropriate expense/asset account | 1,000 | |
|   Income transfers from temporary funds (536) | | 1,000 |
| To record general fund charges paid for by temporary fund. | | |

Expenditures of temporary funds for purposes and activities not normally considered within the scope of hospital operations are charged directly against Temporary Fund Balance (340). When such items are paid for from general fund cash, the entries are:

GENERAL FUND:

| | | |
|---|---|---|
| Due from other funds (111) | 1,000 | |
|   Cash (100) | | 1,000 |
| To record payment of reimbursable expenses | | |
|   by general fund. | | |

TEMPORARY FUND:

| | | |
|---|---|---|
| Temporary fund balance (340) | 1,000 | |
|   Cash (140) | | 1,000 |
| To record transfer of cash to general fund. | | |

GENERAL FUND:

| | | |
|---|---|---|
| Cash (100) | 1,000 | |
|   Due from other funds (111) | | 1,000 |
| To record receipt of cash as reimbursement | | |
|   for charges paid for other funds. | | |

When such items are paid for directly from temporary fund cash, no entries are required in any other fund.

4. *Income and expenditures applicable to endowment funds.* Profits on sales of investment assets are credited to principal, and losses are debited to principal. Separate subaccounts are maintained for each endowment fund balance. In order to keep endowment fund principal intact, a portion of the gross income received on investment real estate, equivalent to the estimated reduction in value of the real estate, may be retained in the endowment fund and not transferred to general, plant, or temporary funds. A portion of the interest received on bonds purchased at a premium should be set aside for the purpose of amortizing the amount of such premium over the remaining life of the bonds. Net income earned on unrestricted endowment funds is recorded as follows:

GENERAL FUND:

| | | |
|---|---|---|
| Cash (100) | 10,000 | |
|   Income from investments (535) | | 10,000 |
| To record receipt of net income from | | |
|   unrestricted endowment fund. | | |

Net income earned on restricted endowment funds is recorded in the following manner:

TEMPORARY FUND:

| | | |
|---|---|---|
| Cash (140) | 5,000 | |
|     Temporary fund balance (340) | | 5,000 |
| To record receipt of net income from | | |
|     restricted endowment fund. | | |

5. *Depreciation in plant assets.* Entries to record depreciation on those plant assets that are depreciable are:

GENERAL FUND:

| | | |
|---|---|---|
| Provision for depreciation (681) | 100,000 | |
|     Due to other funds (208) | | 100,000 |
| To record depreciation on plant assets. | | |

PLANT FUND:

| | | |
|---|---|---|
| Due from other funds (174) | 100,000 | |
|     Accumulated depreciation—Asset | | 100,000 |
| To record accumulated depreciation on plant | | |
|     assets in the plant fund. | | |

Under this system of entries the general fund must replace the physical assets used up by hospital general operations. If the depreciation is to be funded, the following entries are required:

GENERAL FUND:

| | | |
|---|---|---|
| Due to other funds (208) | 100,000 | |
|     Cash (100) | | 100,000 |
| To record transfer of cash to plant fund | | |
|     for funding depreciation charges. | | |

PLANT FUND:

| | | |
|---|---|---|
| Assets restricted for improvement, | | |
|     replacement and expansion of plant (173) | 100,000 | |
|     Due from other funds (174) | | 100,000 |
| To record receipt of cash for replacing | | |
|     assets used up in plant operation. | | |

6. *Retirement of plant assets.* When plant assets are retired, at least three possibilities arise and must be recorded:

a. The asset is sold for book value—

PLANT FUND:

| | |
|---|---|
| Assets restricted for improvement, | |
|     replacement and expansion of plant (173) | 15,000 |

| | | |
|---|---:|---:|
| Accumulated depreciation—Asset | 10,000 | |
|     Plant Asset | | 25,000 |
| To record disposal of plant asset at book value. | | |

    b. The asset is sold for less than book value—

PLANT FUND:

| | | |
|---|---:|---:|
| Assets restricted for improvement, | | |
|     replacement and expansion of plant (173) | 12,000 | |
| Accumulated depreciation—Asset | 10,000 | |
| Due from other funds (174) | 3,000 | |
|     Plant asset | | 25,000 |
| To record disposal of plant asset for less than book value. | | |

GENERAL FUND:

| | | |
|---|---:|---:|
| Miscellaneous expenses (687) | 3,000 | |
|     Due to other funds (208) | | 3,000 |
| To record amount due to plant fund for asset retired at less than book value. | | |

    c. The asset is sold for more than book value—

PLANT FUND:

| | | |
|---|---:|---:|
| Assets restricted for improvement, | | |
|     replacement and expansion of plant (173) | 18,000 | |
| Accumulated depreciation—Asset | 10,000 | |
|     Plant asset | | 25,000 |
|     Due to other funds (268) | | 3,000 |
| To record disposal of plant asset for more than book value. | | |

GENERAL FUND:

| | | |
|---|---:|---:|
| Due from other funds (143) | 3,000 | |
|     Miscellaneous revenues | | 3,000 |
| To record amount due from plant fund for asset retired at more than book value. | | |

    7. *Replacement of plant assets.* When assets are to be replaced, there are two general situations to be considered:

    a. Depreciation has been funded—

PLANT FUND:

| | | |
|---|---:|---:|
| Plant asset | 50,000 | |
|     Assets restricted for improvement, | | |
|     replacement and expansion of plant (173) | | 50,000 |
| To record replacement of plant asset. | | |

▶ NOTE: There is no increase in the total of the Capital—Invested in Plant account (360).

b. Depreciation has not been funded—

GENERAL FUND:

| | | |
|---|---:|---:|
| Due to other funds (208) | 50,000 | |
|   Cash (100) | | 50,000 |
| To record transfer of cash to plant fund | | |
|   for replacement of plant asset. | | |

PLANT FUND:

| | | |
|---|---:|---:|
| Assets restricted for improvement, | | |
|     replacement and expansion of plant (173) | 50,000 | |
|   Due from other funds (174) | | 50,000 |
| To record receipt of transfer of cash from | | |
|   general fund for replacement of plant asset. | | |

The replacement entry would then be the same as if the depreciation were funded.

8. *Expansion or improvement of plant assets.* When plant assets are to be expanded or improved, there are also two general situations to be considered:

a. Assets have already been received for the plant expansion—

PLANT FUND:

| | | |
|---|---:|---:|
| Plant asset | 100,000 | |
|   Assets restricted for improvement, | | |
|     replacement and expansion of plant (173) | | 100,000 |
| To record the addition to plant assets. | | |
| Reserves for plant improvement and | | |
|     expansion (361) | 100,000 | |
|   Capital—Invested in plant (360) | | 100,000 |
| To record the new capital invested in plant. | | |

b. Assets have not been received for the plant expansion—

GENERAL FUND:

| | | |
|---|---:|---:|
| General fund capital (300) | 100,000 | |
|   Cash (100) | | 100,000 |
| To record transfer of cash to plant fund | | |
|   for expansion or improvement of plant. | | |

PLANT FUND:

| | | |
|---|---|---|
| Assets restricted for improvement,<br>    replacement and expansion of plant (173) | 100,000 | |
| Reserves for plant improvement and<br>    expansion (361) | | 100,000 |

To record the transfer of cash from general
fund for expansion or improvement of plant.

The expansion or improvement entries would then be the same as under (a) above.

**Financial Statements.** The balance sheet and the income statement are the two principal statements for a hospital. A combined balance sheet, showing all the hospital funds, is illustrated in Figure 5. An income statement, which is prepared only for the general fund, is shown in Figure 6. Supplementary schedules support the income statement.

### SOCIAL SERVICE ORGANIZATIONS [3]

For the purposes of this section, a social service organization may be defined as a private, non-profit institution whose aim is to improve the mental, moral, and physical well-being of humanity. The specific areas in which these institutions function are numerous and varied—from individual care to international relations, including assistance to the needy, research beneficial to mankind, the furtherance of education and learning, and general welfare projects for the underprivileged. Organized charities, philanthropic institutions, and private welfare agencies of all types fall within the scope of the term.

**Types of funds—dual entity concept.** A social service organization has a dual entity—one that receives and accounts for *donor-unrestricted* contributions and sundry other income, and another that acts as custodian for *donor-restricted* contributions, which must be used and accounted for as the donors have prescribed. Basically, funds are classified according to these two groups of contributions. Separate ledger accounts are maintained in which to record the assets, liabilities, income, and expenses of each group. Subdivisions can be made, as indicated below.

---

[3] This section adapted from: Louis Englander, *Accounting Principles and Procedures of Philanthropic Institutions.* The New York Community Trust, 1957. Financial statements for this section furnished by: S. Edward Tomaso, Chairman of a Committee of the Los Angeles Chapter of the California Society of CPA's, which prepared a "Statement of Accounting Principles for Social Service Organizations" for the Los Angeles Social Service Commission in 1957.

# A HOSPITAL
## Balance Sheet
### As of June 30, 19____

| Assets | | | Equities | | |
|---|---|---|---|---|---|
| **GENERAL FUND:** | | | **GENERAL FUND:** | | |
| Cash | | $ 19,000 | Liabilities— | | |
| Accounts and Notes Receivable | $ 152,650 | | Accounts Payable | $ 27,540 | |
| *Less* Allowance for Uncollectibles | 5,000 | 147,650 | Salaries, Wages and Fees Payable | 159,970 | |
| | | | Withholding Taxes Payable | 30,760 | |
| Inventory—Supplies (at cost) | | 83,400 | Social Security Taxes Payable | 14,560 | |
| Prepaid Expenses | | 21,480 | Notes and Loans Payable | 20,000 | |
| Due from Temporary Funds | | 1,230 | Accrued Expenses Payable | 3,870 | |
| | | | Deferred Income | 4,670 | $ 261,370 |
| | | | Capital | | 11,390 |
| Total | | $ 272,760 | Total | | $ 272,760 |
| **TEMPORARY FUNDS:** | | | **TEMPORARY FUNDS:** | | |
| Cash | | $ 7,860 | Due to General Fund | | $ 3,650 |
| Investments—U.S. Treasury Bonds | | 10,000 | Fund Balances | | 14,790 |
| Accrued Interest Receivable | | 580 | | | |
| Total | | $ 18,440 | Total | | $ 18,440 |
| **ENDOWMENT FUNDS:** | | | **ENDOWMENT FUNDS:** | | |
| Cash | | $ 6,800 | Principal: | | |
| Investments, at book value | | | For General Purposes— | | |
| (market value $568,760) | | 547,000 | Donated | $ 396,700 | |
| | | | Created by Governing Board | 25,000 | $ 421,700 |
| | | | For Restricted Purposes— | | |
| | | | Donated | | 132,100 |
| Total | | $ 553,800 | Total | | $ 553,800 |

PLANT FUNDS:

| | | |
|---|---|---|
| Land | | $ 150,000 |
| Building (at cost) | $1,500,000 | |
| Fixed Equipment (at cost) | 490,000 | |
| Automobiles and Trucks (at cost) | 45,680 | |
| Major Movable Equipment (at cost) | 134,650 | |
| Minor Equipment (Non-depreciable) (at cost) | 43,890 | |
| Total Building and Equipment | $2,214,220 | |
| Less Accumulated Depreciation | 393,560 | 1,820,660 |
| | | $1,970,660 |
| Assets Restricted for Improvement, Replacement and Expansion of Plant | | 495,870 |
| Total | | $2,466,530 |
| Grand Total | | $3,311,530 |

PLANT FUNDS:

| | | |
|---|---|---|
| Liabilities— | | |
| Bonds Payable | $ 200,000 | |
| Mortgages Payable | 100,000 | $ 300,000 |
| Capital and Reserves— | | |
| Fund Capital | $2,064,220 | |
| Reserves for Plant Improvement and Expansion | 102,310 | 2,166,530 |
| Total | | $2,466,530 |
| Grand Total | | $3,311,530 |

Fig. 5. Combined Hospital Balance Sheet for All Funds.

A HOSPITAL
Income Statement
For Period Ending June 19___

| | | | |
|---|---:|---:|---:|
| Revenue from Services to Patients: | | | |
| Revenue from Routine Services to Inpatients | | $ 790,000 | |
| Revenue from Special Services to Inpatients (See Schedule A) | | 1,057,890 | $1,847,890 |
| Revenue from Routine Services to Outpatients | | $ 356,700 | |
| Revenue from Special Services to Outpatients (See Schedule B) | | 568,990 | 925,690 |
|     Total | | | $2,773,580 |
| Deductions from Revenue: | | | |
| Adjustments and Allowances— Contracting Agencies | $ 3,450 | | |
| Adjustments and Allowances— Noncontractual Patients | 1,780 | | |
| Adjustments and Allowances— Contractual Patients | 6,780 | | |
| Adjustments and Allowances— Employees | 4,920 | $ 16,930 | |
| Provision for Uncollectible Receivables | | 4,500 | 21,430 |
|     Net Revenue from Services to Patients | | | $2,752,150 |
| Other Operating Revenue: | | | |
| Revenue from School of Nursing | | $ 48,760 | |
| Revenue from Telephone and Telegraph Service | | 4,560 | |
| Revenue from Special Meals | | 57,800 | |
| Revenue from Rental of Rooms to Employees | | 2,400 | |
| Revenue from Supplies Sold to Employees | | 4,620 | |
| Purchase Discounts | | 54,900 | |
| Revenue from Meals Sold | | 61,870 | $ 234,910 |
|     Total Operating Revenue | | | $2,987,060 |

**Fig. 6. Income Statement for Hospital.**

Operating Expenses:

| | | |
|---|---|---|
| Administration and General | $ 325,550 | |
| Dietary | 284,600 | |
| Household and Property (See Schedule C) | 490,340 | |
| Professional Care of Patients (See Schedule D) | 1,560,730 | |
| Provision for Depreciation | 93,000 | |
| Rental of Hospital Land and Buildings | 22,000 | |
| Real Estate and Other Property Taxes | 13,500 | |
| Outpatient Department | 71,700 | |
| Total Operating Expenses | | $2,861,420 |
| Net Income from Operations | | $ 125,640 |

Other Revenue:

| | | |
|---|---|---|
| General Contributions | $93,750 | |
| Grants from Community Chest, Foundations, and Governmental Agencies | 54,800 | |
| Donated Commodities | 3,590 | |
| Income from Investments | 37,660 | $ 189,800 |

Other Expenses:

| | | |
|---|---|---|
| Interest | $15,000 | |
| Fund-Raising | 27,800 | |
| Miscellaneous | 9,700 | $ 52,500 |
| Net Nonoperating Income (or Loss) | | $ 137,300 |
| Net Income (from Operating and Nonoperating Sources) | | $ 262,940 |

**Fig. 6. Income Statement for Hospital. (Continued.)**

**General or operating fund.** This fund consists of unrestricted contributed income and all non-contributed income. It is used for the general purposes of the institution, as authorized by the directors.

**Special unrestricted funds.** If unrestricted funds are earmarked for special purposes, each resulting fund is treated as a separate entity. The assets of the general fund may be set aside for:

1. The creation of an *investment* or *endowment fund,* whose income will become a secondary source of income for current operations.

2. The creation of a *temporary fund* for some particular self-liquidating objective that cannot be financed entirely out of current contributions.

3. The creation of a *revolving fund* that can be utilized as the need occurs according to the decision of the directors.

In some instances, special types of unrestricted income, such as unrestricted legacies, are not placed in the general fund but are immediately segregated and recorded in an earmarked fund—either a *legacy fund* or the *general endowment fund.*

**Restricted funds.** Restricted funds arise from monies contributed for special purposes only, or whose manner of use is restricted by the donor. At times these funds may require augmentation to enable the institution to carry out their purposes. The directors may authorize the transfer from some earmarked funds to meet the requirements. Types of restricted funds are *research funds, endowment funds,* and *building funds.*

▶ ACCOUNTING FOR TRANSFERS: Transfers between unrestricted and restricted funds are recorded as income for one and expense for the other. Transfers between any two unrestricted funds do not affect income or expense.

**Standards of recording.** Following are distinctive principles of record-keeping for social service organizations:

1. Accounts are set up not only by natural classifications in nominal accounts, but also are subdivided by functional classifications into categories.

2. The principle of matching costs against revenues is applicable only to earned income (see page 1152). Contributed and other income must first be released or raised in order to provide the means of meeting all expenditures, whether for current operational costs or for capital outlays. Therefore, the matching process consists of relating the contributed and other income to all expenditures made in the same fiscal period, whether or not the expenditures have been wholly consumed during the period. Income and expense may be recorded on a cash, accrual, or a modified accrual basis, as long as there is full disclosure of material facts. The majority of institutions use the modified accrual basis of accounting.

▶ NOTE: The modified accrual basis as used by social service organizations differs in some respects both from the modified accrual basis for governmental units (see Chapter 31) and the modified accrual basis generally used in other types of institutions. Variations from the usual procedures of accrual accounting include the following:

    a. *Income is reported on a cash basis.* Therefore, pledges are not normally included as income and are not set up in the balance sheet, except as indicated on this page under *Contributed Income.* Interest on investments is reported as received; hence accrued interest receivable is not set up either.

    b. *Minor prepayments are ignored.* Unless they represent a significant outlay, long-term insurance premiums are charged directly to expense in the year of payment.

    c. *Fixed assets are not usually capitalized, but are treated as expense at the time of acquisition.* Even if the buildings are capitalized, moreover, no depreciation is taken as an operating expense.

    d. *All minor accruals are ignored.*

    3. Normally expenditures are not prorated by accounting periods, but are recorded as expense in the year they are incurred. This includes payments for capital expenditures and other items whose useful life extends beyond the current accounting period.

    4. Expenses are allocated among functional classifications or categories to show their purpose as well as their nature. Those methods of allocation should be applied that best fit the various types of expenditure. The purpose for which the expenditure was made serves as a guide for its classification.

**Major categories of income accounts.** The major categories of income accounts for a social service organization are:

    1. *Contributed income.* All contributions received as a result of appeals to the public are included in this category, with the results of each appeal recorded separately. If certain contributions cannot be identified with a particular appeal, they are recorded in a separate general contribution account. Legacies and memorial gifts, grants from foundations and governmental agencies, and other special types of financial assistance are recorded in individual accounts. If unpaid pledges are included in income, the pledges receivable are set up with a corresponding provision for uncollectible amounts. Contributions of food, clothing, and other property should be recorded at fair market value of the items received.

    2. *Income from affiliated organizations.* Two types of income are included in this category: (a) the income received by a national institution from its branches, and (b) the income received by a participating institution that is a member of a fund-raising agency.

3. *Endowment income.* This category includes the income from investments, interest earned on savings bank deposits, and earnings of restricted funds whose income is designated to be used for operations. Whether the investments of an institution are held as part of the assets of the operating fund or an endowment fund, all income derived from monies not presently required for current operating purposes should be reported in this category. In some restricted funds the income may be designated for general purposes or for some activity of the social service program. Where this is so, the income is transferred to the operating fund and is reported in that category.

4. *Earned income.* This category includes any income derived from the sales of products or services.

5. *Membership dues.* This classification should be used where a dues system exists.

6. *Other income.* This category will include any other type of income not included in the other categories.

**Functional classification of expenses.** As noted previously, expenses are allocated among functional classifications to show not only their nature but also their purpose. These classifications are:

1. *Social service program.* The social service objectives of an institution are translated into a program of activities or projects beneficial to the public. All costs, direct or indirect, in connection with these projects are included in this category.

2. *Fund-raising costs.* This category includes all expenses whose primary purpose is the solicitation of contributions. It should include publicity and promotion expenses incurred in connection with starting a campaign, all campaign costs, and all the necessary clerical and office expenses necessary to implement the campaign. Both direct and allocated expenses are included. If several types of fund-raising effort are used, the expenses of each are recorded separately. In connection with special affairs and functions, only the indirect expenses should be included—the direct costs are deducted from gross income. Public education materials and services that are used in connection with fund-raising efforts should be charged to public information and education rather than to fund-raising.

3. *Public information and education costs.* These costs include all expenses for keeping the public informed of the services being offered, and how and where these services can be obtained. In health organizations, it includes the cost of mass education of the general public with respect to a particular disease.

4. *Administration costs.* This category covers costs that deal with planning and directing institutional policies and finances, including (a) the expenses of the board of directors, who set policies and prepare and ap-

prove budgets, (b) the expenses of the executive directors, who carry out and interpret the policies to the staff, to other institutions, and to the public, and (c) the costs of financial management and control. Part of these costs may be incurred directly for one of the other categories and should be so allocated. The costs remaining in the administration category will be those not directly applicable to any other function.

5. *Payments to affiliated organizations.* This category applies to fund-raising agencies, and to the chapters, divisions, or branches of national institutions. The payments made by fund-raising agencies to the participating members of the agency are included in this category—these payments represent the net cash available after all expenses of the fund-raising agency have been deducted. Contributions received by the national body for the account of a chapter are credited to the branch. On the books of the chapter, all payments (either in cash or through credits) to the national institution are recorded in this category.

6. *Chapter expansion costs.* National institutions, in attempting to increase the scope of their activities and to render service to more communities, either expand existing chapters or create new chapters. On the books of the national body, all costs expended for these purposes are charged to this category.

7. *Central service costs.* This category is used primarily by fund-raising agencies and by national institutions. To it are charged all costs of services performed for the benefit of participating institutions and chapters. In fund-raising agencies, all costs are apportioned between those applicable to the agency itself and those applicable to its participating members. In national institutions, special services such as central purchasing, record keeping, and preparation of fund-raising and public information materials may be performed.

8. *Capital expenditures.* This category is used by institutions that do not capitalize their expenditures for fixed assets. It includes all expenditures for furniture, fixtures, and equipment.

**Doctrines of reporting.** Financial data are recapitulated in terms of annual fiscal periods. While this is the ordinary procedure in any line of business, there is a particular reason for following it in social service organizations. The major source of income is contributions that are received in the main as a result of annual fund-raising activities, which makes an annual accounting period convenient and logical.

Distinctive doctrines of reporting for social service organizations are:

1. Actual results of operations should be compared with budgeted figures. In this way the public is afforded the opportunity of judging how well the implied promises of the budget have been fulfilled.

2. A statement concerning the methods of expense allocation should be included as part of the financial report. Although a detailed report of the bases used need not be included, those who read the report should be assured by the auditor that the methods employed were investigated and found to be satisfactory.

3. Fixed assets may be reported at a nominal value that is less than cost. There is justification for this doctrine as applied to social service organizations. No profits are involved, so there is no improper reduction of profits. The hidden reserve created applies only to the plant or building fund, which were created through contributed income. The expenditure of that income will have been reported in the year it was received, thereby fulfilling the obligation of the institution to account for income received. The building may be regarded as a necessary tool for the implementation of program over subsequent years. While it is true that there is an intrinsic value not recorded among the assets, thereby creating a hidden reserve, that reserve normally cannot be used for the current purposes of the institution. If desired for the purpose of full disclosure, the original cost of the assets recorded at a nominal value may be noted in the report.

**Financial statements.** The balance sheet is presented as a group of individual statements—one for each fund, or each main category of funds. If the latter method is used, the details of the individual funds in each group are presented in separate supporting schedules. Statements of changes in balances of individual funds or related groups of funds may be shown in the same manner. If income is reported on a cash basis, the amount of pledges receivable should be disclosed. If buildings are set up at a nominal cost, the purchase price of buildings or the fair market value of donated buildings should be shown. Figure 7 illustrates a typical balance sheet for a social service organization.

The operating statement is either a statement of cash receipts and disbursements or a statement of income and expenses. Income, other than contributed income and endowment income, should be related to the costs necessary to obtain it. Therefore, membership dues are related to membership costs and expenses, and the costs and expenses of sales or services rendered are segregated and applied against earned income from those sales or services. Unlike the balance sheet, operating statements are reported in only two groups—restricted funds and unrestricted funds. The income and expenses applicable to each subdivision of the groups can be reported either in columnar form in the proper exhibit or as separate schedules of the exhibits. Figures 8 and 9 show typical operating statements for a social service organization.

# AFFILIATE OF A NATIONAL HEALTH AGENCY
## Balance Sheet
### June 30, 19___

| *Assets* | | | | *Liabilities and Fund Balances* | | | |
|---|---|---|---|---|---|---|---|
| **GENERAL FUND:** | | | | **GENERAL FUND:** | | | |
| Cash | | $ 36,000 | | Due to National Office: | | | |
| Investments in Savings and Loan | | | |   Contributions | $19,200 | | |
|   Associations—at cost | | 40,100 | |   Literature and material | 400 | $ 19,600 | |
| Due from Chapters and Committees: | | | | Due to Chapters | | | 200 |
|   Campaign contributions—Chapters | $17,000 | | | Due to others | | | 700 |
|   Campaign contributions—Committees | 7,800 | | | Payroll taxes payable | | | 600 |
|   Education and campaign material | 200 | | | General Fund Balances | | | 85,200 |
|   Other | 3,200 | 28,200 | | | | | |
| Inventories and prepaid expenses—at cost | | 2,000 | | | | | |
| | | | | TOTAL LIABILITIES AND GENERAL | | | |
| | | | |   FUND BALANCE | | $106,300 | |
| TOTAL GENERAL FUND ASSETS | | $106,300 | | | | | |
| **RESEARCH FUND:** | | | | **RESEARCH FUND:** | | | |
| Cash | | $ 1,100 | | Research Fund Balance | | $ 2,800 | |
| Due from Chapters | | 1,700 | | | | | |
| TOTAL RESEARCH FUND ASSETS | | $ 2,800 | | TOTAL RESEARCH FUND BALANCE | | $ 2,800 | |
| **SPECIAL AND RESTRICTED FUNDS:** | | | | **SPECIAL AND RESTRICTED FUNDS:** | | | |
| Cash | | $ 100 | | Special and Restricted Fund | | | |
| | | | |   Balance | | $ 100 | |
| TOTAL SPECIAL AND RESTRICTED | | | | TOTAL SPECIAL AND RESTRICTED | | | |
|   FUNDS ASSETS | | $ 100 | |   FUNDS BALANCE | | $ 100 | |

**Fig. 7. Balance Sheet of a Social Service Organization.**

### AFFILIATE OF A NATIONAL HEALTH AGENCY
Statement of Changes in Fund Accounts
for the Year Ended June 30, 19___

|  | General Fund | Research Fund | Special and Restricted Funds |
|---|---|---|---|
| BALANCE, JULY 1, 19___ | $ 51,200 | $2,900 | $100 |
| INCOME | | | |
| Share of 19___ contributions after deducting $93,200 retained by chapters and $73,000 paid to National office | $127,400 | $ — | — |
| Research grant from Chapter | — | 2,700 | — |
| Interest on investments | 900 | — | — |
| TOTAL INCOME | $128,300 | $2,700 | — |
| INTERFUND TRANSFERS | | | |
| Allocation to Research Fund | $ (4,200) | $4,200 | — |
| EXPENDITURES | | | |
| Research | $ — | $7,000 | — |
| Education | 25,930 | — | — |
| Organization and development of local units | 17,510 | — | — |
| Fund raising | 33,220 | — | — |
| Administration | 13,440 | — | — |
| TOTAL EXPENDITURES | $ 90,100 | $7,000 | — |
| BALANCE, JUNE 30, 19___ | $ 85,200 | $2,800 | $100 |

**Fig. 8. Statement of Changes in Funds of a Social Service Organization.**

## RELIGIOUS INSTITUTIONS [4]

**Types of funds.** The following funds are recommended for a religious institution:

1. *Current fund.* This fund is used to record transactions pertaining to general operations and not specifically allocated to some other fund.

2. *Benevolent and designated funds.* Benevolent and designated funds are established for the express purpose of carrying out specified benevolent and other designated programs.

3. *Special project funds.* These funds are used to account for specific projects that are important enough to require individual handling. Examples are building a new unit or carrying out some special activity.

[4] This section adapted from: Lowell E. Larson, "Church Accounting," *The Journal of Accountancy*, May 1957, Vol. 103, No. 5, pages 28–35.

AFFILIATE OF A NATIONAL HEALTH AGENCY

Statement of Expenditures by Funds Allocated by Functions

for the Year Ended June 30, 19____

| | Total | Education | Organization and Development of Local Units | Fund Raising | Administration |
|---|---|---|---|---|---|
| GENERAL FUND | | | | | |
| Salaries and wages | $45,900 | $13,500 | $12,030 | $11,580 | $ 8,790 |
| Travel expenses | 12,600 | 1,750 | 3,480 | 6,230 | 1,140 |
| Rent and building maintenance | 400 | — | — | 400 | — |
| Telephone and telegraph | 3,200 | 860 | 1,110 | 680 | 550 |
| Stationery, printing and office supplies | 7,100 | 1,740 | 410 | 4,570 | 380 |
| Postage, shipping and mailing | 3,300 | 890 | 110 | 1,740 | 560 |
| Rental and service of equipment | 400 | 160 | 30 | 60 | 150 |
| Insurance and bonding | 100 | — | — | — | 100 |
| Retirement plan | 200 | 60 | 70 | 40 | 30 |
| Legal and accounting services | 800 | — | — | — | 800 |
| Furniture and equipment | 700 | 140 | — | 10 | 550 |
| Educational and campaign material | 9,800 | 2,520 | — | 7,310 | 10 |
| Local bulletins and publications | 1,200 | 1,170 | — | 20 | 10 |
| Exhibits and other audio-visual materials | 500 | 500 | — | — | — |
| Meetings | 1,000 | 750 | 40 | 50 | 160 |
| Publicity expense | 600 | 360 | — | 210 | 30 |
| Speaker honoraria and travel | 800 | 770 | — | — | — |
| Scholarships | 500 | 500 | — | — | — |
| Payroll taxes | 1,000 | 260 | 230 | 320 | 190 |
| TOTAL GENERAL FUND EXPENDITURES | $90,100 | $25,930 | $17,510 | $33,220 | $13,440 |
| RESEARCH FUND | | | | | |
| Research grants paid | $ 7,000 | | | | |

Fig. 9. Statement of Expenditures for a Social Service Organization.

4. *Plant funds.* Transactions pertaining to fixed assets and related mortgage or notes payable accounts are recorded in plant funds. Sizeable plant projects are carried until completion under special project funds. Then the special fund is dissolved and the fixed assets are picked up in the proper plant fund.

**Special features of the accounting system.** The cash basis of accounting is normally used, with budget control on a memorandum basis only. Required books of account are a cash receipts journal and a cash disbursements journal. A general ledger, while not essential, is a useful and desirable addition to the basic system. If a general ledger is introduced into the system, the accrual basis of accounting can be substituted for the cash basis merely by employing a general journal. Another possible refinement is the use of budgetary accounting similar to that employed in governmental general funds, as described in Chapter 31.

**Handling accounts.** If the cash basis is used, columnar groupings in the cash journals are by the various funds. The sources of cash receipts are indicated by appropriate columnar headings as follows: (1) pledge, (2) plate, (3) designation (for designated funds only), and (4) miscellaneous. Columnar headings in the cash disbursements journal indicate: (1) the object of the expenditure (current and special project funds), (2) the program affected (benevolent and designated funds), and (3) the specific property or related liability account (plant funds). When the accrual basis is employed in conjunction with formal budget entries in the general ledger, this information is reflected in appropriate revenue and expense accounts in the general ledger, and in subsidiary accounts.

**Control of cash.** Records of members' accounts are maintained by the financial secretary. These accounts consist primarily of contributions received from the members of the congregation. Pledges and collections are recorded in a subsidiary ledger with a separate account being maintained for each individual contributor. To identify contributors properly, envelopes should be provided for the regular Sunday worship services. The cash received in these envelopes should be counted as soon as possible after the services, and a report rendered as shown in Figure 10.

Disbursements are authorized through approval of the budget by the congregation, after which the officers of the church can act within the provisions of the budget. Any changes must be authorized by the congregation or whatever group is given such specific authority. Disbursements should be made by check only. A petty cash system can be installed for small incidental expenditures.

A CHURCH
Receipts Summary Report
Date: February 15, 19___

| | Current Funds | Benevolent and Designated | | Plant Funds | Total |
|---|---|---|---|---|---|
| | | Item | Amount | | |
| Sunday offering: | | | | | |
| Pledges | $1,456 | Welfare | $145 | $127 | $1,728 |
| Plate offering | 567 | Memorial | 72 | 10 | 649 |
| Total Sunday offering | $2,023 | | $217 | $137 | $2,377 |
| Other receipts: | | | | | |
| Winter festival | $ 346 | | | $346 | $ 692 |
| Church basketball | 150 | | | | 150 |
| Total other receipts | $ 496 | | | $346 | $ 842 |
| TOTAL RECEIPTS | $2,519 | | $217 | $483 | $3,219 |

| Deposited: | | Signed: |
|---|---|---|
| Name of bank | *First National Bank* | JOHN H. GREEN, *Treasurer* |
| Date | *February 16, 19___* | JOEL N. HOPE, *Deacon* |
| Amount | *$3,219 ** | |

\* The total of the deposit and the receipts summary must agree.

**Fig. 10. Church Receipts Summary Report.**

**Financial statements.** Monthly reports can be prepared directly from the columnar totals in the journals if the cash basis is followed. Annual financial statements can then be prepared from a summation of the monthly totals. Under the accrual system, regular governmental or institutional procedures are followed. Statements are set up by funds as in the case of edutional institutions and hospitals, and comparisons with the budget are included.

Monthly statements are usually limited to an analysis of cash receipts and disbursements. Any other interim reports, such as semi-annual or quarterly statements, are similar to the monthly statement. In the annual report a balance sheet and certain statistical data that are of interest to the congregation should be added. This statistical data might include:

1. Contributions per member.
2. Local disbursements per member.
3. Benevolent disbursements per member.
4. Relation of benevolent disbursements to local disbursements.

▶ SUGGESTION: The statistical information can be presented graphically for the current year and four or five previous years.

# 33

# Health and Welfare, and Pension Benefit Funds

**PERCY A. LOCKITCH**

*Certified Public Accountant; Seattle, Washington*

# CHAPTER THIRTY-THREE

# Health and Welfare, and Pension Benefit Funds

This chapter will consider in a general way the social and economic significance of health and welfare, and pension benefit funds (hereafter, for the sake of brevity, the term *welfare and pension benefit funds—or plans—* will be used). It will define and describe welfare and pension benefit plans. It will also summarize the laws through which the Federal government and some state governments exercise control over these plans. Finally, there will be detailed discussions of the areas that are of direct interest to the accountant—the accounting system, auditing procedures, and the tax status of the funds.

## THE IMPORTANCE OF WELFARE AND PENSION BENEFIT FUNDS

**Economic significance.** The tremendous growth of welfare and pension benefit funds in the past decade has been an amazing facet of our modern economy. To the accountant, this growth means a wider, and in many cases, a completely new field of activity.

The latest information released by the Secretary of Labor and by the Bureau of Internal Revenue indicates that there are at least 102,400 health and welfare benefit plans, 54,450 pension benefit plans, and 700 combination plans. The assets of plans registered with the Department of Labor amount to almost $58 billion. A recent survey of a group of representative companies, conducted by the Chamber of Commerce of the United States, showed that these companies were paying out an average of approximately 8% of their total payrolls for employee welfare and pension benefits that are not legally required. This comes to about $370 per year for each employee.

These figures are staggering. But they represent only a beginning upsurge in the popularity of welfare and pension benefit plans.

**Reasons for growth.** What's behind the rapid growth, and why can we expect far greater growth in the immediate future? The following reasons provide the answer.

1. *Unions now seek fringe benefits almost as actively as they do increased wages.* Unions have always been interested in the welfare of their members, but for a long time they were suspicious of benefit plans sponsored by employers or arrived at through collective bargaining. They were afraid that employers would use these plans as a device for holding down wages and keeping the employees "tied" to one company, especially with respect to pension plans. Also, there was a lack of confidence in the soundness of plans established on a company basis. Experience has proved that these fears were groundless. Since most unions have already obtained health and welfare benefit plans for their memberships, they now have the goal of increasing the benefits derived from these plans, and adding pension plans.

▶ NOTE: Welfare and pension benefit plans obtained by collective bargaining, usually as part of the labor contract, are called *negotiated* plans. The company agrees to pay into a benefit fund a specified amount of money per hour or per shift worked, or a stated flat sum per month for each employee.

2. *Companies want to attract and hold non-union personnel.* Companies are recognizing the fact that they must establish plans for their salaried and supervisory personnel so that a parity will be maintained between union and non-union employees. This type of plan is known as a *management* plan.

3. *Favorable tax treatment enables companies having qualified plans to immediately deduct the cost of the plans.* Health and welfare contributions made by an employer can be deducted by him as a necessary business expense. Contributions to a *qualified* pension fund are also deductible. In addition, the fund set up for either type of plan can qualify as a tax-exempt organization. Instructions on how to qualify a plan plus a more detailed discussion of the tax status of welfare and pension benefit plans will be found on pages 1193 to 1197.

▶ OBSERVATION: In the long run, employees receive more "take home pay" from a tax-exempt welfare or pension benefit plan than they would from a salary increase. Contributions made by an employer to either type of plan are not taxable to the employee. Benefits received from a health and welfare plan are not taxable to the beneficiary. Pension benefits are not taxed until they are received, so the beneficiary will usually gain by being in a lower tax bracket as a pensioner than he would have been as an employee. Lump-sum pension payments can usually be reported by the beneficiary as a gain from the sale or exchange of a capital asset held for more than six months.

## DEFINITIONS AND GENERAL INFORMATION

**What is a health and welfare benefit plan?** A health and welfare benefit plan gives a participant, his dependent, or his beneficiary all of any of such things as medical benefits, pay while ill or unemployed, and death benefits. These plans carry sufficient funds to take care of reserves for benefits earned and expenses incurred. Any excess funds are used to acquire better benefits for the participants.

**What is a pension benefit plan?** A pension benefit plan provides retirement benefits for participants. Most pension plans begin pension payments about one year after inception of the plan. Pension benefits at the outset are usually modest, thus enabling the plan to build up toward complete funding of the past service liability. The funds continue to increase until such time as the past service liability is completely funded and sufficient funds are available to cover future liability. This generally takes from ten to fifteen years.

▶ NOTE: Profit-sharing plans that provide benefits at retirement are includible as pension benefit plans.

**Negotiated versus management plans.** *Negotiated* welfare or pension benefit plans and *management* welfare or pension benefit plans were defined on page 1163. An analysis of the two types of plans follows:

1. *Size distinction.* Management plans are usually single employer plans. They are started by the management of a concern for the sole benefit of the employees of that firm. In contrast to this is the industry-wide or regional nature of most negotiated plans. For example, fifteen thousand employers in the Pacific Coast region contribute to a teamster pension fund that covers about 120,000 employees.

▶ COMMENT: There are, however, some instances where employers in a similar line of work will pool their resources and establish a multi-employer management plan. The advantages of large combined plans are discussed on page 1166.

2. *Accounting and operational differences.* The single employer management plan presents no particular problem to the accountant. Records are usually maintained by the regular accounting staff of the organization. This staff is thoroughly familiar with the firm's policies and has available all necessary payroll and personnel data to process claims quickly and accurately. For this reason, subsequent consideration of the accounting system and of auditing procedures (see pages 1172 to 1193), while encom-

passing the single employer type of plan, will deal mainly with the multi-employer negotiated plan.

The same line of reasoning can be applied to the area of operational problems. A single employer plan by its very nature is easier to control than is a multi-employer plan. Also, information concerning the operational features of a single employer plan is readily available to the independent accountant through employees, company manuals, and similar material that would be referred to for an ordinary audit engagement. Therefore, the following discussion will relate primarily to the operation of multi-employer negotiated plans.

**How a negotiated plan operates—the trust agreement.** Management of a negotiated plan is usually vested in a board of trustees, generally an equal number from labor and management. The basic document for a negotiated plan is the written conformed trust agreement. In addition to providing for the establishment of the plan, the trust agreement should:

1. Specify the class or type of employee eligible for coverage.

2. State the basis for employers' and employees' contributions.

3. Guarantee that all funds will be used only for employee benefits and trust expenses, and that no *direct* cash payments will be made to employees except as pension benefits under a trusteed plan.

4. Provide for a board of trustees and designate a third party who would decide matters when the board was deadlocked. If no third party is named, some sort of arbitration machinery should be set up.

5. Describe in detail the functions and powers of the board of trustees, and outline the procedures that the board is to follow.

6. Cover all general provisions regarding the operation of the trust and the rights and obligations of the employers, the employees, and the trustees.

▶ OBSERVATION: The design of the trust agreement will have an important bearing on the cost of the plan. In the trust agreement for a health and welfare benefit plan, for example, a clause discontinuing loss-of-time coverage during layoff, leave of absence, or strike could make quite a difference in the eventual cost of the plan.

▶ WARNING: A trust agreement is a legal document and is properly the work of an attorney.

**The trustees.** Members of the board are normally top-rated executives of either a labor organization or a management concern, and, as such, have little time for the daily routine operation of the plan. They select, with the consent of the union members, the way the plan is to be funded, and they usually appoint an administrator. In addition to the administrator, they delegate various trust functions to consultants, brokers, carriers, corporate trustees and nominees, attorneys, and actuaries.

**Methods of funding a negotiated health and welfare benefit plan.** Health and welfare benefit plans are usually funded by an insurance contract between the trust and an insurance carrier or a health insurance group. However, there are self-insured plans where the trust itself pays the medical bills and other benefits of the covered employees. These self-insured plans often place a great deal of emphasis on measures to prevent sickness and accidents.

**Methods of funding a negotiated pension benefit plan.** The two types of negotiated pension benefit plans most commonly used are the *insured* plan and the *trusteed* plan. If the trustees adopt an insured plan, all funds in excess of current expenses are remitted to an insurance carrier. The carrier guarantees a rate of interest on these funds. When a participant retires, an annuity policy is purchased for him from these accumulated funds. Trusteed plans, usually through the medium of a corporate trustee, invest the funds and pay benefits directly from the plan.

▶ COMMENT: The investment of these monies requires great caution, and corporate trustees invariably follow the "prudent man" rule. Therefore, they acquire only high-grade securities. The charge has been levelled that pension trusts create scarcity in high-grade investment securities and thus keep prices abnormally high.

**Function of the administrator.** The administrator is responsible for maintaining the records for the plan and carrying out the dictates of the board of trustees. The administrator could be the trust department of a bank, an individual, or a corporation that serves on a fee basis (usually a percentage of employers' contributions). In some cases, the administrative function is carried out by the trust itself with a salaried staff. The interests of all parties are best served if all administrative activities are removed from both the management and the union offices. A competent independent administrator should be appointed.

**Advantages of large combined plans.** In negotiated health and welfare benefit plans, the cost of carrier retention is far lower for large plans than for small ones because the larger the plan, the less expense the carrier has. A large pension trust has better investment opportunities than a small pension trust, with the result that its rate of earnings would normally be higher. In addition, the administrative costs are proportionally lower for a large plan, whether it be health and welfare or pension benefit, than they would be for a small one.

▶ COMMENT: There is a tendency for all similar craft local unions in an area to join forces in one large plan; also, related craft unions often unite in a single plan. A laborers' health and welfare plan in western Washington covers the membership from fifteen scattered local unions. There are approximately 1,600 employers making contributions for the benefit of about 11,000 workers. In Alaska all the building laborers and ironworkers are joined in one plan. Another large plan has combined auto painters, sheet-metal workers, and light-metal fabricators.

**Related or overlaid pension plans.** A negotiated health and welfare benefit plan may be local in scope, but a related or overlaid pension plan—that is, one that covers the same people—might be expanded so that it embraces several states. Such pension plans are often the "open end" type of plan.

▶ EXAMPLE: The Automotive Machinists' Health and Welfare Plan in Seattle is overlaid with a pension plan. Soon after the establishment of the pension plan in Seattle, the Spokane membership joined and soon thereafter the rest of the membership in the State of Washington and all in the State of Oregon joined. Subsequently, memberships in Utah, Montana, Colorado, and Idaho were added. The door is open for all the memberships in the fourteen western states to be welded into one strong pension plan.

**Reciprocity agreements.** These agreements allow a worker who has insufficient eligibility in either of two negotiated health and welfare benefit plans, but has sufficient eligibility in both plans combined, to borrow from one plan so that he may obtain benefits in the other. This is done by transferring hours from one plan to the other. The agreements are very common in the construction crafts since many workers follow the work and, as a result, compile work hours in more than one jurisdiction.

## FEDERAL AND STATE CONTROL

The Federal government and some state governments have become increasingly interested in welfare and pension benefit plans as a result of the plans' rapidly expanding social and economic significance. The accountant should recognize this governmental influence, and he should acquaint himself with the pertinent provisions of certain laws that have been enacted. These laws are:

1. The Labor Management Relations (Taft-Hartley) Act.
2. The Labor-Management Reporting and Disclosure (Labor Reform) Act, also known as the Landrum-Griffin Act.

3. The Welfare and Pension Plans Disclosure Act.
4. Individual state disclosure laws.

**The Taft-Hartley Act.** Section 302 of this law makes it illegal for an employer to give any money to a representative of his employees for the purpose of establishing a welfare or pension fund (or for the union to accept the money) unless certain conditions are met. One of these conditions is that the fund must be audited annually.

**The Landrum-Griffin Act.** Section 502 provides, in part, that a representative or employee of a trust in which a labor organization is interested must be bonded if he handles funds or other property of the trust. This rule applies only to labor organizations that have property and annual financial receipts exceeding the value of $5,000. The amount of the bond must be equal to at least ten per cent of the funds handled by the representative or employee, and his predecessor, during the preceding fiscal year. In no case, however, need the bond be for more than $500,000. If it is the trust's first year, the amount of the bond must be at least $10,000.

**The Welfare and Pension Plans Disclosure Act.** This Act, when it first became effective, was unique in that it was limited to disclosure and reporting and did not go into the field of regulation. The Secretary of Labor had no real power to enforce compliance with the provisions of the Act. Subsequent amendments by Congress, however, have added teeth to the Act—the Secretary now has direct enforcement powers, and there are provisions for criminal penalties.

The Act provides that the administrator of a plan that has 26 or more participants must file two copies of a plan description with the Labor Department; if the plan covers 100 or more participants, the administrator must also file two copies of an annual report. The Secretary of Labor is authorized to prescribe, by regulations, the form and detail of the plan descriptions and annual reports. Forms D-1 and D-2, issued by the Secretary, embody the requirements for such form and detail.

*The plan description—Form D-1.* Within 90 days after the establishment of a plan, the administrator must issue a description of the plan. This is, in essence, a registration statement. Among other things, it must show: (1) the name, address, official position, relation to the employer or union, and other offices of the person or persons *defined* as the administrator (see below), (2) the names, titles, and addresses of any trustee who is not the administrator, (3) the name, address, and description of the plan and type of administration, (4) a schedule of benefits, the source of financing, and the identity of the organization through which the benefits are provided, (5) the basis of accounting, that is, whether records are kept on a calendar year basis, or on a policy or fiscal year basis, (6) whether the plan is referred to in a collective bargaining agreement, and (7) the procedures to be followed in presenting claims for benefits, and the remedies available for redress of denied claims.

Along with the description of the plan, the administrator must furnish copies of the plan or of the bargaining agreement, contract, or other instrument under which the plan was established and is operated.

Any changes that are made in the plan must be reported to the Labor Department within sixty days after the change has been made.

▶ OBSERVATION: The plan description must be signed and sworn to by the *administrator*. Under this Act he is defined as the person or persons designated by the terms of the plan or collective bargaining agreement with responsibility—or in the absence of such designation, the person or persons actually responsible—for the *ultimate* control, disposition, or management of the money received. Therefore, the trustees are often considered the administrators, and must sign as such and bear the responsibility for complying with the provisions of the Act.

*The annual report—Form D-2.* The administrator must file two copies of the annual report within 150 days after the end of the plan's accounting year. However, the Secretary of Labor may require reports to be filed more frequently than annually, if he thinks it is necessary.

The following information must be included in every annual report:

1. A detailed summary of assets broken down to specify the amount in each of the following: cash, government bonds, non-government bonds, debentures, common stocks, preferred stocks, common trust funds, real estate loans and mortages, operated real estate, other real estate, and other assets.

2. A statement of the amount contributed by *each* employer.

3. The amount, if any, contributed by employees.

4. The number and amount of benefits paid.

5. The number of employees covered by the plan.

6. A statement of liabilities, disbursements, receipts, and other financial activities; and a detailed statement of salaries, fees, and commissions paid, to whom and for what purpose.

If the Secretary of Labor determines that an investigation of a plan is required, he may require the filing of a detailed supporting schedule of assets and liabilities.

▶ REMEMBER THIS: This above information must be either sworn to by the administrator, or "certified to by an *independent certified or licensed public accountant,* based upon a comprehensive audit conducted in accordance with accepted standards of auditing."

Additional data must be furnished, dependent upon the type of plan. If the benefits are provided by insurance, the annual report should divulge (1) premiums paid to each carrier, (2) number of persons covered by each class of benefits, (3) claims paid by the carrier, (4) all dividends, retroactive rate adjustments, commissions, and other fees or specific costs paid by the insurance company, (5) amounts held by the insurance company to provide benefits after retirement and the remainder amount of premiums, and (6) the names and addresses of the brokers, agents, or other persons to whom commissions or fees were paid, the amount paid to each, and for what purpose. If the insurance carrier does not maintain separate experience records covering the specific group, the annual report must include a statement as to the basis of the premium rate, the amount of premiums paid, a copy of the financial report of the carrier, and a detailed statement of any specific costs incurred by the carrier in connection with the acquisition or retention of the plan.

Trusteed pension plans must also report the type and basis of pending actuarial assumptions used, the amount of current and past liability, and the number of employees, retired and not retired, covered by the plan.

▶ HOW TO OBTAIN FORMS: You can obtain copies of Forms D-1 and D-2 by writing to the Welfare and Pension Reports Division, Bureau of Labor Standards, U.S. Department of Labor, Washington 25, D.C. A *Guide in Using Plan Description and Annual Report Forms* is also available.

*Bonding and enforcement provisions of the Act.* Bonding of administrators, officers, and employees of welfare and pension plans is required under the Act. The minimum bond is $1,000 and the maximum is 10% of funds handled in excess of $10,000, up to $5,000,000.

The Secretary of Labor is authorized to make an investigation of any plan that he believes is in some way in violation of the Act, but he may act only when he has first required a certification of the annual report by an independent certified or licensed public accountant.

An administrator of a plan is required not only to file copies of a plan description and an annual report with the Labor Department, but he must also (1) make copies available for examination by any participant or beneficiary at the plan's principal office, and (2) mail a copy of the plan description and an adequate summary of the latest annual report to any participant or beneficiary who makes a written request. This data must be provided within 30 days of the request. The administrator may have to pay $50 to the one making the request for each day of failure or refusal to comply, plus costs and reasonable attorney fees.

Any person who wilfully violates or fails to comply with the provisions of the Act may be fined $1,000 and imprisoned for six months for each offense.

Any person who embezzles or steals any funds or property from a trust fund may be subject to a fine of $10,000 and imprisonment for five years. A similar penalty attaches to anyone who makes a false statement or knowingly fails to disclose any fact required to be disclosed.

Any employee of a plan, any officer, counsel, agent or employee of a sponsoring employer, and any person or representative of a benefit service who offers or receives any fee, kickback, commission, gift, loan, or thing of value with the intent to influence or be influenced with respect to the plan's affairs is subject to three years in jail and a $10,000 fine.

**State disclosure laws.** Five states have welfare and pension fund disclosure laws. These state laws are all different from one another; however, every one of them requires that an annual report be filed by the plans that come under their coverage. The standard reporting form adopted by the National Association of Insurance Commissioners is used, with minor modifications, in all states having a disclosure law.

Other principal provisions of the various state disclosure acts are summarized in the following chart:

| State | Type of plan covered | Must the plan be registered? | Who administers the law? | Is an examination required? |
|---|---|---|---|---|
| Connecticut | Trusteed | Yes | Insurance Commission | No (3) |
| Massachusetts | All | Yes | (1) | No (4) |
| New York | Negotiated | Yes | (2) | Yes |
| Washington | Trusteed | Yes | Insurance Commission | Yes |
| Wisconsin | All | Yes | Insurance Commission | Yes |

(1) A three man interdepartmental board composed of the Commissioners of Labor and Industries, Banks, and Insurance.
(2) The Superintendent of Banks if the fund is managed by a corporate trustee, the Superintendent of Insurance if it is not.
(3) The Insurance Commissioner may conduct an examination only if requested to do so by the interested parties.
(4) The Board must have the approval of a probate court judge before it can examine a fund.

## THE ACCOUNTING SYSTEM

**Interested parties.** Many diverse factions are interested in the accounting for welfare and pension benefit funds. A listing of the interested parties will demonstrate how important it is to maintain adequate records and controls.

1. *The employer.* The employer wants to be sure that he is getting the maximum benefits for his employees with a minimum of expense.

2. *The employees.* In most cases, employees accept a benefit plan in lieu of a wage increase. Since effort was expended to obtain these benefits, and since the benefits are a form of compensation to the employees, they also want to make certain that "their money" is working to the best advantage.

3. *The board of trustees.* Members of the board usually delegate much of their authority, so they must depend on good accounting methods and thorough auditing for the assurance that funds under their trusteeship are functioning properly.

4. *The Federal government.* The Federal government makes a substantial financial sacrifice because of the provisions of the Internal Revenue Code relating to tax-exempt plans (see page 1193). In addition, the Government is concerned with the protection of the plans' participants, as was indicated in the discussion on Federal and state control.

5. *State governments.* If they have their own income tax laws, state governments also have a direct financial interest. Protection of the participants in plans operating within their jurisdiction is another consideration.

▶ OBSERVATION: In most cases, many employers make contributions to a fund and many participants share in the benefits. The interests of all the concerned groups are best served by the establishment of a trust fund that is operated independently of the employer group and the employee group.

**Chart of accounts.** The following chart lists the account titles that have been used in many welfare and pension benefit funds. Also shown are the books that would be the source of entries to these accounts. This is a basic chart; the administrator or accountant can select those accounts that best serve the purpose of his particular plan, or he can add other accounts as the occasion warrants. The chart is designed for either cash basis or accrual basis accounting.

▶ COMMENT: A great many accounts are affected by general journal entries. Pension trusts in particular usually employ a corporate trustee or nominee, or an insurance carrier. In the case of a trusteed plan, the corporate trustee has control of the cash. In the case of an insured plan, the insurance carrier has all the money and all interest and annuities purchased have to be recorded by means of journal entries. Therefore, the only funds usually available to an administrator for pension funds are an operation fund that is reimbursed monthly by the corporate trustee and a pension payment fund from which pension payments are made, and which is also reimbursed by the corporate trustee. Only by use of the general journal can a complete explanation of each transaction be made.

## BALANCE SHEET ACCOUNTS.

| ASSETS | Debits from | Credits from |
|---|---|---|
| Cash Accounts (a ledger sheet for each bank) | Cash Receipts or General Journal | Cash Disbursements or General Journal |
| Accounts Receivable | General Journal | Cash Disbursements or General Journal |
| Accrued Interest Receivable | General Journal | General Journal |
| Investments—U. S. Bonds | Cash Disbursements or General Journal | Cash Receipts or General Journal |
| Investments—Other Government Bonds | Cash Disbursements or General Journal | Cash Receipts or General Journal |
| Investments—Corporate Bonds | Cash Disbursements or General Journal | Cash Receipts or General Journal |
| Investments—Preferred Stocks | Cash Disbursements or General Journal | Cash Receipts or General Journal |
| Investments—Common Stocks | Cash Disbursements or General Journal | Cash Receipts or General Journal |
| Mortgages Receivable | Cash Disbursements or General Journal | Cash Receipts or General Journal |
| Furniture and Fixtures | Cash Disbursements Journal | Cash Receipts or General Journal |
| Depreciation Reserve | General Journal | General Journal |
| LIABILITIES | | |
| Premiums Payable | Cash Disbursements Journal | General Journal |

| LIABILITIES *(Cont.)* | Debits from | Credits from |
|---|---|---|
| Other Accounts Payable | Cash Disbursements Journal | General Journal |
| Accrued Taxes and Expenses | Cash Disbursements Journal | General Journal |
| SURPLUS | | |
| Reserve for Future Benefits and Expense | General Journal | General Journal |

## INCOME AND EXPENSE ACCOUNTS.

INCOME

| | Debits from | Credits from |
|---|---|---|
| Employers' Contributions | Cash Disbursements or General Journal | Cash Receipts Journal |
| Employees' Contributions | Cash Disbursements or General Journal | Cash Receipts Journal |
| Interest—Savings Banks | General Journal | General Journal |
| Interest—U. S. Bonds | General Journal | Cash Receipts or General Journal |
| Interest—Premium Deposits | General Journal | Cash Receipts or General Journal |
| Interest—Other Government Bonds | General Journal | Cash Receipts or General Journal |
| Interest—Corporate Bonds | General Journal | Cash Receipts or General Journal |
| Interest—Mortgages | General Journal | Cash Receipts or General Journal |
| Dividends—Stocks | General Journal | Cash Receipts or General Journal |
| Experience Rating Refunds | General Journal | Cash Receipts Journal |
| Gain or Loss on Sale or Redemption of Securities | Cash Receipts or General Journal | Cash Receipts or General Journal |
| Suspended Annuity Payments | General Journal | General Journal |

EXPENSES

| | | |
|---|---|---|
| Refunds to Contributors or Other Trust | Cash Disbursements Journal | General Journal |

| EXPENSES *(Cont.)* | *Debits from* | *Credits from* |
|---|---|---|
| Accrued Interest Purchased | Cash Disbursements or General Journal | General Journal |
| Administration Fees | Cash Disbursements Journal | General Journal |
| Audit Fees | Cash Disbursements Journal | General Journal |
| Bank Charges | Cash Disbursements or General Journal | General Journal |
| Investment Counsel Fees (or Corporate Trustee Fees) | Cash Disbursements Journal | General Journal |
| Legal Fees | Cash Disbursements Journal | General Journal |
| Actuarial Fees | Cash Disbursements Journal | General Journal |
| Salaries | Cash Disbursements Journal | General Journal |
| Taxes—F.I.C.A., State and Federal Unemployment, Industrial Insurance, Personal Property | Cash Disbursements Journal | General Journal |
| N.S.F. Check Losses | General Journal | General Journal |
| Printing and Office Supplies and Expense | Cash Disbursements Journal | General Journal |
| Rent | Cash Disbursements Journal | General Journal |
| Utilities | Cash Disbursements Journal | General Journal |
| Postage | Cash Disbursements Journal | General Journal |
| Rent of Equipment | Cash Disbursements Journal | General Journal |
| Insurance—General | Cash Disbursements Journal | General Journal |
| Insurance Consultant's Fees | Cash Disbursements Journal | General Journal |
| Trustees' Fees | Cash Disbursements Journal | General Journal |

|  | Debits from | Credits from |
|---|---|---|
| EXPENSES (*Cont.*) | | |
| Trustees' Travel Expense | Cash Disbursements Journal | General Journal |
| Depreciation | General Journal | General Journal |
| Telephone and Telegraph | Cash Disbursements Journal | General Journal |
| Deposit Administration Remittance | Cash Disbursements Journal | General Journal |
| Insurance Premiums—Carrier | Cash Disbursements Journal | General Journal |
| Insurance Premiums—Health Care Contractor | Cash Disbursements Journal | General Journal |
| Benefits Paid Direct From Fund | Cash Disbursements Journal | General Journal |
| Fidelity Bonds | Cash Disbursements Journal | General Journal |
| Maintenance and Repair of Office Equipment | Cash Disbursements Journal | General Journal |
| Pensions Paid (if a self-insured Plan) | Pension Register | General Journal |
| Retirement Annuities Purchased (if an insured Plan) | Cash Disbursements Journal | General Journal |
| Mortgage Service Cost | Cash Receipts or General Journal | General Journal |

▶ NOTE: In many instances (cash refunds, for example), credits to expense accounts can come from the Cash Receipts Journal.

**Accounting records.** The accounting records should be simple books of original entry and a general ledger supported by subsidiary ledgers. As indicated in the chart of accounts, the books of original entry are the Cash Receipts Journal, the Cash Disbursements Journal, the Pension Register, and the General Journal. Figure 1 shows how the first three of these books might be set up.

The General Ledger is supported by the following subsidiary ledgers:

1. *The Investment Ledger.* This is the usual type of investment record.

2. *The Employer Contributor Ledger.* All employers' contributions are detailed by employer in this ledger. If a punched-card system is in operation, a deck of punched cards can serve as the Employer Contributor Ledger.

CASH RECEIPTS JOURNAL

| CONTRIBUTION | Dr. AMOUNT | Cr. EMPLOYER CONTRIBUTION | Cr. EMPLOYEE CONTRIBUTION | Cr. DIVIDENDS | Cr. INTEREST | Cr. OTHER EXPLANATION | AMOUNT |
|---|---|---|---|---|---|---|---|
| | | | | | | | |
| | | | | | | | |

CASH DISBURSEMENTS JOURNAL

| DATE | ITEM | CHECK # | Cr. AMOUNT | Dr. PREMIUMS PURCHASED | Dr. OFFICE SUPPLIES | Dr. REFUNDS | Dr. OTHER ITEM | AMOUNT |
|---|---|---|---|---|---|---|---|---|
| | | | | | | | | |
| | | | | | | | | |

PENSION REGISTER

| DATE | NAME | CHECK # | AMOUNT | COMMENTS |
|---|---|---|---|---|
| | | | | |
| | | | | |

**Fig. 1. Cash Receipts Journal, Cash Disbursements Journal, and Pension Register.**

3. *The Employees' or Participants' Ledger.* The prime purpose of the Employees' or Participants' Ledger is to determine eligibility. The form of the employees' eligibility records, which make up the Employees' or Participants' Ledger, depends upon the eligibility requirements of the particular plan. A deck of punched cards could be used as the Employees' or Participants' Ledger.

There are numerous ways in which eligibility requirements can be determined. For example, the requirements for insurance coverage, especially in the case of health and welfare benefit plans, have about as many variations as there are plans in existence. Some of the most common are:

a. *Current month coverage.* The employee works one month, the employer remits the next month, and the employee is covered for the month in which the employer made his remittance.

b. *Lag month coverage.* The employee works one month, the employer remits the next month, and the employee is covered for the month subsequent to the one in which the employer made his remittance.

c. *Deposit premium coverage.* The employer deposits a month's premium in advance. This advance premium is used *only* if the employer does not pay into the fund when he should. It is refundable if he withdraws as a contributor.

d. *Hour bank coverage.* An employee may build up more working hours than are necessary for coverage, and save the excess hours for future use. For example, if eligibility called for 120 work hours a month and an employee had accumulated 480 extra work hours, he would be covered for the next four months, even though he did not work during that period.

e. *Cast back method.* An employee may "cast back" any deficiency to previous months in which he had accumulated more hours than were needed for eligibility. This method is commonly used in the construction industry because of the peaks and valleys of construction employment.

The infinite variety of the eligibility requirements dictates the setting up of adequate controls so that *all* eligible participants and *only* eligible participants will obtain benefits.

**Accounting controls and procedures.** *Cash receipts.* Direct banking provides the best means of control for contributions. When the contributor mails his remittance directly to the bank, there is no need for the administrator, or anyone on his staff, to handle funds. Not only does this constitute good control, but it also saves time for the administrator's staff, and eliminates the necessity of bonding them under the provisions of the Landrum-Griffin Act.

With his remittance, the contributor forwards to the bank an *Employer Remittance Report.* The bank makes the deposit to the appropriate fund or funds and sends the deposit slip and the Employer Remittance Report to the administrator. Figure 2 shows an Employer Remittance Report, which would be prepared by the contributor, for a health and welfare benefit plan. In situations where employment is stable, a pre-billing form of the Employer Remittance Report can be used. The administrator prepares the pre-billing type of report on the basis of the previous month's figures. Then it goes to the employer who makes the required additions or deletions and mails the corrected version along with his remittance to the bank. Figure 3 is an example of the pre-billing form of the Employer Remittance Report.

EMPLOYER REMITTANCE REPORT

PAGE____OF____PAGES

*Construction Industry Health and Security Trust Fund*

Check here if you need more forms ☐

**IMPORTANT INSTRUCTIONS – PLEASE FOLLOW:**

1. Mail reports and remittances to, and make check payable to
CONSTRUCTION INDUSTRY TRUST FUND, care of First National Bank, P.O. Box 49, Seattle, Washington
2. Complete all reports in triplicate, retain third copy (pink) for your files and mail first two copies to the Bank, with your remittance.
3. List all employees covered by this Plan who worked during the period covered. Please be sure names and Social Security Numbers are correct.
4. In computing compensable hours, include all paid hours including any overtime hours, since last report. Your report is to be Monthly to include the payroll period closing nearest to first of the month. Adjust to nearest half hour or hour. Please use separate report forms for separate months. DO NOT COMBINE.
5. Do not include on this report any other occupations except those covered by this "Construction Workers' Plan." Other crafts have separate report forms.
6. Add total compensable hours reported for all employees, multiply this figure by 10¢, and remit amount due. Explain adjustments on reverse side of form. The 10¢ per hour contribution is not subject to payroll or withholding tax.
7. Please be sure your firm name is the one you use in conducting your business. Explain any change in firm name from last report.
8. Your report is due before the 15th of the month, following close of payroll. Please send it in as early as you can.
9. Address all inquiries for information to: CONSTRUCTION INDUSTRY HEALTH AND SECURITY TRUST FUND, 2700 First Ave., Seattle 1, Wash., or telephone Seattle MAin 4-5154. No collect telephone calls or telegrams will be accepted.
10. If no contributions are due the Fund, please check block at right, state reason on face of report, sign and return . . . . . . . . . . . . . . . ☐
11. Due to present Internal Revenue regulations self-employed, sole proprietors or partners are not allowed to contribute on their own behalf for benefits under this Plan.

This report covers payroll period beginning _____, 196__, Ending _____, 196__.
(See Par. 4 above)

| NAME OF EMPLOYEE (Type or print) | | | SOCIAL SECURITY NUMBER (Must be accurate) | TOTAL COMPENSABLE HOURS FOR PERIOD |
|---|---|---|---|---|
| Last Name | First Name | Middle Initial | | |
| | | | | |

IF ADDRESS SHOWN BELOW IS A CHANGE FROM THAT SHOWN ON LAST REPORT, PLEASE CHECK HERE ☐

"The undersigned employer agrees to be bound by the terms of the Trust Agreement dated August 1, 1956, entitled "Construction Industry Health and Security Trust Fund" and any amendments thereto and as an individual employer to make contributions to said Trust Funds as provided by the agreement of August 1, 1956, between certain Employer Associations and Local Unions of the Construction Industry Workers of America."

_____
Employer's Name

_____
Address          City          Zone

_____
Report Prepared by          Title

Phone No._____ Date _____,196__

TOTAL HOURS

Earned Contribution @ .10 per Hour          $_____

Adjustments – Explain on Reverse Side          $_____

REMITTED HEREWITH          $_____

White Original – Yellow Duplicate – Pink Triplicate
SEND WHITE AND YELLOW COPIES TO BANK WITH REMITTANCE

**Fig. 2. Employer Remittance Report.**

When the administrator or his staff receive the Employer Remittance Report and the bank deposit slip from the bank, they process them in the following manner:

1. The amount on the deposit slip is checked against the amount reported on the corresponding remittance report.

2. The deposit slip is used as the basis for posting to the Cash Receipts Journal.

ADMINISTRATIVE OFFICE

## METAL WORKERS' PENSION TRUST FUND
### c/o WELFARE AND PENSION SERVICE, W.S.L.C.
### SEATTLE, WASH.

IMPORTANT — FOLLOW CAREFULLY
THE INSTRUCTIONS ON REVERSE SIDE
WHEN COMPLETING THIS REPORT.

| EMPLOYEE NAME | SOCIAL SECURITY NUMBER | * MONTHLY RATE OR COMPENSABLE HOURS | NEW EMPLOYEE/BEGIN DATE | TERMINATION DATE |
|---|---|---|---|---|
| | | | | |
| | | | | |
| | | | | |

TOTAL COMPENSABLE HOURS

TOTAL COMPENSABLE HOURS @ . PER HOUR | * $

| | | | |
|---|---|---|---|
| TOTAL AMOUNT DUE ON EMPLOYEES ON MONTHLY RATE BASIS | FULL MONTH . | WEEKLY RATE . | DAILY RATE . | * $ |

ADJUSTMENTS MUST BE EXPLAINED (SEE INSTRUCTIONS ON REVERSE SIDE) | $

AMOUNT OF REMITTANCE | $

I CERTIFY THIS INFORMATION IN THIS REPORT IS TRUE AND CORRECT.

SIGNATURE

TITLE

DATE

* PLEASE REFER TO YOUR LABOR AGREEMENT AND SEE INSTRUCTION 4
ON REVERSE SIDE OF THIS FORM.

| PERIOD COVERED | | REPORT DUE DATE | | | EMPLOYER NUMBER |
|---|---|---|---|---|---|
| MONTH | YEAR | MONTH | DAY | YEAR | |
| FROM | TO | | | | |

IF REPORT COVERS OTHER THAN FIRST TO LAST DAY OF
MONTH, INDICATE DATES COVERED IN SPACES AT LEFT.

EMPLOYER REMITTANCE REPORT
MAIL REPORTS AND REMITTANCES TO AND MAKE CHECKS PAYABLE TO
**METAL WORKERS' PENSION TRUST FUND**
C O FIRST BANK OF PORTLAND
P O BOX 19, PORTLAND, OREGON

**Fig. 3. Pre-Billing Form of Employer Remittance Report. (Front.)**

## INSTRUCTIONS FOR PREPARING THIS REPORT

**1.** Mail reports and remittances to, and make check payable to:
METAL WORKERS' PENSION TRUST FUND, c/o the bank address shown on the face of this form.

**2.** List all new employees covered by this Trust who worked during the period covered. Please be sure names and Social Security numbers are correct.

**3.** Dates of New Hires, Rehires, and Terminations of Employment must be shown in the respective columns designated.

**4.** Please refer to the labor agreement when computing payments to the fund.
  A. If you are paying a monthly rate, the appropriate rate per employee is shown on the face of this report.
  B. If you are paying an hourly rate, the correct hourly rate is shown on the face of this report. In computing compensable hours, include all paid time, including overtime, holidays, and vacation time. Multiply total hours by hourly rate, adjust to the nearest half hour or hour, and remit amount due.

**5.** Reports must be submitted each and every month. If payroll period ends on date other than the last day of the calendar month, compute as of the pay period nearest the end of the month. If there was no compensable employment during the month write NONE in total box, explain on face of report, sign report, and return.

**6.** Contributions are not subject to payroll or withholding tax.

**7.** Any adjustments necessary by reason of error on any previous report shall be detailed on a separate sheet of paper, specifying each individual concerned and attached to this report.

**8.** Do not include on this report any other occupation except those covered by this Trust. In case of doubt, contact the local union or the Administrative Office.

**9.** Your report is due before the date shown on the face of this report. Please send it in as early as you can.

**10.** Please be sure your firm name is the one you use in conducting your business. Explain any change in firm name from last report.

**11.** Complete all reports in triplicate, retain third copy (pink) for your files, and mail first two copies, together with your remittance payable to the Trust.

**12.** Address all inquiries for information c/o WELFARE AND PENSION SERVICE, W.S.L.C., Seattle 1, Washington.

**Fig. 3. Pre-Billing Form of Employer Remittance Report. (Back.)**


3. The amount on the Employer Remittance Report is posted to the appropriate page in the Employer Contributor Ledger.

4. The information in the Employer Remittance Report is used to record in the Employees' or Participants' Ledger the hours worked or the equivalent eligibility factor for each employee.

5. The postings to the Employees' or Participants' Ledger are cross-checked to the postings in the Employer Contributor Ledger and the record of the bank deposit in the Cash Receipts Journal.

6. The Employer Remittance Reports are filed alphabetically by employer. These reports are often referred to, particularly when questions arise concerning the eligibility of employees.

If direct banking is not used, essentially the same procedure would be followed, except that the deposit slip would be prepared by the administrator's staff upon receipt, directly from the employer, of the remittance report and the payment. Then, of course, the money should be deposited in the bank, and the deposit slip and remittance report would be processed in the same manner as above.

Receipts from other sources such as interest, dividends, experience rating refunds, repayment of mortgage loans, and proceeds from the sale of securities, are controlled and recorded on the same basis as contributions.

*Cash disbursements.* Disbursements should be made by check only, retaining a duplicate voucher check with each invoice or statement. The best procedure is to have the checks signed by two trustees. If the plan is negotiated, one labor trustee and one management trustee would ordinarily be authorized to sign. However, the trustees sometimes delegate this authority to the administrator, or to the administrator and one trustee. The original invoice or statement should accompany the check for signature and should be initialled by the trustees.

▶ WARNING: Paid invoices should be cancelled either by machine or by *indelible* stamping, so that there will be no chance of their being successfully sent through for payment again.

*Other transactions.* Often a corporate trustee or nominee is delegated to make investments when cash is available, to receive dividends and interest, to liquidate holdings, and to otherwise manage the investment portfolio. The corporate trustee must notify the administrator in writing in complete detail about every such transaction, so that the transactions can be reflected in the accounting records by means of journal entries.

**Application of accounting machines.** Small funds usually have totally hand operated and posted systems. Their very smallness makes it impractical to acquire bookkeeping or accounting machines. Medium-sized funds use some form of bookkeeping machinery in order to speed up the operation and to get more accurate results. There are instances, particularly when a complicated eligibility formula is involved, when it is advisable for both small and medium-sized funds to employ the services of a data processing service bureau.

Large funds generally use punched-card accounting systems. The many small transactions, coupled with the great need for accuracy and timeliness, make the punched-card system the most economical and workable one for a large fund. See Chapter 22 for information on punched-card accounting systems.

▶ COMMENT: Punched-card accounting equipment is a great aid to the auditor. The principal time-consuming procedures for the auditor are the verification of employers' contributions, the examination of eligibility records, and the determination of liability for future premiums, which is based on the hours worked by participants before the end of the audit period. These three areas embrace over 90% of a plan's receipts and expenses, and practically all of its liabilities. When the necessary data are readily available on punched cards, work that would normally be expected to take days can be completed in hours.

## AUDIT PROCEDURES [1]

**Suggested audit program.** As has been indicated earlier, there are many individuals and groups concerned with the operation of welfare and pension benefit funds. Therefore, extreme care should be exercised in any audit of these funds. The following program covers the particular aspects of welfare and pension benefit fund audits. It assumes the implementation of the usual footing, cross-checking, reconciling, and verification steps—and cut-off procedures—that would be part of any audit.

1. Read and excerpt the trust agreement and all other documents that would be included in the permanent audit file.

2. Read and excerpt the minutes of each meeting of the board of trustees. These minutes contain the trustees' decisions on such matters as the selection of brokers, carriers, actuaries, attorneys, auditors, and consultants; salary increases; administration fee increases; and changes in benefits. The auditor should be aware of the trustees' decisions and intentions, so that he will be able to determine if actual trust business is being carried out in accordance with these decisions and intentions.

3. Obtain direct positive confirmation of *all* employers' contributions. A letter should be sent to each contributor showing the total amount of his payments during the period under audit. An adding machine tape or a tabulation of his monthly remittances should be attached to the letter. The contributor is asked either to confirm the total amount or state his objections in the space provided. Of course, a self-addressed stamped envelope should be included. Figure 4 illustrates a typical letter of confirmation for employers' contributions.

---

[1] Portions of this section were adapted by the author from his published article: "Audit and Tax Problems of Health and Welfare Funds," *The Journal of Accountancy,* January 1958, Vol. 105, No. 1, pages 45, 46.

▶ OBSERVATION: Some employers (notably contractors) contribute to as many as twenty different plans, and the confirmation often discloses that the contributor's staff has made remittances to the wrong plan. If many such errors come to light, the administrator should be advised to take immediate steps to correct his bookkeeping and record keeping procedures. Naturally, the money should be transferred and the records adjusted when any error is discovered.

Gentlemen:

An Annual Audit is being made of the financial transactions of this Trust for the period beginning March 1, 19___ and ending February 28, 19___.

The records show that you contributed $7,967.84. This represents only the amount of cash you actually remitted. A tabulating machine listing of these payments is attached.

Will you please confirm this direct to our Auditor, Mr. Allen Jones, 1110 20th Avenue, Seattle, Washington. A stamped addressed envelope is enclosed for your convenience.

Very truly yours,

Trustee

The above is correct.  Firm Name _____

By _____ Date _____

The above does not agree with our records, which show _____

_____

_____

_____

Firm Name _____

By _____ Date _____

**Fig. 4. Letter of Confirmation for Employers' Contributions.**

4. Obtain direct confirmation from all depositaries as to account balances and rates of interest. The interest received on savings account balances should be proved by independent computation.

5. Make a physical inspection of all securities owned by the plan. If a physical inspection would be too time-consuming for the auditor and for bank personnel, a *detailed* certification by the custodian, signed by an executive officer, will suffice. The audit report should explain which method was used to verify the securities. Look up cost values as of dates of purchase in order to satisfy yourself that the proper prices were paid for securities. Figure 5 shows excerpts from an audit work paper reflecting the verification of securities owned.

Construction Industry Health and Welfare Fund — Securities Owned FY 3/31/—

| | # Shares or Maturity Value | Cost | Market | Source of Market Value | Method of Confirmation |
|---|---|---|---|---|---|
| **U.S. BONDS** | | | | | |
| Federal Land Bank 4% Bonds Due 5/1/— | 16000000 | 16097912 | 15895280 0 | Wall St. Jr. 4/1/— | Letter – National Bank of Commerce – Corporate Nominee |
| F N M A Bonds 4⅜% Due 4/10/— | 30000000 | 2910193 | 29622000 | " " | " – Chase Manhattan Bank, NYC |
| Treasury Bonds of 11/51/— Due 4/10/— | 60000000 | 5929582 | 5836800 | Federal Res. Bank | Physical Inspection Safe Dep. Box of Administration Office |
| Series K U.S. Bonds | 20000000 | 20000000 | 19360000 | | |
| TOTAL | | 44937487 | 44011800 | | |
| **CORPORATE BONDS** | | | | | |
| Grace Line 4¼% Due 7/1/— | 5000000 | 5000000 | 4637500 | Trust Dept. Nat Bk of Com. | National Bank of Commerce |
| Phillips Petroleum 4¼% Conv Deb Due 2/15/— | 100000 | 100000 | 106375 | Wall St. Jr. 4/1/— | " |
| Southern Counties Gas 4% Refunding 5/1/— | 6000000 | 6159375 | 5687500 | Trust Dept. N B of C | " |
| TOTAL | | 21946685 | 20769875 | | |
| **COMMON STOCKS** | | | | | |
| Wellington Fund | 4834607 | 6757774 | 6685891 | Wall St. Jr. Bd 4/1/— | Letter Wellington Fund |
| Aluminum Co of America | 100 | 966805 | 910000 | " | " N B of C |
| American Metal Climax | 100 | 542732 | 440000 | " | " |
| Central Illinois Public Service | 200 | 543750 | 965000 | " | " |
| General Electric | 200 | 1429742 | 1797500 | " | " |
| Goodyear Tire and Rubber Co | 365 | 698009 | 1314000 | " | " |
| Southern California Edison | 200 | 1083750 | 1167500 | " | " |
| Westinghouse Electric | 400 | 1755797 | 1990000 | " | " |
| TOTAL | | 30941128 | 33810291 | | |

Fig. 5. Audit Work Paper Reflecting Verification of Securities Owned by Plan.

6. Check all bond interest and all dividend income to make certain that the correct amounts have been received and have been properly accounted for.

7. Confirm by direct communication with insurance carriers: (a) the amount of premiums paid to the carrier, (b) what agents or brokers participate in commissions paid by the carrier as a result of trust business, and (c) the amount of experience rating refund, if any, that the carrier remitted to the trust. The carrier should be requested to provide a copy of the commission schedule for payments to the broker (see Figure 6). This schedule should be included as part of the audit report. The carrier should also be asked to indicate whether the broker has a vested interest in the commissions. Figure 7 shows a letter of confirmation that could be sent to an insurance carrier.

| *Annual Volume* | *Average of First Year and Renewal Commission Over a Ten-Year Period* | |
|---|---|---|
| | *From* | *To* |
| $ 20,000 | 3.2% | 4.1% |
| $ 30,000 | 3.0% | 3.7% |
| $ 50,000 | 2.6% | 3.2% |
| $ 100,000 | 1.7% | 2.3% |
| $ 150,000 | 1.3% | 2.0% |
| $ 250,000 | .8% | 1.8% |
| $ 500,000 | .5% | 1.2% |
| $1,000,000 | .3% | .8% |
| $2,500,000 | .2% | .5% |
| $5,000,000 | .1% | .4% |

**Fig. 6. National Association of Insurance Commissioners Approved Commission Schedule for Brokers.**

Paul Revere Life Insurance Company
Group Department
Worcester 8, Massachusetts

Gentlemen:

*Group Number OB-35872*

The financial records of this Trust are being audited for the fiscal year ended June 30, 19___. The records show the following premiums paid to you during the year:—

| July 19___ | $3,645.11 | February 19___ | $3,545.00 |
|---|---|---|---|
| August | 3,500.90 | March | 3,998.76 |
| September | 3,803.87 | April | 3,800.24 |
| October | 3,910.22 | May | 3,800.24 |
| November | 3,908.32 | June | 4,076.75 |
| December | 3,892.41 | | |
| January 19___ | 3,949.13 | Total | $45,830.95 |

An experience rating refund of $3,397.98 was paid to the Trust in November 19___. The broker of record is Mr. F. W. King.

**Fig. 7. Letter of Confirmation to Insurance Carrier.**

Will you please confirm all the above direct to our Auditor:—

> Mr. Allen Jones
> 1100 20th Avenue
> Seattle, Washington

Please also furnish him with a copy of the commission schedule for payments to the broker, for inclusion with his report, and advise whether the broker has a vested interest in this case.

A stamped addressed envelope is enclosed. Your co-operation will be greatly appreciated.

> Very truly yours,
>
> Trustee

**Fig. 7. Letter of Confirmation to Insurance Carrier. (Continued.)**

In the case of an insured pension plan, (a) amounts remitted to the carrier, (b) interest earned on the deposits, and (c) annuities purchased from accumulated funds should be obtained from the carrier. It is also advisable to obtain a statement from the carrier as to brokerage arrangements and commissions.

8. Verify the computation of any experience rating refunds. Special emphasis should be given to the disposition of the reserve retained by the carrier for claims that were incurred but not settled at the beginning of the audit period.

9. Obtain direct confirmation from all brokers stating that they have not engaged in fee-splitting nor made any questionable deals. Figure 8 is an example of this type of confirmation letter.

James and Kingston, Inc.
1521 18th Avenue
Seattle, Washington

Gentlemen:

An audit is being made of the records of this Trust for the year ended June 30, 19___.

Will you please confirm direct to our auditor:—

> Mr. Allen Jones
> 1120 18th Avenue
> Seattle, Washington

that your firm served as sole broker of record for the Trust, and that no one else shared in the commission received from this business.

A stamped addressed envelope is enclosed for your convenience. Your co-operation will be greatly appreciated.

> Very truly yours,
>
> **Trustee**

**Fig. 8. Letter of Confirmation to Broker.**

▶ SUGGESTION: If a broker balks at giving such information, he can be prodded through notification that his refusal will be referred to in the audit report, and that the board of trustees will be requested to probe into the matter.

10. Investigate the reasons for any change in carriers during the audit period. First-year commissions are usually higher than those for subsequent years.

11. Thoroughly check at least three months' eligibility records to determine that premiums are being paid only on eligible members (see Figure 9). In the case of a pension benefit plan, verify future service credits by ex-

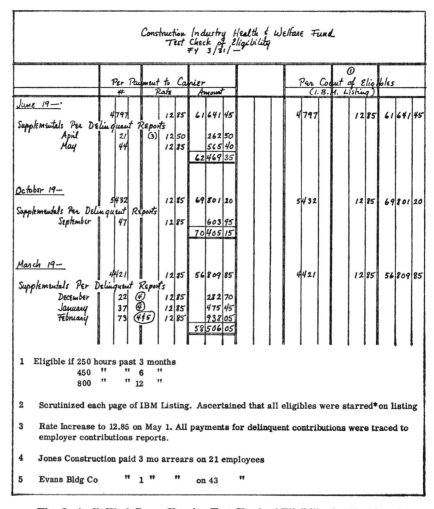

Fig. 9. Audit Work Paper Showing Test Check of Eligibility for Health and Welfare Benefit Plan.

amining the eligibility records. These records should be kept in perpetuity because they can be the basis for determining the amount of a retiree's pension.

12. Prove all administration fees that were paid during the year. Figure 10 is an audit work paper illustrating this step.

Construction Industry Health and Welfare Fund.
Administration Fees
Fiscal Year Ended 3/31/—

| | Employer Contributions Month | Amount | Rate of Fee | Per Books Amount Paid | Per Computation Amount Paid | Month Paid |
|---|---|---|---|---|---|---|
| | Mar 19— | 62744 00 | 3.2% | 2007 80 | 2007 80 | April |
| | Apr " | 58439 00 | " | 1870 05 | 1870 05 | May |
| | May " | 67395 00 | " | 2156 64 | 2156 64 | June |
| | June " | 72773 00 | " | 2328 74 | 2328 74 | July |
| | July " | 74798 00 | 3.7% (1) | 3131 39 | 3131 39 | Aug |
| | Aug " | 81428 00 | " | 3012 84 | 3012 84 | Sept |
| | Sept " | 77654 00 | " | 2932 40ok | 2873 20 (2) | Oct |
| | Oct " | 74421 00 | " | 2753 58 | 2753 58 | Nov |
| | Nov " | 71241 00 | " | 2635 92 | 2635 92 | Dec |
| | Dec " | 68837 00 | " | 2546 97 (3) | 2546 97 | Jan |
| | Jan 19— | 63004 00 | " | 2289 71 ok | 2331 15 | Feb |
| | Feb " | 61449 00 | " | 2273 61 | 2273 61 | Mar |
| Total Per General Ledger | | | | 29989 65 | | |

(1) See minutes of June 16, 19— authorizing administration fee increase retroactive to June 1, 19— collections

| | | |
|---|---|---|
| .5% of | 72 773 00 | 363 87 |
| 3.7% of | 74 798 00 | 2767 52 |
| | | 3131 39 |

(2) Law firm collected $ 3,200.00 from delinquent employer contributors and remitted $ 1,600.00, retaining 1/2 for fees. Administrator serviced entire amount and is entitled to fee based on entire contributions. See auditors' J.E.6

Legal fees                                        1600 00
Employers' contributions                                        1 600 00
    To record fee retained by Bell and Jones, attorneys for collections from Anderson Construction Co. Inc.

(3) Administration fee includes fee for Johnson Supply Co. December contribution. This contribution was not processed but was refunded to General Laborers' Trust. See auditors' J.E.7

Employer contributions                                        1 120 00
Refunds                                        1 120 00
    To correct distribution for December employer contribution of Johnson Supply Co. This was refunded to General Laborer Trust

**Fig. 10. Audit Work Paper for Proof of Administration Fees.**

13. Review all payroll records of the plan.

14. Examine all expense vouchers, cancelled checks, and authorizations.

▶ OBSERVATION: Particular care should be taken during the examination of cancelled checks to make sure that they are signed by authorized persons and are properly indorsed. All bank reconciliations for the period should be checked and the cut-off statement should be reconciled.

15. Verify the adequacy of all fidelity bonds. In particular, they should be checked for conformity with the bonding provisions of the Landrum-Griffin Act and the Welfare and Pension Plans Disclosure Act. Also ascertain that everyone who should be bonded is bonded. Figure 11 illustrates this step.

Construction Industry Pension Fund
Fidelity Bond
3/31/—

| # | Co. | From | To | Coverage | | Premium |
|---|---|---|---|---|---|---|
| 288 8 36 | Fid & Dep. Co of Md. | 3/8/— | 3/8/— | 30 0 0 00 00 | Each of Eight Trustees | 4 6 22 07 |

Purchased through Elmer Burns and Co.

This is a blanket type Labor Organization Fidelity Bond—Consolidated Form. It is in strict conformity with the provisions of the Landrum-Griffin Act.

Check next audit—possible sufficient increase in receipts to warrant additional coverage and premium. This is a 3 year policy.

**Fig. 11. Audit Work Paper for Verification of Adequacy of Fidelity Bond.**

16. Check about 5% of the claims paid (under a health and welfare benefit plan) against the eligibility records.

17. Verify pension payments by examining either the past service records at the employer's office or the membership records at the union office. Figure 12 is an audit work paper analysis of pension payments.

▶ NOTE: Past service credit is usually allowed if the employee has an unbroken record of union membership during the required period.

18. Compute the unliquidated liability for future premiums earned prior to the end of the accounting year. Determine the solvency of the plan by comparing the amount of this liability with the surplus reserves. If the liability is larger than the reserves, the trustees should be notified and advised to take one of the following steps:

a. Reduce the benefits and thereby obtain a reduction in premium costs.
b. Get competitive bids from a number of carriers with a view toward finding a carrier who will supply coverage at a lower cost.

Construction Industry Pension Fund
Analysis of Pensioners who began receiving Pensions
During Current Fiscal Year
March 31, 19—

| # | Pensioner Name | Union Local | (1) Member (2) Beneficiary | (a) Life Annuity (2) Temporary Annuity | Options | 1. Disability 2. Service 3. Old-Timer 4. Early Retir. | Social Security Number | Date of Birth | Proof of Age | Date of Union Membership | Past Service (Union Office) | Future Service (Administration) | Pension Amount |
|---|---|---|---|---|---|---|---|---|---|---|---|---|---|
| 71 | J. A. Mitchell | 81 | — | — | Normal | 1 | 052 28 7994 | 4/7/— | S.S. Award | 2/7/— | 15 " | 2 " | 36 00 |
| 72 | Peter Berger | 81 | — | — | Normal | 1 | 590 12 8163 | 8/2/— | Birth Cert. | 12/29/— | 17 " | ½ " | 35 50 |
| 73 | John Creighton | 504 | — | — | Normal | 1 | 124 26 2506 | 4/4/— | Birth Cert. | 9/15/— | 18 " | — " | 36 00 |
| 74 | Norman Kautor | 81 | — | — | Normal | 1 | 477 21 1747 | 3/1/— | S.S. Award | 9/16/— | 13 " | 2 " | 32 00 |
| 75 | N. A. Miller | 504 | — | — | Normal | 1 | 119 31 6432 | 1/24/— | Naturalizen | 10/30/— | 17 " | 2 " | 42 00 |
| 76 | Thomas Armstrong ① | 504 | — | — | Normal | 2 | 529 63 7945 | 12/17/— | Birth Cert. | 9/7/— | 17 " | ½ " | 35 50 |

| # | Pensioner Name | Union Local | (1) Member (2) Beneficiary | (a) Life Annuity (2) Temporary Annuity | Options | Type | Social Security Number | Date of Birth | Proof of Age | Date of Union Membership | Past Service | Future Service | Pension Amount |
|---|---|---|---|---|---|---|---|---|---|---|---|---|---|
| 99 | S. L. Scorso ② | 81 | — | — | Normal | 2 | 573 62 4121 | 6/5/— | S.S. Award | 10/1/— | 17 " | 2 " | 40 00 |
| 100 | John Fitler ② | 81 | — | — | Normal | 2 | 568 37 7212 | 8/7/— | Naturalizen | 1/10/— | 18 " | 3 " | 45 00 |
| 101 | Robert Handy | 504 | • | • | 50% | 2 | 543 74 4357 | 11/14/— | Birth Cert. | 11/5/— | 13 " | 2 " | 26 24 |

① 5/1/— Trnsfr to 81   11/1/— Trnsfr to 504   4/1/— Trnsfr to 81   9/1/— Trnsfr to 504 — records checked OK

② 5/1/— Trnsfr from 504   OK

③ For other years' retirees see File 4/23 for 19—, File 729 for 19—, File 944 for 19—, and File 1166 for 19—

Fig. 12. Audit Work Paper for Analysis of Pension Payments.

c. Tighten eligibility requirements in order to eliminate the coverage for marginal workers.

d. Increase employer contributions.

19. Investigate and try to determine the amount of any delinquency in employer contributions.

▶ OBSERVATION: Supplemental payments to the carriers usually arise from the fact that some employers were delinquent in their contributions. This could indicate a deficiency in the accounting system, and steps should be taken to remedy the situation.

20. Investigate all undistributed employers' remittances.

21. Finally, an old accounting maxim: "Wherever the trail leads, pursue it."

**The permanent audit file.** The permanent audit file for a health and welfare benefit plan should consist of: (1) a copy of the trust agreement and all amendments to it, (2) a benefit booklet, (3) a specimen copy of the insurance policy, (4) a copy of the agreement with the administrator, (5) a copy of the labor agreement providing for the benefits, (6) copies of the agreements with any other concerns or individuals receiving fees, such as the corporate trustee or nominee or the brokerage firm, and (7) a copy of the tax exemption letter.

A pension plan permanent audit file should contain: (1) a copy of the trust agreement, (2) a copy of the plan, (3) a copy of the master contract with the carrier, more commonly known as the Group Annuity Contract or the Deposit Administration Contract, (4) a copy of the labor agreement providing for pensions, (5) copies of commission agreements, (6) a copy of the certificate by the carrier to retirees, (7) all original data submitted to the Internal Revenue Service for tax exemption, and (8) a copy of the tax exemption letter.

**The audit report—cash versus accrual basis.** The accrual method of accounting should be used on the audit report if the books can be made to reflect clearly and accurately the results of the necessary adjustments. Some of the factors that should be taken into account when reporting on an accrual basis are:

1. Trust departments of banks, which often serve as administrators, maintain plan records on a cash basis. There is no way of compelling a bank to make retroactive adjustments or reversals.

2. Corporate trustees carry securities at cost on their records. They seldom make provision for amortization of bond premiums and discounts, nor for interest accruals and deferments.

3. Most of the assets due at the end of an accounting period are offset by the liabilities inherent in these assets. Employers' contributions would be offset by the amount of the premiums due and the administration fees applicable to the contributions. Also, an accrual for an experience rating refund would be complicated by the fact that a few bad experience months can more than offset favorable claims experience for a few months.

4. Trustees and participants can more easily understand cash basis reports.

▶ SUGGESTION: If the cash basis is used, all the known unrecorded assets, liabilities, and contingencies can be disclosed in a series of notes that would be appended to the audit report. In the event of an actuarial review, these notes will be of value to the actuary.

**Form of the audit report.** Whenever possible, the long-form audit report containing an unqualified opinion should be used. The Appendix to this chapter illustrates an audit report of this type, prepared on a cash basis. The audit report should leave no doubts about the financial position of the plan, and it should be an aid to the trustees in the formulation of policy.

## TAX EXEMPTION FOR WELFARE AND PENSION BENEFIT PLANS

A welfare or pension benefit plan can attain the status of a tax-exempt organization under the provisions of Section 501 of the Internal Revenue Code. We will consider the advantages of qualifying for, the requirements for, and methods of obtaining tax exemption.

**Advantages of qualifying a plan.** When either a welfare or a pension benefit plan qualifies as a tax-exempt organization, the trust is not taxed on contributions to its corpus or on income earned. This is particularly advantageous in the case of a pension benefit plan. If the contributions and the investment income of a pension trust were taxed, less than 40% of any anticipated pension could be paid. The ability continuously to compound tax-free investment income provides enough funds for the payment of adequate pensions. A tax-exempt health and welfare benefit plan has the advantage of being able to buy additional coverage for its participants without raising contribution rates.

**Requirements for qualification for a pension benefit plan.** A pension benefit plan qualifies as a tax-exempt organization under Section 501(a) of the Internal Revenue Code if it meets the requirements for qualification listed in Section 401(a) of the Code. These requirements are:

1. The plan must operate as a trust that is created, organized, and maintained in the United States.

2. It must be established by an employer for the exclusive benefit of his employees and their beneficiaries. However, contributions may be made by the employees as well as by the employer.

3. The sole purpose of the plan must be to distribute to the employees or their beneficiaries the corpus and income of the fund that is accumulated by the trust in accordance with the plan.

4. The trust agreement must provide that no part of the corpus or income can be used for, or diverted to, purposes other than for the exclusive benefit of the employees or their beneficiaries.

5. The plan must cover: (a) 70% or more of all the employees, or (b) 80% or more of the eligible employees (this applies only if at least 70% of all the employees *are* eligible), or (c) such employees as qualify under a *non-discriminatory* (see next requirement) classification set up by the employer; for example, the employer could limit coverage to a certain department, certain age groups, etc.

▶ NOTE: Employees who have not been employed for the minimum period prescribed by the plan (which cannot be more than five years), and those whose customary employment is for not more than twenty hours in any one week or five months in any calendar year are excluded in both (a) and (b).

6. Contributions or benefits provided under the plan must not discriminate in favor of officers, shareholders, those engaged in supervisory work, or highly compensated employees.

The Regulations amplify the Code as follows:

1. The plan must be a written program. It must provide systematically for the payment of definitely determinable benefits after the employee's retirement, and it must be communicated to the employee.

2. Plan contributions and benefits cannot be dependent upon employer's profits. This, of course, does not apply in the case of a profit-sharing plan that provides retirement benefits.

3. The plan must be actuarially sound.

4. The plan cannot provide for the payment of lay-off, sick, accident, hospitalization, or medical benefits. Incidental death benefits can be provided.

5. The plan must imply a permanent program. Termination for any reason other than business necessity might be construed as evidence that the plan was not bona fide. This is especially true if the plan is abandoned

soon after pensions have been fully funded in favor of a select segment of those covered.

6. The plan cannot amount to a subterfuge for the distribution of profits to shareholders.

7. Self-employed persons or partners cannot participate in the plan for their own benefit.

**How to qualify a pension benefit plan.** Verified copies of all the instruments constituting or evidencing the plan (trust indenture, group annuity contracts, specimen copy of each type of individual contract, etc.), a statement describing the plan, and other required information must be submitted to the District Director of Internal Revenue in order to qualify the plan.

The statement describing the plan should identify the plan and set forth: (1) the name or names of the employers, (2) the effective date of the plan, (3) the method of distribution or of disbursing benefits, (4) the dates when the instruments were executed, and the date the employees were furnished descriptions of the plan, (5) employee eligibility requirements, (6) the rules relating to employer contributions and employee contributions, (7) the basis or formula for determining the amount of benefits to be paid, (8) the vesting or non-vesting provisions, (9) the medium of funding, and (10) the rules covering discontinuance or modification of the plan.

A tabulation showing the names, positions, duties, dates of birth, percentages of stock ownership, years of service, and compensation of the 25 highest-paid employees covered by the plan must be submitted. A schedule grouping employees with respect to their eligibility and coverage at the end of the year is also required, as is a detailed analysis of all the methods, factors, and assumptions used in determining costs—in other words, an actuarial review.

Obviously, competent legal advice should be sought when drawing up the trust agreement. It is essential that this agreement contain all the necessary provisions and present them properly.

▶ SUGGESTION: The required documents and information should be submitted to the District Director *before* the plan is put into effect. The District Director will make an advance determination on the qualification of a pension benefit plan. Thus, if the plan is defective in any way, there is an opportunity to revise it before it becomes operative.

**Filing an annual tax return for a tax-exempt pension plan.** A tax-exempt pension trust must file Form 990-P annually. If trust funds are invested in the stock or securities of the employer or related parties, or if they are loaned to the employer or related parties, these investments or loans must be reported and explained.

The trust also has to report annually the same information that is required for qualification (see page 1195). However, if the employer files such information on his tax return, the trust may merely attach to Form 990-P a letter from the employer to this effect. It is advisable for the trust to actually report the information on its return if there are many employer contributors. Any income of the trust that is derived from activities not related to trust business, as defined in Code Section 513, should be reported on Form 990-T.

**Requirements for qualification for a health and welfare benefit plan.** Section 501(c)(9) of the Internal Revenue Code grants tax-exempt status to a voluntary *employees'* beneficiary association, if:

1. It is organized for the purpose of providing for the payment of sickness, accident, death, or other benefits for its members or their dependents.

2. No part of its net earnings goes to a private shareholder or individual except through the payment of normal benefits.

3. At least 85% of its income consists of amounts collected from members and amounts contributed by the employer.

**How to qualify a health and welfare benefit plan.** Exemption Application Form 1027 must be filed with the District Director of Internal Revenue in order to obtain qualification. A conformed copy of the original trust agreement or articles of association, information similar to that on an audit report, and a schedule of benefits must accompany the application.

▶ NOTE: A health and welfare benefit plan must have been in operation for a complete year before it can file for exemption. It *cannot* get an advance determination as to whether it qualifies.

**Filing an annual tax return for a tax-exempt health and welfare benefit plan.** A tax-exempt health and welfare benefit plan must file Form 990 annually. An analysis of gross income, receipts, and disbursements has to be shown along with other pertinent information. Form 990-T should be used to report income from an unrelated trade or business as defined in Code Section 513.

**Special tax problems of health and welfare benefit plans.** Many negotiated health and welfare benefit plans provide for participation by what are called associate employees. This term usually refers not only to salaried and supervisory personnel, but also to self-employed craftsmen who are union members in good standing. As a result, self-employed carpenters, plumbers, barbers, and similar craftsmen often obtain coverage under a union plan by paying their entire premium into the fund. But under the 1954 Internal Revenue Code, only a voluntary association of *employees* can qualify for tax exemption. Plans in which self-employed persons participate *cannot qualify,* because such persons are not employees.

Of course, health and welfare benefit plans that have self-employed participants can eliminate these participants from coverage and thereby qualify for exemption. Many plans have done this. There are cases, however, where it has been found not feasible to eliminate the self-employed because a large percentage of the participants belong to this group. In 1957 the Director of the Tax Rulings Division issued a ruling that, in effect, excluded contributions and experience-rating refunds from the taxable income of a non-exempt negotiated health and welfare *trust* if the exemption had been denied to the trust for having self-employed participants. With contributions and experience rating refunds excluded, the only remaining taxable income would be investment income. Since trust expenses and administration costs are usually far in excess of investment income, the majority of these non-exempt trusts have not been required to pay any taxes.

▶ WARNING: Subsequent rulings by the Director of the Tax Rulings Division are at variance with the 1957 ruling, in that they state that some non-exempt trusts are not true trusts within the meaning of the Internal Revenue Code.

▶ WHAT TO DO: Even if all conributions, all experience rating refunds, and all investment income are held to be taxable, it is possible to minimize the tax liability by setting contribution rates at about the same level as premium and administrative costs.

There is one other area where a welfare benefit plan can experience tax trouble. A plan can receive only 15% of its income from sources other than employers' contributions if it is to maintain exempt status. A poor employment year or a year beset by strikes could impair the balance between investment income and employers' contributions, and thus cause a plan to become a taxable entity.

**CONCLUSIONS**

The Landrum-Griffin Act and the Federal Disclosure Act practically abolish captive union memberships. These memberships have new rights and privileges. Too frequently the exercise of these rights and privileges will take the form of harassment caused by dislike of a business agent or a trustee or an administrator. It follows, then, that administrators should keep complete and accurate accounting records, that audit programs should be thorough, and that audit reports should be comprehensive and informative.

# APPENDIX

### Long-Form Audit Report for Health and Welfare Fund

ALLEN JONES
CERTIFIED PUBLIC ACCOUNTANT
1100 20TH AVENUE
SEATTLE, WASHINGTON

May 11, 19___

Construction Industry Health
  and Security Fund
123 Cedar Street
Seattle, Washington

Gentlemen:

In accord with your request I have made an examination of the Balance Sheet of Construction Industry Health and Security Fund for the fiscal year ended March 31, 19___, and of its Statement of Cash Receipts and Disbursements for the year then ended. This examination was made as explained below in the Scope of Examination section of this report, and included all tests of the accounting records and supporting information I considered necessary.

In my opinion the Balance Sheet and Statements of Receipts and Disbursements fairly present the financial condition of the Trust on March 31, 19___, and the results of its operation for the year then ended, in conformity with generally accepted accounting principles.

*Scope of Examination*

Cash on deposit with the National Bank of Commerce in both checking and investment accounts was verified by direct confirmation with the depositary. The checking account was reconciled for the entire year under review. There are sixteen savings bank accounts, and a confirming letter was obtained from each as to the balance on March 31, 19___. Interest credited to the accounts during the year was checked for accuracy.

All securities owned by the Trust were confirmed by certification of the National Bank of Commerce, nominee for the Trust, by the Chase Manhattan Bank, and by Wellington Fund Inc.

There were 858 employer contributors who made covering payments to the Trust during this fiscal year. Their contributions amounted to $773,730.54. A letter was sent to each, detailing his contributions. He was asked to sign if cor-

**1198**

rect or state his exceptions if incorrect. There were returned 657 confirmations, amounting to $618,958.90. Percentagewise, 76.57% of the employer contributors confirmed 80.0% of the dollar contributions. It is assumed that those contributors who did not answer are satisfied with their statement of account.

A letter was sent to the Western Mutual Life Insurance Company asking them to confirm all payments this Trust made to them, and to disclose the broker of record for the Trust, data regarding experience rating refund, and manner of payment to the broker. They replied that premium payments are in accord with the Trust records. They stated that the only broker of record is Evans and Lane, Inc., and that there is an understanding between Evans and Lane Inc. and Mr. John Green whereby Mr. Green shares in the commission derived from this business. They also stated that the basis of commission paid to Evans and Lane Inc. is 1% of all premiums received. They also confirmed that no experience rating refund was returned to the Fund during the year.

Mr. Daniel Evans of Evans and Lane Inc. in reply to a request for information regarding brokerage arrangements stated that his firm was the only broker for this Trust, and that 50% of the commission derived from this business went to Mr. John Green. Mr. Green, in response to a letter asking for information, stated that no one shares in his commission.

Administration fees paid to the Welfare and Pension Administration Service were proved in their entirety and found to be in accord with the contractual agreement.

All paid invoices were examined and found to be proper charges of this Trust. Authorizations all bore the signature of one employer and one employee Trustee, as did the checks which paid for these Trust disbursements.

Eligibility records for three months were thoroughly checked. Benefits are being purchased in strict accord with the eligibility requirements of this Trust.

The National Bank of Commerce has received investment counsel fees on a semi-annual basis. I checked the computation of these fees as shown by the records kept at the National Bank of Commerce. The fee is in accord with the agreement entered into between the Trustees and the Bank.

All minutes of the Trust were read in their entirety. All actions taken by the Trust are in strict accord with these minutes and with the Trust agreement.

The Fund is protected against dishonesty by a fidelity bond issued by the Indemnity Insurance Company of North America. This bond is for $100,000.00 per employee or Trustee, and is for a period which ends on April 8, 19___. During the year the Trustees of the Construction Industry Pension Fund were also covered under this policy. In addition the Fund is protected by a fidelity bond in the amount of $50,000.00 which covers the Administrator and his employees. This bond is paid for by the Administrator. Effective April 8, 19___ there was acquired a new blanket type of Labor Organization Fidelity Bond issued by the Peerless Insurance Company covering each of eight trustees for three years for $160,000.00. Cost of this bond will be $2,508.45. It is in strict conformity with the provisions of the Landrum-Griffin Act.

## Comment

Your auditor wishes to call your attention to the following:

(1) Exhibit D attached is a condensed statement of income and expense for all the years this Trust has operated. It is hoped that this will be of value and interest to the Trustees.

(2) Since this Trust operates on a cash basis of accounting, no reserves have been established for unliquidated liability for premium payments based on hours worked before March 31, 19___. There is appended Exhibit E, delineating this liability. It may be of interest to the Trustees to know that the run-off shows a liability of $437,692.80. To meet this liability there is a surplus of $1,275,455.64. It would seem that the Trust is in excellent financial condition.

(3) There is also appended Exhibit F, which is a comparison of administrative expenses and investment income. During the year investment income amounted to 123.42% of administrative costs.

(4) Appended to the financial statements is a series of Notes which should be read in conjunction with the statements.

I am pleased to report that your Administrator maintains a complete and clean set of records for the Trust. The Administrator's and his staff's help during the past year are greatly appreciated.

/s/   *Allen Jones*
Certified Public Accountant

## EXHIBIT A

CONSTRUCTION INDUSTRY HEALTH AND SECURITY FUND
BALANCE SHEET AS AT MARCH 31, 19___
*(Prepared on a Cash Basis of Accounting)*

### ASSETS

*Cash*

| | |
|---|---:|
| Cash in Transit | $      192.00 |
| Cash—National Bank of Commerce, Checking Account | 90,501.56 |
| Cash—National Bank of Commerce, Investment Account | 34,738.58 |
| Cash in Sixteen Savings Accounts (Schedule 1) | 171,779.50 |
| Total Cash | $ 297,211.64 |

*Investments*

| | |
|---|---:|
| Corporate Bonds at Cost, per Schedule 2 (market value $207,698.75) | $ 219,456.85 |
| Corporate Stocks at Cost, per Schedule 3 (market value $338,102.91) | 309,412.28 |
| Federal Land Bank 4% Bonds due 5.1.62 (market value $158,528.00) | 160,979.12 |

F.N.M.A. 4⅜ % Bonds at Cost due 4.10.69
(market value $29,622.00)                                              29,101.93
Treasury Bonds of 11.15.61 at Cost, 2½ %
(market value $58,368.00)                                              59,293.82
U. S. Series K Bonds at Cost
(market value $193,600.00)                                            200,000.00

    Total Investments                                  $   978,244.00

    Total Assets                                       $1,275,455.64

### NET WORTH

Surplus—a Reserve for future benefits                                $1,275,455.64

## EXHIBIT A—SCHEDULE 1

CONSTRUCTION INDUSTRY HEALTH AND SECURITY FUND

CASH IN SAVINGS ACCOUNTS, AS AT MARCH 31, 19___

*(Prepared on a Cash Basis of Accounting)*

| Bank | City | Rate of Interest | Interest Earned | Balance on March 31, 19___ |
|---|---|---|---|---|
| Prudential Mutual Savings Bank | Seattle | 3½% | $ 477.82 | $ 11,888.73 |
| Puget Sound Mutual Savings Bank | Seattle | 3½% | 391.95 | 11,860.59 |
| United Mutual Savings Bank | Tacoma | 3½% | 392.84 | 11,887.40 |
| Washington Mutual Savings Bank | Seattle | 3½% | 373.84 | 11,784.78 |
| Metropolitan Federal Savings Bank | Seattle | 4% | 330.09 | 8,873.48 |
| Seattle Federal Savings Bank | Seattle | 4% | 486.00 | 10,100.00 |
| Washington Federal Savings Bank | Seattle | 4% | 486.08 | 10,100.00 |
| Union Federal Savings Bank | Seattle | 4% | 487.45 | 10,100.00 |
| First Federal Savings Bank | Seattle | 3½% | 350.00 | 10,000.00 |
| Alaska Federal Savings Bank | Juneau | 3% | 320.78 | 10,934.41 |
| First Federal Savings Bank | Anchorage | 4% | 436.20 | 11,233.98 |
| First National Bank of Ketchikan | Ketchikan | 2% | 209.16 | 10,615.20 |
| First Bank of Sitka | Sitka | 2% | 209.16 | 10,615.20 |
| First Savings and Loan | Seattle | 4% | 375.00 | 10,000.00 |
| City National Bank | Anchorage | 3% | 320.00 | 10,907.53 |
| Alaska National Bank | Fairbanks | 3% | 309.68 | 10,878.20 |
| Total | | | $5,956.05 | $171,779.50 |

*EXHIBIT A—SCHEDULE 2*

CONSTRUCTION INDUSTRY HEALTH AND SECURITY FUND
CORPORATE BONDS OWNED AS AT MARCH 31, 19___
*(Prepared on a Cash Basis of Accounting)*

|  | Due Date | Maturity Value | Cost | Market Value on March 31, 19___ |
|---|---|---|---|---|
| Grace Line U. S. Government Insured 4¼ % | 7. 1.78 | $ 50,000.00 | $ 50,000.00 | $ 46,375.00 |
| Phillips Petroleum 4¼ % Convertible Debentures | 2.15.87 | 1,000.00 | 1,000.00 | 1,063.75 |
| Sears Roebuck 4¾ % Sinking Fund Debentures | 8. 1.83 | 50,000.00 | 52,687.50 | 50,750.00 |
| Southern Counties Gas 4% Refunding | 5. 1.83 | 65,000.00 | 61,993.75 | 56,875.00 |
| Southern Pacific Series 2, 3¼ % Equipment Trust Certificates | 3. 1.71 | 60,000.00 | 53,775.60 | 52,635.00 |

Total Maturity Value      $226,000.00

Total Cost Value per Balance Sheet      $219,456.85

Total Market Value on March 31, 19___      $207,698.75

*EXHIBIT A—SCHEDULE 3*

CONSTRUCTION INDUSTRY HEALTH AND SECURITY FUND
COMMON STOCKS OWNED AS AT MARCH 31, 19___
*(Prepared on a Cash Basis of Accounting)*

|  | Number of Shares | Cost | Market Value on March 31, 19___ |
|---|---|---|---|
| Addressograph-Multigraph | 50 | $ 5,354.81 | $ 6,125.00 |
| Allied Chemical and Dye | 200 | 8,544.98 | 9,800.00 |
| Aluminum of America | 100 | 9,668.05 | 9,100.00 |
| American Metal Climax | 200 | 5,427.32 | 4,400.00 |
| American Trust-Wells Fargo Bank | 220 | 8,750.00 | 11,852.50 |
| Central Illinois Public Service | 200 | 5,437.50 | 9,650.00 |
| Consolidated Natural Gas | 200 | 9,434.76 | 9,300.00 |
| Continental Can | 100 | 4,361.13 | 4,400.00 |
| Crown Zellerbach | 200 | 10,420.04 | 8,800.00 |
| General America | 40 | 6,190.00 | 6,300.00 |

*EXHIBIT A—SCHEDULE 3—(Continued)*

CONSTRUCTION INDUSTRY HEALTH AND SECURITY FUND
COMMON STOCKS OWNED AS AT MARCH 31, 19——
*(Prepared on a Cash Basis of Accounting)*

| | Number of Shares | Cost | Market Value on March 31, 19__ |
|---|---|---|---|
| General American Transportation | 200 | 6,203.66 | 12,800.00 |
| General Electric | 200 | 14,297.42 | 17,975.00 |
| General Motors | 200 | 7,240.87 | 8,900.00 |
| General Public Utilities | 315 | 7,539.37 | 7,402.50 |
| Goodyear Tire and Rubber | 365 | 6,980.09 | 13,140.00 |
| International Paper | 102 | 11,775.43 | 11,449.50 |
| Libby-Owens-Ford | 200 | 10,421.84 | 11,925.00 |
| National Cash Register | 210 | 12,656.48 | 12,337.50 |
| National Lead | 100 | 9,909.98 | 9,700.00 |
| Phillips Petroleum | 200 | 7,192.15 | 8,450.00 |
| Puget Sound Power and Light | 200 | 7,075.00 | 6,575.00 |
| Puget Sound Pulp and Timber | 500 | 11,750.00 | 12,000.00 |
| Southern California Edison | 200 | 10,837.50 | 11,675.00 |
| Standard Oil of California | 210 | 7,992.95 | 9,135.00 |
| Standard Oil of New Jersey | 100 | 5,809.23 | 4,400.00 |
| Union Carbide | 50 | 6,556.01 | 6,675.00 |
| Wellington Fund | 4,834.617 | 67,577.74 | 66,185.91 |
| Westinghouse Electric | 400 | 17,557.97 | 19,900.00 |
| Weyerhaeuser Timber | 200 | 6,450.00 | 7,750.00 |

Total Cost Value per Balance Sheet $309,412.28

Total Market Value on March 31, 19__ $338,102.91

*EXHIBIT B*

CONSTRUCTION INDUSTRY HEALTH AND SECURITY FUND
SURPLUS ANALYSIS AS AT MARCH 31, 19——
*(Prepared on a Cash Basis of Accounting)*

Surplus on April 1, 19__ $1,215,270.89

ADD

Net Employers' Contributions $773,730.54
Interest, Dividends and Other Income 42,435.59

Total Trust Income 816,166.13

Total $2,031,437.02

DEDUCT

| | | |
|---|---|---|
| Net Premiums Paid | $721,599.78 | |
| Administrative Expenses | 34,381.60 | |
| Total Trust Expenses | | 755,981.38 |
| Surplus on March 31, 19__ | | $1,275,455.64 |

## *EXHIBIT C*

CONSTRUCTION INDUSTRY HEALTH AND SECURITY FUND
STATEMENT OF RECEIPTS AND DISBURSEMENTS
FISCAL YEAR ENDED MARCH 31, 19__
*(Prepared on a Cash Basis of Accounting)*

| | | | |
|---|---|---|---|
| Cash Balance on April 1, 19__ | | | $ 335,531.26 |

RECEIPTS

| | | | |
|---|---|---|---|
| Employers' Contributions | $774,686.29 | | |
| Less Refunds | 955.75 | | |
| Net Contributions | | $773,730.54 | |

INCOME RECEIPTS

| | | | |
|---|---|---|---|
| Dividends | $ 11,828.51 | | |
| Interest on Corporate Bonds | 9,092.50 | | |
| Interest on Savings Accounts | 5,956.05 | | |
| Interest on U.S. Bonds | 15,528.43 | | |
| Profit on Sale of U.S. Bonds | 30.10 | | |
| Total Investment Income | | 42,435.59 | |
| Total Trust Income | | | 816,166.13 |
| Total Available | | | $1,151,697.39 |

DISBURSEMENTS

| | | | |
|---|---|---|---|
| Premiums—Western Mutual Life | | $721,599.78 | |

ADMINISTRATIVE EXPENSES

| | | | |
|---|---|---|---|
| Accrued Interest Purchased | $ 120.31 | | |
| Administration Fees | 29,490.10 | | |
| Audit Fees | 1,243.29 | | |
| Bank Charges | 1.95 | | |
| Investment Counsel Fees | 2,481.15 | | |
| Legal Fees | 46.25 | | |

*EXHIBIT C—(Continued)*

CONSTRUCTION INDUSTRY HEALTH AND SECURITY FUND
STATEMENT OF RECEIPTS AND DISBURSEMENTS
FISCAL YEAR ENDED MARCH 31, 19—
*(Prepared on a Cash Basis of Accounting)*

ADMINISTRATIVE EXPENSES *(Cont.):*

| | | |
|---|---|---|
| N.S.F. Checks | 504.00 | |
| Printing and Office Supplies | 494.55 | |
| Total Administrative Expenses | 34,381.60 | |
| Total | | 755,981.38 |
| Balance before Security Transactions | | $ 395,716.01 |

OTHER CASH TRANSACTIONS

| | | |
|---|---|---|
| U.S. Securities Redeemed | | 212,371.64 |
| | | $ 608,087.65 |

DEDUCT

| | | |
|---|---|---|
| Purchase of Common Stocks | $208,624.66 | |
| Purchase of U.S. Securities | 102,251.35 | |
| Total New Investments Acquired | | 310,876.01 |
| Balance on March 31, 19— | | $ 297,211.64 |

## EXHIBIT D

### CONSTRUCTION INDUSTRY HEALTH AND SECURITY FUND

### STATEMENT OF RECEIPTS AND DISBURSEMENTS AND GROWTH OF SURPLUS

APRIL 1, 19___ TO MARCH 31, 19___

*(Prepared on a Cash Basis of Accounting)*

| | Year Ended 3.31.___ | Year Ended 3.31.___ | Year Ended 3.31.___ | Year Ended 3.31.___ | Year Ended 3.31.___ | Year Ended 3.31.___ | Year Ended 3.31.___ | Seven-Year Total | % of Income |
|---|---|---|---|---|---|---|---|---|---|
| **RECEIPTS** | | | | | | | | | |
| Employers' Contributions | $551,542.83 | $593,148.63 | $648,786.67 | $816,237.33 | $811,586.06 | $730,014.90 | $774,686.29 | $4,926,002.71 | |
| Less Refunds | 133.70 | 3,543.08 | 1,938.90 | 459.63 | 4,983.86 | 1,299.50 | 955.75 | 13,314.42 | |
| Net Employers' Contributions | $551,409.13 | $589,605.55 | $646,847.77 | $815,777.70 | $806,602.20 | $728,715.40 | $773,730.54 | $4,912,688.29 | 97.12 |
| **OTHER INCOME** | | | | | | | | | |
| Dividends | | | $ 4,515.60 | $ 5,885.58 | $ 6,336.01 | $ 8,309.60 | $ 11,828.51 | $ 36,875.30 | .73 |
| Interest on Savings Accounts | | $ 644.77 | 3,858.44 | 5,159.94 | 7,708.65 | 5,324.83 | 5,956.05 | 28,652.68 | .57 |
| Interest on U.S. Bonds | | 3,395.62 | 8,280.00 | 8,322.80 | 7,878.95 | 24,613.49 | 15,528.43 | 68,019.29 | 1.34 |
| Interest on Corporate Bonds | | | | | | 2,455.50 | 9,092.50 | 11,548.00 | .23 |
| Refund of Expenses | | 93.65 | | | | 267.93 | | 361.58 | .01 |
| Sale of Rights | | | 76.00 | 70.45 | | | | 146.45 | |
| Profit on Sale of U.S. Bonds | | | | | | | 30.10 | 30.10 | |
| Total Other Income | $ None | $ 4,134.04 | $ 16,730.04 | $ 19,438.77 | $ 21,923.61 | $ 40,971.35 | $ 42,435.59 | $ 145,633.40 | 2.88 |
| Total Income | $551,409.13 | $593,739.59 | $663,577.81 | $835,216.47 | $828,525.81 | $769,686.75 | $816,166.13 | $5,058,321.69 | 100.00 |
| **EXPENSES** | | | | | | | | | |
| Premiums Paid | $129,359.16 | $415,395.67 | $537,026.77 | $658,026.54 | $721,231.05 | $670,642.19 | $721,599.78 | $3,853,281.16 | |
| Less Experience Rating Refund | | 86,855.00 | | 130,927.00 | | 54,843.00 | | 272,625.00 | |
| Net Premiums Paid | $129,359.16 | $328,540.67 | $537,026.77 | $527,099.54 | $721,231.05 | $615,799.19 | $721,599.78 | $3,580,656.16 | 70.79% |

# EXHIBIT D—(Continued)

## CONSTRUCTION INDUSTRY HEALTH AND SECURITY FUND
### STATEMENT OF RECEIPTS AND DISBURSEMENTS AND GROWTH OF SURPLUS
#### APRIL 1, 19___ TO MARCH 31, 19___
*(Prepared on a Cash Basis of Accounting)*

| | Year Ended 3.31___ | Year Ended 3.31___ | Year Ended 3.31___ | Year Ended 3.31___ | Year Ended 3.31___ | Year Ended 3.31___ | Year Ended 3.31___ | Seven-Year Total | % of Income |
|---|---|---|---|---|---|---|---|---|---|
| **ADMINISTRATIVE EXPENSES** | | | | | | | | | |
| Accrued Interest Purchased | | $ 136.18 | | | | $ 1,014.78 | $ 120.31 | $ 1,271.27 | .03 |
| Administration Fees | $ 8,814.86 | 19,060.43 | $ 24,423.14 | $ 30,845.72 | $ 30,662.70 | 27,874.04 | 29,490.10 | 171,170.99 | 3.38 |
| Audit Fees | | 1,228.90 | 1,337.89 | 1,505.18 | 1,582.88 | 1,577.05 | 1,243.29 | 8,475.19 | .17 |
| Bank Charges | 193.50 | 29.13 | .60 | | | | 1.95 | 225.18 | |
| Fidelity Bonds | | 1,223.40 | | | 1,223.40 | | | 2,446.80 | .05 |
| Investment Counsel Fees | | 312.50 | 1,006.49 | 1,124.81 | 1,327.86 | 2,224.74 | 2,481.15 | 8,477.55 | .17 |
| Legal Fees | | | | | | 250.33 | 46.25 | 296.58 | |
| Loss on Sale of Securities | | | | | | 3,246.00 | | 3,246.00 | .06 |
| N.S.F. Check Losses | | | | | | | 504.00 | 504.00 | .01 |
| Printing and Office Expenses | 1,720.81 | 722.52 | 392.34 | 1,266.91 | 648.82 | 850.38 | 494.55 | 6,096.33 | .12 |
| Total Administrative Expenses | $ 10,729.17 | $ 22,713.06 | $ 27,160.46 | $ 34,742.62 | $ 35,445.66 | $ 37,037.32 | $ 34,381.60 | $ 202,209.89 | 3.99 |
| Total Expenses | $140,088.33 | $351,253.73 | $564,187.23 | $561,842.16 | $756,676.71 | $652,836.51 | $755,981.38 | $3,782,866.05 | 74.78 |
| Net Surplus Increase for Year | $411,320.80 | $242,485.86 | $ 99,390.58 | $273,374.31 | $ 71,849.10 | $116,850.24 | $ 60,184.75 | | |
| Grand Total Surplus Increase | | | | | | | | $1,275,455.64 | 25.22% |

## EXHIBIT E

CONSTRUCTION INDUSTRY HEALTH AND SECURITY FUND
STATEMENT OF UNLIQUIDATED PREMIUM LIABILITY
AS AT MARCH 31, 19___
*(Prepared on a Cash Basis of Accounting)*

| Month | Number of Premiums | Rate | Amount |
|---|---|---|---|
| April 19___ | 4,570 | $12.70 | $ 58,039.00 |
| May 19___ | 4,420 | 12.70 | 56,134.00 |
| June 19___ | 4,340 | 12.70 | 55,118.00 |
| July 19___ | 4,185 | 12.70 | 53,149.50 |
| August 19___ | 3,932 | 12.70 | 49,936.40 |
| September 19___ | 3,684 | 12.70 | 46,786.80 |
| October 19___ | 3,254 | 12.70 | 41,325.80 |
| November 19___ | 2,570 | 12.70 | 32,639.00 |
| December 19___ | 1,905 | 12.70 | 24,193.50 |
| January 19___ | 1,255 | 12.70 | 15,938.50 |
| February 19___ | 304 | 12.70 | 3,860.80 |
| March 19___ | 45 | 12.70 | 571.50 |
| Total | 34,464 | $12.70 | $437,692.80 |

## EXHIBIT F

CONSTRUCTION INDUSTRY HEALTH AND SECURITY FUND
COMPARISON OF ADMINISTRATIVE EXPENSE AND INVESTMENT INCOME
FISCAL YEAR ENDED MARCH 31, 19___
*(Prepared on a Cash Basis of Accounting)*

ITEMS OF EXPENSE

| | |
|---|---|
| Purchase of Accrued Interest | $ 120.31 |
| Administration Fees | 29,490.10 |
| Audit Fees | 1,243.29 |
| Investment Counsel Fees | 2,481.15 |
| Legal Fees | 46.25 |
| Office Supplies and Printing | 494.55 |
| Bank Charges | 1.95 |
| N.S.F. Check Loss | 504.00 |
| Total Administrative Expense | $34,381.60 |

*EXHIBIT F—(Continued)*

CONSTRUCTION INDUSTRY HEALTH AND SECURITY FUND
STATEMENT OF UNLIQUIDATED PREMIUM LIABILITY
AS AT MARCH 31, 19___
*(Prepared on a Cash Basis of Accounting)*

ITEMS OF INCOME

| | |
|---|---|
| Dividends | $11,828.51 |
| Interest on Corporate Bonds | 9,092.50 |
| Interest on Savings Accounts | 5,956.05 |
| Interest on U.S. Bonds | 15,528.43 |
| Profit on Sale of U.S. Bonds | 30.10 |
| Total Investment Income | 42,435.59 |
| Excess of Investment Income over Administrative Expense | $ 8,053.99 |
| Percentage of Investment Income to Administrative Expense | 123.42% |

CONSTRUCTION INDUSTRY HEALTH AND SECURITY FUND
NOTES TO FINANCIAL STATEMENTS
FISCAL YEAR ENDED MARCH 31, 19___

*Note 1.* There is due to the Administrator the sum of $1,566.34 for administrative services rendered in March 19___. This Amount is payable in April 19___.

*Note 2.* All investments are shown at cost for Balance Sheet purposes. Series K bonds are redeemable at a price lower than cost if such redemption occurs before maturity.

*Note 3.* These statements have been prepared on a cash basis of accounting, therefore no reserve has been established for insurance premiums due after March 31, 19___ and based on eligibility hours worked before March 31, 19___. There is an apparent liability (per Exhibit E) of $437,692.80.

*Note 4.* No provision has been made for employers' delinquent contributions to be received, or for administration fees and premium costs which will attach to these delinquent contributions when received. The nature of the construction industry precludes any such determination.

*Note 5.* No provision has been made for a possible experience rating refund from the carrier. This refund will accrue to the Fund, if earned, at the expiration of the policy year.

*Note 6.* There is a contingent asset amounting to $14,031.00. This is a fluctuating reserve held by the carrier, Western Mutual Life Insurance Company, and bears interest at the rate of 2¾ %. Commencing January 1, 19___ the interest rate becomes 4%. It is the intention to build this reserve to $35,000.00 or approximately 5% of a year's premiums. In the event that the policy is cancelled before the end of the policy year, the carrier can use the reserve to offset any losses.

# 34

# Accounting Under SEC Regulations

**CHARLES B. HELLERSON**

*Certified Public Accountant; Partner, Hurdman and Cranstoun, New York*

**1211**

CHAPTER THIRTY-FOUR

# Accounting Under
# SEC Regulations

The influence of the Securities and Exchange Commission (SEC) on certain segments of the public accounting profession has been considerable for a good many years. Today, many small and medium-sized practitioners are finding that the rush among close corporations to "go public" is, for the first time, making it essential for them to become familiar with the extensive body of law and the regulations and pronouncements that govern the public sale of securities.

Anyone who is familar with the scope of the SEC's activities will immediately realize that a chapter such as this cannot provide all-inclusive coverage. Rather, it is intended to serve as an introduction for the practitioner who has had little or no experience in SEC work, and as a refresher and reference for the practitioner who is experienced in SEC work. On this basis, the substantive matter that is provided concerns those areas with which the public accountant will most frequently be concerned—specifically, Form S-1, Forms 10 and 10-K, and Regulation S-X. To complement the substantive material, there are suggestions and guides that will enable the accountant to delve further into the subject matter.

Throughout the chapter, we have used SEC terminology even though in some cases it conflicts with modern accounting terminology. Also, although we have simplified some of the "legal jargon," we have retained much of it in the interest of technical accuracy. It is probably just as well that the reader get used to it if he intends to take on SEC engagements.

The chapter will begin with an introduction to the SEC itself. Then we will proceed to a more detailed discussion of the SEC in the accounting field.

## AN OVERALL LOOK AT THE SEC

The public accountant will not become involved in all areas in which the SEC functions. However, he should have some idea of the scope of its activities and the basis for its operations. This section will provide the information that comprises the background for the public accountant's work. It will also touch on some items of more general interest.

Specifically, we will discuss:

1. Origin and structure of the SEC.
2. Laws administered by the SEC.
3. Enforcement powers of the SEC.
4. SEC procedures.

**Origin and structure of the SEC.** The SEC was created in 1934 by act of Congress. Its inception can be traced to the Senate investigations following the stock market crash of 1929. These investigations revealed the many abuses existing at the time in the distribution of and trading in securities, thus underlining the need for legislation to protect the public. Although many states had their own laws for the regulation of security transactions, these "blue sky" laws were in many cases ineffective and, furthermore, had no application to transactions in interstate commerce. Therefore, during the 1930's and in the year 1940, Congress passed a series of laws designed to guard the public with respect to securities sold in interstate commerce or listed on a national securities exchange.

The SEC was established to administer these laws. An independent regulatory agency responsible to the Congress, it performs a quasi-judicial function in conjunction with its administrative function. Five men, appointed by the President with the consent of the Senate, serve as Commissioners for five-year terms. They are assisted by a professional staff, which is organized into appropriate operating sections. As will be seen later in the chapter, the public accountant will be concerned principally with (1) the Division of Corporate Finance, and (2) the Office of Chief Accountant.

**Laws administered by the SEC.** The significance of the SEC becomes obvious upon even a brief review of the laws it administers. These laws are:

1. *Securities Act of 1933.* This law protects the investor by requiring the issuer of a security to make full disclosure of the material facts concerning the security and the company. A *material fact* is defined as a fact that the average prudent investor would be expected to rely on. Disclosure is accomplished by means of a registration statement and a prospectus that must be filed with the Commission for review. Copies of the prospectus must be furnished to potential investors, and the registration statement is available for examination by the public. In its review, the Commission determines whether there has been compliance with its rules, regulations,

and instructions, and whether there has been full disclosure of matters of significance to potential investors. However, any decision as to the relative value of the security as an investment is left to individual buyers.

Section 3(b) of the Act allows the Commission to exempt from registration offerings of an aggregate value of less than $300,000. Certain special types of offerings are exempt under Section 3(a) of the Act. Furthermore, the jurisdiction of the Act is limited to securities to be sold in interstate commerce or through the mails in such a way as to constitute a *public offering.*

▶ WARNING: The determination of what is and what is not a public offering frequently involves complex legal considerations in individual cases. The accountant should not attempt to offer advice on this question, but should suggest that the matter be referred to a qualified lawyer.

▶ NOTE: Before 1934, the 1933 Act was administered by the Federal Trade Commission.

2. *Securities Exchange Act of 1934.* Any company that desires listing on a national securities exchange, the securities exchanges themselves, and various brokers and dealers are required to file registration statements with the Commission under the provisions of this Act. The 1934 Act, then, protects the public in the *trading* in securities, while the 1933 Act protects the public in the *distribution* of securities. The two Acts thus complement each other and form the backbone of the Commission's work.

The registration statements required by the 1934 Act are kept up-to-date by means of periodic reports that must be filed with the Commission subsequent to the date of registration. Companies that register under the 1933 Act may become subject to the reporting requirements of the 1934 Act even though their securities are not listed on a national exchange (see page 1222). The 1934 Act also gives the SEC jurisdiction over the registrant's proxy solicitation material.

3. *Public Utility Holding Company Act of 1935.* As the name indicates, this Act pertains to a special field. It provides for registration of companies included in holding company systems in the electric utility and retail gas fields. The Commission is granted broad regulatory powers with regard to the financial and operating structures of these companies.

4. *Trust Indenture Act of 1939.* The purpose of this Act is to protect corporate creditors by requiring that evidences of corporate indebtedness (bonds, notes, etc.) be offered to the public only under a trust indenture that has qualified with the Commission.

5. *Investment Company Act of 1940.* This law protects the small investor who attempts to obtain diversification by purchasing shares in an

investment company. Investment companies must register with the SEC, which also has regulatory powers under the Act.

6. *Investment Advisers Act of 1940.* This law provides for the registration of certain individuals engaged in the business of advising others on investment matters.

**Enforcement powers of the SEC.** The Acts just described provide the Commission with considerable powers with which to enforce their provisions. In addition, where fraud or willful violation of an Act is involved, the Justice Department may institute criminal proceedings based on evidence supplied by the SEC.

▶ NOTE: If fraud is involved in the sale of securities in interstate commerce or through the mails, exemptions under the 1933 Act do not apply and the SEC has jurisdiction.

In order to carry out its functions, the Commission has the following direct powers:

1. It can prevent the distribution of a security being offered for sale.
2. It can stop the trading in a security.
3. It can take disciplinary actions (fines, suspension of privileges, etc.) against individuals and organizations.

However, the Commission's orders may be appealed to the courts.

**SEC procedures.** The SEC is authorized to define terms used in certain of the laws it administers, and it can prescribe the way in which the information required by the laws is to be reported. In this regard, the SEC has issued rules and regulations under the various Acts. These rules and regulations provide essential information concerning SEC procedures. Of particular concern to the accountant are:

1933 ACT:
Rules of general applicability (Rules 170 and 171).
Regulation A—general exemption to registration.
Regulation C—rules applicable to registration.

1934 ACT:
Sections of Regulation 12 pertaining to formal requirements and general requirements as to contents.
Sections of Regulation 13 pertaining to requirements of annual and other reports.
Regulation 14—rules relating to solicitation of proxies.
Sections of Regulation 15 relating to reports of registrants who have registered under the 1933 Act.

*Registration procedures.* The procedures to be followed in preparing and filing the registration statement are the major area of interest to the public accountant, since a registration statement must include a great deal of financial information. Furthermore, much of this financial data must be accompanied by an opinion of an independent public accountant. The nature of the financial information will be discussed later on in the chapter. Our concern here is with procedures relating to the filing of the registration statement itself.

▶ OBSERVATION: Detailed financial information is not required under the Trust Indenture Act of 1939 and the Investment Advisers Act of 1940, so the public accountant will not be concerned with these laws. Two of the Acts that do require the filing of detailed financial information—the Public Utility Holding Company Act of 1935 and the Investment Company Act of 1940—apply to special types of businesses. Therefore, most public accountants will be involved only with the Securities Act of 1933 and the Securities Exchange Act of 1934.

The rules governing the requirements for registration are set forth in Regulation C, the instructions to the form used, and Regulation S-X. Under the 1933 Act, the first step in the registration procedure is to file the appropriate form with the office of the SEC in Washington, D.C. This should be done twenty days before the anticipated effective date of the registration. The registration statement is thoroughly reviewed by the Division of Corporate Finance. As we have previously indicated, this review is aimed toward determining whether there has been full disclosure of matters of significance to potential investors; the Commission does not pass judgment on the merits of the security as an investment. In fact, the front page of a prospectus must contain a statement in bold-face type to the effect that the securities have not been approved or disapproved by the SEC.

Upon completion of its review, the Commission sends a letter of comments (popularly known as a *deficiency letter*) to the registrant. This letter sets forth the particular parts of the registration statement that the SEC believes require amendment. In order to minimize the number and the extent of such deficiencies, accountants and others experienced in SEC work make it a practice to discuss matters on which they have doubts or questions with members of the Commission's staff before the registration statement is actually filed. Often, a problem can be resolved over the telephone. In other cases, a conference is required. The SEC's staff is extremely cooperative and helpful and should be consulted whenever a problem cannot otherwise be solved. But it should be remembered that they are busy men and should not be queried indiscriminately.

Discussion with members of the staff may be advisable after the letter of comments has been received. There may be some questions or problems concerning the means or even the desirability of complying with the Commission's suggestions. Again, some matters can be cleared up over the telephone, while others can be resolved only through a conference. When agreement has been reached, an amendment must be filed. This amendment is handled by the Division of Corporate Finance in the same manner as the original registration statement was handled. The twenty-day waiting period starts all over again. However, the Commission can agree upon request to "accelerate" the amendment by treating it as if it were filed as of the filing date of the original registration statement. If an amendment does not correct the deficiencies to the satisfaction of the Commission, another letter of comments is sent and the cycle is repeated.

Normally, a registration statement becomes effective twenty days after it has been filed, but the Commission has the power to consent to an earlier effective date (Sec. 8(a), 1933 Act). Therefore, it is necessary to file an amendment as quickly as possible. When an amendment is not filed within the allotted time, the Commission can take the following courses of action, depending on the circumstances: (1) if the deficiencies are not material, it can allow the registration statement to become effective in deficient form but without acceleration, or (2) if the deficiencies are material, it can refuse to permit the registration statement to become effective, thereby prohibiting sale of the securities to the public.

▶ WHAT TO DO: If deficiencies in the registration statement cannot be corrected in time, a *delaying amendment* should be filed. In order to avoid the necessity of filing successive delaying amendments, a *blanket delaying amendment* can be filed (Rule 473). This blanket delaying amendment is worded as follows:

> The registrant hereby amends this registration statement on such date or dates as may be necessary to delay its effective date until the registrant shall file a further amendment which specifically states that this registration statement shall thereafter become effective in accordance with Sec. 8(a) of the Securities Act of 1933 or until the registration statement shall become effective on such date as the Commission, acting pursuant to said Sec. 8(a), may determine.

The registration statement must not contain an untrue statement or omission of a material fact *when it becomes effective* (Sec. 11, 1933 Act). Therefore, the accountant must remember to keep currently abreast of the financial affairs of his client after the registration statement has been filed. An authoritative discussion of the accountant's responsibility for disclosure of events subsequent to the date of the financial statements, with suggestions for making a review of the client's affairs, can be found in *Statement on Auditing Procedure No. 25,* issued by the Committee on Auditing Procedure of the American Institute of Certified Public Accountants.

▶ COMFORT LETTER: Frequently, the underwriter will require a "comfort letter" from the accountant. In this letter, the accountant indicates that he has made a review, but not an audit, of financial statements for periods subsequent to the date of the statements filed, and that he has read minutes, made inquiries of officers, and the like; and that, based on this review, no knowledge came to his attention of any changes in capital stock or any material adverse changes in the financial position of the company.

The SEC also reviews registration statements and annual reports filed under the 1934 Act. In general, the procedure is the same as under the 1933 Act—deficiency letters are sent and, if necessary, amendments are filed. However, since there is usually no effective date involved in filings under the 1934 Act, delaying amendments are not required. In fact, deficiency letters relating to annual reports filed under the 1934 Act sometimes consist merely of suggestions by the Commission that should be incorporated in the annual report for the next year.

## THE SEC IN THE ACCOUNTING FIELD

Because of the importance of financial information to the potential investor, the SEC has a considerable interest in accounting practices and procedures. The Acts themselves place a great deal of emphasis on accounting matters, to such an extent that the Commission—although it has chosen not to do so—could make itself the authoritative body in the accounting field. The activities and pronouncements of the Commission in this area are, of course, the primary concern of this chapter. We will consider:

1. Background—guides to SEC thinking on accounting matters, and the SEC position on accounting principles and practices.
2. Financial statements required by the SEC.
3. The accountant's duties and responsibilities.
4. Form and content of financial statements.

### BACKGROUND

**Guides to SEC thinking on accounting matters.** The public accountant engaged in SEC work must be conversant with the requirements of the appropriate law, and he must also have a thorough knowledge of the

Commission's views on accounting and auditing theory and practice. These views are expressed through a number of media, as follows:

1. *Regulation S-X*. This is the major accounting regulation. It governs the form and content of the financial statements that must be filed under the various Acts. An up-to-date copy of Regulation S-X is the most essential tool for any accountant engaged in SEC work. Copies can be obtained by writing to the SEC, 425 Second Street NW, Washington 25, D.C.

2. *Accounting Series Releases*. Opinions of the Chief Accountant on major accounting and administrative questions are published in these releases. Notices of changes in Regulation S-X and other matters of interest to accountants are also made known through Accounting Series Releases. Past releases can be obtained from the Superintendent of Documents, U. S. Government Printing Office, Washington 25, D.C. You will be placed on the current mailing list if you send a written request to the main office of the SEC.

3. *SEC Decisions and Reports*. The Accounting Series Releases were not issued before 1937. For information on Commission decisions and opinions that were reached prior to that date, it is necessary to refer to the bound volumes of SEC Decisions and Reports. These are available from the Superintendent of Documents.

4. *Annual Reports of the SEC*. At the end of each fiscal year, the SEC sends its annual report to Congress. This report summarizes the Commission's activities for the year and provides a valuable insight into its procedures and policies. Copies can be obtained from the Superintendent of Documents.

5. *Speeches and articles by the Commissioners and members of the staff*. Those officially connected with the SEC are often called upon to give talks on accounting subjects. Professional publications frequently print these speeches and also publish articles by the Commissioners and members of the staff.

**The SEC position on accounting principles and practices.** The SEC has not invoked the authority given to it by Congress to the extent that it dictates the accounting principles to be applied in the preparation of the financial section of the registration statement. It has left this area primarily to the discretion of the accounting profession by requiring that financial statements be prepared in accordance with generally accepted accounting principles. However, the Commission reserves the right to use "its own judgment of what is sound accounting practice." In this connection, the Commission has had to point out many times that tax accounting does not necessarily represent generally accepted accounting practice. And in Accounting Series Release No. 56, the Commission stated that the standard is the accepted accounting practice at the date of the particular transaction, not at the filing date. This is especially important in cases where it is necessary to reconstruct accounts.

▶ OBSERVATION: If there is "no substantial authoritative support" for the accounting principles on which the statements are based, the deficiency will not be corrected by mere disclosure of this fact in footnotes or in the accountant's report. This point was brought out in Accounting Series Release No. 4. For more detail on the accountant's report and the accountant's responsibility, see pages 1230 to 1234.

## FINANCIAL STATEMENTS REQUIRED BY THE SEC

The requirements as to what financial statements must be filed for registration are shown on the appropriate registration or reporting form and in the instruction booklet for the form. Certain terms defined in Regulation S-X are used in the instructions to the various forms; we will refer to these definitions in the following discussion when it is necessary for clarification. Also, reference will be made to various provisions, rules, and regulations under the Acts that are of particular significance to the accountant.

Most of the forms prescribed by the SEC are for use only by special types of issuers or apply only to particular kinds of securities. Our discussion will concentrate on those forms that have general applicability and, therefore, are most frequently used, as follows:

1. Form S-1, for registration under the 1933 Act.
2. Form 10, for registration under the 1934 Act, and Form 10-K, for annual reports under the 1934 Act.

**1. Form S-1.** Companies registering under the 1933 Act that do not fall within the "special" categories should use Form S-1. Thus, commercial or industrial concerns will usually file on Form S-1. The form itself is divided into two sections: Part I is for information required in the prospectus; Part II is for information not required in the prospectus. In preparing the statements required for Form S-1 and other forms, the preparer should keep in mind the provisions of Rule 3-06 of Regulation S-X to the effect that information required with respect to any statement is a minimum requirement to which must be added any additional information necessary to make the financial statements not misleading. Also, attention should be paid to General Instruction D for Form S-1, which permits cross-referencing instead of repeating the same information in several parts of the prospectus.

**Part I of Form S-1.** The financial information required in Part I of Form S-1 is:

1. *Summary of earnings.* Item 6 on the form requires that a summary of earnings be furnished in comparative columnar form for the registrant or the registrant and its subsidiaries consolidated, or both, depending on for whom balance sheets must be filed. This summary, which is actually a condensed profit and loss statement, is probably the single statement most frequently referred to by investors. It should include, depending on the type of business, (a) net sales or operating revenues, (b) cost of goods sold or operating expenses (or gross profit), (c) interest charges, (d) income taxes, (e) net income, (f) special items (see page 1252), and (g) net income and special items. If common stock is being registered, the earnings applicable to common stock, earnings per share, and dividends declared should be shown; if long-term debt is being registered, the annual interest requirements on the debt should be shown; and if preferred stock is being registered, the annual dividend requirements on the stock should be shown.

However, the trend in recent years has been to present more and more information in the summary of earnings. In fact, there is a tendency to reflect all the required income, expense, and sometimes even earned surplus information in the summary of earnings, thus eliminating entirely the separate profit and loss and earned surplus statements.

The summary must cover the preceding five fiscal years, unless the company and its immediate predecessors have not been in business that long. It must also cover (1) the period between the end of the latest fiscal year and the date of the latest balance sheet filed, and (2) the corresponding period of the preceding fiscal year. These interim periods are commonly referred to as *short periods.* The SEC further requires that data for additional years should be furnished if such data are necessary to keep the summary "from being misleading." In the case of an initial offering, the underwriters frequently demand that the summary cover a ten-year period.

▶ Note: When data for unaudited short periods are included in the summary, a statement should be made in a footnote that all adjustments necessary to a fair statement of the results for such periods have been made. In addition, the SEC must be furnished, in a separate letter, with the details of any adjustments, other than normal recurring accruals, entering into the determination of the results shown.

Because of the importance of the summary of earnings, any information or explanation that is of material significance to investors in appraising the results shown should be reflected, or reference should be made to such information or explanation if it is set forth in another section of the prospectus. This is usually done by means of footnotes.

▶ COMMENT: The summary of earnings is a comparative statement covering a substantial period of time. Therefore, retroactive adjustments may be an important factor in its preparation. The SEC requires that the summary reflect "the retroactive adjustment of any material items affecting the comparability of the results."

2. *Balance sheet of the registrant.* Item 21 on the form, as supplemented by the instruction book for the form, sets forth the requirements as to what financial statements should be filed. The first of these is the balance sheet of the registrant. This should reflect the accounts as of a date within 90 days prior to the filing date of the registration statement unless all of the following conditions are present, in which case a date within a six-month period is allowed:

a. The registrant files annual and other reports pursuant to Section 13 or 15(d) of the 1934 Act. Section 13 requires any company whose securities are listed on a national securities exchange to file these reports. Section 15(d) brings certain companies covered under the 1933 Act but whose securities are not listed on a national exchange under the same requirements; however, the aggregate value of the securities offered under the 1933 Act and all other securities of a substantially similar character must be at least $2,000,000.
b. The total tangible assets of the registrant and its subsidiaries, less any valuation or qualifying reserves, amount to $5,000,000 or more.
c. The registrant is not in default on long-term debt.

The requirements as to what information should be included in the financial statements are contained in Regulation S-X (see pages 1235 to 1253).

3. *Profit and loss statements of the registrant.* These should be filed for each of the last three complete fiscal years and for the period between the end of the latest of these years and the date of the latest balance sheet filed. As pointed out previously, the information required in the profit and loss statement can be included in the summary of earnings.

Under Rule 5-02(35d) of Regulation S-X, a surplus statement must be filed for each period for which a profit and loss statement is required. It may be either a separate statement or it may be a continuation of the related profit and loss statement. The information relating to retained earnings can also be included in the summary of earnings.

▶ OMISSION OF REGISTRANT'S STATEMENTS: If consolidated statements of the registrant and one or more of its subsidiaries are filed and the consolidated group meets certain requirements, the individual financial statements of the registrant may be omitted. The conditions that must be met are that either:

a. The registrant is primarily an operating company and all subsidiaries included in the consolidation are totally-held subsidiaries—that is, substantially all their outstanding securities and long-term debt (over one year) are owned by or owed to the registrant, either directly or through other totally-held subsidiaries—*or*

b. The registrant's total assets and total gross revenues (except for investments in, advances to, and interest and dividends received from the consolidated subsidiaries) amount to 85% or more of the comparable items as shown on the consolidated statements that are filed.

When the registrant's statements are omitted, the appropriate reason must be given in the listing of financial statements that have been included in the registration statement (Part II, Item 31). For example:

Financial statements of the registrant are omitted as the registrant is primarily an operating company and its subsidiaries, whose accounts are included in the consolidated financial statements filed, are totally-held subsidiaries.

4. *Consolidated statements.* A consolidated balance sheet and a consolidated profit and loss statement for the registrant and its subsidiaries should be filed as of the same dates as the corresponding statements filed for the registrant. If the registrant's statements are omitted, the consolidated statements should be filed as of the dates that would have been required if the registrant's statements had been filed.

The principles and practices to be followed in consolidation are set forth in Regulation S-X. These principles and practices are summarized in Chapter 3, *Consolidated Financial Statements.*

5. *Statements of unconsolidated subsidiaries.* For each of its majority-owned subsidiaries not consolidated, the registrant should file the balance sheets and profit and loss statements that would be required if the subsidiary itself were a registrant. In Rule 1-02 of Regulation S-X, a *majority-owned subsidiary* is defined as a subsidiary that has more than 50% of its outstanding voting securities owned by the registrant and/or one or more of the registrant's other majority-owned subsidiaries.

The statements should be as of the same dates and for the same periods as those of the registrant. In cases where it is not feasible to provide the balance sheet of any unconsolidated subsidiary as of a date within 90 days of filing, a *certified* balance sheet (see page 1231) as of the end of the subsidiary's latest annual or semi-annual fiscal period will suffice.

Under Rule 4-03 of Regulation S-X, the statements of majority-owned subsidiaries not included in the main consolidation may be consolidated or combined in one or more separate groups.

6. *Statements of 50%-owned persons.* The term *person,* as defined in the 1933 Act, covers not only individuals but also every form of commercial organization that can issue securities. A *50%-owned person* is one whose voting securities are owned directly or indirectly as follows: (1) approximately 50% by the registrant, and (2) approximately 50% by another *single* interest.

The registrant should file the same financial statements for any 50%-owned person that would be required if the person were a registrant. The other single interest should be identified on these financial statements.

▶ SIGNIFICANT SUBSIDIARY RULE: The financial statements of all majority-owned subsidiaries and 50%-owned companies that do not in the aggregate constitute a *significant subsidiary* do not have to be filed. As defined in Rule 1-02 of Regulation S-X, a subsidiary is considered significant if it (or, if it is itself a parent, it and its subsidiaries) meets any *one* of the following conditions:

a. The assets of the subsidiary exceed 15% of the assets of the registrant and the registrant's subsidiaries on a consolidated basis.
b. The investments in and advances to the subsidiary by the registrant and the registrant's other subsidiaries exceed 15% of the assets of the registrant and the registrant's subsidiaries on a consolidated basis.
c. The sales and operating revenues of the subsidiary exceed 15% of the sales and operating revenues of the registrant and the registrant's subsidiaries on a consolidated basis.

▶ NOTE: When the financial statements of majority-owned subsidiaries and 50%-owned companies are omitted, the reason for the omission must be given. This is usually done in a footnote to the financial statements.

7. *Statements of affiliates whose securities are collateral for the issue being registered.* For any of its affiliates whose securities are pledged as collateral for more than 20% of the principal amount of the securities being registered, the registrant should file the same financial statements that would be required if the affiliate were a registrant. The measure of the value of the securities of the affiliate is the greatest of principal amount, par value, book value, or market value.

8. *Special statements.* Under certain special conditions, additional statements or information must be provided. If the registrant has emerged from a reorganization in which substantial changes have occurred in its accounts or has succeeded to another business (by means other than purchase) during the period for which profit and loss statements are required, explanation of the resulting changes should be set forth in notes or in supporting schedules. If the registrant is about to emerge from such a reorganization or is about to succeed to another business, a balance sheet giving effect to the plan of reorganization or succession must be filed. The financial statements of the businesses that are about to be succeeded to should also be provided. And if necessary in order to achieve comparable profit and loss data over the required three-year period (or, if the profit and loss data are included in the summary of earnings, the required five-year period), the profit and loss statements of businesses that have been succeeded to must be filed, or the pertinent data must be reflected through combined statements.

When control of a business has been directly or indirectly acquired by the registrant after the date of the latest balance sheet filed or is about to be acquired by the registrant, the same financial statements that would be required if the business were a registrant must be provided.

▶ NOTE: The above requirements do not apply if the registrant succeeds to or acquires the business of one of its totally-held subsidiaries. Also, the statements of any businesses acquired (not those succeeded to) that do not in the aggregate constitute a significant subsidiary may be omitted. However, the Commission may call for additional statements not specifically required by the instructions, in the interest of adequate disclosure and investor protection.

9. *Supplementary profit and loss information.* The information required by Schedule XVI (see page 1259) should be filed in support of all profit and loss statements in which sales and operating revenues are of a "significant amount." As this information is required in the prospectus, it can be presented either through footnotes or through a separate schedule.

**Part II of Form S-1.** The financial information includible in Part II of Form S-1—that is, information that does not have to be shown in the prospectus—consists of historical data and schedules that support items reported in the financial statements in Part I. It should be remembered that the supplementary profit and loss information called for by Schedule XVI (see preceding paragraph) must be included in the prospectus and need not be duplicated in Part II of the registration statement. The historical financial information, as required in Part E of the instructions to the Form, should be furnished for the seven-year period preceding the period for which profit and loss statements are filed, so that taken together they cover a ten-year period. This historical information should reveal:

1. Any material increases or decreases resulting from the revaluation of investments, property, plant and equipment, or intangible assets.

2. Any material restatements of capital shares that resulted in transfers from capital share liability to surplus or reserve; also, any proceeds from an original issue of capital shares that were credited to accounts other than capital share accounts.

3. Any material amount of debt discount and expense that was written off earlier than required under a periodic amortization plan.

4. Any material amount of premium paid on retirement or discount and expense remaining unamortized on long-term debt or preferred shares that were retired.

5. Any material increases or decreases in surplus, other than those arising either from transactions listed above, from the closing of the profit and loss account, or from the declaration or payment of dividends.

▶ NOTE: The historical information should be provided even if the applicable accounts are not presently carried on the books. Also, it should be provided for any predecessors of the registrant. However, if the required historical information has been furnished previously pursuant to the 1933 and 1934 Acts, it does not have to be resubmitted. Part E does not require an audit, but only a review of the accounts specified.

The rules for the supporting schedules are set forth in Article 5-04 of Regulation S-X. For convenience, they are covered in this chapter under the appropriate balance sheet and profit and loss statement headings on pages 1240 to 1253.

**Pro-forma financial statements.** In addition to the financial statements required to be furnished in the registration statement, it is often advisable to include pro-forma financial statements in order to clarify an otherwise complicated situation; the SEC can require that such statements be provided if they are omitted. Pro-forma statements can be used to present many kinds of situations, such as the financial position that would result from a proposed recapitalization or merger, the acquisition of two or more companies, or the incorporation of a partnership. In the latter two situations, a pro-forma profit and loss statement might be appropriate as well as a pro-forma balance sheet. However, it is important to remember that what purports to be a pro-forma statement of income should not in fact be a projection of future earnings.

Rule 170 under the 1933 Act pertains to pro-forma statements. It reads as follows:

> Financial statements which purport to give effect to the receipt and application of any part of the proceeds from the sale of securities for cash shall not be used unless such securities are to be offered through underwriters and the underwriting arrangements are such that the underwriters are or will be committed to take and pay for all of the securities, if any are taken, prior to or within a reasonable time after the commencement of the public offering, or if the securities are not so taken, to refund to all subscribers the full amount of all subscription payments made for the securities. The caption of any such financial statement shall clearly set forth the assumptions upon which such statement is based. The caption shall be in type at least as large as that used generally in the body of the statement.

▶ WHAT TO DO: Study the underwriting agreement and ascertain if the underwriting commitment complies with Rule 170 before including in the prospectus a pro-forma balance sheet that gives effect to the sale of the securities being registered.

**Post-effective amendments.** In certain instances, such as the existence of warrants or convertible debentures, it is necessary to bring the prospectus up to date periodically—that is, a new prospectus must be filed with and processed by the SEC. This is so because of the requirements of Section 10(a)(3) of the 1933 Act: when a prospectus is used more than nine months after the effective date of the registration statement, the information it contains can be no more than sixteen months old.

The prospectus is brought up to date annually by filing a *post-effective amendment*. As far as the financial statements are concerned, this involves filing the required information for the most recent fiscal year and dropping out the information that, as a result of the new information, is no longer required under the instructions to the Form. Thus, the balance sheet as of the end of the most recent fiscal year is substituted for the balance sheet previously filed; and the profit and loss and surplus statements and the summary of earnings for the most recent fiscal year are substituted for the corresponding statements for the earliest fiscal year for which such statements were previously filed. In other words, the new prospectus will contain the balance sheet at the end of the most recent year, profit and loss and surplus statements for the most recent three years, and a summary of earnings for the most recent five years. Supplementary profit and loss information must also be brought up to date, but it is not necessary to file the other supporting schedules, because they will be filed annually with Form 10-K. The new prospectus must be accompanied by an accountant's report and consent on the same basis as the original prospectus (see page 1231).

**Generally available statement.** Because of the liability provisions under Section 11(a) of the 1933 Act, it is important that the accountant be familiar with what is commonly known as a *generally available statement.* Section 11(a) provides that an investor may sue various persons, including the certifying accountant, who were involved with the registration statement, if the investor can show that an untrue statement of material fact was made in the registration statement or that a required material fact was omitted from the registration statement. It is not necessary for the investor to show that he relied on the untrue statement or relied on the registration statement not knowing of the omission.

However, Section 11(a) further provides that if the issuer has made generally available to its security holders an earnings statement covering a period of at least twelve months beginning after the effective date of the registration statement, the investor's right of recovery is conditioned on his furnishing proof that he acquired the security relying on the untrue statement in the registration statement or on the registration statement without knowledge of the omission. The advantage of furnishing a generally available statement, then, is obvious. While the generally available statement does not need to be accompanied by an accountant's opinion, the accountant is usually requested to review it.

**Regulation A offerings.** As we have already pointed out, the 1933 Act gives the SEC the authority to exempt from registration offerings of an aggregate value of less than $300,000. Under this authorization, the Commission has issued Regulation A, which specifically provides for the exemption from registration of securities for which the gross proceeds from sale within any twelve-month period do not exceed the $300,000 amount. However, such securities must be qualified by filing four copies of a notification (Form 1-A) with the regional SEC office along with four copies of the offering circular. The offering circular must include the following financial statements, which must be prepared in accordance with generally accepted accounting principles:

1. Balance sheet as of a date within 90 days prior to the date of filing of the notification. However, upon request the Commission may extend the period up to six months.

2. Profit and loss statements and analyses of surplus for at least two fiscal years prior to the date of the balance sheet and for the period between the close of the last fiscal year and the date of the balance sheet.

These statements do not have to be accompanied by an accountant's opinion. But the underwriter will usually insist that they be reviewed by an independent accountant.

▶ NOTE: There is a ten-day waiting period after the notification has been filed before the securities can be offered for sale. This gives the SEC an opportunity to review the notification and the offering circular.

**2. Forms 10 and 10-K.** Most companies listing securities on a national securities exchange for the first time will use Form 10 to register with the SEC. A summary of earnings is not required on Form 10, but otherwise the requirements for financial statements are virtually the same as those previously described for Form S-1. However, the balance sheets on Form 10 should reflect the accounts at the close of the latest fiscal year, unless such fiscal year has ended within 90 days prior to the date of filing *with the exchange*. In this latter situation, the balance sheets may be stated as of the close of the preceding fiscal year. Profit and loss statements should be filed for each of the three fiscal years immediately preceding the date of the corresponding balance sheet that is filed.

▶ NOTE: When statements as of the preceding fiscal year are filed, an amendment to the registration statement must be filed within 120 days after the date of filing. This amendment must provide the appropriate balance sheets and profit and loss statements as of the end of the latest fiscal year.

▶ OBSERVATION: When a company wants to list additional classes of securities, Form 8-A should be used. The financial information required on Form 8-A pertains to businesses acquired by the registrant or any of its majority-owned subsidiaries.

Rule 12B-23 (1934 Act) permits the incorporation of financial statements required to be filed as part of Form 10 by reference to the financial statements included in an earlier 1933 Act filing (Form S-1). Material incorporated by reference must be clearly identified in the reference. If the material to be incorporated by reference includes the accountant's report, a current accountant's consent (see page 1234) must be filed.

Any company having securities registered on a national securities exchange, and certain companies registered under the 1933 Act (see explanation of Section 15(d) of the 1934 Act on page 1222), must file an annual report with the SEC. Form 10-K is the form most frequently used for this annual report. The financial information required is similar to that required on Form 10 except, of course, that it covers only the latest fiscal year.

▶ COMMENT: In addition to the requirements of the SEC, the listing company must also adhere to the rules of the particular exchange. These can be obtained from the exchange itself.

**Forms 8-K and 9-K.** From time to time, the accountant will also be concerned with Form 8-K, a current report of certain important events or changes within the company, and Form 9-K. Form 9-K is a mid-year report of sales and gross revenues, net income before and after taxes, extraordinary and special items, and charges and credits to earned surplus. Form 8-K requires financial statements only when the purpose of the report is to disclose the acquisition of a *significant* amount of assets. In such a case, a balance sheet as of a date reasonably close to the date of acquisition and profit and loss statements for each of the last three fiscal years and for the period between the close of the latest fiscal year and the date of the latest balance sheet filed are required.

**Proxy statements.** Regulation 14 under the 1934 Act contains the SEC's rules relating to the solicitation of proxies. Schedule 14A under Regulation 14 sets forth the requirements for proxy statements.

Ordinarily, financial statements are not required in the proxy statement unless the matters to be acted upon by the stockholders relate to (a) authorization or issuance of securities otherwise than for exchange, (b) modification or exchange of securities, or (c) mergers, consolidations, acquisitions, and similar matters. In such cases, the company must furnish financial statements such as would be required in an original application for the registration of securities under the 1934 Act (see requirements for Form 10, page 1229). All schedules other than the schedule of supplementary profit and loss information may be omitted. The statements must be prepared and certified in accordance with Regulation S-X.

### THE ACCOUNTANT'S DUTIES AND RESPONSIBILITIES

In general, the public accountant who follows the requirements as to accounting and auditing set forth by the American Institute of Certified Public Accountants will usually be meeting SEC standards. However, there are a number of significant factors in the area of duties and responsibilities that the independent accountant should be aware of when engaged in SEC work. We will discuss these, as follows:

1. What statements should be certified.
2. Who may certify the statements.
3. The accountant's certificate.
4. The accountant's consent.

▶ NOTE: The question of the accountant's liability under the 1933 and 1934 Acts is covered in Chapter 29, *Reporting on Audit Findings*. Also, see the discussion of the *generally available statement* on page 1228 of this chapter.

**What statements should be certified.** More often than not, financial statements filed with the SEC must be accompanied by an accountant's report or opinion, which the Commission refers to as a "certificate." The specific instructions with regard to what statements must be certified are contained in the instructions to the various forms. We will briefly outline the certification requirements for the most frequently used forms—S-1, 10, and 10-K.

1. *Form S-1.* Balance sheets and profit and loss and surplus statements, including consolidated statements, should be certified. Ordinarily, the balance sheets required to be filed with the registration statement will be certified. However, if they are not certified, either (a) an additional balance sheet as of a date within one year prior to the filing date, or (b) an additional balance sheet for a fiscal year that ends within one year and 90 days prior to the filing date should be filed and certified.

Profit and loss and surplus statements should be certified up to the date of the latest corresponding certified balance sheet filed. The summary of earnings does not have to be certified. But if the summary includes the information required in the profit and loss statement and therefore a separate profit and loss statement is not filed (see page 1221), the summary must be certified on the same basis as a profit and loss statement.

2. *Form 10.* The balance sheets and profit and loss and surplus statements that are filed in accordance with the instructions (see page 1229) must be certified.

3. *Form 10-K.* Balance sheets and profit and loss and surplus statements must be certified.

▶ AMENDMENTS: If, after certified financial statements are filed, they, or any notes to them, are amended (as a result, for example, of an SEC letter of comments), the certifying accountant must certify to them in their amended form. This always requires signing a new consent (see page 1234) that generally refers to the registration statement being "as amended." In addition, depending on the circumstances, a new certificate may have to be signed.

▶ SCHEDULES: In all cases, supporting schedules should be certified if the statements they support are certified (Rule 5-04, Regulation S-X).

**Who may certify the statements.** Certification of financial statements filed with the SEC must be made by an independent certified public accountant or public accountant. However, "independence" is governed by the requirements of the SEC, not those of state CPA societies or the American Institute of Certified Public Accountants. The SEC does not consider an accountant independent if during the period covered by his report he has any direct financial interest in the business of his client, or any material indirect financial interest, or is connected with the client as either a promoter, underwriter, director, officer, employee, or voting trustee. The SEC considers all relevant circumstances in determining the accountant's independence with respect to a particular client. Thus, circumstances and relationships that do not have any direct connection with the filing of reports with the Commission are taken into account. For example, failure to make adequate disclosure in reports other than reports filed with the SEC may be grounds for questioning the independence of the accountant.

In practice, the question as to whether an accountant is independent is one of fact, depending on the particular circumstances of the case.

▶ WHAT TO DO: The SEC has covered the question of independence in the following Accounting Series Releases: Numbers 2, 22, 28, 37, 44, 47, 68, 79, 81, and 82. If you have any doubts about your position with regard to a particular client, review these Releases. Some of them cite actual cases in which the Commission has ruled on the independence of certain accountants, and there may be a case similar to yours. If you do not find the answer, then refer the matter to the Commission. But be sure to obtain a definite decision *before* you begin work on the registration statement. This will avoid the possibility of putting the client in a position where he must pay a new accountant to go over work you have already done, with a consequent delay in the date of filing with the SEC.

**The accountant's certificate.** The technical requirements applicable to the accountant's report are set forth in Article 2 of Regulation S-X. The certificate must contain these elements:

1. *It must be dated.*
2. *It must be manually signed.* If the accountants signing the certificate are a partnership, the firm name should be signed.
3. *The financial statements must be identified.* The accountant is expected to identify in his certificate the financial statements covered by his opinion. A detailed enumeration is not required—for example, a statement or statements, to the effect that the balance sheets and the related statements of profit and loss and surplus and the supporting schedules have been examined, is sufficient.

4. *The scope of the audit must be revealed.* The accountant must state in the certificate whether the audit was made in accordance with generally accepted auditing standards. He must designate any auditing procedures recognized as normal, or considered necessary under the circumstances of the particular case, that have been omitted, and he must give the reasons for their omission.

5. *The accountant's opinions must be expressed.* The accountant must clearly state in the certificate: (a) his opinion as to the financial statements covered by the certificate and the accounting principles and practices reflected in those statements; (b) his opinion as to any material changes in accounting principles or practices, or in the method of applying them; (c) his opinion as to any material retroactive adjustments of the accounts (see Rule 3-07 on page 1236); and (d) the nature of, and his opinion as to, any material differences between the accounting principles and practices reflected in the financial statements and those reflected in the accounts after the entry of adjustments for the period under review.

▶ IMPORTANT: As indicated above, the accountant must specifically and clearly identify any matters to which he takes exception. Furthermore, he must state the effect of each exception on the related financial statements. But in practice the SEC will not accept a filing in which the accountant states exceptions to an accounting practice or as to the scope of his examination.

The standard report recommended by the American Institute of Certified Public Accountants meets the SEC requirements. An example, based on the assumption that there are no exceptions, follows:

> We have examined the balance sheet of X Company as of December 31, 19___ and the related statement(s) of income and surplus for the year then ended. Our examination was made in accordance with generally accepted auditing standards, and accordingly included such tests of the accounting records and such other auditing procedures as we considered necessary in the circumstances.

> In our opinion, the accompanying balance sheet and statement(s) of income and surplus fairly present the financial position of X Company at December 31, 19___, and the results of its operations for the year then ended, in conformity with generally accepted accounting principles applied on a consistent basis.

The above example makes no reference to the supporting schedules, which, as we have already pointed out, should also be certified if the basic financial statements are required to be certified. In the case of a registration statement, it is customary to furnish a separate opinion on the schedules. This is so because the schedules are included in Part II of the registration statement but not in the prospectus. Typical wording of such an opinion would be as follows:

> In connection with our examination of the financial statements of X Company as of December 31, 19___ and for the three years then ended, which are included in the prospectus, we have also examined the supporting schedules.
>
> In our opinion, these schedules fairly present the financial data required to be submitted under the regulations of the Securities and Exchange Commission.

It is not uncommon for more than one accounting firm to be involved in a single registration statement. When the principal accountant relies on an examination made by another accountant, the report of the other accountant must be filed. However, if the principal accountant accepts responsibility for the other accountant's examination, either through making no reference to it in his certificate or through an express statement in his certificate that he does accept responsibility, the other accountant's report need not be filed.

To show that he has relied on (but does not accept responsibility for) the examination of another accountant, the principal accountant should include in his certificate a statement similar to the following:

> . . . The financial statements of the Company's Canadian subsidiary which are included in the consolidated financial statements were examined by Roe and Doe, Chartered Accountants, whose report appears elsewhere in this prospectus.
>
> In our opinion, based upon our examination and the report of Roe and Doe referred to above, the consolidated financial statements enumerated above fairly present . . .

▶ OBSERVATION: In its letter of comments to the registrant the SEC may cite the accountant's certificate itself for deficiencies. Thus, it is important to have a thorough knowledge of the Commission's requirements as to the form of certificate and the extent of the opinions and information that must be included.

**The accountant's consent.** The SEC requires that the certifying accountant "consent" to the use of his opinion(s) on the financial statements and schedules. In fact, this consent must cover any reference made to the accountant in the registration statement. The consent, which must be dated and signed, may be incorporated in the accountant's certificate. Usually, however, it appears separately in **Part II** of the registration statement. An example follows:

We hereby consent to the use of our opinion, dated February 24, 19___, in the Prospectus constituting a part of the within Registration Statement. We also consent to the reference to our firm as set forth under the captions "Summary of Earnings" and "Experts" in said Prospectus.

## FORM AND CONTENT OF FINANCIAL STATEMENTS

As we indicated previously, the instructions governing the actual preparation of financial statements to be filed with the SEC are contained in Regulation S-X. The Regulation also defines certain terms, as explained throughout the discussion of Form S-1, and prescribes the technical requirements for the certification of financial statements, as indicated in the previous section. In addition, it sets forth rules with regard to consolidated and combined statements, which are covered in Chapter 3, *Consolidated Financial Statements.*

We will consider here the following parts of Regulations S-X:

1. Article 3, *Rules of general application.*
2. Article 5, *Commercial and industrial companies* (form and content of financial statements).
3. Article 11, *Content of statements of surplus.*
4. Article 12, *Form and content of schedules.*

▶ NOTE: Articles 1, 2, and 4 cover the subjects referred to in the first paragraph of this section (definitions, certification, and consolidations). Because of their technical nature, the definitions should be constantly referred to in considering the meaning and applicability of other rules. Articles 6 through 10 apply to special kinds of businesses or forms of organization—for example, management investment companies, insurance companies, and banks.

**Rules of general application.** Article 3 covers a variety of subjects. The explanation of general terms defined in the article will be incorporated into the discussion on the form and content of financial statements, under the next heading. Comments on other rules contained in the article follow.

Article 3 permits financial statements to be presented in such form and order, with "generally accepted terminology," as will best express their significance and character in accordance with the provisions of Regulation S-X (Rule 3-01(a)). Money amounts may be shown in even dollars or thousands of dollars. When amounts are rounded to the nearest thousand, the fact must be indicated either beneath the caption of the statement or schedule, or at the top of each money column (Rule 3-01(b)).

Any item that is not material does not have to be shown separately (Rule 3-02). However, it is important to remember that in Accounting

Series Release No. 41, the SEC pointed out that the significance of an item is not necessarily dependent on the amount of money involved. Furthermore, individual captions and entire financial statements need not be shown or filed if they are not applicable to the particular company (Rule 3-03). But, under Rule 3-03(c), the financial statements that have been omitted and the reasons for their omission should be mentioned in the listing of financial statements on the appropriate form (Form S-1, Item 31, and Form 10-K, Item 10—see page 1223 for an example). Also, footnote information need not be duplicated—cross reference may be made from one statement or schedule to another (Rule 3-04).

▶ IMPORTANT: It should be kept in mind that the information required by Regulation S-X is a minimum requirement to which should be added any additional information necessary to make any financial statements filed not misleading (Rule 3-06).

Disclosure should be made of (1) any changes in accounting principles and practices, or in the method of applying them, that affect the comparability of the financial statements filed with those of prior periods, and the effect of the change on the net income for each period for which financial statements are filed, and (2) any material retroactive adjustments affecting the financial statements filed and the effect of the adjustments on net income of prior periods (Rule 3-07). Disclosure of required information as to accounting principles and practices can be accomplished either through notes to the appropriate financial statements or within a single statement summarizing the accounting principles and practices reflected in the statements. In practice, disclosure is usually made through notes.

Article 3 further requires that certain items be specifically set forth in the balance sheet and profit and loss statements, or in notes to the statements. These requirements are covered in Rules 3-19 and 3-20, and they should always be reviewed to assure that these important rules have been complied with. The following chart lists and explains these items, and provides an example in each case.

CHART OF REQUIRED GENERAL NOTES TO
FINANCIAL STATEMENTS, WITH EXAMPLES

| ITEM | EXAMPLE |
|---|---|
| BALANCE SHEET (RULE 3-19): | |
| *Assets subject to lien* should be designated and the secured obligations should be identified. | Under a loan agreement, the company has assigned $1,000,000 principal amount of its installment accounts receivable as collateral for the note payable to the bank. |

The effect upon any balance sheet item of *intercompany profits or losses* should be stated. If the effect cannot be accurately determined, an estimate or explanation should be given.

The facts and amounts concerning any *default* in principal, interest, sinking fund, or redemption provisions with respect to any issue of securities or credit agreements, or any breach of covenant of a related indenture or agreement, should be stated. The effect of the default or breach should be noted.

If *preferred shares* are callable, the date or dates and the amount per share at which they are callable should be stated. Any arrears in cumulative dividends should be stated, both as an amount per share and in total for each class. Any preferences on involuntary liquidation other than par or stated value should be revealed; if the excess over par or stated value is material, the amount should be shown and the effect on junior shares and on surplus should be indicated.

A brief description of the essential provisions of any employee *pension or retirement plan* should be given. The estimated annual cost of the plan should be stated. If the plan has not been funded, the estimated amount that would be necessary to fund or

All intercompany accounts and transactions have been eliminated in consolidation, except that an indeterminate amount of profit is included in the cost of work in process inventories. Such amount is impracticable of determination, but is not material in relation to the total amount of inventories shown.

As of December 31, 19__, dividends are in arrears on the 5% cumulative preferred stock in the amount of $10 per share. Under such circumstances, each share of such preferred stock is entitled to equal voting rights with each share of common stock until the dividends in arrears are paid.

Authorized 30,000 shares of 5% cumulative preferred stock of $100 par value, of which 1,080 shares are held in the treasury of the company and 28,920 shares are outstanding. There are no arrears in the payment of dividends. An amount equal to $100 per share plus accrued and unpaid dividends must be paid to holders of the preferred stock in the event of liquidation, dissolution, or winding up, whether voluntary or involuntary, before any distribution may be made to the holders of common stock. The preferred stock is redeemable on 60 days' notice upon payment of $100 per share plus accrued and unpaid dividends. The holders of the preferred and common stock have equal voting rights per share and have no preemptive rights nor cumulative voting rights.

The company and its subsidiaries have in effect a non-contributory retirement plan covering all of its employees with more than five years continuous service. Costs charged to operations for the current year amounted to $250,-000. The plan does not require pay-

CHART OF REQUIRED GENERAL NOTES TO
FINANCIAL STATEMENTS, WITH EXAMPLES—(*Continued*)

| ITEM | EXAMPLE |
|---|---|

**BALANCE SHEET (RULE 3–19)** *(Cont.):*

otherwise provide for the past service cost of the plan should be disclosed.

ments on the past service liability, estimated to be approximately $2,000,000 at the end of the year.

Any *restrictions that limit the availability of surplus for dividends* should be described, with the source, the pertinent provisions and, where appropriate and determinable, the amount restricted briefly indicated. Restrictions reported in the note on preferred shares do not have to be covered again.

The loan agreement with the XYZ Insurance Company restricts the payment of dividends (other than stock dividends) to 75% of consolidated net earnings subsequent to January 31, 19___, plus $500,000. At January 31, 19___, the amount of retained earnings available for payment of dividends was approximately $505,000.

Any *contingent liabilities* not reflected in the balance sheet should be described in a brief statement.

The company is contingently liable on notes receivable discounted in the amount of $1,000,000 at December 31, 19___.

**PROFIT AND LOSS STATEMENT (RULE 3-20):**

The basis of taking profits into income on *installment or deferred sales* should be stated.

Profits on installment sales are taken into income at the time of the sale. Carrying charges on such sales are deducted from selling and administrative expenses.

The amount of *intercompany profits or losses* should be stated. If the amount cannot be accurately determined without unreasonable effort and expense, an estimate or explanation should be given.

Intercompany purchases and sales have been eliminated in consolidation, except intercompany sales and purchases of certain materials charged to construction. The amount involved is impracticable of determination but is not material in amount.

The accounting treatment of *depreciation, depletion, obsolescence, and amortization* should be described. The methods and rates used to determine annual provisions should be stated; and the treatment of maintenance, repairs, renewals, and betterments should be indicated. The adjustment of accumulated reserves when properly

It is the policy of the company and its consolidated subsidiaries to make annual provisions for depreciation on a straight-line basis at rates that will extinguish the gross amount of depreciable assets over their estimated useful lives. Rates used are as follows: buildings, $3\frac{1}{3}\%$ to $5\%$; machinery, $6\frac{2}{3}\%$ to $10\%$; furniture and fixtures, ties are retired or otherwise disposed of should be explained.

10% to 20%; automobiles and trucks, 25% to 33⅓%.

Leasehold improvements are amortized on a straight-line basis over the period from date of acquisition to termination of lease, or over their estimated useful lives, whichever is less.

Maintenance and repair of properties are charged to expense as incurred. Renewals and betterments to properties are capitalized.

Upon sale or other disposition of fixed assets, cost and related accumulated depreciation are removed from the asset and reserve accounts, respectively, and any resulting gain or loss is credited or charged to income.

For *capital stock optioned to officers and employees,* the title and amount of securities subject to option, the year or years during which the options were granted, and the year or years during which the options are exercisable should be stated. The number of shares under option at the balance sheet date, the number of shares that became exercisable during the period, and the number of shares on which options were exercised, should be shown. The option price and fair value, per share and in total, should be shown as of the dates options were granted, the dates options became exercisable, and the dates options were exercised. The basis of accounting for the option arrangements, and the amount of charges, if any, in income for such options should also be reported.

On January 1, 19__, the company granted options to certain of its officers and key employees to purchase 20,000 shares of common stock at $20.00 per share, which is not less than 95% of the fair market value of the stock on that date. These options are exercisable ratably in the five years succeeding the date of grant and expire six years from such date.

At the balance sheet date, there were 12,000 shares under option not yet exercised at $20.00 per share (total $240,000). At the date of grant, the fair market value was $20.50 per share (total $246,000). During the year, options for 4,000 shares became exercisable, at which date the fair market value was $25.00 per share (total $100,000). Options for 4,000 shares were exercised during the year. The fair market values at dates of exercise ranged from $24.00 to $26.00 per share (total $99,500).

The excess of the option price over par value of common stock is credited to capital surplus. No charges were reflected in income for options.

**Commercial and industrial companies (form and content of financial statements).** Article 5 sets forth specific provisions with regard to the form and content of financial statements of commercial and industrial companies. It also covers the requirements as to what schedules should be filed in support of these statements. It is important to remember that the term "financial statements" includes all supporting schedules (Rule 1-01(b)). We will present this material in the form of a chart, showing the balance sheet captions and the profit and loss statement captions, with the appropriate schedule listed alongside the related caption. The caption numbers are those prescribed in Regulation S-X. Generally, our wording is either identical or similar to that used in the Regulation; however, in some cases additional comments of a clarifying nature have been included. Also, material relating to public utility companies that is included in Article 5 has been omitted in our discussion.

▶ NOTE: Article 5A, which deals with commercial, industrial, and mining companies in the promotional, exploratory, or development stage, is not covered in the following chart.

CHART OF FINANCIAL STATEMENT CAPTIONS
WITH SUPPORTING SCHEDULES

| CAPTION | SUPPORTING SCHEDULE |
|---|---|

### BALANCE SHEET

ASSETS AND OTHER DEBITS

CURRENT ASSETS:

In general, as defined in Rule 3-13, current assets should be realizable within one year. However, if the trade practice for items such as installment receivables and the processing of certain inventories is longer than one year, the longer period may be followed provided an explanation is made. If it is practicable, an estimate of the amount not realizable within one year should be given.

1. *Cash and cash items.* State separately (a) cash on hand, demand deposits, and time deposits; (b) call loans; and (c) funds subject to withdrawal restrictions.

2. *Marketable securities.* Include only securities having a ready market. Securities of affiliates should not be shown | Schedule I, *Marketable Securities— Other Security Investments,* should be filed in support of this caption if (a)

under this caption. State the basis of determining the amount at which the securities are carried. Also state, parenthetically or otherwise, the aggregate cost and the aggregate market value.

**3.** *Notes receivable (trade).*

**4.** *Accounts receivable (trade).*

**5.** *Reserves for doubtful notes and accounts receivable (trade).* Notes and accounts receivable known to be uncollectible should be excluded from the assets as well as from the reserve accounts. Rule 3-11 provides that reserves should be shown as deductions from the specific assets to which they apply.

**6.** *Inventories.* State separately, if practicable, the major classes of inventory, such as finished goods, work in process, raw materials, and supplies. The breakdown may be made in a footnote referred to under the caption. State the basis of determining the amounts. If a basis such as *cost, market,* or *lower of cost or market* is used, a general indication of the method of determining the cost or market should be given—for example, *average cost, first-in, first-out,* or *last-in, first-out.*

**7.** *Other current assets.* State separately (a) total of current amounts (other than trade accounts subject to the usual trade terms) due from directors, officers, and principal holders of equity securities other than affiliates; (b) total of current amounts due from parents and subsidiaries; and (c) any other amounts in excess of 10% of total current assets, with an indication of any such amounts that are due from affiliates other than parents and subsidiaries.

the value of the marketable securities, at the greater of cost or market, constitutes 15% or more of total assets, or (b) this value plus the amount at which other security investments are carried in the balance sheet constitutes 20% or more of total assets. The Schedule should be filed as of the date of the latest balance sheet filed.

Schedule XII, *Reserves,* should be filed in support of this caption (and Caption 33) for each period for which a profit and loss statement is filed.

Schedule II, *Amounts Due From Directors, Officers, and Principal Holders of Equity Securities Other Than Affiliates,* should be filed with respect to any of the named persons whose aggregate indebtedness is more than either $20,000 or 1% of total assets. This Schedule should be filed for each period for which a profit and loss statement is filed.

CHART OF FINANCIAL STATEMENT CAPTIONS
WITH SUPPORTING SCHEDULES—(*Continued*)

CAPTION                                        SUPPORTING SCHEDULE

## BALANCE SHEET

### ASSETS AND OTHER DEBITS (CONTINUED)

CURRENT ASSETS (*Cont.*):

The indebtedness of a parent, a subsidiary, or an affiliate should not be considered as current unless their net current asset position justifies such treatment. In the registrant's balance sheet, a breakdown should be made of indebtedness eliminated and not eliminated in the related consolidated balance sheet.

In Accounting Series Release No. 41, the SEC pointed out that amounts due from officers and directors are of a special nature and origin. Therefore, they should be set forth separately, even if they are relatively small in amount.

8. *Total current assets.*

INVESTMENTS:

9. *Securities of affiliates.* State the basis of determining the amounts. State separately the amounts that in the related consolidated balance sheet are (a) eliminated and (b) not eliminated.

Schedule III, *Investments in Securities of Affiliates,* should be filed in support of this caption for each period for which a profit and loss statement is filed. However, it may be omitted if (a) neither the sum of *Securities of affiliates* and *Indebtedness of affiliates* —*not current* nor the amount of *Indebtedness to affiliates*—*not current* exceeds 5% of total tangible assets, or (b) the information has not changed from that reported on a previous filing.

10. *Indebtedness of affiliates—not current.* State separately the indebtedness that in the related consolidated balance sheet is (a) eliminated and (b) not eliminated.

Schedule IV, *Indebtedness of Affiliates —Not Current,* should be filed in support of this caption for each period for which a profit and loss statement is filed. It may be omitted under the same conditions that allow Schedule III to **be omitted.**

11. *Other security investments.* State the basis of determining the amount. If available, show parenthetically or otherwise the aggregate market value.

Schedule I, *Marketable Securities—Other Security Investments,* should also (see Caption 2, page 1240) be filed in support of this caption if (a) the amount at which the other security investments are carried in the balance sheet constitutes 15% or more of total assets, or (b) this amount plus the value of marketable securities (Caption 2), at the greater of cost or market, constitutes 20% or more of total assets.

12. *Other investments.* State separately, by class of investments, any items in excess of 10% of the amount of all assets other than fixed and intangible.

FIXED ASSETS:

13. *Property, plant, and equipment.* State separately each major class of fixed asets, such as land, buildings, machinery and equipment, and leaseholds. The breakdown may be made in a footnote referred to under the caption. Also state the basis of determining the amounts.

Schedule V, *Property, Plant, and Equipment,* should be filed in support of this caption for each period for which a profit and loss statement is filed. The Schedule may be omitted if the total of the property, plant, and equipment does not exceed 5% of total tangible assets and if neither the additions nor deductions during the period exceed 5% of total tangible assets.

14. *Reserves for depreciation, depletion, and amortization of property, plant, and equipment (or reserves in lieu thereof).* As indicated previously, reserves should be shown as deductions from the specific assets to which they apply.

Schedule VI, *Reserves for Depreciation, Depletion, and Amortization of Property, Plant, and Equipment,* should be filed in support of this caption for each period for which a profit and loss statement is filed. If Schedule V may be omitted, Schedule VI may also be omitted.

INTANGIBLE ASSETS:

15. *Patents, trade marks, franchises, goodwill, and other intangible assets.* State the basis of determining the amounts. In Accounting Series Release No. 50, the Commission stated that it disapproved of the practice of writing off purchased goodwill by charges to capital surplus.

Schedule VII, *Intangible Assets,* should be filed in support of this caption for each period for which a profit and loss statement is filed.

CHART OF FINANCIAL STATEMENT CAPTIONS
WITH SUPPORTING SCHEDULES—(*Continued*)

CAPTION                                    SUPPORTING SCHEDULE

BALANCE SHEET

ASSETS AND OTHER DEBITS (CONTINUED)

INTANGIBLE ASSETS (*Cont.*):

16. *Reserves for depreciation and amortization of intangible assets.* See Caption 14.

Schedule VIII, *Reserves for Depreciation and Amortization of Intangible Assets*, should be filed in support of this caption for each period for which a profit and loss statement is filed.

DEFERRED CHARGES:

17. *Prepaid expenses and other deferred items.* State separately any material items. Prepayments of services to be received within one year may be included under Caption 7.

18. *Organization expense.* State the method of amortization, if any.

19. *Debt discount and expense.* State the method of amortization. In Accounting Series Release No. 10, the SEC stated that the unamortized balance of debt discount and expense of bonds that were retired prior to maturity, through the proceeds from a sale of capital stock, should be written off to earnings or to earned surplus.

20. *Commissions and expense on capital shares.* State the method of amortization, if any. These items may be shown as deductions from surplus.

OTHER ASSETS:

21. *Other assets.* State separately (a) total of amounts due from directors, officers, and principal holders of equity securities other than affiliates; (b) each pension or other special fund; and (c) any other item in excess of 10% of the amount of all assets other than fixed and intangible.

See Caption 7 for the SEC's opinion regarding amounts due from officers and directors, as set forth in Accounting Series Release No. 41.

Schedule II, *Amounts Due From Directors, Officers, and Principal Holders of Equity Securities Other Than Affiliates*, should be filed with respect to any of the named persons whose aggregate indebtedness is more than either $20,000 or 1% of total assets. This Schedule should be filed for each period for which a profit and loss statement is filed. It is also used to support items under Caption 7.

## LIABILITIES, CAPITAL SHARES, AND SURPLUS

CURRENT LIABILITIES:

In general, as defined in Rule 3-14, current liabilities should be due and payable within one year. However, generally recognized trade practices may be followed with respect to the exclusion of items such as customers' deposits and deferred income, provided an appropriate explanation of the circumstances is made.

22. *Notes payable.* State separately amounts payable (a) to banks, (b) to trade, and (c) to others.

23. *Accounts payable (trade).*

24. *Accrued liabilities.* State separately (a) payrolls, (b) tax liability, (c) interest, and (d) any other material items.

25. *Other current liabilities.* State separately (a) dividends declared; (b) bonds, mortgages, and similar debt; (c) total of current amounts due to parents and subsidiaries (in the registrant's balance sheet, a breakdown should be made of the amounts eliminated and not eliminated in the related consolidated balance sheet); (d) total of current amounts, (other than items arising in the ordinary course of business) due directors, officers, and principal holders of equity securities other than affiliates; and (e) any other item in excess of 10% of total current liabilities, with an indication of any such amounts that are due to affiliates other than parents and subsidiaries.

All other items may be shown in one amount.

26. *Total current liabilities.*

DEFERRED INCOME:

27. *Deferred income.*

LONG-TERM DEBT:

Rule 3-15 provides that any *reacquired evidences of indebtedness* should be shown separately as a de-

CHART OF FINANCIAL STATEMENT CAPTIONS
WITH SUPPORTING SCHEDULES—(*Continued*)

| CAPTION | SUPPORTING SCHEDULE |
|---|---|

## BALANCE SHEET

### LIABILITIES, CAPITAL SHARES, AND SURPLUS (CONTINUED)

LONG-TERM DEBT (*Cont.*):

duction under the appropriate liability caption. However, if the evidences of indebtedness are reacquired for pension or other special funds, they may be shown as assets of such funds. When they are shown as assets of a fund, a parenthetical statement of their face value, their cost, and the amount at which they are carried on the books must be included.

28. *Bonds, mortgages, and similar debt.* State separately each issue or type of obligation and such information as will indicate (a) the general character of each type of debt, including the rate of interest; (b) the date of maturity (if maturing serially, a brief indication of the serial maturities should be given—for example, "maturing serially from 19__ to 19__."); (c) the total annual amounts of maturities and of sinking fund requirements for each of the 5 years following the date of the balance sheet; (d) any contingencies relating to the payment of principal or interest; (e) priority; and (f) the basis of conversion for any convertible issues. The breakdown may be made in a footnote referred to under the caption.

Schedule IX, *Bonds, Mortgages, and Similar Debt,* should be filed in support of this caption as of the date of the latest balance sheet filed.

29. *Indebtedness to affiliates—not current.* State separately indebtedness that in the related consolidated balance sheet is (a) eliminated and (b) not eliminated.

Schedule X, *Indebtedness to Affiliates —Not Current,* should be filed in support of this caption for each period for which a profit and loss statement is filed. This Schedule and Schedule IV may be combined. The Schedule may be omitted under the same conditions that allow Schedules III and IV to be omitted (see page 1242, Captions 9 and 10).

30. *Other long-term debt.* Include all amounts of long-term debt not provided for in Captions 28 and 29. State separately (a) total amounts due banks; (b) total amounts due directors, officers, and principal holders of equity securities other than affiliates; and (c) other long-term debt, specifying any material item.

If any of the items under this caption are secured, the information required under Caption 28 should be provided for them.

OTHER LIABILITIES:

31. *Other liabilities.* State separately any amount in excess of 10% of the total of liabilities other than long-term debt.

32. *Commitments and contingent liabilities.* The rules for these items are set forth in Article 3. For the method of reporting contingent liabilities not reflected in the balance sheet, see page 1238.

The pertinent facts relative to firm commitments of a material amount for the acquisition of permanent investments and fixed assets and for the purchase, repurchase, construction, or rental of assets under long-term leases should be stated briefly under this caption or in a footnote referred to under this caption (Rule 3-18(a)). Where the rentals or obligations under long-term leases are material, the amounts of annual rentals should be shown with an indication of the periods for which they are payable, together with any important obligation assumed or guarantee made in connection with such leases. If the rentals are conditional, the minimum annual amounts should be stated (Rule 3-18(b)).

RESERVES, NOT SHOWN ELSEWHERE:

33. *Reserves, not shown elsewhere.* State separately each major class and indicate clearly its purpose.

Schedule XII, *Reserves,* should be filed in support of this caption for each period for which a profit and loss statement is filed.

CHART OF FINANCIAL STATEMENT CAPTIONS
WITH SUPPORTING SCHEDULES—(*Continued*)

| CAPTION | SUPPORTING SCHEDULE |
|---|---|

## BALANCE SHEET

### LIABILITIES, CAPITAL SHARES, AND SURPLUS (CONTINUED)

CAPITAL SHARES AND SURPLUS:

Rule 3-16 provides that *reacquired shares* should be shown separately as a deduction from capital shares, or from the total of capital shares and surplus, or from surplus, at either par or stated value, or cost, as circumstances require. *Discount on capital shares,* or any unamortized balance, should be shown separately as a deduction from capital shares or from surplus, as circumstances require (Rule 3-17).

| | |
|---|---|
| 34. *Capital shares.* State for each class of shares title of issue, the number of shares authorized, the number of shares outstanding and the related capital share liability, and the basis of conversion for any convertible issues. Also state the dollar amount of capital shares subscribed but unissued, and of any subscriptions receivable. | Schedule XIII, *Capital Shares,* should be filed in support of this caption as of the date of the latest balance sheet filed. Schedule XIV, *Warrants or Rights,* should be filed with respect to warrants or rights granted by the registrant. This Schedule should also be filed as of the date of the latest balance sheet filed. |

35. *Surplus.* Separate captions should be shown for (a) paid-in surplus, (b) surplus arising from revaluation of assets, (c) other capital surplus, and (d) earned surplus (with a further breakdown into appropriated earned surplus and unappropriated earned surplus). If undistributed earnings of subsidiaries are included, the amount should be stated parenthetically or otherwise (in a consolidated statement, this applies only to the undistributed earnings of subsidiaries not consolidated in such statement). Any description of earned surplus subsequent to the effective date of a quasi-reorganization should indicate the point of time from which the new

earned surplus has accumulated, and for a period of at least 3 years should indicate the total amount of the deficit eliminated.

The analysis of each surplus account required by Article 11 (see page 1253) should be referred to under this caption.

*Schedules not related to a particular caption:*

Schedule XI, *Guarantees of Securities of Other Issuers,* should be filed with respect to any such guarantees by the registrant. It should be filed as of the date of the latest balance sheet filed.

Schedule XV, *Other Securities,* should be filed if there are any classes of securities not included in Schedules IX, XI, XIII, and XIV. However, information need not be set forth as to notes, drafts, bills of exchange, or bankers' acceptances, having a maturity at the time of issue not exceeding 1 year. The Schedule should be filed as of the date of the latest balance sheet filed.

## PROFIT AND LOSS STATEMENT

For all practical purposes, the SEC has adopted the principal of the *all-inclusive income statement.* All items of profit and loss given recognition in the accounts during the period should be included in the profit and loss (or income) statement. For a full discussion of the all-inclusive income statement, see Chapter 1.

1A. *Gross sales less discounts, returns, and allowances.* State separately, if practicable, (a) sales to parents and subsidiaries, and (b) sales to others.

2A. *Cost of goods sold.* State the amount of cost of goods sold as regularly computed under the system of accounting followed. Indicate the amount of opening and closing inven-

CHART OF FINANCIAL STATEMENT CAPTIONS
WITH SUPPORTING SCHEDULES—(*Continued*)

CAPTION                                          SUPPORTING SCHEDULE

## PROFIT AND LOSS STATEMENT (CONTINUED)

tories used in the computation, and state the basis of determining such amounts. Merchandising organizations, both wholesale and retail, may include occupancy and buying costs under this caption; however, publicity costs should be included under selling, general, and administrative expenses (Caption 4) or shown separately.

1B. *Operating revenues.* State separately, if practicable, (a) revenues from parents and subsidiaries, and (b) revenues from others. This caption and Caption 1A (gross sales) may be combined if either of the items is not more than 10% of the sum of the two items.

2B. *Operating expenses.* State separately, if practicable, (a) purchases from and services rendered by parents and subsidiaries, and (b) purchases from and services rendered by others. If Captions 1A (gross sales) and 1B (operating revenues) are combined, this caption may be combined with Caption 2A (cost of goods sold).

3. *Other operating expenses.* State separately any material item not included under Caption 2A or 2B.

4. *Selling, general, and administrative expenses.*

5. *Provision for doubtful accounts.*

6. *Other general expenses.* Include items not normally included as selling, general, and administrative expenses (Caption 4).

OTHER INCOME:

7. *Dividends.* State separately, if practicable, the amount of dividends from

Schedule **XVII,** *Income From Dividends—Equity in Net Profit and Loss*

(a) securities of affiliates, (b) market-able securities, and (c) other security investments.

However, dividends on a company's own stock held in its treasury or in a sinking fund or other special funds should not be included in income (Accounting Series Release No. 5).

of *Affiliates,* should be filed for each period for which a profit and loss statement is filed. Dividends from securities of affiliates, marketable securities, and other security investments should be shown. However, the schedule may be omitted if neither the sum of *Securities of affiliates* (balance sheet, Caption 9) and *Indebtedness of affiliates—not current* (balance sheet, Caption 10) nor the amount of *Indebtedness to affiliates—not current* (balance sheet, Caption 29) exceeds 5% of total tangible assets.

8. *Interest on securities.* State separately, if practicable, the amount of interest from (a) securities of affiliates, (b) marketable securities, and (c) other security investments.

9. *Profits on securities.* Profits should be stated net of losses. No profits on the securities of the registrant or the registrant's affiliates should be included under this caption. State the method followed in determining the cost of securities sold—for example, *average cost, first-in, first-out,* or *identified certificate.* This statement may be made in a footnote referred to under the caption.

10. *Miscellaneous other income.* State separately any material amounts, indicating clearly the nature of the transactions out of which the items arose.

INCOME DEDUCTIONS:

11. *Interest and debt discount and expense.* State separately (a) interest on bonds, mortgages or similar debt; (b) amortization of debt discount and expense or premiums; and (c) other interest.

12. *Losses on securities.* Losses should be stated net of profits. The rules for Caption 9 (exclusion with regard to

CHART OF FINANCIAL STATEMENT CAPTIONS
WITH SUPPORTING SCHEDULES—(*Continued*)

CAPTION                                    SUPPORTING SCHEDULE

## PROFIT AND LOSS STATEMENT (CONTINUED)

INCOME DEDUCTIONS (*Cont.*):

securities of registrant and registrant's affiliates, and statement of method of determining cost) also apply to this caption.

13. *Miscellaneous income deductions.* State separately any material amounts, indicating clearly the nature of the transactions out of which the items arose.

14. *Net income or loss before provision for taxes on income.*

15. *Provision for income taxes.* State separately (a) normal income and surtax, and (b) other income taxes. If the registrant pays its taxes as a member of a consolidated group, a note should be included on the registrant's own statement disclosing the estimated amount of taxes that the registrant would have paid on an individual basis.

Only those state taxes that are clearly taxes on income should be reported under this caption.

16. *Net income or loss.*

17. *Special items.* This caption is used for those items of profit or loss that are given recognition in the accounts but are not included in the determination of net income or loss. Many accountants, for purposes other than filing with the SEC, might treat such items as direct charges or credits to earned surplus.

18. *Net income or loss and special items.*

*Schedules not related to a particular caption:*

Schedule XVI, *Supplementary Profit
and Loss Information*, should be filed
as indicated on page 1225.

**Content of statements of surplus.** The analysis of surplus must be given
for each class of surplus shown in the balance sheet (Caption 35) for each
period for which a profit and loss statement is filed. However, as we indicated previously, the analysis of earned surplus may be presented either
as a separate statement or as a continuation of the profit and loss statement. As set forth in Article 11, a statement of surplus should contain:

1. *Balance at beginning of period.* This may be the balance as per
the accounts. If the surplus statement is filed as part of an annual or other
periodic report (for example, on Form 10-K) and the beginning balance
differs from the closing balance reported on the previous report, the difference should be noted and explained.

2. *Net income or loss (or net income or loss and special items) from
profit and loss statement.*

3. *Other additions to surplus.* State separately any material amounts,
indicating clearly the nature of the transactions out of which the items arose.

4. *Deductions from surplus other than dividends.* State separately any
material amounts, indicating clearly the nature of the transactions out of
which the items arose.

5. *Dividends.* For each class of shares state the amount per share and
the aggregate amount. Show separately (a) dividends paid in cash, and (b)
dividends other than those paid in cash, specifying the method of payment
in each case.

6. *Balance at close of period.* The amount as of the close of the most
recent period should agree with the corresponding amount under Caption
35 of the balance sheet.

**Form and content of schedules.** While Rule 5-04, as we have already
pointed out, covers the requirements as to what schedules should be filed,
it does not contain instructions concerning the form and content of the
schedules. This information can be found in Article 12, where each
schedule is illustrated with explanatory notes. We will list the schedules
required by Rule 5-04 and show the applicable illustration and explanation
exactly as set forth in Article 12, except that specific references to companies other than ordinary commercial and industrial ones have been
omitted.

## SCHEDULE I, MARKETABLE SECURITIES—OTHER SECURITY INVESTMENTS

| Col. A | Col. B | Col. C | Col. D |
|---|---|---|---|
| Name of Issuer and Title of Issue (Note 1) | Number of Shares or Units—Principal Amount of Bonds and Notes | Amount at Which Carried in Balance Sheet (Note 2) | Value Based on Current Market Quotations at Balance Sheet Date |

Note 1. Each issue shall be stated separately, except that reasonable groupings, without enumeration, may be made with respect to (1) securities issued or guaranteed by the United States Government and (2) investments as to which the aggregate amount carried in column C is not more than two percent of total assets.

    2. State the basis of determining the amounts in column C. Column C shall be totaled to agree with the respective balance sheet captions.

## SCHEDULE II, AMOUNTS DUE FROM DIRECTORS, OFFICERS, AND PRINCIPAL HOLDERS OF EQUITY SECURITIES OTHER THAN AFFILIATES

| Col. A | Col. B | Col. C | Col. D | | Col. E | |
|---|---|---|---|---|---|---|
| Name of Debtor | Balance Receivable at Beginning of Period (Note 1) | Additions | Deductions | | Balance Receivable at Close of Period | |
| | | | (1) Amounts Written Off | (2) Collections (Note 2) | (1) Current | (2) Not Current |

Note 1. The balance at the beginning of the period of report may be as per the accounts.

    2. If collection was other than in cash, explain.

## SCHEDULE III, INVESTMENTS IN SECURITIES OF AFFILIATES

| Col. A | Col. B | | Col. C | | Col. D | | Col. E | |
|---|---|---|---|---|---|---|---|---|
| Name of Issuer and Title of Issue (Note 1) | Balance at Beginning of Period (Note 2) | | Additions | | Deductions | | Balance at Close of Period | |
| | (1) Number of Shares or Units. Principal Amount of Bonds and Notes | (2) Amount in Dollars | (1) Number of Shares or Units. Principal Amount of Bonds and Notes | (2) Amount in Dollars (Note 3) | (1) Number of Shares or Units. Principal Amount of Bonds and Notes | (2) Amount in Dollars (Note 4) | (1) Number of Shares or Units. Principal Amount of Bonds and Notes | (2) Amount in Dollars |

Note 1. (a) Group separately securities of (1) subsidiaries consolidated; (2) subsidiaries not consolidated; and (3) other affiliates, showing shares and bonds separately in each case. Within each group major investments shall be stated separately. Reasonable grouping without enumeration may be made of other investments.

    (b) Those foreign investments, the enumeration of which would be detrimental to the registrant, may be grouped.

    2. The balance at the beginning of the period of report may be as per the accounts.

    3. If the cost of additions in column C represents other than cash expenditures, explain. If acquired from an affiliate (and not an original issue of that affiliate) at other than cost to the affiliate, show such cost, provided the acquisition by the affiliate was within two years prior to the acquisition by the person for which the statement is filed.

    4. State: (a) Cost of items sold and how determined; (b) amount received (if other than cash, explain); and (c) disposition of resulting profit or loss.

## SCHEDULE IV, INDEBTEDNESS OF AFFILIATES—NOT CURRENT

| Col. A | Col. B | Col. C |
|--------|--------|--------|
| Name of Affiliate (Note 1) | Balance Receivable at Beginning of Period (Note 2) | Balance Receivable at Close of Period |

**Note 1.** Affiliates shall be grouped as in the related schedules required for investments in securities of affiliates. The information called for may be shown, however, in total for each column for any two or more totally-held subsidiaries, provided the number of subsidiaries so grouped is stated.
   2. The balance at the beginning of the period of report may be as per the accounts.

## SCHEDULE V, PROPERTY, PLANT, AND EQUIPMENT (NOTE 1)

| Col. A | Col. B | Col. C | Col. D | Col. E | Col. F |
|--------|--------|--------|--------|--------|--------|
| Classification (Note 2) | Balance at Beginning of Period (Note 3) | Additions at Cost (Note 4) | Retirements or Sales (Note 5) | Other Changes—Debit and/or Credit—Describe (Note 6) | Balance at Close of Period |

**Note 1.** If the financial statements are being filed as part of an annual or other periodic report, comment briefly on any significant and unusual additions, abandonments, or retirements, or any significant and unusual changes in the general character and location, of principal plants and other important units, which may have occurred within the period.
   2. Show by major classifications such as land, buildings, equipment, or leaseholds. If such classification is not present or practicable, this may be stated in one amount. The additions included in column C shall, however, be segregated in accordance with an appropriate classification. If property, plant, and equipment abandoned is carried at other than a nominal amount indicate, if practicable, the amount thereof and state the reasons for such treatment. Items of minor importance may be included under a miscellaneous caption.
   3. The balance at the beginning of the period of report may be as per the accounts. If neither the total additions nor the total deductions during the period amount to more than 10% of the closing balance and a statement to that effect is made, the information required by columns B, C, D, and E may be omitted: *Provided* That the totals of columns C and D are given in a footnote, and *Provided further,* That any information required by Notes 4, 5 and 6 shall be given and may be in summary form.
   4. If the changes in property accounts in column C represent anything other than additions from acquisitions, state clearly the nature of the changes and the other accounts affected. If cost of property additions represents other than cash expenditures, explain. If acquired from an affiliate at other than cost to the affiliate, show such cost, provided the acquisition by the affiliate was within two years prior to the acquisition by the person for which the statement is filed.
   5. If changes in column D are stated at other than cost, explain if practicable.
   6. State clearly the nature of the changes and the other accounts affected. If provision for depreciation, depletion, and amortization of property, plant, and equipment is credited in the books directly to the asset accounts, the amounts shall be stated in column E with explanations, including the accounts to which charged.

## SCHEDULE VI, RESERVES FOR DEPRECIATION, DEPLETION, AND AMORTIZATION OF PROPERTY, PLANT, AND EQUIPMENT (NOTE 1)

| Col. A | Col. B | Col. C | | Col. D | | Col. E |
|--------|--------|--------|--------|--------|--------|--------|
| | | Additions | | Deductions from Reserves | | |
| Description (Note 2) | Balance at Beginning of Period (Note 3) | (1) Charged to Profit and Loss or Income | (2) Charged to Other Accounts—Describe | (1) Retirements, Renewals, and Replacements | (2) Other—Describe | Balance at Close of Period |

**Note 1.** (a) If other reserves are created in lieu of depreciation reserves, the same information shall be given with respect to them.

(b) Insofar as amounts for depreciation, depletion, and amortization are credited to the property accounts, such amounts shall be shown in the schedule of property, plant, and equipment, as there required.

**2.** If practicable, reserves shall be shown to correspond with the classifications of property set forth in the related schedule of property, plant, and equipment, separating especially depreciation, depletion, amortization, and provision for retirement.

**3.** The balance at the beginning of the period of report may be as per the accounts.

## SCHEDULE VII, INTANGIBLE ASSETS (NOTE 1)

| Col. A | Col. B | Col. C | Col. D | | Col. E | Col. F |
|---|---|---|---|---|---|---|
| | | | Deductions (Note 5) | | | |
| Description (Note 2) | Balance at Beginning of Period (Note 3) | Additions at Cost— Describe (Note 4) | (1) Charged to Profit and Loss or Income | (2) Charged to Other Accounts— Describe | Other Changes— Debit and/or Credit—Describe | Balance at Close of Period |

**Note 1.** If in the accounts it is not practicable to separate intangible assets from property, plant, and equipment, the information here required may be included in the schedule for property, plant, and equipment. In such event state in the balance sheet any known amount of intangibles so included with an indication that a further unknown amount of intangibles is also so included.

**2.** Show by major classifications, such as patents, or goodwill. If such classification is not present or practicable, this may be stated in one amount. The additions included in column C shall, however, be segregated in accordance with an appropriate classification. Items of minor importance may be included under a miscellaneous caption.

**3.** The balance at the beginning of the period of report may be as per the accounts. If neither the total additions nor the total deductions during the period amount to more than 10% of the closing balance and a statement to that effect is made, columns B, C, D, and E may be omitted by any company other than a public utility company. Any information required by note 4 or 5 shall, however, be given and may be in summarized form.

**4.** If the changes in accounts in column C represent anything other than additions from acquisitions, state clearly the nature of the changes and the other accounts affected. If cost of additions represents other than cash expenditures, explain. If acquired from an affiliate at other than cost to the affiliate, show such cost, provided the acquisition by the affiliate was within two years prior to the acquisition by the person for which the statement is filed.

**5.** If provision for depreciation and amortization of intangible assets is credited in the books directly to the intangible asset accounts, the amounts shall be stated in column D with explanations, including the accounts to which charged.

## SCHEDULE VIII, RESERVES FOR DEPRECIATION AND AMORTIZATION OF INTANGIBLE ASSETS (NOTE 1)

| Col. A | Col. B | Col. C | | Col. D | Col. E |
|---|---|---|---|---|---|
| Description (Note 2) | Balance at Beginning of Period (Note 3) | Additions | | Deductions from Reserves— Describe | Balance at Close of Period |
| | | (1) Charged to Profit and Loss or Income | (2) Charged to Other Accounts— Describe | | |

**Note 1.** Insofar as amounts for depreciation and amortization are credited to the intangible asset accounts, such amounts shall be shown in the schedule of intangible assets, as there required.

**2.** If practicable, reserves shall be shown to correspond with the classification in the related schedule of intangible assets.

**3.** The balance at the beginning of the period of report may be as per the accounts.

## SCHEDULE IX, BONDS, MORTGAGES, AND SIMILAR DEBT (NOTE 1)

| Col. A | Col. B | Col. C | Col. D | | Col. E | Col. F | Col. G | Col. H | |
|---|---|---|---|---|---|---|---|---|---|
| Name of Issuer and Title of Each Issue (Note 2) | Amount Author- ized by Indenture | Amount Issued and not Retired or Cancelled (Note 3) | Amount Included in Col. C Which is | | Amount Included in Sum Extended Under Caption "Bonds, Mortgages and Similar Debt" in Related Balance Sheet (Note 4) | Amount in Sinking and Other Special Funds of Issuer Thereof (Note 5) | Amount Pledged by Issuer Thereof (Note 5) | Amount Held by Affiliates for Which Statements are Filed Here- with (Note 6) | |
| | | | (1) Held by or for Account of Issuer Thereof | (2) Not Held by or for Account of Issuer Thereof | | | | (1) Persons Included in Con- solidated State- ment (Note 7) | (2) Others |

**Note 1.** Indicate in a note to the most recent schedule filed for a particular person or group any significant changes since the date of the related balance sheet. This information need not be given, however, if the schedule is filed as part of an annual or other periodic report.

**2.** Include in this column each issue authorized, whether issued or not and whether eliminated in consolidation or not. For each issue listed give the information called for by columns B to H, inclusive.

**3.** Indicate by means of an appropriate symbol any issues of which additional amounts may be issued.

**4.** This column is to be totaled to correspond to the related balance sheet caption.

**5.** Indicate by means of an appropriate symbol any amounts not included in sub- column D (1).

**6.** Affiliates for which statements are filed herewith shall include affiliates for which separate financial statements are filed and those included in consolidated or combined statements, other than the issuer of the particular security.

**7.** Include in this subcolumn only amounts held by persons included in the con- solidated statement in support of which this schedule is being filed. If not eliminated in the consolidation, explain in a note.

## SCHEDULE X, INDEBTEDNESS TO AFFILIATES—NOT CURRENT

| Col. A | Col. B | Col. C |
|---|---|---|
| Name of Affiliate (Note 1) | Balance Payable at Beginning of Period (Note 2) | Balance Payable at Close of Period |

**Note 1.** Affiliates shall be grouped as in the related schedules required for investments in securities of affiliates. The information called for may be shown, however, in total for each column for any two or more totally-held subsidiaries, provided the number of subsidiaries so grouped is stated.

**2.** The balance at the beginning of the period of report may be as per the accounts.

## SCHEDULE XI, GUARANTEES OF SECURITIES OF OTHER ISSUERS (NOTE 1)

| Col. A | Col. B | Col. C | Col. D | Col. E | Col. F | Col. G |
|---|---|---|---|---|---|---|
| Name of Issuer of Securities Guaranteed by Person for Which State- ment is Filed | Title of Issue of Each Class of Securities Guaranteed | Total Amount Guaranteed and Outstand- ing (Note 2) | Amounted Owned by Person or Persons for Which State- ment is Filed | Amount in Treasury of Issuer of Securities Guaranteed | Nature of Guarantee (Note 3) | Nature of any Default by Issuer of Securities Guaranteed in Principal, Interest, Sink- ing Fund or Redemption Provisions, or Payment of Dividends (Note 4) |

**Note 1.** Indicate in a note to the most recent balance sheet filed for a particular person or group any significant changes since the date of the related balance sheet. This information need not be given, however, if the schedule is filed as part of an annual or other periodic report. If this schedule is filed in support of consolidated statements or group statements, there shall be set forth guarantees by any person included in the consolidation or group.

2. Indicate any amounts included in column C which are included also in column D or E.

3. There need be made only a brief statement of the nature of the guarantee, such as "Guarantee of principal and interest," "Guarantee of interest" or "Guarantee of dividends." If the guarantee is of interest or dividends, state the annual aggregate amount of interest or dividends so guaranteed.

4. Only a brief statement as to any such defaults need be made.

## SCHEDULE XII, RESERVES

| Col. A | Col. B | Col. C | | Col. D | Col. E |
|---|---|---|---|---|---|
| Description (Note 1) | Balance at Beginning of Period (Note 2) | Additions | | Deductions from Reserves—Describe | Balance at Close of Period |
| | | (1) Charged to Profit and Loss or Income | (2) Charged to Other Accounts— Describe | | |

**Note 1.** List, by major classes, all reserves not included in specific schedules. Identify each class of reserves by descriptive title. Group (a) those reserves which are deducted in the balance sheet from the assets to which they apply and (b) those reserves which support the balance sheet caption **Reserves, not shown elsewhere.** Special contingency reserves may be grouped in one total. Reserves as to which the additions, deductions, and balances were not significant may be grouped in one total and in such case the information called for under columns C and D need not be given.

2. The balance at the beginning of the period of report may be as per the accounts.

## SCHEDULE XIII, CAPITAL SHARES (NOTE 1).

| Col. A | Col. B | Col. C | Col. D | | Col. E | | Col. F | | Col. G | Col. H |
|---|---|---|---|---|---|---|---|---|---|---|
| Name of Issuer and Title of Issue (Note 2) | Number of Shares Authorized by Charter | Number of Shares Issued and Not Retired or Cancelled | Number of Shares Included in Col. C Which are | | Shares Outstanding as Shown on or Included in Related Balance Sheet Under Caption "Capital Shares" | | Number of Shares Held by Affiliates for Which Statements are Filed Herewith (Note 4) | | Number of Shares Reserved for Officers and Employees | Number of Shares Reserved for Options, Warrants, Conversions, and Other Rights |
| | | | (1) Held by or for Account of Issuer Thereof | (2) Not Held by or for Account of Issuer Thereof | (1) Number | (2) Amount at Which Carried (Note 3) | (1) Persons Included in Consolidated Statements (Note 5) | (2) Others | | |

**Note 1.** Indicate in a note to the most recent schedule filed for a particular person or group of any significant changes since the date of the related balance sheet. This information need not be given, however, if the schedule is filed as part of an annual or other periodic report.

2. Include in this column each issue authorized, whether issued or not, and whether eliminated in consolidation or not, *provided* that when this schedule is filed in support of a consolidated statement, the information required by columns A–H inclusive need not be given as to any consolidated subsidiary if all of the outstanding shares of each issue of capital shares (other than directors' qualifying shares) of such subsidiary are held by one or more of the persons included in such consolidated statement; if the answer to columns G and H would be none; and if a footnote indicating such omission is given. For each issue listed give the information called for by columns B to H, inclusive.

3. This column is to be totaled to correspond to the related balance sheet caption.

In the case of consolidated subsidiaries only the minority interest need be set forth.

4. Affiliates for which statements are filed herewith shall include affiliates for which separate financial statements are filed and those included in consolidated or combined statements, other than the issuer of the particular security.

5. Include in this subcolumn only amounts held by persons included in the consolidated statement in support of which this schedule is being filed. If not eliminated in the consolidation, explain in a footnote.

## SCHEDULE XIV, WARRANTS OR RIGHTS (NOTE 1)

| Col. A | Col. B | Col. C | Col. D | Col. E | Col. F | Col. G |
|---|---|---|---|---|---|---|
| Title of Issue of Securities Called for by Warrants or Rights | Amount of Securities Called for by Each Warrant or Right | Number of Warrants or Rights Outstanding (Note 2) | Aggregate Amount of Securities Called for by Warrants or Rights Outstanding | Date from Which Warrants or Rights are Exercisable | Expiration Date of Warrants or Rights | Price at Which Warrant or Right Exercisable |

**Note 1.** Indicate in a note to the most recent schedule filed for a particular person or group any significant changes since the date of the related balance sheet. This information need not be given, however, if the schedule is filed as part of an annual or other periodic report.

2. State separately amounts held by persons for which separate statements are filed or which are included in consolidated or combined statements, other than the issuer of the particular security.

## SCHEDULE XV, OTHER SECURITIES

(A separate illustration for this Schedule is not included in Article 12 because, depending on the type of securities, the information should correspond to that required in Schedules IX, XI, XIII, or XIV.)

## SCHEDULE XVI, SUPPLEMENTARY PROFIT AND LOSS INFORMATION (NOTE 1)

| Col. A | Col. B (Note 2) | | Col. C (Note 2) | | Col. D |
|---|---|---|---|---|---|
| | Charged Directly to Profit and Loss | | Charged to Other Accounts | | Total |
| Item | (1) To Cost of Goods Sold (rule 5-03-2A) or Operating Expenses (rule 5-03-2B) (Note 3) | (2) Other | (1) Account | (2) Amount | |
| 1. Maintenance and repairs. | | | | | |
| 2. Depreciation, depletion, and amortization of fixed and intangible assets (or charges in lieu thereof). | | | | | |
| 3. Taxes, other than income and excess profits taxes. (Note 4) | | | | | |
| 4. Management and service contract fees. | | | | | |
| 5. Rents and royalties. (Note 5) | | | | | |

**Note 1.** State for each of the items noted in column A the total called for in column D and, if practicable, set forth the details called for in columns B and C.

    **2.** Totals may be stated in the respective columns under column B without further designation of the accounts to which charged. If practicable, designate in column C the accounts to which charged.

    **3.** Do not include in this column amounts deducted in the profit and loss statement under the caption **Other operating expenses.**

    **4.** State separately each material item.

    **5.** If the aggregate amount of rents and royalties is not material, a statement to that effect will suffice. State rents and royalties separately if either amount is material.

## Schedule XVII, Income From Dividends—Equity in Net Profit and Loss of Affiliates

| Col. A | Col. B | | | Col. C |
|---|---|---|---|---|
| Name of Issuer and Title of Issue (Note 1) | Amount of Dividends (Note 2) | | | Amount of Equity in Net Profit and Loss for the Period (Notes 2 and 4) |
| | (1) Cash | (2) Other (Note 3) | (3) Total of Related Captions of Profit and Loss or Income Statement | |

**Note 1.** The shares of affiliates shall be listed as in the related schedules required for investments in securities of affiliates. Dividends from (1) marketable securities and (2) other security investments shall also be included, and may be shown in separate aggregate amounts: **Provided, however,** That securities held in issuers as to which securities representing exactly fifty percent of the voting power are held directly or indirectly by the person for which the statement is filed and those representing the other fifty percent are held by another single interest, shall be separately stated and are, within the group, to be listed separately as to each major investment, the balance to be stated in a single aggregate.

    **2.** The information called for in columns B and C may be shown in total for each column for any two or more totally-held subsidiaries included in a consolidated statement.

    **3.** State as to any dividends other than cash, the basis on which they have been taken up as income, and the justification, if any, for such action. If any such dividends received from affiliates have been credited to income in an amount differing from that charged to income or earned surplus by the disbursing company, state the amount of such difference and explain.

    **4.** (a) The information required by column C need be furnished only (1) as to affiliates and (2) as to issuers securities of which representing exactly fifty percent of the voting power are held directly or indirectly by the person for which the statement is filed and those representing the other fifty percent are held by another single interest. If the answer required in column B is in the negative as to any particular person, the information called for in column C shall nevertheless be furnished.

    (b) The equity in the net profit and loss of each person required to be listed separately shall be computed on an individual basis. In addition, there may be submitted the information required as computed on the basis of the statements of each such person and its subsidiaries consolidated.

# 35

# Accounting for Government Contracts

**HENRY W. SWEENEY, Ph.D.**

*Certified Public Accountant; Senior Partner, Henry W. Sweeney & Co., New York; Adjunct Professor of Accounting, Columbia University; Former Special Assistant to Assistant Secretary of Defense; Author, "Stabilized Accounting"*

**1261**

# CHAPTER THIRTY-FIVE

# Accounting for Government Contracts

The entire problem of accounting for Government contracts, and the difference between normal accounting-and-administrative procedures and Government-contract procedures, can be briefly summed up in the words of Oliver Wendell Holmes, former Justice of the Supreme Court of the United States:

> "Men must turn square corners when they deal with the Government."

This quotation helps explain why some companies find Government contracts a source of substantial and profitable business, while others find them a source of great financial loss. To rephrase Justice Holmes' statement, the Government is a special type of customer, and unless it is treated as such, it can be very difficult to do business with.

The firm that wishes to go into Government work must, first of all, know what to do to satisfy Government regulations and to meet the problems that inevitably arise. Because many of these regulations and problems revolve about costs, the public accountant, with his specialized knowledge of costs, cost systems, and auditing, is in a strategic position to be of great service to the client wishing to enter the field of Government contracts.

With this in mind the present chapter introduces the subject of accounting for Government contracts by delineating the different types of contracts and the procedures involved in obtaining them. The problems peculiar to performing Government-contract work profitably are considered next, especially the Government's definition of allowable and unallowable costs and the termination and price renegotiation of Government contracts. Finally, the last section offers suggestions for designing systems to maximize cost recovery and for expediting necessary auditing under Government contracts.

## INTRODUCTION TO GOVERNMENT CONTRACTS
### TYPES OF CONTRACTS

Government contracts fall into the following seven main categories:

1. Firm fixed-price.
2. Fixed-price with escalation.
3. Fixed-price with price redetermination.
4. Fixed-price incentive.
5. Cost-reimbursement.
6. Cost-plus-incentive-fee.
7. Cost-plus-percentage-of-cost.

**Firm fixed-price.** A firm fixed-price contract provides for a price that is not subject to adjustment, regardless of the cost experience of the contractor in the performance of the contract. The use of this type of contract is suitable when stable and reasonably definite specifications are available, when fair and reasonable costs can be obtained, and when the time allowed for performance is reasonably adequate under the prevailing conditions. Currently the Department of Defense is stressing the desirability of more open bidding on defense contracts, and less negotiating.

**Fixed-price with escalation.** A fixed-price contract with escalation provides for the upward and downward revision, or only downward revision, of the stated contract price upon the occurrence of certain contingencies, which are specifically defined in the contract. The use of this type of contract is appropriate where there is serious doubt as to the stability of market and labor conditions that will exist during an extended period of production, and where contingencies that would otherwise be included in a firm fixed-price contract are identifiable and can be covered separately by escalation. Escalation provisions are generally of two broad types:

1. Price escalation that provides for adjustment of the contract price on the basis of increases or decreases from an agreed-upon level in published or established prices of specific items.

2. Labor-and-material escalation that provides for adjustment of the contract price on the basis of increases or decreases from agreed standards or indices in wage rates and specific material costs, or in either.

**Fixed-price with price redetermination.** A fixed-price contract providing for the redetermination of price calls for the negotiation of firm fixed prices after completion of the contract or at stated periods of contract performance. The use of price-redetermination clauses is generally appropriate where fair and reasonable prices cannot be negotiated at the time of contract negotiations. There are three types of fixed-price redeterminable contracts, namely, (1) prospective price redetermination at a stated time or times during performance, (2) retroactive and prospective price redetermination at a stated time during performance, and (3) retroactive price redetermination after completion.

The first type, prospective price redetermination at a stated time or times during performance, provides for the negotiation of a firm fixed price for an initial period of contract deliveries or performance and for prospective price redetermination, either upward or downward, at a stated time or stated times during the performance of the remainder of the contract. This kind of contract is appropriate where (1) negotiation has shown that a firm fixed-price contract does not fulfill the requirements established by the conditions surrounding the procurement, (2) the contractor's accounting system is adequate for price-redetermination purposes, (3) the prospective pricing period can be made to conform with the operation of the contractor's accounting system, and (4) there is reasonable assurance that price-redetermination action will be taken promptly at the time or times specified.

The second type of fixed-price redeterminable contract, namely, retroactive and prospective price redetermination at a stated time during performance, provides for a price ceiling and for retroactive and prospective redetermination of prices either (1) upward or downward or (2) only downward at a designated time early in the contract performance. This kind of contract is not to be used on or after January 1, 1963. Until then it is to be used only when (1) negotiation has shown that the use of any other type of fixed-price contract is impracticable, (2) the estimated value of the procurement is in excess of $500,000, (3) the initial negotiated price is a reasonable estimate sufficient to establish a billing price, (4) there is sufficient time of contract performance to accomplish the price redetermination prior to completion of forty percent (40%) of the contract on a cost-incurred basis, (5) the contractor's accounting system is adequate for price-redetermination purposes, (6) reasonable assurance exists that price-redetermination action will be taken at the time specified, (7) a ceiling price is established, and (8) written approval has been received from the Office of the Deputy Chief of Staff for Logistics or Offices of the Heads of the Technical Services, for the Army; the Office of Naval Material, for the Navy; Headquarters, Air Force Systems Command or Headquarters, Air Force Logistics Command, for the Air Force; and the Executive Director, Procurement and Production, for the Defense Supply Agency.

The third type of fixed-price redeterminable contract, namely, retro-active price redetermination after completion, provides for a ceiling price and retroactive price redetermination after completion of the contract. It is not to be used unless the procurement is for research and development at an estimated cost of $100,000 or less, or unless, until January 1, 1963, the procurement is of an urgent nature and the total period of contract performance is six months or less; and in either case conditions (5), (6), (7), and (8) cited in the immediately preceding paragraph must be met.

**Fixed-price incentive.** A fixed-price incentive contract provides for (1) adjustment of total "target" profit (which is the amount of profit agreed upon by both parties as a fair goal at which to aim) and (2) establishment of the final contract price by a formula based on the relationship that final negotiated total cost bears to total target cost. There are two types of fixed-price incentive contracts, namely, "initial target" and "successive targets."

*Initial-target type of contract.* Under the initial-target type contract, a target cost, a target profit, a price ceiling, and a final profit-and-price-adjustment formula are negotiated at the outset. The use of this kind of contract is appropriate where firm targets and a formula for establishing final profit and price can be negotiated at the outset so as to provide a fair and reasonable incentive.

*Successive-targets type of contract.* Under the successive-targets type of contract, an initial-target cost, an initial-target profit, a price ceiling, a formula for fixing the firm-target profit, and a production point at which the formula will be applied are negotiated at the outset. The use of this kind of contract is appropriate where available cost-and-pricing informa-tion is not sufficient to permit negotiation of realistic firm targets at the out-set. Enough information, however, should be available to permit negotia-tion of initial targets. Furthermore, there should be reasonable assurance that additional reliable information will become available at an early point in the performance of the contract so as to permit negotiation then of either a firm fixed price or of firm targets and a final profit-and-price formula that will provide fair and reasonable incentive.

▶ COMMENT: A fixed-price incentive contract should not be used un-less the contractor's accounting system is adequate for price-revision pur-poses and permits satisfactory application of the profit-and-price-adjust-ment formulas. In no case should such a type of contract be used where (1) cost-or-pricing information adequate for firm targets is not available at the time of initial contract negotiation or at a very early point in performance, or where (2) the sole or principal purpose is to shift substantially all cost responsibility to the Government. Furthermore, the firm-target profit or the formula for final profit-and-price is not to be established prior to negotiation of the firm-target price. Finally, neither type of fixed-price incentive contract is to be used unless there has been a determination, by proper authority, that such method of contracting is likely to be less costly than other methods; or that to secure supplies or services of the kind or quality required is not practicable without its use.

**Cost-reimbursement.** This type of contract provides for payment to the contractor of his allowable costs incurred in the performance of the contract to the extent prescribed in the contract. It is suitable for use only when the uncertainties involved in contract performance are of such magnitude that cost of performance cannot be estimated with sufficient reasonableness to permit use of any type of fixed-price contract. In addition, the contractor's cost accounting system must be adequate for the determination of costs applicable to the contract, and appropriate surveillance by Government personnel during contract performance must be capable of providing reasonable assurance that inefficient or wasteful methods are not being used by the contractor. This type of contract establishes an estimate of total cost for the purpose of obligating Government funds and setting a ceiling that the contractor may not exceed (except at his own risk) without prior approval or subsequent ratification by the contracting officer. It is a contract type that may be used only after a determination, by proper authority, that such method of contracting is likely to be less costly than other methods, or that to obtain supplies or services of the kind or quality required is not practicable without its use. There are several categories of cost-type contracts.

1. The *cost contract* is a cost-reimbursement type of contract under which the contractor receives no fee.
2. The *cost-sharing* contract is a cost-reimbursement type of contract under which the contractor not only receives no fee, but is reimbursed for only an agreed portion of his allowable costs.
3. The *cost-plus-a-fixed fee (CPFF)* contract is a cost-reimbursement type of contract under which the contractor is paid a fixed fee that, when once negotiated, does not vary with actual cost, but may be adjusted as a result of any subsequent changes in the work or services to be performed under the contract.
4. The *time-and-material (T&M)* contract provides for procurement of supplies or services on the basis of (a) direct labor hours at fixed hourly rates that include direct and indirect labor costs, overhead, and profit, and

(b) material at cost, often plus a small percentage, such as 5%, for material handling (such allowance for handling having been excluded, of course, from the overhead costs that form part of the hourly rates).

**Cost-plus-incentive-fee (CPIF).** This type of contract is a cost-reimbursement type with provision for a fee that is adjusted by formula in accordance with the relationship that total allowable costs bear to target cost.

▶ COMMENT: The Department of Defense recommends the use of incentive-type contracts (fixed-price-incentive and cost-plus-incentive-fee contracts) whenever they are appropriate, while placing drastic limitations on the use of cost-plus-a-fixed-fee (CPFF) contracts.

**Cost-plus-percentage-of-cost (CPPC).** This type of contract was banned in 1940 from use in United States Government contracts and subcontracts. It had been used widely during World War I and subsequently, usually in the form of "cost plus 10%." But it was generally considered to cause wasteful use of materials, manpower, and facilities—hence, excessive costs—because the greater the contractor's cost, the greater the contractor's profit.

▶ NOTE: It is mentioned here for the sake of completeness and for the reason that, until shortly after the outbreak of World War II in Europe, it was the prevailing kind of cost-type Government contract—and at times probably the prevailing kind of Government defense contract.

## OBTAINING A PRIME CONTRACT OR SUBCONTRACT

For a company that has engaged only in commercial work, the problem of acquiring a Government contract may, at first, seem insurmountable. Actually, however, the Government's rules and procedures in respect to procurement are logically and well conceived, especially considering the tremendous scope and volume of Government procurement. If the prospective contractor takes the time to become familiar with and to follow these rules and procedures correctly, the task of obtaining Government contracts can become almost routine.

Rules and procedures involved in obtaining a Government contract are treated under the following headings:

1. Government policy in choosing contractors.
2. Formal-advertising procurements.
3. Negotiated contracts.

**Government policy in choosing contractors.** It is the policy of the United States Government to make purchases, by contract, from responsible prospective contractors. In addition to any specific requirements relating to a particular procurement, a responsible prospective contractor can be defined as one that meets the following minimum standards:

1. Is a manufacturer, construction contractor, or regular dealer.
2. Has adequate financial resources, or ability to obtain them.
3. Will be able to comply with the proposed delivery schedule.
4. Has a satisfactory performance record.
5. Has a satisfactory record of integrity.
6. Meets the requirements of the standard non-discrimination clause.
7. Is otherwise qualified and eligible to receive an award under applicable laws and regulations.

The Government contracting officer has the authority to determine the responsibility of a prospective contractor. This determination may be based on information obtained from the Government files, from credit and other publications, from banks and similar references, and from the prospective contractor himself. When such sources are not sufficient, a pre-award survey is required to be made in order to determine whether the contractor meets the minimum standards for a responsible prospective contractor. Part of the pre-award survey may include advice from military auditors regarding (a) the acceptability of the contractor's accounting system for proper accumulation of contract costs and audit verification, and (b) the contractor's financial condition.

*Debarred contractors.* Each procurement agency is required to maintain a list of firms and individuals that it has debarred or suspended. This is a form of blacklist. Contract awards of any character, including sales, will not be made to them; nor will bids or proposals be solicited from them. Lists of debarred firms and individuals are furnished to the Department of the Army, which is responsible for issuing a joint consolidated list for the Department of Defense. This consolidated list of debarments is furnished, in turn, to the General Services Administration, which has the responsibility for securing such lists from all Federal Government agencies and compiling an overall consolidated list of debarments.

The bases for including the names of contractors on the Defense Department list of debarred, ineligible, or suspended bidders are:

1. Violation of Section 3 of the Walsh-Healey Public Contracts Act (41 USC 37).
2. Violation of Section 3 of the Davis-Bacon Act (40 USC 276a-2(a)).

3. Violation of Section 3a or 3b of the Buy American Act (Public Law 428, 72nd Congress, 47 Stat. 1520; 41 USC 10b (b)).

4. Non-qualification as "manufacturer" or "regular dealer" under the Walsh-Healey Public Contracts Act (ASPR 12-603(a)).

5. Conviction for criminal offenses or clear and convincing evidence of violation of contract provisions, where the violation is of a character so serious as to justify debarment action.

6. For other cause of such serious and compelling nature as may justify debarment, to be determined by the Secretary of the Department concerned.

In order to afford contractors considered for debarment a fair opportunity to present information in their own behalf, they must be given written notice of such intentions, complete with the reasons for this action. If debarment is then decided upon, the contractors must also be advised of this decision. The debarment and suspension of a contractor entail formal procedures that are generally conducted in strict observance of the applicable laws and statutes.

*Small business concerns.* It is the policy of the Defense Department to place a fair proportion of its total purchases with small business concerns. The Small Business Administration (SBA), established under the provisions of Public Law 85-536 (known as the Small Business Act), assists small business concerns through financing and other business aids. One of the principal activities of the SBA is close liaison with the Department of Defense in order to assure small business that it will secure its fair share of Government contracts. For purposes of this Act, a small business concern is defined as one independently owned and operated, not dominant in its field of operation, and, with its affiliates, employing not more than 500 employees—or one certified as a small business concern by SBA. In addition, the SBA has the statutory authority to certify the competence of any small business concern as to capacity and credit.

*Depressed-area firms.* In addition to its policy on small business concerns, the Defense Department also endeavors, as a matter of policy, to place contracts with business establishments located in areas that the Department of Labor has determined to have substantial labor surpluses and in areas where entire industries are designated as depressed by the Office of Civil and Defense Mobilization.

**Formal-advertising procurements.** Generally, as a preliminary to the procurement of supplies and services, formal advertising is required of every department of the Federal Government. Procurement by negotiation is permitted in lieu of formal advertising only in certain instances. These exceptions to the general rule will be discussed in the next section on negotiated contracts.

In accordance with this advertising requirement, procurements must generally be made by soliciting bids from all qualified sources of supplies or services deemed necessary by the contracting officer to assure full and free competition consistent with the procurement of the required supplies or services. The four basic steps in such procurement are:

1. Preparation of the invitation for bids.
2. Publicizing the invitation for bids.
3. Submission of bids by prospective contractors.
4. Awarding the contract.

*Invitation for bids.* The procurement agency prepares the invitation for bids, describing the requirements clearly and accurately and avoiding unnecessarily restrictive specifications or requirements that might unduly limit the number of bidders. The "invitation" includes a complete assembly of related documents (whether attached or incorporated by reference) furnished to prospective bidders for the purpose of obtaining bids.

*Publicizing the invitation.* Publicizing the invitation for bids is usually done sufficiently in advance of actual purchase to enable all interested contractors to be aware of the opportunity. This publicity is accomplished by means of distribution to prospective bidders (whose names are taken from a bidders' mailing list that each procurement activity is required to establish and maintain on a current basis) and to builders' exchanges and other organizations that maintain plan-display rooms for free use by the public when the solicitations relate to non-confidential construction work; posting in public places; and publication in newspapers and trade journals.

A handy reference chart of sources of information on new Government business follows:

| TITLE | CONTENTS | WHERE TO WRITE |
|---|---|---|
| *Commerce Business Daily*<br>DAILY    $20 Annually | 1. Proposed govt. procurement<br>2. Contracts awarded (over $10,000)<br>3. Proposed sales of govt. property | U. S. Dept. of Commerce<br>Administrative Service Office<br>Room 1300, New Post Office Bldg.<br>433 W. Van Buren St.<br>Chicago 7, Ill. |

| Title | Contents | Where to Write |
|---|---|---|
| *Federal Procurement & Subcontracts Daily*<br>DAILY    $194 Annually | 1. Proposed govt. procurement<br>2. Subtract opportunities with defense contractors<br>3. Contracts awarded (by product listing and to whom)<br>4. Contracts awarded by industry to subcontractors<br>5. Trends and developments giving indications of future procurement possibilities | Federal Procurement Publications, Inc.<br>10–42 47th Rd.<br>Long Island City 1, N. Y. |
| *Federal Subcontracts Weekly*<br>WEEKLY    $40 Annually | Material is drawn primarily from information contained in the *Federal Procurement & Subcontracts Daily* | Same as above |
| *U. S. Government Advertiser*<br>DAILY    $198 Annually | Essentially same as *Federal Procurement & Subcontracts Daily* | Ardole Publishing Co., Inc.<br>669 Eighth Ave.<br>New York 36, N. Y. |
| *Dodge Reports*<br>DAILY    Price varies according to usage. | Covers activity during the various stages of development through which a construction project passes. (From proposed construction through the awarding of subcontracts) | F. W. Dodge Corp.<br>119 W. 40th Street<br>New York 18, N. Y. |
| *Engineering News-Record*<br>WEEKLY    $6 Annually | Includes bids asked, low bidders, contracts awarded (over $50,-000). Construction only | Engineering News-Record<br>330 W. 42nd Street<br>New York 36, N. Y. |

*Submission of bids.* To be considered for award, the bid submitted by a contractor must comply in all material respects with the invitation for bid. The submitted bid, filled out and executed, must be received in the designated office not later than the exact time set for the opening of bids. All bids received prior to the time of opening are kept secure and unopened in a locked box or safe.

*Awarding the contract.* The official designated as the bid-opening officer decides when the time set for bid opening has arrived. He then personally and publicly opens all bids received prior to that time, and, when practicable, reads them aloud to the persons present, and has them recorded. Within the time for acceptance specified in the bid or bid extension, the contracting officer must then make the award to the responsible bidder whose bid conforms to the invitation for bids and is determined to be most advantageous to the Government. This determination is based not only on price, but on all other pertinent factors. Contracts awarded after formal advertising must be of the firm fixed-price type, except that fixed-price contracts with escalation may be used when some flexibility is necessary and feasible.

**Negotiated contracts.** The Department of Defense may enter into contracts through negotiation, without formal advertising, in the following instances:

1. National emergency.
2. Public exigency.
3. Contracts not exceeding $2,500.
4. Personal or professional services.
5. Services of educational institutions.
6. Purchases outside the United States.
7. Medicines or medical supplies.
8. Supplies purchased for authorized resale.
9. Perishable or non-perishable subsistence supplies.
10. Supplies or services as to which competition by formal advertising is impracticable.
11. Experimental, development, or research work.
12. Classified purchases (procurements that may, in general, be regarded as confidential or secret).
13. Technical equipment requiring standardization and interchangeability of parts.
14. Technical or specialized supplies requiring substantial initial investment or extended period of preparation for manufacture.
15. Negotiation after formal or informal advertising.
16. Purchases in the interest of national defense or industrial mobilization.
17. Other exceptions authorized by law.

In this type of procurement, contractors are required to submit price quotations supported by cost and other data needed by the contracting officer to enable him to negotiate effectively. Fewer contractors are solicited than in formal-advertising procurement. In these conditions, the contracting officer may conduct negotiations with one or more or all of the contractors submitting price quotations.

*How sources of price quotations are selected.* In the research and development field, for example, the Defense Department sponsors a continuous search for information regarding sources of potential contractors competent to perform research and development work. This search is a cooperative effort by technical personnel, small business specialists, and contracting officers to obtain information and recommendations on potential contractors and to consider the desirability of seeking additional sources by advance publication or proposed procurements.

The selection of sources of solicitation of price quotations is based on discussions with potential contractors (either singly or in a group), correspondence, and surveys and recommendations made by technically qualified Government personnel. Recommendations are made after review of relevant data furnished by contractors seeking this type of work.

When a product is covered by a *qualified-products list,* bids and proposals will be accepted only from manufacturers whose products have already been "qualified." Each procurement agency establishes a qualified-products list by testing products submitted by manufacturers for qualification. Therefore, it is important to find out which products are covered by qualified-products lists and to submit them for qualification well in advance of contract bids.

*Bidding on contracts: Preparation of cost summaries.* Depending on their intended use, cost summaries may be prepared on the basis of either historical costs or estimates of costs, or on both. A full knowledge of all the requirements of the invitation to bid is a prerequisite to effective cost-summary preparation. This includes a complete comprehension of such matters as the technical aspects of the supplies or services covered by the bid invitation, the delivery schedules, the inspections and approvals by Government representatives, Government-furnished materials or facilities, and the like.

Because of the importance of proper cost presentation and the many technical and other problems involved, responsibility for the preparation of cost figures should be vested in an officer, other key employee, or head of a contract-administration department in the contractor's establishment. For only then may the necessary planning, control, direction, and eventual coordination of the data required to be furnished by the various departments concerned be assured.

Cost estimates prepared for initial-pricing purposes are generally submitted on DD Form 633, and for price-redetermination purposes on DD Form 784.

▶ SUGGESTION: Negotiations can be materially expedited if the required cost analyses ("breakdowns") are submitted and the general and special instructions on the reverse side of the forms are complied with. This is particularly true with respect to requested supporting cost data and details.

*Submission of brochures containing supplementary information.* Brochures prepared for the purpose of furnishing information on a contractor's facilities, product capabilities, and key personnel are an important part of procurement by negotiation and should be made available to Government procurement activities before or with the submission of bids. Care should be exercised to ensure disclosure of factual data in sufficient detail to provide (1) ready understanding of the plant and its individual facilities, (2) complete informaticn about all products manufactured and services available, and (3) information concerning the education, experience, and careers of management and key personnel. Pictures depicting special facilities, products, and the like enhance the brochure presentation.

*Negotiation of fees or profits.* In the case of cost-plus-a-fixed-fee contracts, 10 USC 2306(d) provides that the fee shall not exceed 10% of the estimated cost of the contract, exclusive of the fee, as determined by the Secretary of the department concerned. Exceptions to this rule are the 15% limitation for experimental, developmental, or research contracts and the 6% limitation for architectural or engineering services related to public works on utility projects (but here the 6% relates to the cost of the entire project, not the cost of merely the architectural or engineering services). However, the Defense Department procurement activities are not authorized to approve fixed fees in excess of 7% of the estimated cost of any contract except that the limitation on an experimental, developmental, or research contract is 10%. The fee limitation on an architectural or engineering contract remains 6%, based on the cost of the entire project.

As to fixed-price-type contracts, a fair and reasonable profit cannot be determined by applying a predetermined percentage to the cost or selling price of a product. In these cases, the Armed Services Procurement Regulation (ASPR) recommends that the profit factor be established as a dollar amount and that the percentage relationship be computed primarily to ensure compliance with the required limitations. Therefore, where effective competition and compliance with requirements as to completion have been present, the reasonableness of the total *price* is the major concern. Otherwise, factors such as degree of risk, nature of work performed or to be performed, extent of Government assistance, contractor's investment, character of business, amount of subcontracting, and the like, as well as costs, must be considered in determining and evaluating profit. Under these circumstances the preparation of profit estimates, as such, is unnecessary.

*Negotiation of contract and clauses.* Particular attention should be paid to the type of contract used and to the clauses or terms that it contains. This is of paramount importance if possible dire consequences are to be avoided. Competent legal advice, therefore, should be obtained as to the precise interpretations of contract clauses and the obligations that are likely to ensue. In order to help determine what type of contract to use in a particular case, reference may be made to the section at the beginning of this chapter, where there is a discussion of each type of contract and when it should be used.

Important clauses customarily found in contracts, some required by statute and others by procurement-activity purchase regulations, comprise the following subjects:

1. Default.
2. Disputes.
3. Assignment of claims.
4. Bonds and insurance.
5. Covenant against contingent fees.
6. Changes.
7. Payments and advance payments.
8. Cost provisions.
9. Documentation.
10. Examination of records.
11. Government property.
12. Gratuities.
13. Inspection and acceptance.
14. Labor policies.
15. Convict labor, eight-hour law, Davis-Bacon Act, Copeland Anti-Kickback Act, Walsh-Healey Public Contracts Act, and Fair Labor Standards Act of 1938.
16. Nondiscrimination in employment.
17. Termination.
18. Renegotiation.
19. Patents and royalties.
20. Utilization of small business concerns.

## PROBLEMS PECULIAR TO GOVERNMENT CONTRACTS

Few businessmen would be so foolhardy as to attempt to enter an unfamiliar field without the necessary research into its special problems and procedures. Nevertheless, many business concerns with no previous experience in Government work think they can enter this special and complex field with no particular preparation—probably because the Government work to be performed is similar to their normal work. Unfortunately, though, the businessman who tries to treat a Government contract as just another part of his business runs the risk of finding the contract a financially and emotionally disillusioning experience, possibly causing him to renounce Government work forever.

The reason for this unfortunate consequence, as previously pointed out in the introduction to this chapter, is that Government regulations and procedures are the cause of many problems rarely, if ever, encountered by businesses exclusively engaged in production for civilian markets. But if the contractor new to Government work prepares well in advance to meet and conquer these problems, Government contracts need hold no fear for him and can become a valuable adjunct to his regular production.

The problems peculiar to Government contracts will be discussed next.

## ADMINISTRATIVE PROBLEMS

**Inspection.** Many of the problems arising in connection with the inspection of Government work by Government representatives can be attributed to the inexperience of contractors' personnel with the strict literal manner in which contract specifications must be followed. For unless the contractor adheres closely and accurately to these specifications, he is likely to find a large percentage of his production rejected by the inspectors. Accordingly, management and other responsible personnel must have full knowledge and understanding of specification requirements, and must establish and maintain high standards of quality. Additionally, a well-run self-inspection system may well help reduce the inspection problem.

Many contracts provide for the inspection to take place at the contractor's plant. In these cases, especially where the contracts require that Government inspectors be provided with suitable working space and facilities to perform their duties, arrangements should be made to ensure that every necessary convenience will be available for the inspectors. Proper arrangements are likely to expedite inspection, hence permit quicker shipments and speedier reimbursements from the Government.

The replacement or correction of supplies rejected by the inspectors requires that appropriate action be taken. For the Government has the right to repair or replace defective articles at the contractor's expense, accept them at lower cost, or even terminate the contract for default.

**Specifications.** As mentioned above in connection with inspection, specifications are generally furnished by the Government, they must be strictly complied with by contractors, and they are rigidly enforced by

Government inspectors when testing and inspecting contract items for approval. Specific written approval should be obtained from the contracting officer before any changes or deviations from approved specifications are authorized.

**Change orders.** Change orders arise from any one of the following causes:

1. Change in drawings, designs, or specifications.
2. Change in the method of shipment or packing.
3. Change in the place of delivery.
4. Faulty specifications.
5. Government property or materials delivered late, in poor condition, or not delivered at all.
6. Acceleration or stretch-out of delivery schedule.

A carefully-maintained historical contract file will be extremely helpful in resolving the problems and negotiating the costs of change orders. This file should contain a briefing of the pertinent contract provisions and requirements, copies of all authorized changes in the basic contract, memoranda of telephone calls and conferences, copies of approvals obtained, and appropriate documentation and commentary on all important factors involved in negotiations and other proceedings prior to the contract award.

▶ WARNING: Written confirmation of all important matters and, in particular, of oral agreements should be obtained. There is the possibility that the contracting officer may have exceeded his authority in making certain oral agreements. And there is the probability that the Government's practice of rotating its officer personnel will result in the replacement of the contracting officer.

**Billings.** *Cost-type contracts.* Reimbursement provisions and billing instructions are set forth in the contract. Billings for costs incurred and for portions of the fixed fee, if any, are prepared and submitted on Standard Forms (SF) 1034 (original) and 1034a (copies—normally 8), commonly termed *Public Vouchers.* Except in special circumstances, it is no longer necessary to list the supporting cost details on Standard Forms 1035 and 1035a.

Billings should be prepared on a cumulative basis by elements of cost, showing the cost of the current performance period separately. Army and Air Force contract billings should be submitted to contracting officers or their designated representatives, whereas Navy billings should be sent to the local office of the audit agency that has "audit cognizance" (jurisdiction) of the contract. For Navy billings also, the cost of all subcontract termination settlements and of any Class 1, 2, 3, or 4 plant property must be set out separately on the public voucher and on the contractor's Cumulative Claim and Reconciliation, which is one of the required terminal documents.

Government contracts require that certain types of cost have specific and administrative approvals. In order to avoid cost suspensions or disallowances by Government auditors or contracting officers, these approvals should be made part of the contract billing file.

Also required are compliance with the patent, royalties, and property clauses of the contract and the submission of terminal documents promptly after physical completion of the contract work, but in no event later than one year from the date of such completion. The terminal documents required are the Completion Voucher (SF 1034 and SF 1034a), Cumulative Claim and Reconciliation, Release of Claims, and Assignment of Refunds, Rebates, Credits, and Other Amounts. As the contractor and the cognizant auditor must reach an understanding on the total costs to be allowed, preparation of the terminal documents should be a joint effort. Such action may be initiated by either party.

*Fixed-price contracts.* Billings for items delivered and accepted under fixed-price contracts are generally based on prices stipulated in the contract. The contractor's own invoice form is usually used for this purpose. Where progress payments are provided for in the contract, invoices should be supported by incurred-cost data in such detail and form as directed by the contracting officer or his representative.

**Subcontract administration.** The administration of subcontracts is the responsibility of the prime contractor. When other than firm-fixed-price subcontracts are involved, this responsibility includes not only the negotiation of an equitable and reasonable price, but also audit of subcontractors' costs (unless the cognizant Government audit agency agrees to perform the audit). With regard to placing a firm-fixed-price subcontract, the prime contractor must be prepared to (1) furnish evidence that effective competition existed, unless the subcontractor was the sole source, (2) show that cost breakdowns or other price-supporting data were obtained and evaluated, (3) explain the reason for the award, and (4) where required, produce written approvals from the contracting officer.

**Other administrative problems.** Other problems peculiar to Government contracts arise from the requirements regarding (1) retention of records for the periods specified in such contracts, (2) retention of documentation for General Accounting Office audit, (3) approvals of accounting system, procurement practices, estimating and bidding procedures, and make-or-buy policies, (4) audit of accounting records and other pertinent data by auditors from various Government agencies, (5) termination, and (6) renegotiation of contracts and subcontracts. The last three such problems will be explored in detail in the following sections.

## ALLOWABLE AND UNALLOWABLE COSTS AND EXPENSES

One of the major problems encountered in any Government contract, except the firm-fixed-price contract, is the problem of determining which costs are allowable and which are not. This determination is based on (1) the specific provisions of the contract, and (2) the rules contained in the Armed Services Procurement Regulation (ASPR). Often businessmen are perplexed upon finding out that ASPR disallows such legitimate and provable expenses of doing business as bad debts, donations, entertainment, advertising (except three specific kinds), and interest and other financial expenses. The Government, however, takes the following positions:

1. *Bad debts* do not occur on Government contracts because the Government never defaults.

2. *Donations* are uncontrollable expenses that should come out of profits.

3. *Entertainment* is not an expense of a Government contract because Government employees are specifically precluded from accepting entertainment or gifts.

4. *Advertising* is not necessary to sell to the Government.

5. *Interest and other financial* expenses are the costs of providing capital (of which the contractor is supposed to possess a sufficient amount already), hence should come out of profit or owners' equity.

It is relatively unimportant whether the contractor agrees with the philosophy behind the allowance or disallowance of costs on a Government contract. But it is vital, both before and after taking a Government contract, that he understand which of his costs and expenses the Government will allow and which it will disallow. (In even a firm-fixed-price contract, this caution may turn out to be important in the event of termination.) The remainder of this section is devoted to effecting such an understanding.

**Applicable regulations.** *1. Cost-reimbursement-type contracts.* Cost-reimbursement contracts for supplies, services, and experimental, developmental, or research work (other than with educational institutions)—not including facilities and construction contracts—specify the use of the cost principles and procedures set forth in ASPR Section XV, Part 2. This Section is to be used as the basis for the following:

1. Determination of reimbursable costs under such contracts, including cost-type subcontracts and cost-reimbursement portions of time-and-material contracts.

2. Negotiation of final overhead rates.

3. Negotiation of costs under terminated cost-reimbursement-type contracts where the contractor elects to "voucher out" his costs, as well as for settlement by unilateral "determination" on the part of the Government.

▶ NOTE: Revision No. 50 to ASPR XV, Part 2, issued as of November 2, 1959, was made mandatorily effective July 1, 1960; its use was permissive prior to that date.

*2. Fixed-price contracts.* Revision No. 50 provided that ASPR XV, Part 2, besides its specified use for cost-reimbursement-type contracts, should be used also for guidance in (1) development and evaluation of contractors' procurement-pricing proposals regarding initial pricing, (2) fixed-price contracts of the price-redeterminable and incentive types, (3) terminated contracts, and (4) conversion of letter contracts to definitive contracts. (Part 6 of ASPR XV sets forth such usage.)

**General principles of cost allowance.** The costs and expenses incurred in performance of a cost-reimbursement contract are allowable provided the individual items of cost meet the following tests for allowability:

1. Reasonable in nature and amount.

2. Allocable to the contract.

3. Within any limitations set forth in Part 2 of ASPR XV or in the contract.

4. Not specifically excluded by Part 2 of ASPR XV or by the contract.

*Reasonableness of costs.* A cost is reasonable if, in its nature and amount, it would be incurred by an ordinary prudent person in the conduct of competitive business.

*Allocable costs.* A cost is properly allocable if it is known or estimated to have been caused by or to have benefited that particular objective, such as a contract, product, product line, process, or class of customer or activity. The allocation must be made, of course, in accordance with relative costs caused or benefits received or other equitable relationship.

*Direct and indirect costs.* Direct costs can be specifically identified with a particular cost objective. They are not necessarily limited to items that are incorporated in the end product, as are costs of direct material and direct labor, but may include items that, although ordinarily chargeable as indirect cost, can be specifically identified with a particular contract.

▶ WARNING: When items ordinarily chargeable as indirect costs are charged directly to Government work, the cost of like items applicable to a contractor's other work must be eliminated from indirect cost pools allocated to Government work.

Indirect costs are those costs that have been incurred for common or joint objectives and, therefore, cannot properly be charged directly to any one job. In addition, certain minor direct costs may be too small to warrant the bother of charging directly, hence are also charged into the pool of indirect costs. After direct costs have been determined and charged directly to the contract or other work, indirect costs are those remaining to be allocated on some equitable basis to the several kinds of work that the contractor performs.

▶ OBSERVATION: Many contractors with large volumes of Government contracts have successfully adopted a system of charging all overhead expenses directly. (See pages 1310 to 1313 for a full explanation of the operation of this type of system.)

**Costs and expenses provided for in the contract.** The reasonableness and allocability of certain costs, with reference to any particular contract, may be difficult to determine. This situation is especially true when such costs are claimed by companies, or separate divisions of a company, that are not subject to effective competitive restraints.

In order to avoid the possibility of subsequent disallowances or disputes based on the unreasonableness or non-allocability of those costs, prospective contractors should seek agreement with the Government *before* incurring special or unusual costs whose reasonableness or allocability is difficult to determine. Any such agreement should be incorporated in cost-reimbursement-type contracts, or made part of the contract file in the case of negotiated-fixed-price contracts. This agreement should govern the particular cost treatment throughout the performance of the contract. However, the absence of an advance agreement regarding any element of cost will not, in itself, make that cost unallowable.

Advance agreements may be particularly important in the following cost areas:

1. Compensation for personal services, especially of management.
2. Use charge for fully-depreciated assets.
3. Deferred maintenance costs.
4. Pre-contract costs.
5. Research and development costs.
6. Royalties.

7. Selling and distribution costs.

8. Travel costs related to special or mass personnel movements.

9. Rentals under leaseback agreements.

10. Special rearrangement or relocation of facilities.

**Costs and expenses requiring special approval.** The contractor has the sole responsibility for obtaining whatever necessary special approvals may be required for allowance of certain costs and expenses. The following list is representative of those items frequently requiring approval:

1. Insurance coverage.

2. Overtime and shift-work premiums.

3. Patents, purchased designs, and royalty payments.

4. Pension and retirement plans.

5. Rentals and other charges under leaseback agreements.

6. Research and development programs.

7. Salaries and wages, bonuses, fringe benefits, and other forms of compensation (including wages or salaries of partners or sole proprietors).

8. Special rearrangement or relocation of facilities.

9. Special security measures.

10. Subcontracts and purchase orders, depending on the amount, type of procurement, and kind of materials, equipment, or services being purchased.

11. Training programs.

12. Items of an unusual nature, such as expenses pertaining to foreign travel, costs of mass or special personnel movements, and lengthy assignments of employees away from their home stations.

**Allowability of specific costs and expenses.** Selected items of costs, together with explanatory comments, are set forth in ASPR 15-205, substantially as follows:

1. *Advertising.* The only allowable advertising expenses are those solely for (a) help-wanted advertising, (b) procurement of scarce items for performance of the contract, and (c) disposal of scrap or surplus materials acquired in performance of the contract. Such expenses must meet the test of reasonableness and must be properly apportioned to applicable Government contracts and any other work.

2. *Bad debts.* Unallowable.

3. *Bidding costs.* Bidding costs of the current accounting period, on both successful and unsuccessful bids and proposals, normally will be treated as allowable indirect costs. In this event, no bidding costs of past accounting periods will be allowable in the current period as direct or indirect charges

to Government contracts. However, if the contractor's established practice is to treat bidding costs by some other method, the results obtained may be acceptable if found to be reasonable and equitable.

4. *Bonding costs.* Costs of bonding required pursuant to the terms of the contract are allowable, as are also the costs of bonding required by the contractor in the general conduct of his business to the extent that such bonding is in accordance with sound business practice and that the rates and premiums are reasonable under the circumstances.

5. *Civil-defense costs.* Reasonable costs of civil-defense measures undertaken on the contractor's premises pursuant to suggestions or requirements of civil-defense authorities are allowable when allocated to all work of the contractor. Costs of capital assets involved in the aforementioned type of measures are allowable through depreciation. Contributions to local civil-defense funds and projects are unallowable.

6. *Compensation for personal services.* This item of cost includes all remuneration, in whatever form and whether paid currently or accrued or deferred, for services rendered by employees to the contractor during the period of contract performance. It includes, but is not limited to, salaries, wages, directors' and executive-committee members' fees, bonuses (including stock bonuses), incentive awards, employee stock options, employee insurance, fringe benefits, and contributions to pension, annuity, and management employee-incentive-compensation plans. Such costs are generally allowable to the extent that the total compensation of individual employees is reasonable for the services rendered and that these costs are not in excess of those allowable by the Internal Revenue Code and regulations thereunder.

7. *Contingencies.* Unallowable for historical costing, but may be given consideration with regard to terminations.

8. *Contributions and donations.* Unallowable.

9. *Depreciation.* Generally, depreciation is an allowable element of contract cost if the amount is computed upon the property-cost basis used by the contractor for Federal income-tax purposes and if spread over useful life on a consistent and reasonable basis. However, depreciation on idle or excess facilities is not allowable unless such facilities are necessary for standby purposes. Depreciation or a use charge will not be allowed on assets that have been fully depreciated if a substantial portion of such depreciation was recovered under Government contracts or subcontracts.

10. *Employee morale, health, and welfare costs and credits.* Allowable if the income generated from these activities is credited against the costs, unless such income has been irrevocably allocated to employee-welfare organizations.

11. *Entertainment costs.* Unallowable.

12. *Excess-facility costs.* Costs of maintaining, repairing, and housing idle and excess contractor-owned facilities, except those reasonably necessary for standby purposes, are unallowable.

13. *Fines and penalties.* Unallowable unless incurred as a result of compliance with specific provisions of the contract or written instructions of the contracting officer.

14. *Food service and dormitory costs and credits.* Allowable providing profits are included as credits to contract costs, except those profits irrevocably set aside for an employee-welfare organization for the benefit of employees.

15. *Fringe benefits.* Generally allowable.

16. *Insurance and indemnification.* Generally allowable with certain requirements and important limitations.

17. *Interest and other financial costs.* Unallowable unless incurred by reason of nonpayment of taxes, where the nonpayment is attributable to the contracting officer.

18. *Labor-relations cost.* Allowable.

19. *Losses on other contracts.* Unallowable. Included in such unallowable losses are costs under other Government contracts and agreements that provide for no reimbursement to the contractor, or only nominal reimbursement, for the actual cost of the work or services supplied.

20. *Maintenance and repair costs.* Generally allowable except those relating to excess facilities.

21. *Manufacturing and production engineering costs.* Generally allowable.

22. *Material costs.* Generally allowable, but with certain restrictions and limitations, particularly with regard to material sold or transferred between plants, divisions, or organizations under common ownership control.

23. *Organization costs.* Unallowable.

24. *Other business expenses.* Allowable when allocated on an equitable basis.

25. *Overtime, extra-pay shift, and multi-shift premiums.* Allowable to the extent approved or permitted by ASPR Section XII.

26. *Patent costs.* Allowable except the costs of preparing documents and any other patent costs relating to the filing of a patent application where title is not conveyed to the Government.

27. *Pension plans.* Generally allowable if the plan is approved by the Internal Revenue Service. This cost is closely related to the reasonableness of gross compensation for individual employees' services.

28. *Plant-protection costs.* Allowable.

29. *Plant-reconversion costs.* Generally unallowable except for the cost of removing Government property and the restoration or rehabilitation costs caused by such removal.

30. *Precontract costs.* Allowable to the extent that they would have been allowable if incurred after the date of the contract.

31. *Professional-service costs: Legal, accounting, engineering, and other.* Generally allowable except those incurred in connection with organization and reorganization, defense of antitrust suits, prosecution of claims against the Government, and patent-infringement litigation.

32. *Profits and losses on disposition of plant, equipment, or other capital assets.* Unallowable.

33. *Recruiting costs.* Generally allowable within certain limitations, except that costs of special benefits or emoluments offered to prospective employees beyond the standard practices in the industry are unallowable.

34. *Rental costs (including sale-and-leaseback of facilities).* Generally allowable. However, rents specified in sale-and-leaseback agreements are allowable to only the extent that such rental costs do not exceed the amounts that the contractor would have received if he had retained legal title to the facilities and leased them to a tenant, unless otherwise specifically provided in the contract.

35. *Research and development.* The costs of independent research, as defined in ASPR 15-205.35, are generally allowable as indirect costs provided that they are allocated to all work of the contractor and follow certain prescribed guide lines. The costs of independent development, as defined in the aforementioned regulation, are generally allowable to the extent that such development is related to the product lines for which the Government has contracts, provided that the costs are reasonable in amount and are allocated as indirect costs to all work of the contractor on such product lines. Research and development costs, regardless of their nature, incurred in accounting periods prior to the award of a particular contract, are unallowable except where allowed as precontract costs.

36. *Royalties and other costs for use of patents.* Generally allowable, with such exceptions as the Government's right to the free use of patents, unenforceable or expired patents, and royalties arrived at as a result of bargaining at less than arm's length.

37. *Selling costs.* Allowable to the extent that they are reasonable and are allocable to Government business. Certain restrictions are placed on salesmen's and agents' compensation, fees, commissions, etc., that are contingent upon the award of contracts.

38. *Service and warranty costs.* Allowable when not inconsistent with the terms of the contract.

39. *Severance pay.* Generally allowable with certain conditions to be met. Normal severance-pay costs are allowable, but must be allocated to all work performed in the contractor's plant. The allowability of abnormal or mass severance-pay costs will be considered on a case-by-case basis.

40. *Special tooling costs.* The cost of special tooling, when acquired for a particular Government contract, or particular Government contracts to which its usefulness is limited, is allowable and must be allocated to the specific Government contract or contracts for which acquired.

41. *Taxes.* Generally allowable except Federal income and excess-profits taxes; taxes connected with financing, refinancing, or refunding operations; and taxes for which exemptions are available to the contractor.

42. *Termination costs.* Certain types of costs are allowable and others unallowable, as explained in the following section on termination.

43. *Trade, business, technical, and professional-activity costs.* Allowable.

44. *Training-and-educational costs.* Generally allowable, except grants to educational or training institutions, inasmuch as such grants are considered contributions and thus unallowable.

45. *Transportation costs.* Generally allowable.

46. *Travel costs.* Generally allowable.

## TERMINATION

The authority of contracting officers to terminate contracts for *convenience of the Government* or *default of the contractor,* and to enter into settlement agreements, is usually found in the termination clause, or in other provisions of the contract. The Government has a contractual right to terminate any contract, whether fixed-price or cost-type, in whole or in part and for its convenience or for default, according to the pertinent circumstances. Default occurs when a contractor fails to perform his obligations under the contract. (Unless otherwise specified, this entire section deals with terminations for *convenience,* inasmuch as they are much more common than terminations for default.)

Settlements of fixed-price and cost-type contracts that have been terminated for *convenience* may be effected by (1) negotiated agreement, between the Government and the contractor, (2) unilateral "determination" by the contracting officer without the contractor's acquiescence, (3) submission of unreimbursed allowable costs to date of termination (by the use of Standard Form 1034, Public Voucher, in the case of cost-type contracts), or (4) a combination of such methods.

A *fixed-price* contract that has been terminated for *default* may not require any such settlement, as when the Government simply cancels for non-delivery and purchases similar items elsewhere. Some correspondence, of course, will unavoidably result. A *cost-type* contract that has been terminated for *default* will, however, usually require a settlement (which is likely to be considerably less favorable to the defaulting contractor than he had expected).

**Government's objective in settling termination claims.** The Government's policy in *convenience* terminations is to compensate the contractor fairly for the work done and the preparations made on the terminated portions of the contract. This policy provides an allowance for profit that is reasonable under the circumstances. Fair compensation, being a matter of judgment, cannot be measured exactly. In a specific case, various methods may be equally appropriate for arriving at fair compensation. The application of standards of business judgment, as distinguished from strict accounting principles, is the heart of a settlement.

The primary objective is to negotiate a settlement by mutual agreement. The parties may agree upon a total amount to be paid to the contractor, without having to agree upon and determine the particular elements of cost and profit comprising this sum. Cost and accounting data are guides, but not rigid measures, for determining fair compensation. In appropriate cases, costs may be estimated, differences compromised, and doubtful questions settled by agreement. Other types of data, criteria, or standards may furnish equally reliable guides to fair compensation. The attempt is made to minimize the amount of record keeping, reporting, and accounting in connection with the settlement of termination claims. But this minimum must be compatible with reasonable protection of the public interest and fairness to contractors.

**Notice of termination.** A termination can be effected only by a written notice to the contractor stating (1) the contract is being terminated for the convenience of the Government, or for default, pursuant to the contract provisions authorizing such termination, (2) the effective date of termination, (3) the extent of termination and, if a partial termination, the portion of the contract to be continued, and (4) any special instructions. A copy of the notice of termination is sent to any known assignee, guarantor, or surety of the contractor.

**What the contractor must do upon receipt of notice.** After receipt of the notice of termination, the contractor must comply with the termination clause of the contract and the notice of termination, except as otherwise directed by the contracting officer. Generally the contractor is required to do the following:

1. Stop work immediately on the terminated portion of the contract, **and** discontinue placing subcontracts under such portion

2. Terminate all subcontracts related to the terminated portion of the prime contract.

3. Immediately notify the contracting officer of any special circumstances precluding the stoppage of work.

4. In the case of a partial termination, continue to perform the unterminated portion of the contract, and submit promptly any request for an equitable adjustment of price with respect to such continued portion, supporting the request by evidence of any increase in the cost of the continued portion.

5. Take such action as may be necessary, or as the contracting officer may direct, to protect and preserve property, in the contractor's possession, in which the Government has or may acquire an interest; and, to the extent directed by the contracting officer, deliver such property to the Government.

6. Promptly notify the contracting officer in writing of any legal proceedings against the contractor growing out of any subcontract or other commitment related to the terminated portion of the contract.

7. Settle all outstanding liabilities and all claims arising out of termination of subcontracts, obtaining any approvals or ratifications required by the contracting officer.

8. Promptly submit his own settlement proposal, supported by appropriate schedules.

9. Dispose of any termination inventory as directed or authorized by the contracting officer.

**Initial conference.** To expedite settlement, the regulations suggest holding an initial conference, which should be held as promptly as possible to develop a definite program for effecting the settlement. If appropriate in the judgment of the contracting officer, principal subcontractors, as well as the contracting officer or his representative, should also be present. The following topics are worthy of discussion at such a meeting:

1. General principles relating to the settlement of the termination claim, including obligations of the contractor under the termination clause of the contract.

2. Extent of the termination, the point at which work stopped, and the status of any plans, drawings, and information that would have been delivered had the contract been completed.

3. Status of any continuing work.

4. Obligation of the contractor to terminate subcontracts, and general principles to be followed in settlement of subcontractor claims.

5. Names of subcontractors involved and the respective dates on which termination notices were issued to them.

6. Contractor's personnel handling the review and settlement of subcontractor claims, and the methods to be followed in such review and settlement.

7. Arrangements for transfer of title, and delivery to the Government, of any materials required by the Government.

8. General principles and procedures to be followed in the protection, preservation, and disposition of the contractor's and subcontractors' termination inventories, including the preparation of termination inventory schedules.

9. Contractor's accounting practices and preparation of DD Form 546 (Schedule of Accounting Information) (ASPR 8-802.9).

10. Form in which the settlement proposals shall be submitted.

11. Accounting review of the settlement proposals.

12. Any requirements for interim financing in the nature of partial payments to the contractor.

13. Tentative time schedule for negotiating the settlement, including submission of settlement proposals, termination inventory schedules, and accounting-information schedules by the contractor and subcontractors.

▶ NOTE: Whenever the contracting officer has reason to suspect fraud or other criminal conduct in connection with the settlement of a terminated contract, he is required to discontinue all negotiations with the contractor and report the facts to higher authority.

**Submission of Termination Settlement Proposals.** Termination settlement proposals are to be submitted within one year from the effective date of termination, unless properly extended by the contracting officer, and are to be submitted on the appropriate Department of Defense standard termination forms. The more important of these forms are:

1. DD Form 540—Settlement Proposal—Inventory Basis.

2. DD Form 541—Settlement Proposal—Total Cost Basis.

3. DD Form 542—Inventory Schedule A—Metals in Mill Product Form.

4. DD Form 542c—Inventory Schedule A—Continuation Sheet.

5. DD Form 543—Inventory Schedule B—Raw Materials.

6. DD Form 543c—Inventory Schedule B—Continuation Sheet.

7. DD Form 544—Inventory Schedule C—Work in Process.

8. DD Form 544c—Inventory Schedule C—Continuation Sheet.

9. DD Form 545—Inventory Schedule D—Dies, Jigs, Fixtures, Etc., and Special Tools.

10. DD Form 545c—Inventory Schedule D—Continuation Sheet.

11. DD Form 546—Schedule of Accounting Information.

12. DD Form 547—Settlement Proposal for Cost-Reimbursement-Type Contracts.

13. DD Form 547's—Notice of Audit Status Date.

14. DD Form 548—Application for Partial Payment.

15. DD Form 831—Settlement Proposal—Short Form.

16. DD Form 832—Inventory Schedule E—Short Form for Use With DD Form 831 Only.

**The two bases for preparing settlement proposals.** The bases to be used for the preparation of settlement proposals are the *inventory basis* and the *total cost basis*. The use of any other basis must have the prior approval of the Secretary of the department concerned. The inventory basis is preferred. But when its use is not practicable or will unduly delay settlement, the total cost basis is to be used if approved in advance by the contracting officer.

*Inventory basis.* Under the inventory basis, the contractor can claim only those costs chargeable or allocable to the terminated portion of the contract. In that case the settlement proposal shall separately itemize:

1. Metals, raw materials, purchased parts, work in process, finished parts, components, dies, jigs, fixtures, and tooling—at purchase or manufacturing cost.

2. Any charges such as engineering costs, initial costs, and general and administrative costs.

3. Costs of settlements with subcontractors.

4. Settlement expenses.

5. Other proper charges.

6. Profit allowance or loss adjustment.

The use of the inventory basis involves the taking of an inventory (known as the termination inventory) and shipping out the finished products with the approval of the contracting officer. Alternately, finished products may be included in the settlement proposal as acceptable finished products. Whether the completed products are shipped or included in the settlement proposal, the contract sales price is used for billing or costing purposes, respectively.

*Total cost basis.* When the total cost basis is used under a complete termination, all costs incurred under the contract up to the effective date of termination must be itemized. The cost of settlements with subcontractors, together with applicable settlement expenses, must be added, plus an allowance for profit or minus an adjustment for loss. The contract price for all "end items" (those to be furnished under the contract) delivered or to be delivered, and accepted for payment, must be deducted. All unliquidated advance and progress payments to the contractor, and all credits from other known sources, must also be deducted.

**Review of settlement proposals by audit agency.** *Prime contracts.* Settlement proposals of $2,500 or over submitted by a prime contractor are referred by the contracting officer or his authorized representative to the cognizant audit agency for examination and recommendation. When the contracting officer deems it necessary, proposals of less than $2,500 may also be referred for audit.

The auditor develops the information specifically requested by the contracting officer and may also make any further accounting review that he thinks is necessary. The audit agency then submits written comments and recommendations to the contracting officer.

*Subcontracts.* Subcontractor settlements are referred to the cognizant audit agency for written comments and recommendations when the settlement involves $25,000 or more, or when the contracting officer considers an audit, in whole or in part, desirable.

Although in other cases the prime contractor or higher-tier subcontractor has the responsibility for performing an accounting review of a subcontractor's termination claim, the military department audit agency should be requested to perform the review in situations where one or more of the following conditions exist:

1. A subcontractor, for reasons relating to competition, objects to an accounting review of its records by the prime contractor or an upper-tier subcontractor.

2. A military department audit agency is currently performing audit work at the subcontractor's plant, or can perform such work more economically or efficiently.

3. Audit by the military department audit agency is necessary for consistent audit treatment and orderly administration.

4. The contractor has a substantial or controlling financial interest in the subcontractor.

The contracting officer may, upon the written request of the prime contractor and under certain other specified conditions, authorize the prime contractor, in writing, to conclude settlements, of $10,000 or less each, of its terminated subcontracts without the approval or ratification of the contracting officer.

▶ OBSERVATION: A subcontractor has no direct contractual rights against the Government upon termination of a prime contract. Its rights are against the prime contractor, or intermediate subcontractor, with whom it has contracted. Upon termination of a prime contract, the prime contractor and each subcontractor are responsible for the prompt settlement of the termination claims of its immediate subcontractors.

**Settlement Review Boards.** Settlement Review Boards, established within each procuring activity, are required to review and approve each settlement agreement and each determination prior to final execution if either of the following conditions exists:

1. The agreement or determination involves $50,000 or more.

2. The fee, as adjusted, in the case of a cost-reimbursement contract or subcontract, is $50,000 or more, whether it applies to a complete termination or to the terminated portion of a contract or subcontract. (The review is limited, where a cost-type contract or subcontract is involved, to just the fee.)

**Applicable cost principles in terminations.** The cost principles set forth in the applicable part of ASPR Section XV are to be used as a guide for the evaluation of cost information in the negotiation of a termination settlement. They are the new cost principles promulgated by Revision No. 50, dated November 2, 1959, and made mandatorily effective July 1, 1960, but permitted to go into effect earlier. Hence, the cost provisions of ASPR Section VIII, previously used, are no longer applicable unless the contract termination clause so provides.

Contract terminations generally cause costs or special cost treatment that would not have arisen had the contract not been terminated. Cost principles covering such items, set forth in ASPR 15-205.42, are explained below. They should be considered in conjunction with the other matters presented in the remainder of this section on termination.

*Common items.* The cost of items reasonably usable in the contractor's other work is not allowable in the termination settlement, unless the contractor submits evidence proving that he could not retain such items at cost without sustaining a loss. In deciding whether they are reasonably usable in other work of the contractor, the contracting officer considers the contractor's plans and orders for current and scheduled production. Contemporaneous purchases of common items by the contractor are usually regarded as evidence that such items are reasonably usable in the contractor's other work. Any acceptance of common items as allocable to the terminated portion of a contract will be limited, moreover, by the excess of such items on hand, in transit, and on order, over the reasonable quantitative requirements of the contractor's other work.

*Costs continuing after termination.* If, in a particular case, despite all reasonable efforts by the contractor, certain costs cannot be discontinued immediately after the effective date of termination. such costs will generally be considered allowable within the limitations set forth in this section. Any post-termination costs that continue due to the negligent or willful failure of the contractor to discontinue them, however, will be ruled unallowable.

*Initial costs.* Subject to the following limitations, initial costs, including "starting load" and preparatory costs, are allowable:

1. Starting load costs are those of a non-recurring nature arising in the early stages of production and, because of the termination, not fully absorbed. They may include the cost of labor, material, and related overhead attributable to such factors as:

    a. Excessive spoilage resulting from inexperienced labor.
    b. Idle time and subnormal production occasioned by testing and changing methods of processing.
    c. Employee training.
    d. Unfamiliarity or lack of experience with the product, materials, manufacturing processes, and techniques.

2. Preparatory costs are those incurred in preparing to perform the terminated contract, including costs of initial plant rearrangement and alterations, management and personnel organization, production planning, and similar activities, but excluding special machinery and equipment and starting load costs.

3. If initial costs are claimed, but have not been segregated on the contractor's books, segregation for settlement purposes must be proved by cost reports and schedules that show high unit production costs incurred during the early stages of the contract.

4. When the settlement proposal is prepared on the inventory basis, initial costs should normally be prorated over the sum of the end items called for by the contract immediately prior to termination. But if the contract includes end items of a diverse nature, some other equitable basis may be employed for allocation, such as estimated machine or labor hours required for performance of the contract.

5. When initial costs are included in the settlement proposal as direct charges, they must not, of course, be included in overhead too.

6. Initial costs attributable to only one contract should not be allocated to other contracts.

*Loss of useful value of special tooling, machinery, and equipment.* A loss of this type is generally allowable provided:

1. Such special tooling, machinery, or equipment is not reasonably capable of being used in the other work of the contractor.

2. The interest of the Government is protected by transfer to the Gov-

ernment of title to the tooling, machinery, or equipment, or by other means deemed appropriate by the contracting officer.

3. The loss of useful value with respect to any one terminated contract is limited to the same proportion of the acquisition cost as the terminated portion of the contract, measured in dollars, bears to (a) the entire contract that was terminated, plus (b) any other Government contracts for which the special tooling, machinery, and equipment were acquired.

*Rental cost under unexpired lease.* This cost is generally allowable where it can be clearly shown to have been reasonably necessary for the performance of the terminated contract—less any residual value of such lease—provided:

1. The amount of the rental claimed does not exceed the reasonable use value of the property that was leased for the period of the contract and for such further period as appears reasonable.

2. The contractor makes all reasonable efforts to terminate, assign, settle, or otherwise reduce the cost of the unexpired lease.

The alterations cost of the leased property may also be included (provided such alterations were necessary for the performance of the contract) and, in addition, the cost of reasonable restoration required by the lease.

*Settlement expenses.* These costs are generally allowable. They consist mainly of the following:

1. Accounting, legal, clerical, and similar expenses reasonably necessary for (a) the preparation and presentation of settlement claims and supporting data with respect to the terminated portion of the contract, and (b) the termination and settlement of subcontracts.

2. Reasonable cost of storage, transportation, protection, and disposition of property acquired or produced for the contract.

*Subcontractor claims.* These claims are generally allowable, including the apportionable portions of claims that are common to both the contract and to any other work of the contractor.

*Profit on the terminated contract.* Profit will be allowed only on preparations made, and work done, by the contractor with respect to the terminated portion of the contract. None is considered allowable on the contractor's settlement expenses. Anticipatory profits and consequential damages, moreover, will not be allowed. Factors to be considered in negotiating the amount of profit are the following:

1. Extent and difficulty of the work done by the contractor as compared with the total work required by the contract. Engineering estimates

of the percentage of completion will not ordinarily be required. However, if these estimates are available, they should be considered.

2. Engineering work, production scheduling, planning, technical study and supervision, and other necessary services involved and performed.

3. Efficiency of the contractor, with particular regard to attainment of quantity and quality production, reduction of cost, and economy in the use of materials, facilities, and manpower.

4. Amount and sources of capital employed and extent of risk assumed. But if interest on borrowed capital is allowed as a cost, profit will not be allowed on that interest.

5. Inventive and developmental contributions, and cooperation with the Government and other contractors in supplying technical assistance on such contributions.

6. Character of the business, including the source and nature of materials and the complexity of manufacturing techniques.

7. Rate of profit that the contractor would have earned if the contract had been completed.

8. Character, extent, and difficulty of subcontracting, including selection, placement, and management of subcontracts, engineering technical assistance, and other services rendered. But the profit allowed to the contractor will not be measured by the sum of the contractor's payments to its subcontractors in settlement of their termination claims.

9. Rate of profit that both the Government and the contractor contemplated when the contract was negotiated.

*Loss on termination.* No profit will be allowed in the negotiation or determination of any settlement if the contractor would have incurred a loss in completing the entire contract. The amount of loss will be negotiated or determined, and the settlement will then be adjusted thus:

1. If the settlement is on an *inventory basis,* the contractor will not be paid more than the sum of the following:

   a. The amount negotiated or determined for settlement expenses.

   b. The contract price, as adjusted, for acceptable completed end items.

   c. The remainder of the full settlement amount agreed upon or determined (including the allocable portion of initial costs), reduced by multiplying such remainder by the ratio of (1) the total contract price to (2) the total cost incurred prior to termination plus the estimated cost to complete the entire contract. Of course, all disposal and other credits, all unliquidated advance and progress payment, and all other amounts previously paid by the Government to the contractor under the contract must also be deducted from the settlement.

2. If the settlement is on a *total cost basis,* the contractor will not be paid more than the sum of the following:

    a. The amount agreed upon or determined for settlement expenses.

    b. The remainder of the full settlement amount agreed upon or determined, reduced by multiplying such remainder by the ratio of (1) the total contract price to (2) that remainder plus the estimated cost to complete the entire contract. Here too all disposal and other credits, unliquidated advance and progress payments, and all other amounts previously paid by the Government to the contractor under the contract are deducted from the settlement payment.

In the estimation of the cost to complete, consideration should be given to expected production efficiencies and all other pertinent factors.

▶ NOTE: The total amount payable to the contractor on account of a settlement, whether through negotiation or by determination, before deduction of disposal and other credits and exclusive of settlement costs, must not exceed the total contract price less payments otherwise made, or to be made, under the contract.

**Election to discontinue public voucher billing.** Under the additional regulations applicable to the settlement of terminated cost-reimbursement types of contracts, the contractor may elect to discontinue the use of Standard Form 1034 (Public Voucher). In the event of such an election, it must be made in the manner required by the contracting officer (in the case of the Navy, for example, by the Contract Audit Division in the office of the Comptroller of the Navy).

Once this election is made, the contractor is not permitted to resume the use of Standard Form 1034. Instead, the contractor must submit, within one year from the effective date of termination (if such period has not been extended by the contract terms), his unvouched costs and claim for fee (if any) on DD Form 547 "Settlement Proposal for Cost-Reimbursement-Type Contracts." This is obligatory unless the head of the procuring activity concerned authorizes modification. On the basis of such a settlement proposal, partial settlements may be made from time to time as appropriate.

▶ IMPORTANT: The proposal should contain only "unvouched costs" and should not include any costs that were finally disallowed or that will be the subject of a reclaim voucher.

**Election to continue public voucher billing.** Where the contractor elects to continue submitting vouchers on Standard Form 1034 for reimbursement of costs, and claims a fee, his settlement proposal will be limited to a claim for an adjusted fee. This proposal must be submitted to the contracting officer within one year from the effective date of termination, unless the period has been extended in accordance with the contract terms. The proposal may be submitted on DD Form 547 or by letter appropriately certified, but the contractor must justify the amount of fee that he claims. The fee to be paid, if any, is required to be established in the manner provided by the contract.

**Termination inventories.** Subject to the exercise of the Government's contractual right to acquire title to any item in the termination inventory and to require delivery of it, the contractor is required to dispose of all termination inventories in the manner most favorable to the Government. This objective may be accomplished by:

1. Purchase or retention by the prime contractor or subcontractor at cost.

2. Return to suppliers.

3. Sale (including purchase or retention at less than cost by the prime contractor or subcontractor).

Under cost-reimbursement-type contracts, the contractor's right to purchase or retain contractor-acquired property at cost, or to return it to suppliers, is subject to the approval of the contracting officer, after adjustment for previously reimbursed costs of such property.

The details of the termination inventory should be submitted on the applicable standard inventory forms as soon as possible after receipt of the termination notice. The inventory schedules must identify each item by adequate commercial description in order to facilitate screening and disposal. The contractor must execute the certificates on these schedules, which, among other things, tender title to the Government of the property listed (unless the Government already has title).

The contractor is required to transfer any common items of material to other work, where reasonably possible. When this is done, the items must not be included in the inventory schedules submitted. As to any items that become usable on other work after submission of the inventory schedules but before final disposition of such items has been made, the contractor is required to direct the transfer of such items at cost and to correct the applicable schedules accordingly. Any withdrawal or sale of Government-furnished property is subject to the approval of the contracting officer.

The "plant-clearance period" begins on the effective date of a termination for convenience. It ends, for each particular property classification at any one plant or location, 90 days after receipt by the contracting officer of acceptable inventory schedules covering all items of that particular classification in the termination inventory at that plant or location. Or it ends on such later date as may be agreed to by the contracting officer and the contractor. The "final phase" of a plant-clearance period is that portion after the receipt of acceptable inventory schedules covering all items of the particular property classification at the plant or location.

**Termination due to default.** *Cost-type contracts.* In the event of default, the procedures applicable to a cost-reimbursement type of contract permit the contractor to be reimbursed for his allowable costs in accordance with the termination clause, plus an appropriately reduced total fee, if any, computed in accordance with the default provisions of the contract. The costs of preparing the contractor's settlement proposal are not allowable in such case. A cost-reimbursement type of contract does not contain any provision for Government recovery of excess costs of reprocurement after termination for default, but there could be a charge against the contractor under the "Inspection of Supplies and Correction of Defects" clause with respect to the contractor's failure to replace or correct defective supplies.

*Fixed-price contracts.* Under fixed-price contracts terminated for default, the Government is not liable for the contractor's costs on undelivered work, and is entitled to the repayment of any advance or progress payments applicable to such work. The Government may elect to accept and take all or part of the completed articles and the manufacturing materials (paragraph (d) of the clause in ASPR 8-707). If so, the Government must then pay the contractor the contract price for such completed articles and the amount agreed upon by the contractor and the contracting officer for such manufacturing materials, plus the cost for protection and preservation of such property. In default, the contractor is liable to the Government for any excess costs of articles and services procured to replace those that were to be provided under the contract terminated (ASPR 8-602.6).

## RENEGOTIATION

The Renegotiation Act of 1951, as amended, provides for the elimination of so-called "excessive profits" on contracts subject to the Act. Determinations required under Renegotiation Regulations are made by the Renegotiation Board set up under the Act and established as an independent part of the executive branch of the Federal Government.

**Contracts subject to renegotiation.** Most of the contracts awarded by the military departments contain a clause stating that the contract is subject to the Renegotiation Act of 1951, as amended. The absence of such a clause in a contract does not, however, necessarily mean that the contract is *not* subject to the Act. The contractor or subcontractor, in the absence of such clause, is charged with the responsibility of ascertaining whether the Act is applicable to his work.

In addition to Defense Department contracts, contracts issued by the Maritime Administration, the Federal Maritime Board, the General Services Administration, the National Aeronautics and Space Administration, and the Atomic Energy Commission are subject to the Renegotiation Act of 1951, as amended. As to subcontracts subject to the Act and as to mandatory exemptions, the applicable regulations go into considerable detail and, therefore, constitute required reading for everyone concerned.

**Exemptions.** Not all contracts subject to the Act must go through renegotiation. If the aggregate of the amounts received or accrued on renegotiable contracts during a fiscal year by a contractor or subcontractor (and by all persons under the control of, or controlling, or under common control with, the contractor or subcontractor) does not exceed $1,000,000 for fiscal years ended after June 30, 1956, such receipts or accruals will not be renegotiated.

Exemptions for *standard commercial articles and services* are also provided by the Act. If a contractor or subcontractor decides to file for such an exemption, the required report is due on or before the first day of the third calendar month following his fiscal-year end or the first day of the fifth month after the fiscal-year end. If the earlier date is selected for submission of such "Standard Commercial Articles Report," the remainder of the financial data required is to be filed by the first day of the fifth month following the end of the fiscal year, or within 30 days after the Board sends written notice of its action on the claim for exemption, whichever date occurs later. Unless the Board notifies the contractor within 60 days after filing that (1) the material submitted is incomplete or defective, (2) additional information is required, or (3) there are material misstatements of facts, the six-months automatic approval period begins to run with the filing of the exemption report. But if such aforementioned notification is received, the six-months approval period does not begin to run until the deficient data have been corrected and accepted by the Board.

**Factors used in determining excessive profits.** The Board considers the following factors in determining excessive profits:

1. *Efficiency of the contractor or subcontractor,* with particular regard to attainment of quality and quantity of production, reduction of costs, and economy in the use of materials, facilities, and manpower.

2. *Reasonableness of costs and profits,* with particular regard to volume of production, normal earnings, and comparison of war and peace time products.

3. *Contractor's or subcontractor's net worth,* with particular regard to the amount and source of public and private capital employed.

4. *Extent of risk assumed,* including risk incident to reasonable pricing policies.

5. *Nature and extent of contribution to the defense effort,* including inventive and developmental contributions and cooperation with the Government and other contractors in supplying technical assistance.

6. *Character of business,* including source and nature of materials, complexity of manufacturing technique, character and extent of subcontracting, and rate of turnover.

**Segregating sales between renegotiable and non-renegotiable.** The major problem in filling out the standard forms for submitting renegotiable data (due on or before the first day of the fifth month following the close of the fiscal year) is the segregation of sales into renegotiable and non-renegotiable. The regulations suggest the following methods:

1. Ascertaining from each customer the percentage of its sales subject to the Act and then applying such percentage to the total sales made to that customer.

2. Using certain governmental, trade association, or other reports that show the proportion of renegotiable business to total business in the industry as a whole.

3. Identifying, one by one, any renegotiable subcontracts with customers (who, therefore, are prime contractors having contracts directly with a Government agency or are higher-tier subcontractors). The first direct indication that sales to a customer are subject to renegotiation is that the contract or sales agreement contains a renegotiation article. The second indication is that it contains a reference to a Government contract number, provided, however, that such reference represents a prime contract under a Government department whose contracts are subject to the Act. The third indication is that it contains a reference to a *CMP* allotment number or to a *DO* rating that can be identified, from the symbols used, as having been issued by any one of the Government departments covered under the Act. A list of such symbols is obtainable from the Board.

Any contractor that cannot determine its renegotiable business should report this fact to the Board, so that an acceptable method of determining the renegotiable sales can be mutually arranged.

**Allowable costs.** The costs allowable against renegotiable business will be those expenditures and expenses allocated as deductions from renegotiable revenue by the contractor's established cost accounting method, if that method satisfactorily reflects recognized accounting principles and practices, and provides acceptable deductions for determining net income for Federal income tax purposes. The Act declares, in effect, that all items allowable as deductions or exclusions for Federal income tax purposes (exclusive of taxes measured by income) shall be allowed as costs in renegotiation to the extent that they are properly allocable to renegotiable business. The allowability of any item of cost appears, consequently, to depend upon affirmative answers to two basic questions. These are:

1. Is the cost a permissible income-tax deduction?
2. Is the cost reasonably allocable to renegotiable business?

**Election to file on consolidated basis.** A contractor desiring to be renegotiated on a consolidated basis may make a written request to the Board for such action. The regulations provide that renegotiation on a consolidated basis will be conducted with a parent corporation and its subsidiary corporations if the group constitutes an affiliated group under the Internal Revenue Code and if all the corporations in the group request renegotiation on such basis and consent to such regulations as the Board shall prescribe with respect to (a) the determination and elimination of excessive profits of the group, and (b) the allocation of such excessive profits to each corporation in the affiliated group.

**Renegotiation Board's procedure with regard to data submitted.** The assignment of contracts for renegotiation is made after receipt of the contractor's renegotiable-data report. If the Board determines that renegotiation proceedings are warranted, the contractor's case is assigned to a Regional Board. Generally, an assignment will be made whenever a contractor's receipts and accruals during a fiscal year exceed the applicable statutory minimum. If an assignment is not to be made, the Board will so notify the contractor. Each case assigned will be classified by the Board as a *Class A* or *Class B* case. A *Class A* case is usually one in which the contractor reported profits of more than $800,000 on renegotiable contracts, and a *Class B* case is one where such profits were reported as $800,-000 or less.

When a Regional Board determines the amount of excessive profits and the contractor agrees to refund the amount so determined, an agreement is entered into by both parties. In *Class A* cases the properly executed agreement, with a report of the case, will be reviewed by the Renegotiation Board. If the Renegotiation Board is not in accord with the determination, the case will be sent back to the Regional Board for further proceedings. But if the Renegotiation Board is in accord with the determination, the agreement becomes conclusive in the absence of fraud, malfeasance, or willful misrepresentation of a material fact. In *Class B* cases the Regional Boards themselves are authorized to make the final determinations without review by the Renegotiation Board.

When the Renegotiation Board fails to reach an agreement with a contractor or subcontractor regarding the elimination of excessive profits, the Board is authorized to issue an order determining the amount of such excessive profits. The contractor or subcontractor is then notified of such action by registered mail. The order becomes final after 90 days, unless, within that period, the contractor or subcontractor files a petition of protest with the Tax Court of the United States. This action is taken under the "unilateral order procedure."

The Tax Court has exclusive final jurisdiction to determine the amount, if any, of excessive profits. Its decision shall not be reviewed or redetermined by any other court or agency. The filing of a petition by the contractor as the result of an order of the Board will operate to stay the execution of collection proceedings, provided the contractor files a bond with the Tax Court in the amount fixed by the Court. Collections by the Board in excess of the amount determined by the Court will be refunded to the contractor with 4% interest per annum from the dates of collection.

The liability of a contractor or subcontractor for any excessive profits earned during a fiscal year covered by the required renegotiable data submitted by him is discharged unless renegotiation proceedings are commenced within one year after the filing of such data in the absence of fraud, malfeasance, or willful misrepresentation of a material fact. If, within two years after the commencement of renegotiation proceedings for a particular year, an agreement is not reached, or an order is not issued determining the amount of excessive profits, any liability for excessive profits in that year is generally discharged, with the same limitations as to fraud, malfeasance, or willful misrepresentation of a material fact.

The Renegotiation Act and Internal Revenue Code provide that the amount of a contractor's Federal income tax applicable to excessive profits realized in a taxable year under renegotiation shall be allowed as a credit against the total amount of excessive profits to be eliminated.

## ARMED SERVICES AGENCY AUDITS

Audits of contractors' accounting records, books, and related supporting data are performed for the Government by the Armed Services Agencies, the General Accounting Office, the Renegotiation Board, and, of course, the Internal Revenue Service.

As its title declares, this section is primarily devoted to discussing the Armed Services Agency audits. Except in the case of firm-fixed-price contracts, this type of audit is a major factor in determining the amount of costs to be reimbursed and the final contract prices. Furthermore, in the event of termination of a firm-fixed-price contract, the Armed Services

Agency audit becomes a significant factor in determining the amount of termination claim allowed.

The General Accounting Office performs post-audits, on a selective basis, of all reimbursements made to contractors under Department of Defense contracts. Its audits also include the evaluation of actions consummated by the Government procurement activities and audit agencies.

As discussed in the previous section, Renegotiation Board audits are concerned with determining whether excessive profits have been made on contracts related to the defense effort. In this connection, Internal Revenue audits have a direct bearing on determinations made by the Renegotiation Board.

**Functions of Armed Services Audit Agencies.** These audit agencies perform a variety of audit and accounting services for the various procurement activities of the military departments. The following are examples of such services:

1. Audit of contractors' incurred and claimed costs under cost-reimbursement contracts for the purpose of determining the allowable costs of performance. (This determination is made in accordance with the applicable section of the Armed Services Procurement Regulation (ASPR XV) and with the terms of the contract.)

2. Review of contractors' procurement pricing proposals and submission of advisory audit reports under fixed-price contracts of the price-redetermination type. (This review is made using ASPR XV, Part 2, for guidance, as provided by Revision 50.)

3. Assistance to procurement activities in connection with initial pricing studies, setting target prices, and negotiation of final prices under incentive-type contracts. (ASPR XV, Part 2, is here also used as guide.)

4. Review of contractors' and subcontractors' claims arising from contract terminations and submission of audit advisory reports on them. (In the case of terminations, the audit agencies are directed to use the cost principles set forth in ASPR 15-205.42 in place of the cost portions of ASPR Section VIII formerly used.)

5. Submission of advisory reports to procurement activities on the financial conditions of prospective contractors.

6. Submission of advisory reports on weaknesses in the financial conditions of contractors and subcontractors performing Government contracts.

7. Submission of advisory reports on contractors' accounting systems, procurement procedures and practices, and estimating procedures.

**Cognizant audit agency.** The performance of all Government defense-contract audit work at any one designated location is under the cognizance of one audit agency representing all the military departments. This is the consequence of the Audit Coordination Program, which was instituted in recent years for the purpose of reducing the overall expense of these audits and confining the use of the contractor's accounting records to one military department.

Audit coordination is performed at locations where contracts of more than one military department are subject to audit. There are many factors in determining the practicability of audit coordination and choosing the audit agency that should be assigned audit cognizance. Some of the more important factors are:

1. Preponderance of audit interest by one particular military department.

2. Accessibility to an established military audit office.

3. Responsibility of one military department for procurement and mobilization planning.

4. Availability of audit personnel.

5. Possibility of significant savings in travel expense.

**Policies and procedures of audit agencies.** The Contract Audit Manual, issued under the authority of Section 401 of the Act of August 10, 1949 (Public Law 216, 81st Congress), prescribes policies and procedures for use by the audit agencies of the Departments of the Army, Navy, and Air Force in auditing procurement-contract costs and in performing other audit assignments. Uniformity in audit policies and procedures has been established except where recognition of the individual procedures of a military department is considered desirable.

*Auditing standards.* The Contract Audit Manual specifies auditing standards that are quite reminiscent of those issued by the AICPA. These standards are as follows:

GENERAL STANDARDS

1. The contract audit should be performed by a person or persons with adequate training and proficiency as an auditor.

2. In all matters relating to the contract audit the auditor should maintain a mental attitude of unbiased judgment and objective consideration of the facts.

3. Due care should be exercised in the performance of the audit and in the preparation of any report concerning it.

STANDARDS OF FIELD WORK

1. The audit program must be adequately planned, and any assistants must be properly supervised. Since the auditor is responsible for the development of an audit program that will protect the interests of the Government, he is to satisfy himself by means of sound and practicable auditing procedures that the contractor's representations as to costs incurred under the contract are determined in accordance with generally accepted accounting principles, contract provisions, and applicable Government regulations. The auditor should not unnecessarily extend the auditing procedures nor needlessly duplicate the work of the contractor.

2. There should be an appropriate study and evaluation of the contractor's system of internal control to determine the extent to which reliance can be placed on it. The information thus developed is to be the basis for planning the audit procedures and the extent of the tests of recorded transactions. Where practicable, as in the case of resident audit staffs, a study and evaluation, once made, should be kept current by periodic review and by observation of the contractor's accounting practices.

3. A representative number of transactions should be audited to determine the extent to which reliance may be placed on the contractor's accounting policies and procedures and on the contractor's representations as to costs incurred under the contract. The determination as to what is a representative number depends upon the auditor's judgment concerning what constitutes a reasonable test of all the recorded transactions. If necessary, the audit work should be expanded or modified on the basis of the results of initial testing, but the extent of such expansion or modification cannot be stated precisely and must be left largely to the auditor's judgment. A detailed audit of every significant transaction may be made when specified by the requesting authority or when authorized by the auditor's supervisory officer.

Sufficient competent evidence should be obtained through inspection, observation, and inquiry to afford a reasonable basis for acceptance, suspension, or disallowance of the contractor's alleged costs incurred under the contract, and for a supporting opinion regarding such action.

*The initial conference.* The initial conference is an important aspect of the audit, and is held between representatives of the Government and the contractor to acquaint the contractor's staff with Government procedures, policies, and requirements. Depending on the type of contract, the subjects of these discussions include procedures to be followed in presenting and collecting claims for reimbursement, requirements as to documentary evidence, and procedures for conducting the audits by either resident or mobile audit groups.

Such conferences also afford the contractor's representatives the opportunity to discuss any questions that they may have. Arrangements for suitable working space and establishment of a cooperative and efficient working relationship are additional accomplishments that usually result from these initial conferences.

*Aid and information obtainable from Government auditors.* Officers and employees of the Government are prohibited by law from acting as agents or attorneys in prosecuting any claim against the United States or aiding or assisting in the prosecution or support of any such claim other than in the proper discharge of their official duties. One of the auditor's official duties, however, is to inform contractors how public vouchers, termination settlement proposals, cost statements, and other financial representations in connection with Government contracts should be prepared and submitted. The auditor may also properly advise contractors as to types of cost considered allowable and unallowable. On request, he may orally express an opinion concerning the acceptability of a specific item of cost.

*Confidential nature of audit data.* Military department auditors must not disclose information about contractors' costs, financial matters, or other business affairs to unauthorized persons, or to anyone that does not establish necessary military-security clearance. Audit work papers, audit reports, contractors' unpublished financial statements, correspondence, files, and other records may contain information that the contractor regards as confidential or information restricted for military-security purposes, or both. Such information is to be used for only official purposes. Consequently, all necessary safeguards over these classes of data will be provided in accordance with military-security regulations.

**Expediting the audit.** Every type of contract that the Government has the right to audit contains provisions requiring the contractor to maintain books, records, and other evidence of contract costs. These records must be readily available for audit purposes, and no limitation or restriction may be placed on the auditor's inspection of them. Moreover, contractors are required to furnish suitable working space and facilities necessary for the Government audit staffs to perform their work.

Over and above these requirements, Government audits and the subsequent related reimbursement and pricing actions can be greatly expedited, with ensuing benefits to both parties, if the contractor fully understands and complies with the many obligations that he is required to meet. Some of these obligations are specified in the contract, while others arise from regulations and instructions in the military departments and audit agencies with which the contractor is dealing. Some ways whereby the contractor may expedite the audit and the related reimbursement and pricing are:

1. Obtain all required approvals on a timely basis.

2. Segregate in the accounting records, and eliminate from claims for reimbursement and from cost representations, the types of costs specified in ASPR XV as unallowable, as well as costs that are otherwise unallowable.

3. Whether overhead is reimbursable under cost-type contracts on the basis of actual cost or application of final negotiated overhead rates, prepare and submit overhead-rate proposals, including supporting overhead schedules, to the cognizant audit office as soon as possible after the close of the accounting year or other period.

4. Notify contracting officers sufficiently in advance when there is a likelihood that costs incurred and to be incurred will exceed the maximum cost fixed in cost-type contracts, thereby affording the contracting officers the opportunity to make timely decisions as to whether additional funds will need to be obligated for use under the contracts.

5. Prepare and submit billings in such detail and form, together with any related documents, as to comply with instructions contained in the contract or furnished by the cognizant audit office.

6. Provide an accounting system that will supply and substantiate the costs incurred under individual contracts. The system should also furnish, under redeterminable and incentive-type contracts, the accumulation of production costs by individual departments or operations, as well as by lots, runs, etc., together with the cost data on each contract item that is to be repriced separately. Costing of the number of units to be completed before the price-redetermination or firm-target point should be established by an adequate number of lots or runs, so as to permit the development of historical data to reflect cost trends satisfactorily. The system should, moreover, yield preproduction costs and sufficient data about scrap, spoilage, rework, and similar requisite figures.

7. Submit cost data on DD Form 784 (used in price redetermination), together with all the supporting details required by the instructions set forth on the reverse side of that form, as soon as possible after the price-redetermination or target point has been reached.

8. Set up and maintain a procurement organization that fully understands and follows principles and practices (including estimating and bid-

ding procedures) acceptable to the cognizant audit office and military department.

9. Prepare and keep readily available, in connection with cost statements submitted for price redetermination and initial-pricing action, priced bills of materials, efficiency and learning curves, and forecast data relating to work backlogs, sales, overhead rates, and work force.

Once again emphasis should be placed upon the advisability of assigning the full responsibility for planning, monitoring, and coordinating all actions taken, or required to be taken, by the various production and administrative departments to a capable defense-contracts administrator or an experienced member of the management team. This is vitally necessary to insure strict and timely compliance with the terms of the contract and with the instructions or requirements of the contracting officer, his duly delegated representative, and the cognizant audit agency.

## DESIGNING ACCOUNTING SYSTEMS AND RECORDS TO MAXIMIZE COST RECOVERY

The contractor's accounting system must provide proper contract costs under (1) Government cost-type contracts and (2) fixed-price contracts of the incentive or redeterminable type. This condition is a prerequisite to the awarding of such contracts by the procurement activities of the Defense Department. However, accounting systems should not be designed merely to cover the minimum requirements set by the Government. On the contrary, systems should be designed to produce a maximum recovery of costs applicable to these contracts. For if the accounting system yields costs that are less than those actually incurred on the contracts, the unrecovered costs will obviously eat into the company's profits. Not so obvious, however, is that the use of a normally designed cost system not specifically tailored for the problems of Government contracts may cause contract costs to erode because of the Government's definition of allowable and unallowable costs, and because of decisions made by individual auditors and contracting officers. (This last point is explained and illustrated on pages 1280 to 1287, pages 1293 to 1297, and pages 1301 to 1302).

After first describing the basic requirements for a contractor's accounting system and records, this section will explain how to set up a system that directly charges, in so far as practicable, expenses that are usually treated as overhead, thereby minimizing the loss of charges correctly allocable to Government contracts. Additionally, reference will be made to the use of standard costs and the allocation of home-office-administration costs.

**Basic Government requirements for accounting system.** Generally a contractor's accounting procedures are considered acceptable if they conform to generally accepted accounting practices and if they produce costs properly supportable as applicable to each Government contract.

Because of difficulties encountered by Government representatives in obtaining (1) ready access to all pertinent records of contractors and (2) contractors' production costs of individual units or production lots under price-redetermination contracts, clauses such as the following are beginning to appear in such contracts:

> a. The contractor agrees to keep books and records pertaining to the costs and expenses incurred by it in the performance of this contract to the extent and in such detail as will properly reflect all such costs and expenses, both direct and indirect, applicable to the production of the items called for in the schedule. Such books and records shall be kept in a manner that will provide the necessary detail for the proper preparation of DD Form 784, "Cost Analysis for Contract Price Redetermination," in accordance with the instruction for preparation of said form as printed on the reverse side thereof, or the preparation of such other form, providing substantially similar information, as may be specifically approved by the Contracting Officer at the request of the contractor. In addition, the books and records shall be kept in such manner that production costs may be readily ascertained by individual units or production lots, as the case may be, of each contract item which is to be repriced separately.
>
> b. The contractor's accounting procedures and practices shall be subject to approval by the Comptroller of the Navy (Contract Audit Division). However, no material change will be required to be made in the contractor's accounting procedures and practices if they conform to generally accepted accounting principles and practices and if the costs properly applicable to this contract, in the detail required by paragraph (a) above, are readily ascertainable therefrom.
>
> c. The contractor agrees to make available at its office at all reasonable times any of its records that relate to the performance of this contract for inspection and audit by any authorized representative of the Department of the Navy.

**Direct charging of expenses usually treated as overhead.** The most common way of charging overhead expenses to products is first, accumulating factory-service, distribution, and administrative expenses by logical cost groups, such as by plants, departments, and kinds of expense, and then allocating such expenses to products on the basis of the estimated causes of the costs incurred or the relative benefits received. Many of these allocations are made on such bases as direct-labor dollars or hours, square feet of floor space used, machine hours, etc. In large companies the determination of the most appropriate means of allocating each expense is often based on exhaustive study and research. Many smaller companies, however, not having elaborate cost procedures for allocating costs to products, are *forced* to make such allocations for a Government contract. They usually do so by allocating all factory overhead on the basis of direct-labor dollars and all distribution-and-administrative expenses on the basis of sales.

▶ EXAMPLE: The Hill Manufacturing Company has gross sales (Government and commercial) of $500M, cost of sales of $300M, direct-labor cost of $100M, factory overhead of $150M, and general and administrative expenses of $60M. Thus, its burden rate is 150% of direct labor ($150M/$100M) and its general and administrative rate is 20% of cost of sales ($60M/$300M). The contractor applies these rates (usually reduced by costs not allowed by the contract and ASPR XV) to the Government-contract direct labor and cost of sales in order to arrive at the respective amounts of manufacturing overhead and general and administrative expenses chargeable to the Government contract.

But because Government contracts require a greater amount of administrative and other indirect costs than are usually required by commercial work, the use of a system that allocates indirect costs and expenses on an overall basis of Government and commercial work is almost certainly going to understate the costs chargeable to Government contracts. On the other hand, even if the contractor is performing only Government contracts, this ordinary method of charging costs can still result in loss as the result of the Government's definition of allowable and unallowable costs and of decisions of individual auditors and contracting officers.

▶ EXAMPLE: The Government auditor and his contracting officer decided that $10,000 spent for research and development on a previous Navy contract was not properly includable in the pool of expense allocated to an Army contract. This decision meant disallowance of $1,500 allocated to the Army contract out of the contractor's pool of manufacturing-overhead expenses. Because the $10,000 item had *not* been charged *directly* to the Navy contract, as it should have been, the Navy contract had absorbed only $8,500 of it. The remaining $1,500 was thus irretrievably lost because the contractor had already signed a final release of all claims against the Navy contract.

*Direct-charging systems.* In a direct-charging system, costs and expenses that are usually charged indirectly to overhead are, wherever practicable, charged directly to Government and commercial production.

▶ EXAMPLE: The Hunt Electronic Company's method of direct charging segregates indirect expenses into five groups; namely, those chargeable (1) directly to individual Government contracts, (2) directly to individual commercial products, (3) directly to Government work, but indirectly to individual Government contracts, (4) directly to commercial work, but indirectly to individual commercial products, and (5) to the residual pool of indirect costs and expenses (those that cannot be identified specifically with either Government or civilian production).

When such so-called "direct charging" is used, the contractor is required to meet the following requirements:

1. The method must be consistently applied to all the contractor's contracts, products, and projects, not merely to Government contracts.
2. Costs of like commercial items charged directly must be eliminated from overhead pools that are allocated to Government contracts.
3. Costs normally considered to be indirect but charged directly must be proved to have been incurred solely and specifically for the particular contracts, products, and projects charged.

A contractor should have little difficulty in proving compliance with the first two aforementioned requirements. Satisfactory evidence of compliance with the third condition, however, is likely to prove difficult, to say the least, unless the contractor installs appropriate procedures before direct costing is put into practice. The reason is that Government auditors require data in the form of time tickets, purchase orders, invoices, and the like, properly identified by reference to contract, product, or project, in support of each item of expense charged directly.

Segregation of a contractor's operations between Government and commercial work, with a separate production administration and cost center for each, is one acceptable way to charge costs directly to Government contracts (and probably obtain fuller recovery of Government-contract costs). An example is to have all Government work performed, where practicable, in a separate plant or building or department and to segregate most selling, administrative, and accounting functions by areas and by personnel, according to the Government or commercial nature of the work done. A minor, and usually preliminary, step is to establish a Government-contracts-administration department. Other helpful approaches are:

1. Establishment of material-handling rates where the quantities and kinds of materials required for Government contracts differ markedly from those required for commercial work.
2. Grouping of indirect salaries and expenses by specific functions per-

formed within various departments, so as to facilitate equitable segregation by Government and commercial activities serviced.

3. Direct charging of the following costs:

a. Special tooling.
b. Starting load.
c. Rearrangement.
d. Special packaging-and-packing.
e. Travel.
f. Consultants' fees.
g. Overtime and shift-premium pay.
h. Salaries of expediters.
i. Freight in and out.
j. Telephone and telegraph.
k. Plant protection.
l. Royalties.

Appropriate direct costing of such items will depend, of course, upon the circumstances and the presence of any specific prohibition in the Government contract.

▶ OBSERVATION: A direct-charging system need not cost too much to operate, increases accuracy of costing, and reduces arguments with Government auditors concerning allocations of indirect expenses to Government contracts. However, before it is instituted, a study should be made to determine whether the additional expense involved is justified.

**Acceptable use of standard costs in Government contract work.** With the possible exception of cost-type research and development contracts, the use of standard costs in Government contract work is acceptable if the standards are properly adjusted for applicable variances and if they result in what appear to be fairly accurate contract costs.

Depending on the circumstances, standard costs have varying degrees of usefulness in Government-procurement contract-pricing. They are of great value in the precontract-award negotiations, particularly when the item to be purchased is similar to others with which the contractor has had prior production-and-cost experience.

Standard costs may be used to control all costs or may be restricted to specific classes of cost. They may be incorporated in the accounts—which is preferable—or they may be used for comparison with historical, recorded costs. In either case the standards should be established by analysis of bills of materials, time studies, and other scientific management techniques. As a practical matter, they should perhaps be based upon the best obtainable objectives and then revised in the light of experience, rather than be based upon theoretically perfect objectives.

For Government contract purposes, standard costs may be considered to consist of two main types of standards: *basic* and *current*. Basic standards are those established at a particular time in the past and not revised unless there is a major change in production methods. Current standards, on the other hand, are revised periodically whenever cost fluctuations or production changes make it necessary. Hence, the use of standard costs in Government contracts is likely to be inappropriate if they were established under conditions substantially different from those existing during the performance of the contract, since significant percentage variations from present actual costs are probably involved.

Differences between standard and actual costs should be accumulated in variance accounts by cost elements, such as the classic cost elements "material, labor, and overhead," perhaps being further "broken down" by price and quantity, and even by direct departments in some instances. Variances should be cleared out at least once a year, with inventories receiving their allocable portions of the variances. When the contractor's Government and commercial products are similar, the variances need not distinguish between costs applicable to these two main classes of products. But if the products differ significantly as to type, production operations, inspection requirements, or the like, overall variance percentages cannot be equitably applied to the standard costs of both Government and commercial products. Only a careful study will yield the proper answers to these questions. (Chapter 10 fully treats the subject of standard and estimated costs.)

**Selling, distribution, general, and administration costs.** Among the acceptable bases of allocation of these costs are the following:

1. Processing cost (direct labor, factory overhead, and any other factory production costs exclusive of direct material).
2. Factory "input cost" (manufacturing cost consisting of processing cost plus the cost of direct material).
3. Cost of goods completed.
4. Cost of sales.
5. Sales or net sales (where no more satisfactory base is available).

In the use of each of these bases, the fairness of the results must be substantiated.

In selection of a particular method or methods of apportionment, special consideration should be given to any unusual factors; such as charges of subcontractors; fixed-asset improvement programs; nature, performance, and location of Government contract work; and so on.

The cost-of-sales and manufacturing-cost bases are used to a great extent in allocating selling, distribution, and general and administrative expenses. However, when there is a considerable increase in commercial inventories during the period under review, Government auditors may question the validity of the cost-of-sales basis. The reason is that manufacturing and administrative expenses related to such substantial inventory increase are unlikely to be afforded proper weight by the use of this method.

**Home-office administration costs.** The allocation of home-office administration costs, as distinguished from selling, distribution, and general and administration expenses, is a particular problem, especially when the Government-contract work at a plant or Government installation is performed by one unit, division, or defense-products group of a multi-unit company. The acceptable bases—preferably a combination of them—for allocation of home-office administration costs are the following:

1. Sales (in dollars).
2. Effort (in percentage of time).
3. Capital employed (in dollars).
4. Total assets (in dollars).
5. Personnel (in dollar cost).
6. Payroll (gross payroll in dollars).

In the use of any one or more of these bases, the fairness of the results must be substantiated. Furthermore, the "readiness to serve" of the home-office corporate staff, as well as the actual services rendered, must be considered.